The Psychology and Management of Workplace Diversity

Edited by
Margaret S. Stockdale and Faye J. Crosby

Blackwell Publishing

BLACKWELL PUBLISHING
350 Main Street, Malden, MA 02148-5020, USA
9600 Garsington Road, Oxford OX4 2DQ, UK
550 Swanston Street, Carlton, Victoria 3053, Australia

First published 2004 by Blackwell Publishing Ltd.

2   2005

Library of Congress Cataloging-in-Publication Data

The psychology and management of workplace diversity / edited
by Margaret S. Stockdale, Faye J. Crosby.
p. cm.
Includes bibliographical references and index.
ISBN 1-4051-0099-0 (alk. paper) – ISBN 1-4051-0096-6 (pbk.: alk. paper)
1. Diversity in the workplace–United States. 2. Psychology,
Industrial–United States. 3. Personnel management–United States.
I. Stockdale, Margaret S. II. Crosby, Faye J., 1947–

HF5549.5.M5P79 2003
658.3'008–dc21
2002156372

ISBN-13: 9781405100991 (alk. paper) – ISBN-13: 978-1-4051-0096-0 (pbk.: alk. paper)

A catalogue record for this title is available from the British Library.

Set in 10/12½ Book Antique
by Graphicraft Ltd, Hong Kong
Printed and bound in the United Kingdom
by TJ International, Padstow, Cornwall

The publisher's policy is to use permanent paper from mills that operate a sustainable forestry
policy, and which has been manufactured from pulp processed using acid-free and
elementary chlorine-free practices. Furthermore, the publisher ensures that the text paper and
cover board used have met acceptable environmental accreditation standards.

For further information on
Blackwell Publishing, visit our website:
www.blackwellpublishing.com

Contents

Figures

Contributors

Mark D. Agars is an Assistant Professor of Psychology at California State University, San Bernardino. He earned his PhD and MS degrees in Industrial and Organizational Psychology in 1999 from Pennsylvania State University, and his BA in Psychology from Siena College in 1992. His research interests are in the study of gender and diversity issues, with primary focus on the workplace. He is interested in multi-disciplinary and multi-level approaches to such topics as diversity management, discrimination, and work–family conflict.

Myrtle P. Bell is a management faculty member at the University of Texas at Arlington (UTA). She has degrees from the University of Notre Dame, Louisiana State University, and UTA. Her research focuses on diversity issues (surface v. deep diversity, sexual harassment, and affirmative action) and has been published in numerous journals and several diversity and gender books. She is an active member of the Gender and Diversity in Organizations division of the Academy of Management.

Heather E. Bullock is an Assistant Professor of Psychology at the University of California, Santa Cruz. Her research focuses on perceptions of economic inequality and how classist stereotypes and attributions for poverty are used to legitimize restrictive welfare policy. She also studies discrimination in the everyday lives of low-income women and the intersections of classism, racism, and sexism. Before joining the faculty at UCSC, she served as an APA Congressional Fellow with the Democratic Office of the Senate Committee on Health, Education, and Labor, and Pensions.

Feng Cao is a doctoral student in the Department of Psychology at Southern Illinois University, Carbondale. He received his BA and MA in Psychology from East China Normal University, Shanghai. Feng's research interests are in work–family linkage (especially work–family conflict), human resources management (especially training needs analysis and evaluation of training effects), and program evaluation. His research in China has been published in Chinese psychological journals.

Donna Chrobot-Mason is an Assistant Professor of Psychology at the University of Colorado at Denver. She earned her PhD from the University of Georgia in 1997 and was employed by the Human Resources Department at Xerox Corporation for almost four years before joining the faculty at CU-Denver in 1998. She conducts research in the areas of identity development, diversity management, and leadership across differences. She also consults on diversity training and climate assessment projects.

Kevin Cokley received his PhD in Counseling Psychology in 1998 from Georgia State University. He is a member of the Counseling Psychology program in the Department of Psychology at Southern Illinois University at Carbondale. His research can be broadly categorized in the area of college student development. He is interested in the ways that racially homogeneous and heterogeneous college environments impact different correlates of African-American student development. These correlates include racial and cultural identity development, academic self-concept, and academic motivation. His research articles have appeared in many professional journals.

Faye J. Crosby PhD LLD (Hon.) is a scholar, writer, consultant, and social activist. She has published numerous articles, reviews, and books in the area of social justice. She was one of the first psychologists to document that women – just like men – benefit from combining paid labor and family roles. Her book *Juggling* (1991) helped change employers' view of working mothers. Recently, Crosby has approached gender and work issues from different angles, including affirmative action and mentoring. She co-edited *Mentoring Dilemmas* (1999) and *Sex, Race and Merit: Debating Affirmative Action in Education and Employment* (2000). Her book *Affirmative Action is Dead; Long Live Affirmative Action* is currently in press. Since 1997, Crosby has been Professor of Psychology at the University of California, Santa Cruz. Previously she was on the faculty at Rhode Island College (1976–7), Yale University (1977–85), the Kellogg School of Management (1992–3), and Smith College (1985–97). Her students have conferred awards and praise on Crosby for her exceptional teaching.

George F. Dreher is a Professor of Business Administration at Indiana University, where he teaches in the MBA and MBA in Accounting programs. He was recently a visiting scholar at Hong Kong University of Science and Technology. He received his PhD in Industrial/Organizational Psychology from the University of Houston. His current research addresses the role of race, ethnicity, age, and gender in accounting for selection, promotion, and retention decisions (with a focus on managerial and executive talent pool management). His research has been published in numerous journals.

Robin J. Ely is an Associate Professor at the Harvard Business School, Boston. She teaches courses on leadership and race and gender relations in organizations, and conducts research on how organizations can better manage their race and gender relations while at the same time increasing their effectiveness. Her research in this area focuses on learning and organizational change with attention to conflict, power, and social identity. She taught at Harvard's John F. Kennedy School of Government and at Columbia's School of International and Public Affairs. She received her PhD in organizational behavior from Yale University and an undergraduate degree from Smith College.

Bernardo M. Ferdman is Professor at California School of Organizational Studies, Alliant International University. He has over 20 years' experience as a consultant, teacher, and writer on issues of diversity and multiculturalism, ethnic and cultural identity in organizations, Latinos/as in the workplace, and organizational behavior and development. He is President (2001–3) of the Interamerican Society of Psychology, a Fellow of the American Psychological Association (Division 9), and a Charter Fellow of the International Academy for Intercultural Research, as well as a recipient of SPSSI's Gordon Allport Intergroup Relations Prize. He received his PhD in Psychology from Yale University in 1987.

Rana Haq holds a BA degree in Economics from York University in Toronto, an MBA from Laurentian University in Sudbury, Canada, and is currently pursuing a PhD in Management at the University of Bradford's School of Management in the UK. A faculty member in the School of Commerce and Administration at Laurentian University for the past three years, she has taught undergraduate and graduate courses in the Human Resources and Marketing streams. She has over eight years of management experience in various public, private, and non-profit organizations. Her research interests are in the areas of managing diversity, gender issues in management, cross-cultural communications, interpersonal skills, organizational behavior, organizational development and change, international human resource management, and consumer behavior.

Rosemary Hays-Thomas is Professor of Psychology at the University of West Florida in Pensacola, where she teaches Industrial/Organizational and Social Psychology, including the Psychology of Workforce Diversity. She received her PhD in Social Psychology from the University of Illinois and completed a postdoctoral fellowship in Industrial/Organizational Psychology at Louisiana State University. She has published articles on the topics of pay equity, the teaching of applied psychology, and the status of the Master's degree. She is a Fellow of the American Psychological Association and the Society for the Psychological Study of Social Issues, and currently serves as editor of the *Psychologist-Manager Journal* and as Administrative Officer for the Southeastern Psychological Association. She is a licensed psychologist and a certified Senior Professional in Human Resources.

Sarah L. Holland is President of the Visibility Project, an organization she founded in 1999 to enable companies to address issues of sexual orientation and niche marketing in order to maximize the bottom-line impact of the lesbian/gay/ bisexual/transgender workforce. She serves on the National Advisory Board of Out&Equal Workplace Advocates, and is a director of the Gay and Lesbian Anti-Violence Project in New York City. A longtime human rights and social activist, she is also an executive coach and vocational mentor, and she speaks frequently on workplace visibility issues.

Evangelina Holvino is Director and Senior Research Faculty at the Center for Gender in Organizations at the Simmons College School of Management. She has over 25 years' experience as an organizational consultant and educator, both in the United States and internationally. Her expertise lies in the areas of race, gender, and class, global diversity, strategic planning, leadership development, and organizational learning and change. She has a doctorate in Education and Organizational Development from the University of Massachusetts and is a member and past board member of the AK Rice Institute and the NTL Institute for Applied Behavioral Sciences.

Janet L. Kottke is a Professor of Psychology at California State University, San Bernardino and founder of the Master of Science program in Industrial and Organizational Psychology offered at CSUSB. She earned her PhD and MS degrees in I/O Psychology from Iowa State University and her BA in Psychology from Wartburg College. Among her research interests she has examined issues in discrimination and sexual harassment. She has recently begun research into diversity management as organizational change.

Christine L. Langlands is an International Compensation Consultant with Organization Resources Counselors, Inc. She carries out consulting projects, specializing in the development and review of international and expatriate compensation programs and advises multinationals on international pay policies. She worked for several years as an international insurance broker at Sedgwick, Inc., and holds a Master of Science in Human Resources from the Institute of Human Resources and Industrial Relations at Loyola University. She is a graduate of the University of Illinois Urbana-Champaign, where she received a BS in Psychology. Her publications include *Co-authoring Organizational Behavior: A Management Challenge, Instructor's Manual* (2001).

Micah E. Lubensky is a PhD candidate in Social Psychology and a Cota Robles Fellow at the University of California, Santa Cruz. His academic research focuses on issues of identity and social justice. Passionate about diversity and pluralism, he is also an advocate and activist for increased awareness and inclusion of racial, economic, and political diversity. Much of this work has centered on the diversity within the lesbian/gay/bisexual/transgender communities. He is co-author of an article on affirmative action in education.

Dan A. Mack (deceased) was an Assistant Professor of Psychology at the University of Tennessee at Chattanooga, where he pursued teaching and research related to diversity and fairness. Much of his scholarship focused on the topics of affirmative action attitudes and ethnic and racial identity. He received his PhD from the University of Georgia in 1999. He published several articles and was a member of the Society for Industrial-Organizational Psychology.

Mary E. McLaughlin is a faculty member in the Department of Management and Organization at Pennsylvania State University. She received her PhD from the University of Illinois-Urbana in 1988. Her research interests include several diversity issues at work: acceptance and adjustment of employees with disabilities, discrimination and harassment on the basis of age, appearance, and obesity, and attitudes toward affirmative action programs. She has also focused on understanding and controlling method effects in self-report measures. Her work is published in various books and journals.

Deborah Merrill-Sands is Associate Dean at the Simmons College School of Management. She is a co-founder of the Center for Gender in Organizations at the School of Management, and is known for her work on gender dynamics in the workplace, women and leadership, women in science, and organizational change. She has consulted with corporations and with several major foundations and development organizations and has also served on the boards of international research organizations. She has published numerous articles, book chapters, and monographs in the fields of gender and organizational change, women and leadership, and research management. She received her PhD in Anthropology from Cornell University.

Amelie Montagliani specializes in international issues such as expatriate selection, training, performance, and cross-cultural adjustment. Her focus also includes the areas of selection, compensation, performance management, and program evaluation. She has designed and implemented business solutions for clients in the private sector as well as the public sector. She is currently completing the final requirements for a PhD at the University of Georgia in Industrial/Organizational Psychology. She received a BA in Psychology from Wake Forest University and an MA in Psychology from the University of Richmond. She has published and speaks on topics of cross-cultural adjustment, program evaluation, and compensation systems. She is a member of the Society for Industrial and Organizational Psychology and the American Compensation Association.

Marian N. Ruderman is a Research Scientist at the Center for Creative Leadership in Greensboro, North Carolina. Her research focuses on the career development of women and the impact of diversity on management development processes. She has written widely on these topics in popular magazines and professional journals. She is co-author of the new book *Standing at the Crossroads: Next Steps for High-Achieving Women* and co-editor of *Diversity in Work Teams: Research Paradigms for a Changing Workplace*. She holds an AB from Cornell University and an MA and PhD in Organizational Psychology from the University of Michigan.

Lynda M. Sagrestano received her PhD in Social Psychology from the University of California at Berkeley, followed by postdoctoral fellowships at UCLA in Health Psychology and at the University of Illinois at Chicago in Prevention and Intervention. She is currently an Assistant Professor in the Applied Psychology Program at Southern Illinois University, Carbondale. Her research examines the role of psychosocial, behavioral, and cultural factors in health promotion and disease prevention in varying contexts, as well as power and the use of social influence in interpersonal relationships. She has published in various journals.

Jennifer M. Sequeira is a doctoral student in the Department of Management at the University of Texas at Arlington. She has degrees from Marquette University and Florida Atlantic University. Her research interests are in entrepreneurship (networking among women, minority and immigrant entrepreneurs), international entrepreneurship, and diversity within small businesses. Her research has been published in the *Journal of Business Ethics* and presented at national Academy of Management conferences.

Patricia A. Simpson is Assistant Professor at the Institute for Human Resources and Industrial Relations at Loyola University, Chicago. She received her PhD from the Institute for Labor and Industrial Relations at the University of Illinois, her MA in Labor History from the University of Pittsburgh, and her BA in History and Philosophy from Brooklyn College, City University of New York. She conducts research on occupational segregation by race and gender, on older workers, and on organizational justice. Her articles have appeared in numerous journals.

Margaret S. Stockdale (PhD, 1990, Industrial and Organizational Psychology, Kansas State University) is an Associate Professor of Psychology at Southern Illinois University at Carbondale (SIUC). She is co-author/editor of three books: *Independent Consulting for Evaluators* (co-edited by A. Vaux and M. Schwerin, 1992), *Sexual Harassment in the Workplace* (B. Gutek, A. Stromberg, and L. Larwood, series editors, 1996), and *Women and Men in Organizations: Sex and Gender Issues in the Workplace* (co-authored with J. Cleveland and K. Murphy, 2000). Her primary research concerns gender issues in the workplace, principally sexual harassment. Her research articles have appeared in numerous peer-reviewed journals. She is also an active applied psychology consultant, having conducted training programs for major corporations, local agencies, and businesses, and needs assessments and program evaluations for both the private and public sector. Stockdale teaches graduate and undergraduate courses in workplace diversity, organizational behavior, industrial and organizational psychology, and needs assessment, and is the director of the Applied Psychology PhD program at SIUC.

Dianna L. Stone received her PhD from Purdue University and is currently a Professor of Management and Psychology at the University of Central Florida. She is a Fellow of the Society for Industrial and Organizational Psychology, and currently serves as the Associate Editor of *Cognition and Human Performance*, and is on the editorial boards of *Human Resources Management Review* and the *Journal of Quality Management*. Her research focuses on a variety of issues, including diversity in organizations (race, ethnicity, and disability), organizational justice, information privacy, and reactions to feedback. Results of her work have been published in many journals.

Eugene F. Stone-Romero is a Professor of Psychology at the University of Central Florida. He is a Fellow of the Society for Industrial and Organizational Psychology, the American Psychological Society, and the American Psychological Association. His work has appeared in many journals. He is also the author of numerous book chapters dealing with issues germane to the related fields of industrial and organizational psychology, human resources management, and organizational behavior. He is the author of *Research Methods in Organizational Behavior*, and the co-author of *Job Satisfaction: How People Feel About Their Jobs and How It Affects Their Performance*.

Linda K. Stroh (PhD Northwestern University) is a Loyola University Faculty Scholar and Professor of Organizational Behavior at Loyola University, Chicago. She has taught and published over 60 articles on issues related to organizational effectiveness and efficiency. She is co-author of two books: *Globalizing People Through International Assignments* and *Organizational Behavior: A Management Challenge*.

Kecia M. Thomas, PhD, is an Associate Professor of Psychology and African-American Studies at the University of Georgia. Her training is in Industrial-Organizational Psychology (Penn State, 1993) and her research focuses on the experiences of women and people of color within the world of work. Her scholarship on recruitment, leadership, and identity has been published as several book chapters and as articles within journals. In 1999 she also served as co-editor of a special issue of the *Journal of Career Development* on Black women's experiences as "organizational outsiders within." She is an active member of the Gender and Diversity in Organizations division of the Academy of Management and the Society for Industrial-Organizational Psychology.

Carolyn Wiethoff is a Clinical Assistant Professor of Management in the Kelley School of Business at Indiana University, Bloomington. She received her PhD in

Organizational Behavior and Human Resources from the Fisher College of Business at Ohio State University. Prior to graduate school she worked for Exxon, Arthur Andersen, and Windes & McClaughry in human resources and consulting capacities. In addition to her research in sexual orientation, she studies the effects of hidden diversity in work teams, the nature of intractability in environmental disputes, and the roles of trust and distrust in organizations.

Foreword

In November 1992, 150 letters were sent from Professor Faye Crosby's office at the J. L. Kellogg School of Management at Northwestern University to American feminist scholars throughout the social sciences. The letters invited the women to come to a "conference-cum-slumber-party." Crosby and co-conspirators, Judy Worell, Janice Steil, and Marianne LaFrance, hoped that five or six women would join them at the Crosby family summer home on Martha's Vineyard for a weekend of discussion. Within a week of the mailing, all the spaces were taken. Indeed, the stampede to be included in the working session forced the original group to double in size. Women agreed to sleep on lawn chairs for an opportunity to talk about some of the problems and promises of working for gender equity in and out of academe.

So great was the demand for honest dialogue that the founders decided to continue the enterprise. Another conference-cum-slumber-party took place on Martha's Vineyard and then another in Bodega Bay under the guidance of Stephanie Shields. In 1994 and 1995, twelve more conferences took place. I attended four of them. For the first time, I saw what a group of feminist scholars, committed to moving beyond platitudes in order to address the truly difficult issues that plagued both our research and our lives, could create with just a little care and feeding (well, OK, a *lot* of care and feeding provided by the seemingly tireless staff of Smith College undergraduates). There was more energy, compassion, and ideas, generated with more humor, laughter, and just plain *fun* than I could have imagined possible – we were, after all, a group of academics. In addition, for me personally as for others I'm sure, from these gatherings sprang collaborations and friendships that I fully expect to last a lifetime.

In the years that followed these early conferences the list of invitees grew longer and more diverse: attendance by American women of color, women from other countries, women outside of academe, women from a range of social class backgrounds, and old and young women has grown steadily. As the membership diversified, so did the topics. Procedures for the conference, which arose organically, became institutionalized. A small but sturdy infrastructure grew to support the dissemination of information about the conferences. And the conferences gained a name: The Nag's Heart Conferences. Now, nearly 10 years and 44 conferences since their inception, this venue has provided literally hundreds of women with an opportunity to seek and speak the truth – and so they do. Many alumnae of the conferences testify to the conferences' transformational qualities, and many come back for more.

And so, it should not be surprising that the product of one such conference is this book. What the Nag's Heart Conferences have managed to create is, to me, the essence of what this book aims to foster: workplaces in which all people can bring all relevant parts of themselves to bear on their work, without fear of reprisal or rejection for who they are, in a way that fosters mutual learning and growth. The conference in which this book was conceived, entitled "Diversity in Organizations: Doing Good Well," was held in May 2001. Led by Peggy Stockdale, it tackled the same difficult issues that this book tackles: Yes, we all want diversity; but in a world divided by race, class, sex, nation, and religion, to name but a few of the more polarizing issues in society today, diversity does not come easily. And effectively managing diversity is a challenge that many organizations – and many of us in organizations – are simply not equipped to meet.

In typical Nag's Heart fashion, the conference participants, most of whom are contributors to this volume, gathered in an informal setting – this time, in Faye's home in Santa Cruz – each prepared to discuss a "dilemma" of personal importance relevant to the conference theme. During the intensive work sessions of these conferences (typically four hours in the mornings of two consecutive days), each participant is allocated one half-hour in which to present her dilemma. Much of the formative thinking for this book occurred in these sessions at the conference. But the "work" of the conference doesn't end there. Free time for relaxation in the afternoons, as well as communal meals and activities in the evenings, provide ample time and opportunity for delving further into the issues at hand, and I have no doubt that the ideas deepened considerably in conversations throughout. Additional contributors to the volume joined later in response to Peg Stockdale's subsequent call for papers.

Thus it was within a spirit of community, collaboration, and fun that this insightful, well-researched book has come to be. It provides a sophisticated and comprehensive view of both the challenges and the opportunities that diversity poses for organizations, their leaders, and their members. It offers guidance for us all – for anyone who can manage diversity effectively can manage just about anything.

Robin J. Ely
Harvard School of Business
Boston, MA

Preface

This book is about diversity in work organizations. People differ from each other on all sorts of dimensions, some, but not all, of which have societal importance. Diverse work organizations are those in which the people who work together differ along the dimensions that society has deemed important.

Diverse work organizations can function well or function poorly. Diversity can create stress and conflict and can make everyone – those who are privileged as well as those who are less privileged – anxious and upset. Yet diverse work organizations can also function beautifully, gaining competitive advantage over homogeneous organization. When leaders "manage diversity" they engage in strategies and processes designed to make sure that differences among workers do not diminish, but rather enhance, organizational functioning.

Learning how to manage diversity is of the utmost importance for American organizations in today's world for two reasons. First, the demographics of the United States are changing, and Americans of European descent make up a smaller and smaller proportion of the population. Currently about 30 percent of the population is of "ethnic minority" heritage, and the percentage may grow. Ethnic minority families tend to enjoy a higher birth rate than White Americans. Most of the contemporary immigration into the United States comes from countries outside of Europe. Second, the world is getting smaller. Recent technological advances have hastened the already quick pace of globalization.

Many American corporations have heeded the warning signs. By 2001, three-quarters of the Fortune 1000 corporations had undertaken some kind of diversity initiative. Some of the initiatives may be superficial or short-lived, but some, like those at IBM or Chase Manhattan Bank, are thoughtful, thorough and effective.

What makes for effective diversity management? Our volume aims to give students a broad and deep understanding of the processes involved in the management of diversity at work and in the creation of multicultural work organizations. We start, in Part I, with basics. Chapter 1 outlines the demographic forces and the legal developments that create the environment in which diversity management is needed. Chapter 2 debunks some myths about the costs of diversifying the workforce and offers in their place solid facts about the advantages and disadvantages of diversity in the contemporary American workplace.

In Part II, students encounter a series of models that describe and explain the processes involved in diversity management. There is a saying among corporate consultants: "So long as you don't know where you are going, any road will do." To avoid facile solutions to the real challenges of diversity, we need strong conceptual grounding. That grounding is provided in chapters 3 through 6.

Once the processes of change have been clarified, we are ready to examine in depth how diversity has, does, and should work with respect to a series of dimensions. The dimensions include gender, race or ethnicity, age, disability, and obesity, sexual orientation, and social class. To the best of our knowledge, no other text includes detailed information on all these dimensions. Yet, as our authors make clear, the dynamics of ageism, for example, differ from those of racism or sexism or homophobia.

The book concludes with a long view. Chapter 12 provides guidance on how organizations can change to become more multiculturally inclusive. Chapter 13 describes diversity management issues around the globe. Finally, chapter 14 brings together the wisdom of all the preceding essays to suggest, among other things, some strategies for managing diversity.

In all chapters save the last, we present additional materials within tinted panels. Our aim is to provoke thought and discussion, and many of the issues are controversial. Students may find themselves disagreeing with other students about the "best" answers to the questions that we pose in the panels. If no disagreements occurred, we would be disappointed. In addition to all the other aspects of diversity that we value is another, about which we have no specific chapter in the book. It is the diversity of opinion, born of people's varying experiences, values, and perspectives. This aspect of diversity we prize. It is our view that the honest exchange of differing opinions is one of the best ways to achieve excellence in thought and in performance. Certainly, working closely with all the different and varied authors, that has been our own experience.

Faye Crosby and Peggy Stockdale

Acknowledgments

This book has been a real pleasure to produce, thanks to the dedication, wisdom, and responsiveness of our contributors. We owe debts of gratitude to many colleagues, students, and family members for fulfilling many important functions. For listening to our ideas and giving wise counsel: Alison Konrad and Margaret Wright. For technical help with the preparation of the manuscript: Dianne Lessman and Valerie Jenni. For research and administrative assistance: Feng Cao. For assistance with editing: David Mastros and Hayley Dawson. For support, encouragement, and sound advice: our acquisitions editor, Phyllis Wentworth. For patience and keeping dinner warm: Marilyn Patton. And for keeping the kids out of my hair: Michael Heck. *Thanks!*

The authors and publishers gratefully acknowledge the following for permission to reproduce copyright material:

Figure 3.1 is from T. H. Cox, Jr. (2001), *Creating the multicultural organization: A strategy for capturing the power of diversity*, copyright 2001, reprinted by permission of John Wiley & Sons, Inc. Figure 3.2 is from R. S. Allen and K. A. Montgomery (2001), Applying an organizational development approach to creating diversity, *Organizational Dynamics*, 30 (2), 149–61, copyright 2001, with permission from Elsevier Science. Figure 4.1 is from *The Social Psychology of Organizations*, 2nd edn. (p. 196), by D. Katz and R. L. Kahn, 1978, New York: John Wiley & Sons, Inc. Copyright 1978 by John Wiley & Sons, Inc. Reprinted with the permission of John Wiley & Sons, Inc.

The publishers apologize for any errors or omissions in the above list and would be grateful to be notified of any corrections that should be incorporated in the next edition or reprint of this book.

Part I

FOUNDATIONS

To borrow a phrase, workplace diversity has had a long past but a short history. Concerns about and efforts to address equal employment opportunity have been part of the American business milieu for 40 years, and debated in public and private forums for many years before. But recognition that diversity could be a valuable asset for organizational growth and development has only been articulated in the last decade and a half. The landmark, but often misunderstood, study by the Hudson Institute, *Workforce 2000* (Johnston and Packer, 1987), has been cited as the impetus for starting the "diversity craze" in both the United States and abroad. Since then, scholars in many disciplines, including management, psychology, sociology, economics, and others, have helped to articulate important concepts needed to better understand and manage the dynamics of workplace diversity, as well as to conduct empirical research that helps to inform these practices.

The chapters in this section elucidate the current state of knowledge about the forces that shape workplace diversity scholarship and management. Chapter 1 examines definitions of diversity, as well as demographic, economic, legislative, and business realities that help explain why workplace diversity scholarship and management has become a modern imperative. Chapter 2 takes a critical look at the backlash against diversity scholarship and management. Myths and misguided metaphors are exposed and re-examined under the lens of modern prejudice. Taken together, these chapters prepare both the student and the seasoned scholar for a more in-depth examination of the exciting domain of diversity in the workplace.

WHY NOW? THE CONTEMPORARY FOCUS ON MANAGING DIVERSITY

Rosemary Hays-Thomas

This chapter introduces the concepts of diversity and its management, reviewing several factors that have brought these issues to prominence in business and scholarship. It reviews narrow and broad definitions of diversity and the implications of each, distinguishing diversity from the concepts of equal employment opportunity and affirmative action. Diversity management has become a concern because of real and perceived changes in the demographic makeup of the workforce. Other important changes in the economy and the nature and context of work include globalization, growth of the service sector, increased use of electronic technology and team approaches, frequent organizational mergers, and the dramatic increase in contingent employment. The chapter also reviews the impact of federal law and regulation, including Title VII of the Civil Rights Act of 1964, the Civil Rights Act of 1991, affirmative action policies, the Age Discrimination in Employment Act, the Americans with Disabilities Act, and sexual harassment law. In sum, good diversity management has emerged as a "bottom line" issue that many believe is critical to the productivity and effectiveness of contemporary organizations.

"It's hard to define what diversity is because everyone has an opinion."
(From an advertisement for Goldman Sachs found in the now-defunct *Working Woman* magazine, October 2000: 37)

During the last decade of the twentieth century, the term "diversity" grew in frequency in business magazines, the popular media, trade books, and eventually in scholarly journals and texts. The cover of the June, 1990 *HR Magazine* announced its feature article, "Diversity in the Workplace" (Lewan, 1990) by stating that leadership by human resources professionals could turn the "perceived disadvantage" of diversity into an "organizational strength." Subsequently a survey conducted by the Society for Human Resource Management (SHRM) found that among Fortune 500 firms, three out of four reported they had "diversity programs" and 8 percent more were planning to implement them within the next year ("SHRM releases new survey," 1998). The American Management Association published a popular trade book, *Beyond Race and Gender*, in which the noted consultant Dr. R. Roosevelt Thomas, Jr., maintained that "diversity includes everyone" (Thomas 1991: 10). A book called *Diversity in the Workplace* by industrial/organizational psychologist Dr. Susan Jackson and Associates (1992) described a range of diversity-related programs in business and public sector agencies, set in perspective by scholarly introductory and concluding chapters. And the number of empirical studies addressing the effects of homogeneity/heterogeneity on workplace outcomes showed a dramatic fourfold increase in the last quarter of the century. According to Wise and Tschirhart (2000: 390), "Although it is still relatively sparse, scholarly research on diversity appears to have gained legitimacy, appearing in top-ranked journals in the 1990s."

What is this thing called "diversity," and how did it come to be such a popular topic in psychology, management, and public discourse? Furthermore, what is diversity management? And why is it so highly touted at a time when there appears to be increasing backlash against one program that has effectively increased diversity: affirmative action (Chavez, 2000)? Panel 1.1 addresses the relationship of equal employment opportunity, affirmative action, and diversity management and presents a thought-provoking case that illustrates the controversial nature of these matters in a contemporary university.

1.1 *Sorting out terms: EEO, affirmative action, and diversity*

Many people are not sure whether and how these three terms differ. Sometimes they are used together or interchangeably in the media or everyday conversation (Cox, 1997). In fact, they are quite distinct in meaning and should be distinct in application. Although related, the three terms differ in origin, referents, and underlying assumptions.

The phrase "equal employment opportunity" (EEO) comes from US federal law and regulation and can be considered a *goal state* in which everyone has an equal chance at employment regardless of race, sex, religion, national origin, or other specified attributes that are not job related. Discrimination is prohibited, but proactive procedures are not required. In theory, this condition could be reached; however, in actuality this condition does not now exist. EEO assumes that different groups of people should be treated "equally," that rewards should be based on "merit," and that decision-makers should be blind to the sex or ethnicity of applicants and employees (Yakura, 1996).

Affirmative action originated in executive orders and federal regulation (see chapter 13 for affirmative action-type programs in other nations). It is a *tool* that can be used to attain equal employment opportunity. In contradiction to EEO, affirmative action proactively *requires* decision-makers to pay attention to characteristics like sex or ethnicity to determine if they affect employment consequences. Special actions, such as hiring the ethnic minority candidate when applicants appear to have equal qualifications, are considered appropriate requirements to remedy the effects of past discrimination and thus attain equal opportunity.

The terms "valuing" and "managing diversity" are rooted in scholarship and practice rather than law. Academic researchers, consultants, and human resource professionals use this term in discussing attitudes, behaviors, intergroup relations, and the procedures and culture of organizations as they relate to significant differences among people. This framework assumes that individuals are unique, and that differences are (or can be) a bottom-line asset to organizations. It does not focus only on those target attributes or group memberships that are listed in law or regulation, but aims at the inclusion of everyone (Yakura, 1996). "Valuing" diversity usually pertains to activities designed to increase information and acceptance of cultural differences. "Managing diversity" is a broader term, which refers to a variety of interventions aimed at overcoming the potential costs of workplace differences so that they become a source of strength for the organization. See below for a fuller explanation of the meaning of diversity.

What's wrong with this picture?
"Diversity at What Cost?" shouts the headline on the first page of the *Chronicle of Higher Education*, a weekly publication for and about universities and colleges. The article (Wilson, 2002) describes the "aggressive push" of new procedures at a southern public university with a military and technical tradition, aimed at "diversifying" the faculty by increasing the proportion of hires who are female or members of ethnic minorities. The associate dean of the college of arts and sciences is pictured next to a caption that proclaims, "Under (her) leadership, nearly all faculty hires in . . . Arts and Sciences this year were female or minority scholars" (p. A1). The feature article, "Stacking the Deck for Minority Candidates?" tells us about the first Black man to be appointed to a tenure-track position in the foreign language and literature department at the university. The first line of the article says that if it were not for efforts to increase the diversity of the faculty, he probably would not be at this university.

The article's first description of the associate dean says that she attended a segregated high school, mentions her "deep-red fingernail polish, long curly hair, jangling earrings, and chain-link belt" (p. A11), and describes her as "part cheerleader and part bulldozer." The first information about the Black faculty member describes "gaffes" that occurred in his campus interview. His "demands for perfect pronunciation" as guest instructor in a Spanish class "intimidated" some female students who left in tears. He made a "factual error" about the date of publication of another scholar's work – although this may have resulted from a question beyond his area of expertise. Other department faculty are quoted as saying that before the new rules, he would have been eliminated after this experience. "The reason (he) got the job is because he's black" (p. A10). There also were concerns about one journal in which the candidate had frequently published, and about the fact that he had been tenured but not promoted at his previous university.

The hiring rules which the associate dean "helped push through" include a requirement that each search committee must itself include women and/or minorities. If the dean determines that the committee lacks diversity, it can be reconstituted by including persons from other departments or even other universities. The search committee chair must review information from candidates to ensure that minority and female applicants are in the pool. If there are too few, the committee may be asked to search more extensively. The dean's office reviews applications of "diverse" candidates; if none of them appears among the search committee's choices of candidates to be interviewed, the committee must provide an explanation. Finally, the dean and the department chairman (*sic*) choose the top candidates and make the job offer. A graph accompanying the article shows that 88 percent of tenure-track hires in the last academic year were "diversity hires," that is, not White males. Over the last five years, 54 hires were White males and 52 (almost half) were women and/or people of color.

The new Black faculty member is quoted as saying, "I don't want anyone giving me any crap or thinking, he got the job because he's black. You hire me because of my color, and I find that out, I'm out of here tomorrow. Period" (p. A10).

Midpoint thought questions

1 What do you think of "diversity" from this case example?
2 What does "diversity" mean? Is this fair? Is it legal? Who benefits from these procedures? Is this how universities ought to operate?
3 What do you think of the associate dean? What do you think of the Black faculty member? And why does our introduction to the associate dean comment on her appearance?

After you have answered these questions, please turn to p. 7 for more information about the associate dean, the Black faculty member, and the diversity culture at this university.

The rest of the picture
To develop a fuller understanding of this situation, you should understand that provisions for diverse search committees and certification of applicant pools are fairly standard hiring procedures at most universities. A second chart in the *Chronicle* article shows that over the last four years, faculty of the college of arts and sciences have numbered between 437 and 473. Women have only increased from 20 percent to 23.5 percent of the faculty during this time, despite the new "diversity" rules and the fact that most retirees in those years would certainly have been White men. Non-Whites (of either sex) increased from 7.7 percent to only 10.8 percent – only 47 of 437 faculty members. Comparison of the two charts shows that in four of the last five years, White males were the largest group of new hires. In a typical year, 25–8 faculty would be hired in the college, but only eight faculty were hired in total in the last year when 88 percent of new faculty were "diversity hires." The "88 percent" consisted of only seven people: two White females, two Blacks (one of each sex), two Asian males, and one Hispanic male.

The associate dean, who holds a doctorate in psychology, helped to set up multicultural affairs offices at two other universities before moving to this one. She has just been hired as the associate provost (a higher level than associate dean) for diversity and dual careers at a large midwestern state university. In response to criticisms from White male department chairmen that she attends to color over quality of job applicants, she says, "Every white man that holds a position (here) is not a rocket scientist . . . They have been privileged by their maleness and their whiteness, while others were being discriminated against and excluded" (p. A11). Her picture on the first page of the *Chronicle* shows a pleasant-faced woman of color, wearing a crisp white tailored jacket and black top, pearl necklace, and stylish earrings that can just barely be seen, sheltered by her thick dark hair. Her belt cannot be seen in the photograph.

Later in the article, we learn that when the Black faculty member was hired, the job was first offered to a White woman who turned it down. The third and only other finalist was a White man whose doctoral degree was not yet completed. However, he was "received very well and people were very comfortable with him."

A later edition of the *Chronicle* contains an informative letter from the department chair who supervised the Black faculty member at his previous university (Doyle-Anderson, 2002). She explains that he is a native of the African country of Ghana and is expert not only in Spanish but also in African languages. She also explains that his scholarship appears in the journal for which it is most appropriate, and that at his previous university most faculty are tenured and then promoted at a later date – exactly the pattern followed by the minority faculty member. His former chair says she was "appalled" by the "misleading" statements about the Black faculty member that appeared in the original article.

So: the Black faculty member's credentials included a completed doctorate, prior successful teaching experience, publications, and expertise in more than one modern language – including African languages. He won out over a White candidate who had not yet graduated or previously held a faculty position, presumably had less teaching experience, but with whom the current faculty were "comfortable."

And what do we learn about the environment at this university that might help us to understand the context surrounding these new hiring procedures? In another department a faculty member of Hispanic ethnicity was asked to add a hyphen to his name and to make this alteration with the Social Security Administration (SSA) in order for the university's computer system to process it. (He did put in the hyphen with the university, but not with the SSA.)

One of the science departments has no Black faculty. The chair of the department, after the associate dean "lowered the boom," acted to diversify search committees but was still unable to identify and hire minority faculty. Out of "desperation," he arranged a lunch at the Cracker Barrel restaurant with a scientist from a historically Black university who was traveling through the area in order to "feel (him) out . . . about a possible job" but found him to have "no charisma and (be) totally self-absorbed" (p. A12). Perhaps this department chair was unaware that this restaurant chain was the target of federal lawsuits alleging systematic racial discrimination against African-American employees (Battaglia, 1999) and customers ("Cracker Barrel customers sue," 2001).

More thought questions

1 What might the African-American science professor think about being asked to stop for lunch at this particular restaurant by a department chair he had never met, for an unspecified purpose?
2 Would you change the ethnic spelling of your name in order to accommodate the computer system of a university?
3 Did your images of the associate dean and the Black faculty member change after reading the second half of this commentary?

Discussion questions

1 Identify elements of affirmative action in this example. Is there justification for developing proactive measures to diversify the faculty at this university? If so, what is it?

2 How is "merit" defined in this situation? By the associate dean? By the science department chair? By the faculty just after the language professor's interview?

3 What should be the focus of "managing diversity" efforts in this context? Have efforts been targeted at the organization's culture? Should they be?

4 Does the diversity of the student body imply anything about the diversity of the faculty at a university? (Note: the Supreme Court is currently wrestling with this question.)

5 If you were working with departments to assist them in becoming more inclusive, what strategies might you recommend?

DEFINING BASIC TERMS

It doesn't take much reading or much conversation with managers, employees, consultants, and scholars to discover that the words "diversity" and "diversity management" connote different things to different people. Some definitions stress specific groups, while others do not. Some definitions emphasize power differentials, whereas others remain mute on the issue of power.

Definitions that focus on differences among employees (or potential employees) in terms of membership in particular demographic groups such as racial, ethnic, or gender categories have long been popular among diversity consultants. When Cox (1994: 6) says, "cultural diversity means the representation, in one social system, of people with distinctly different group affiliations of cultural significance," he focuses on racioethnicity, gender, and nationality as the bases for difference. He does so because he believes these dimensions to be particularly important in social interaction, because these bases of identity (unlike religion or age) do not change, and because there is substantial social science research on on these dimensions.

Others of the same orientation as Cox also focus on differences between specific groups to draw attention to the harsh consequences of power imbalances. Such imbalances historically have been quite severe and have affected large numbers of people in our society; they also have been sensitive to discuss and extremely difficult to alter. Thus, the diversity consultant Elsie Cross, who identifies herself as a small black woman, says, "When people today tell me that managing diversity is about 'all kinds of difference' I just look at them with amazement. Obviously, all difference is not treated the same" (Cross 2000: 23). Similarly, Linnehan and Konrad (1999) argue powerfully against the tendency to treat all dimensions of difference as if they were equivalent, for they are opposed to any loss of focus on the contamination of intergroup relations by privilege, power inequality, and stigmatization. An emphasis on demographic group membership in understanding diversity has also come about because many "managing diversity" programs have developed in the context of the social policy of affirmative action, or of civil rights laws such as Title VII of the Civil Rights Act of 1964. In many organizations the individuals charged with managing diversity are also the EEO/AA managers, or the two functions may be located in the same office. The legal context emphasizes membership in "protected categories," that is, groups enumerated in and covered by law or regulation, as the basis for recourse. Thus most legal remedies for unfair discrimination at work require that we identify people in terms of their demographic group memberships. It is ironic that in order to use legal means to reach a condition of equal treatment regardless of group membership, we must begin by categorizing people into groups.

Recently, a number of scholars and consultants have moved away from the focus on specific definitions toward more abstract conceptualizations. Jackson, May, and Whitney (1995: 217) define diversity as "the presence of differences among members of a social unit." For Roosevelt Thomas (1996), diversity refers to the similarities and differences among individuals in a collection, whether they are employees, jelly beans, competitor companies, organizational products or functions, strategic priorities, or any other complex mixture. Diversity increases as the number and variety of the elements in the mixture increase.

Advocates of the broader definition of diversity tend also to define "diversity management" in inclusive ways. In the spirit of inclusiveness, and also to gain the support of White men, researchers and practitioners like diversity consultant Roosevelt Thomas note that effective diversity management does not benefit one group over others. "Managing diversity," says Thomas, "is a comprehensive managerial process for developing an environment that works for all employees" (1991: 10).

Inclusive definitions may help people remember that diversity is not a code word for affirmative action (Ivancevich and Gilbert, 2000; SHRM, 2002). In a survey of employees in a regional office of a federal agency, fully 45 percent of White men believed that "Diversity management is the current terminology for affirmative action" (Soni, 2000: 399). Surprisingly, 18–28 percent of minority and/or female respondents shared that view! When diversity management appears to be a way of sneaking quotas into business, resentment and backlash are likely to be common responses (Hemphill and Haines, 1997).

The broad definitions of diversity and of diversity management also lead us to consider the relevance of social science research that might otherwise be overlooked. For example, there is a long history of research in the field of group dynamics on the effects of heterogeneity within small groups (e.g., Jackson, 1992; McGrath, 1998). Usually the basis of difference in these studies is a nondemographic variable such as ability level, personality, or informational resources. However, what has been learned about effective management of these differences is certainly relevant to contemporary diversity management. Jackson, May, and Whitney (1995) present the example of a team of White men who cannot reach consensus on solutions to organizational problems. "An organization that recognizes only sex and ethnicity as important dimensions of diversity may not consider diversity as a possible cause for the team's problems" (p. 248).

A broad definition also encourages us to recognize that the law is only one factor leading us to attend to organizational diversity. For example, in organizational theory, the differences among functional departments are seen as important sources of both innovation and conflict for organizations; they are certainly significant in understanding organizational effectiveness. Federal law does not protect people from being treated differently because of their weight (Roehling, 1999), their looks, their age (if old enough to work but under 40), their sexual orientation (Kovach and Millspaugh, 1996), their personality, or their preferences in music or in office lighting. Yet differences such as these can certainly be the source of many problems or of many valuable perspectives in the workplace.

It is also useful to remind ourselves that categories are socially constructed rather than inherent essential properties of the things around us. Constructivism assumes that we actively create our reality as we give meaning to the world we encounter. This process is inherently social and relies on language. Those in power in a society have greater influence than others on the development of language, the communication of ideas through the media, and the sharing of ideas that we call education (Hare-Mustin and Marecek, 1988).

For example, although most US citizens and the US Census Bureau have until recently thought of people as being White, Black, Hispanic, Asian/Pacific Islander, or Native American, with each generation it becomes more obvious that these categories do not fit the tremendous variety among our citizens. Multiracial citizens are beginning to object that no category describes them (Finn, 1997), and the 2000 census revised its racial and ethnic categories to take this into account (Rockquemore and Brunsma, 2002). The professional golfer Tiger Woods is the son of a Thai mother and an African-American father; he is said to have described himself as "Cablinasian," or Caucasian, Black, Indian, and Asian (Leland and Beals, 1997).

A final rationale for the inclusive definition of diversity and diversity management derives from its link to other processes of management. Indeed, Thomas (1996) sees diversity management as one aspect of the kind of cognitive task required in contemporary organizations. When there are many items and the differences among them are great, more cognitive and behavioral resources are required to deal with them. We must pay closer attention to our environment and make larger or faster changes in our behavior in order to adapt successfully. The greatest challenge is to consider simultaneously both the similarities and the differences among the elements, especially when many different dimensions simultaneously define this variation.

By conceptualizing diversity in terms of environmental complexity and change, Thomas takes a powerful conceptual leap. He shows us that the challenges posed by diversity management are just one aspect of life in an increasingly complex organizational world. Complexity of thought and flexibility of behavior are required for success in contemporary organizations. An important consequence of this perspective is that diversity management is seen as a form of organizational development and change as well as a set of processes for increasing effectiveness and harmony in a workforce that varies along important dimensions.

In sum, scholars and practitioners take two different approaches to defining "diversity" and "diversity management." One approach emphasizes the position of groups who have traditionally been victims of discrimination. It acknowledges power differentials among groups. The newer approach downplays power differentials and treats all bases of difference as more or less equivalent in terms of systemic analyses. Both approaches have strengths.

Our Working Definition

Because this volume addresses diversity management in the workplace from a psychological perspective, we will use the term "diversity" to refer to differences among people that are likely to affect their acceptance, work performance, satisfaction, or progress in an organization. When we speak of "managing diversity" we mean the purposeful use of processes and strategies that make these differences among people into an asset rather than a liability for the organization. Thus, "diversity management" involves systematic and planned programs or procedures that are designed (a) to improve interaction among diverse people, especially people of different ethnicities, sexes, or cultures; and (b) to make this diversity a source of creativity, complementarity, and greater organizational effectiveness, rather than a source of tension, conflict, miscommunication, or constraint on the effectiveness, progress, and satisfaction of employees.

The Diversity Zeitgeist

Several factors have converged to bring the concept of diversity management to the fore in the discourse on contemporary organizations. The USA continues to experience large demographic changes, and there is a widespread perception of a rapidly changing workforce. We are also undergoing changes in the economy having to do with globalization, the rapid growth in the service sector and decline of manufacturing, the growth in technology, and other related changes in work functions. Finally, almost 40 years of legal initiatives are now coming to fruition.

Demographic changes

Real changes

The figures from the 2000 census show a country that is becoming ever more ethnically diverse. Over the decade since the 1990 census, the proportions of the population identified as Hispanic or Asian have grown, while the proportion of non-Hispanic Whites has dropped and that of Blacks/African Americans has remained fairly constant. Of course, the absolute number of persons in every group has increased, which means that each of us will encounter a more diverse demographic environment.

Persons identified as Hispanic, who may be of any race, have increased about 58 percent over the last decade, from 22.4 million in 1990 to 35.3 million in 2000. Non-Hispanic Blacks have increased over 20 percent to about 35.4 million. Thus across the nation the relative size of these two minority groups is now approximately the same ("Diversity in US on upswing," 2001). The smaller population of Asian descent, now about 11.6 million, has grown faster at over 70 percent, but from a smaller base. The population of non-Hispanic Whites, although still the majority at over 198 million, has grown much more slowly at just over 5 percent.

With the latest census, although there was no "multiracial" category, for the first time respondents could indicate more than one race (Rockquemore and Brunsma, 2002). This in itself is an indicator of increasing demographic complexity. About 2.5 percent of respondents, or 6.8 million persons, chose two or more races, with the most common choice being "White" and "some other race" ("Diversity in US on upswing," 2001). According to Census Bureau estimates, between 11 and 12 million immigrants entered the US in the last decade. Furthermore, about 30 million residents or 11 percent of the population are foreign-born ("Census: 12 million immigrants," 2001).

Current trends are projected to continue in the near future. Based on the current population and assumptions about growth, the Census Bureau makes estimates of the size of various age cohorts for various dates in the future. By July 1, 2015, the 16–64 age group that represents most employed persons is estimated to be about 65 percent White (non-Hispanic); about 15.4 percent Hispanic (of any race); about 13 percent Black; about 5.4 percent Asian/Pacific Islander; and only 0.8 percent American Indian (Population Projections Program, 2000).

Perceptions of change

A major stimulus for the diversity movement was the publication in 1987 of a book by the non-profit Hudson Institute (Johnston and Packer, 1987). Ironically, part of the impact of this report stemmed from a widespread misinterpretation of some of its statistics, which captured the attention of the media around the country. The report outlined four trends expected to impact on employment: (a) the economy was expected to grow; (b) manufacturing was expected to decrease and service industries to increase; (c) new jobs in service industries were expected to require increasing levels of skill; and (d) the workforce was expected to grow slowly, become older, more female, and less White. The publication of *Workforce 2000* was followed by a deluge of books, articles, training catalogs, and workshops on the topic of "managing diversity."

Workforce 2000 included an illustration with one bar graph portraying the 1985 labor force percentages of six demographic groups, and next to it, a bar graph labeled "Increase, 1985–2000" for the same six groups (Johnston and Packer, 1987: figure 3-7, p. 95). The second graph indicated the *net* new entrants in each group, that is, those who enter the labor force minus those who leave due to retirement, death, or other factors. Neither graph actually showed the percentage of the projected 2000 workforce estimated to fall in each category. Unfortunately, misinterpretations of these graphs in the media were widespread, and many concluded that the proportion of White males in the workforce would drop precipitously, perhaps from 47 percent to 15 percent, by the turn of the century.

As later pointed out by DiTomaso and Friedman (1995), direct comparison of the two graphs was erroneous. Because White men made up 47 percent of the labor force in 1985, and because the majority of this group were already in the labor force, most White male entrants would simply replace others who were leaving. The other gender/ethnic groups each constituted smaller percentages in 1985 but would provide the majority of the net new workers. However, White men would still be a strong presence even if only a small percentage of net new entrants were White men. According to calculations made by DiTomaso and Friedman, even if only 15 percent of the net new workers were White males, White men would constitute 41 percent of the workforce in 2000.

In 1997 the Hudson Institute published a sequel, *Workforce 2020*. The authors of the later report noted how the first publication had stimulated "a diversity craze" (Judy and D'Amico, 1997: xiv) and were cautious to note that their new projections should be seen as tentative, being based on assumptions about fertility, mortality, and immigration and subject to large regional variations. The report predicted three changes in workforce demographics. First, the average age of the workforce was expected to rise until about 2020, when it would reach a plateau as many of the baby boomers reached retirement age. Second, the size of the workforce was expected to increase only slowly, barring significant changes in the rate of labor force participation or of immigration. And third, the workforce was expected to become more ethnically diverse and more female, but only incrementally so. Women were expected to constitute about half the workforce. By 2020 about two-thirds of workers were projected to be non-Hispanic Whites, about 14 percent Hispanic (of any race), 6 percent Asian, and about 11 percent Black. (American Indians, a very small percentage of the population, were not mentioned.)

Changes in the economy and work

In addition to changes in the composition of the workforce, the last several decades have brought alterations in how work is accomplished. Changes in workforce demographics may be easy for managers to see as they interact with employees. Less visible but equally important changes have also come about in the nature of work, the way it is structured, and the social context in which it is performed.

Globalization

Many companies today are "global," or at least international (Jackson and Alvarez, 1992; Judy and D'Amico, 1997). Treaties such as the North American Free Trade Alliance (NAFTA) and structures such as the European Union (EU) are breaking down commercial barriers among nations. On January 1, 2002, 12 countries in Europe completed the switch to a common currency, the Euro. Collectively these countries constitute one-sixth of the world's economy ("After years of planning," 2002). Labor pools, consumer preferences, and standards for products, services, and communication are increasingly global (SHRM, 2000).

Companies compete and form strategic alliances across national boundaries. According to Cascio (1995: 928), "global competition is the single most powerful economic fact of life in the 1990s . . . there is no going back." In 1999 there were more than 10,000 acquisitions of foreign companies by US firms, and over 7,000 purchases of US companies by interests in other countries (Harrison, 2000; Sikora, 2000). For example, in the financial sector a London firm, Old Mutual, agreed in June 2000 to buy the US investment firm United Asset Management, and Pioneer Group was purchased by an Italian bank (Boitano, 2000). At the turn of the century, 12 percent of US manufacturing employees worked for foreign-owned firms, and US business interests invested heavily overseas, particularly in Europe, Asia, and Latin America (SHRM, 2000).

The fact of globalization highlights the increasing need to understand how culture, language, and history affect present-day interactions. In addition, the need for effective interaction skills across geographic boundaries will only increase in the future. This recognition is one stimulus for the recent and growing interest in the management of diversity at work.

Growth of the service sector

The part of our economy that is growing most rapidly involves service jobs, including "services hidden within manufacturing," such as the human resources and other support staff in a company that makes a tangible product (Jackson and Alvarez, 1992: 14; Judy and D'Amico, 1997). The proportion of US workers employed in service industries rose from just over half in 1950 to 80 percent at the end of the century ("Current labor statistics," 1999; McCammon and Griffin, 2000), and three-quarters of the gross domestic product comes from the service sector of our economy (US Department of Commerce, 1999).

Manufacturing is often done at a distance by people who never see the customers who use their products. However, when services are provided, there is direct interaction between the provider and the consumer of services (Gutek, 1995). The provider must be able to understand the needs of customers, communicate well with them, and leave them satisfied with the interaction. If you have ever been a student challenged by an instructor's accent or vocabulary, a taxi rider struggling to communicate with the driver who only speaks a different language, or a patient speaking a language different from that of your healthcare provider, you can easily understand the importance of bridging diversity when services are provided. Cultural, language, or personality differences between provider and customer may impair understanding, communication, and the provision of high-quality service; thus, the importance of good management of demographic and other diversity is highlighted in service occupations.

Electronic revolution

The possibilities for communication across the boundaries of time and space have increased enormously just in the last decade. Large amounts of data can be widely and rapidly shared, the flow of information depends not only on physical proximity but on electronic access and technological savvy, and time zones become less relevant as services are provided 24 hours a day (Cascio, 1995; SHRM, 2000). This means that workers are communicating with people from vastly different backgrounds, across regions, nations, and language groups. Managers may be responsible for the work of people they have never met. There is more opportunity for collaboration with people who are widely separated geographically but less opportunity for the face-to-face development of group norms, working procedures, and interpersonal trust. The normal cues of appearance and speech upon which we rely in direct communication are absent in cybertalk. Some have heralded the "race-free" nature of electronic communication, but others have noted a "default whiteness" that may be offensive to minority individuals (Young, 2001). Even among workers who see each other frequently, the reliance on electronic mail for communication creates new challenges for effective interaction. And finally, although there are non-hierarchical aspects to electronic communication, it is clear that there is a class-based "digital divide" both at home and at work as a function of income levels and type of work. Thus information and other technology have much relevance for the management of diversity.

Other aspects of restructured work

The contemporary focus on the diversity issue arises from other aspects of group work as well. Groups or teams of employees are increasingly used to accomplish work that formerly was organized around individual workers or accomplished by assembly lines (Ilgen, 1999). Some of these teams are diverse in terms of demographic characteristics like gender or ethnic background, but most of them include persons of varying skills and prior work experience. For example, cross-functional teams are often used to improve coordination across areas of an organization and to increase speed and innovation in work (Denison, Hart, and Kahn, 1996). People are increasingly required to interact effectively with others in order to get their work done.

In addition, recent years have seen increased numbers of mergers among companies. Corporations have formed new combinations for what they have seen as strategic advantage. During the 1970s an average of 1,200 completed mergers and acquisitions was recorded each year. During the 1990s the average was more than 6,200 yearly, and over 10,000 mergers occurred in 1998 alone ("35-year profile," 2000). Although this number dropped to about 9,000 annually during 1999 and 2000, this is a remarkable increase in a ten-year period ("2000 M&A profile," 2001). Every time two companies merge, their different cultures, technologies, and ways of working pose challenges to management and to employees. Struggling through this process of blending two entities calls attention to the difficulty of dealing effectively with differences.

Another change in the work scene that affects diversity initiatives is the increase in contingent workers. These are individuals who do not have a specific or implied contract for conventional long-term employment; the term includes temporary workers and sometimes those who work part-time. During the last two decades of the twentieth century, when total employment increased 41 percent, part-time, temporary, and contract employment rose 577 percent (Robinson, 2000). A survey by the US Bureau of Labor Statistics (BLS) in February 1999 found that 5.6 million workers held "contingent" jobs, and perhaps 8 million more worked as independent contractors or in some other form of alternative arrangement. Although some contingent employees are long term, the increase in the proportion of workers with somewhat tenuous attachment to their employers has been dramatic. The inevitable result is greater diversity in the identities and indeed the very presence of the individuals who are at work from day to day. In addition, companies may have different policies, wage scales, and benefit structures for contingent employees and the core workforce of longer-term, full-time employees. Variations may occur even when the same or very similar work is being done by both groups, and is a possible source of frustration and resentment.

To make matters even less stable, "permanent" employees do not stay in one organization as long as workers did in earlier generations. According to the US Bureau of Labor Statistics (2000), from ages 18 to 34 the average worker in the US holds 9.2 different jobs. In February 2000, government data showed that approximately one quarter of all employees had been with their present employer for a year or less, and the median employee tenure was only about 3.5 years (Employee tenure summary, 2000). The combined effects of downsizing, decreases in employee loyalty accompanying new organizational cultures, increasing technological change leading to skill obsolescence, and the tight labor market at the turn of the century produced lower job tenure and more frequent career or job changes. As workers move through jobs more rapidly, everyone will have to adapt to new people and new faces at work more often than before.

Legal issues

Both the progress and the dilemmas of diversity are rooted in the civil rights legislation and policy of the 1960s and the changes in the legal climate that have resulted from politics, elections, and the development of case law. There is widespread public misunderstanding about just what is legally required in the area of fair employment. For example, in a study of affirmative action beliefs and attitudes, Kravitz and Platania (1993) found that many undergraduates at their multicultural university held incorrect beliefs about requirements for the use of "quotas," the hiring of minorities regardless of qualifications, and the circumstances in which affirmative action is legally required. Although "real" legal requirements may prevail in regulation and the courts, what people believe to be true will affect their motivation, their judgment and decision-making, and their behavior in organizations.

Over the last 40 years a number of laws and regulations have been enacted to make the American workplace more open to women and to people of color than was true in the era before the civil rights movement. According to Paskoff (1996), the corporate focus on diversity began during a period in the 1980s when early progress under fair employment law was stalled by conservative judicial appointments, unfavorable court decisions, and disincentives in procedures and remedies. "Diversity programs came into being in part as a response to this legal vacuum. Astute business people realized there were problems of discrimination in the workplace, and the law was not then a significant force in addressing them" (Paskoff, 1996: 47). Thus, directly and indirectly, legal factors have contributed to the contemporary interest in the management of diversity. Although the application of fair employment law is extremely complex, and a detailed account of all the laws is beyond the scope of this book, here we outline several important pieces of legislation and of case law.

Title VII of the Civil Rights Act (CRA) of 1964

Title VII was the first major piece of federal legislation to prohibit discrimination in employment for those in specified groups called "protected classes." It also established the Equal Employment Opportunity Commission (EEOC) to monitor and enforce the law. Under Title VII employers cannot discriminate against or segregate workers on the basis of their sex, national origin, religion, color, or race, and the law is broadly written to cover hiring, pay, promotion, and other conditions of employment. Covered entities include federal, state, and local governments, educational institutions, employers with more than 15 employees, labor unions, and employment agencies. Private clubs and Indian reservations are exempt, as are religious organizations in the case of faith-based discrimination.

Over the years, the CRA has been extended to become more inclusive. In 1978 Congress amended the 1964 CRA with the Pregnancy Discrimination Act, clarifying that pregnancy, childbirth, and related medical conditions should be treated the same as other temporary disabilities to prevent differential treatment of women. Two years later the 1980 EEOC Guidelines defined sexual harassment as a form of sex-based discrimination and thus a violation of Title VII (EEOC, 1980a). The Civil Rights Act does not address discrimination on the basis of sexual orientation, a topic that is introduced in panel 1.2 and covered in more detail in chapter 10 of this volume.

1.2 *Sexual orientation as a dimension of diversity*

One of the most fundamental aspects of our identity is our sexual orientation. According to Zuckerman and Simons (1996), this term encompasses a variety of factors that are associated with being attracted to individuals of one's own or of the other sex. Unlike other bases of diversity such as gender, ethnicity, age, and even disability, sexual orientation is not a visible attribute of employees, and thus co-workers are usually unaware of someone's sexual orientation unless that individual chooses to disclose it. Furthermore, employees who are tolerant of other differences among their co-workers may hold very strong negative attitudes towards gay, lesbian, or bisexual individuals, perhaps based in their own religious and moral beliefs; they may also feel free to express their negative views more openly than they would towards other minorities.

According to Zuckerman and Simons (1996), in larger organizations it is likely that between 3 percent and 12 percent of employees are gay, lesbian, or bisexual persons. Others report that from 4 percent to 17 percent of the workforce is gay or lesbian (Gonsiorek and Weinrich, 1991). These percentages are higher than those for some other minorities and indicate that sexual orientation is a relatively common diversity dimension within work organizations.

Neither Title VII nor the ADA nor any other federal statute at this time provides protection against discrimination based on sexual orientation. In 2001 there were only 12 states (California and Nevada in the west, Minnesota and Wisconsin in the midwest, east coast states from Delaware and New Jersey to Vermont and New Hampshire, Hawaii, and the District of Columbia) with laws barring workplace sexual orientation discrimination (Barrier, 2001). However, ordinances in certain municipalities (e.g., Atlanta) and voluntary policies in many large companies (e.g., IBM, Marriott Corporation) have provided some protection (Gray, 2001; Kovach and Millspaugh, 1996).

The political resistance to legislation such as the Employment Non-discrimination Act (ENDA; Kovach and Millspaugh, 1996) and the relative lack of attention to this issue in the diversity literature attest to the contradictory nature of attitudes about sexual orientation and the difficulty of studying this form of discrimination. Because sexual orientation is not directly observable, gay or lesbian employees may experience hostile environment harassment even if co-workers do not know or suspect their sexual orientation.

Organizations differ in diversity climate with respect to sexual orientation. Zuckerman and Simons (1996: 21) developed a quick "thermometer" that employees can use to assess their organizations. Your organization would have a "warm and receptive" climate if you answered positively to items such as these:

Partners of gays, lesbians, bisexuals, and straight people are always recognized on company invitations and so on.
We offer health and other benefits to non-married, live-in partners or employees, regardless of sexual orientation.

In contrast, a positive response to items such as these would indicate a "cold and forbidding" environment:

One or two people are known to be gay, but no one talks about it.
People often tell antigay and AIDS jokes.
Persons who came out as gay, lesbian, or bisexual have been shunned, harassed, fired, or physically injured.

In contrast to other dimensions, sexual orientation has been addressed very little in the diversity literature (but see chapter 10, this volume). The workbook by Zuckerman and Simons (1996) contains exercises, information, and case studies for individuals or groups who wish to learn about sexual orientation as a diversity dimension. Ragins and Cornwell (2001) developed and tested a model of the antecedents and consequences of workplace sexual orientation discrimination. They mailed surveys to more than 2,900 members of national gay rights organizations; the researchers were eventually able to analyze the responses provided by an ethnically diverse sample of 534 gay men and women to determine the variables most related to participants' perceptions of workplace discrimination and the degree of their disclosure of sexual orientation at work. The existence of supportive organizational policies and practices was by far the most important factor, although the existence of protective legislation and the presence of other gay co-workers were also significant. The most impactful organizational practice was welcoming same-sex partners at social events. Also important were policies that forbade sexual orientation discrimination, inclusion of sexual orientation in organizational definitions of diversity, and domestic partner benefits.

Confirmation of the importance of organizational policies was found in another survey of 537 lesbian and gay employees in 38 different organizations (Button, 2001). Employees who perceived more sexual orientation discrimination were likely to manage this aspect of their identities by *counterfeiting* (communicating to others an inaccurate heterosexual identity) or by *avoidance* (revealing as little as possible and staying away from conversations and situations in which sexual orientation might become apparent). When less discrimination was perceived, employees were more likely to adopt an *integration* strategy of revealing sexual orientation directly or indirectly and dealing with the consequences of that revelation.

Both studies showed, not surprisingly, that gay employees who perceived more discrimination also held more negative attitudes toward job and career. They reported lower job satisfaction and organizational commitment (Button, 2001), lower satisfaction with promotion opportunities and career commitment, and higher intentions to leave the organization. Those who perceived discrimination also reported fewer promotions but not lower levels of compensation (Ragins and Cornwell, 2001).

Many people have never considered sexual orientation to be important for the management of diversity, or believe that sexual orientation should not be mentioned at all in the workplace. It is easy to overlook the degree to which sexual orientation is *already* part of the culture of most organizations, simply because the predominant orientation is heterosexual and this seems so *normal*. Desk photos of spouses, discussions of dating and other social activities, the jokes that are told at work – these are indications of sexual orientation, which is generally presumed to be heterosexual (Zuckerman and Simons, 1996). For many gay, lesbian, or bisexual individuals, considerable mental energy may be required to suppress a part of the individuality that heterosexual employees can express freely. In some cases this may divert energy away from more productive work-related goals.

Often when a program or policy is altered for the benefit of a workplace minority, it is later found to be to the benefit of others as well. Domestic partner benefits are one such program; this term refers to the extension of health, leave, and other benefits of employment that are available to spouses. Employees who share households and financial responsibilities on a long-term basis with others to whom they are not married (e.g., a relative, partner, or good friend) thus have access to health and leave benefits on the same basis as married employees.

In Montana, a female faculty member became the lead plaintiff in a lawsuit against her university, claiming that denial of health and other benefits to same-sex partners violated the state constitution. Two days after the suit was filed, she received a piece of anonymous hate mail containing a powdery substance. Two days later, her home was set on fire during the night; she escaped through a window with her partner and their infant child but the house was gutted (Morgan, 2002).

If her employer had routinely provided domestic partner benefits on the same terms as spousal benefits, this lawsuit would not have been necessary and this crime might not have occurred. In addition, the employer would have created a more inclusive climate that "works for everyone."

Discussion questions

1 How does your school or work environment measure up on questions like those of Zuckerman and Simons?
2 List examples of policies or customs in your work or school organization that presume everyone is heterosexual.
3 What arguments can be made *against* domestic partner benefits? Do you find these arguments convincing?
4 In Ragins and Cornwell's study, gay employees did not report lower levels of compensation than their heterosexual colleagues. What might account for this apparent non-discrimination in pay, even though the employees report other forms of sexual orientation discrimination?

As suits were brought and case law developed under Title VII, two legal scenarios were distinguished: *disparate treatment* and *adverse impact* (Gutman, 2000). Under disparate treatment analysis, the plaintiff (the person complaining of discrimination and bringing the suit) claims that he or she was treated differently because of membership in a protected class. Because the treatment is alleged to be explicitly different, this is sometimes referred to as "intentional discrimination." Thus advertisements specifying applicant sex, use of different cutoff scores or methods of selection as a function of race or sex, or clear preferential treatment on the basis of sex, race, or religion would likely be found a violation of the law. Evidence might consist of documents or statements showing discriminatory policies or intent to discriminate. Disparate treatment cases are usually brought by individuals (though class action suits are possible) and usually involve only the most egregious discrimination because the standards of evidence are so high.

In the second scenario, adverse or disparate impact cases involve a claim that an apparently neutral employment policy or procedure in fact has a different and negative impact on members of a protected category. For example, requiring a high school diploma, a minimum height, or a particular passing score on an employment test would be suspect if it screened out disproportionate numbers of minority or female applicants or employees. In such cases the plaintiff making a claim of discrimination uses statistical evidence to show that the success rate (e.g., the percent who are hired or promoted) of majority individuals is significantly higher than that of minorities. The defendant (employer) must then show either that the plaintiff is in error, or that the practice, though discriminatory, is justified because it is job-related or a business necessity. In early Title VII adverse impact cases, this was generally interpreted to mean that the procedure must be shown to be valid as a predictor of job performance. To prevail, the plaintiff must then show that an equally valid alternative procedure with less adverse impact could have been used. Thus the plaintiff must show adverse impact at step one, and the defendant must provide evidence of validity or business necessity at step two.

What does all this imply for the management of diversity? It should be noted that fair employment laws often have the positive effect of alerting organizations to examine and sometimes change practices that directly or indirectly disadvantage various groups. There are pitfalls and unintended consequences, however. First, the entire basis for recourse under the law rests on proof of membership in a class of people on a dimension that proscribes discrimination (sex, national origin, religion, color, and race). The law does not protect against discrimination on the basis of other dimensions including appearance, social class, personality, political belief, or sexual orientation. Furthermore, any diversity practices that appear to give preferential treatment to members of one covered demographic group are suspect as disparate treatment. Finally, validity is only an issue if adverse impact is first shown; the law does not prohibit the use of invalid practices per se. Thus a company that can avoid the appearance of discrimination, perhaps by hiring women or minorities "by the numbers" without concern for qualifications, may never be challenged even if its decision rules are completely invalid and unrelated to job performance. By the same token, an employer may be hesitant to use a well-validated procedure that does have adverse impact (such as most cognitive ability tests; Bobko, Roth, and Potosky, 1999) in order to avoid legal challenge.

The Civil Rights Act of 1991 (CRA '91)

With the American system of checks and balances, the legislature can provide as many corrections to the courts as the courts provide to legislative statutes. And both the courts and the legislature can shape the outcomes of regulations made by the executive branch. In the Civil Rights Act of 1991 the legislative branch passed a law that they saw as providing correction for some of the overly conservative rulings of the Supreme Court, while simultaneously correcting for some overly liberal consequences of affirmative action. In response to Supreme Court decisions (e.g., *Wards Cove v. Atonio*, 1989) that contradicted earlier Title VII case law and made the plaintiff's burden much more difficult, Congress reinstated the pre-*Wards Cove* standards for adverse impact cases. CRA '91 also provided for jury trials and expanded monetary damages in cases of intentional discrimination and unlawful harassment. Because juries are thought to be more sympathetic than judges to plaintiffs' arguments, and because plaintiffs can now win compensatory and punitive damages (not merely back pay and appropriate remedy), the number of Title VII cases has increased (Paskoff, 1996).

The 1991 Civil Rights Act also contained a provision that many saw as an attempt to curtail affirmative action. After the Civil Rights Act of 1964 and the establishment of affirmative action in 1965, a very progressive Supreme Court rendered an important decision in the case of *Griggs v. Duke Power Company* (1971). *Griggs* in effect prohibited employers from using employment-screening tests, educational requirements, or other measures that eliminated disproportionately more applicants from the protected classes than majority applicants (i.e., procedures with adverse impact) unless the employer could demonstrate a compelling business need. This was generally interpreted as requiring demonstration that the procedure was a valid predictor of job performance. To reduce the threat of lawsuits and ensure more opportunity to underrepresented groups while retaining some of the advantages of selection through valid measures, the practice of within-group scoring was developed. When within-group scoring is used, one selects a certain number of the highest scorers among one group (e.g., White applicants) and a comparable proportion of the highest scorers among another group (e.g., people of color). Thus, two candidates might have the same within-group score but different absolute levels of performance on the selection device. This procedure was used by the US Employment Service in screening applicants for blue collar jobs (Hartigan and Wigdor, 1989) and the practice came to be called "race-norming" (or "two-list cutoff").

Perceptions of unfairness can arise when those selected from the minority group have scores below the scores of some rejected from the majority group. Even the recognition that the tests have limited powers of prediction, or that all candidates are "qualified," does not seem to eradicate the perceptions of unfairness if the predictive power of the tests is similar for majority and minority applicants (Sackett and Wilk, 1994). CRA '91 prohibited employers from adjusting or altering scores or from using different cutoff scores on employment tests on the basis of race, color, religion, sex, or national origin; such practices may be psychometrically appropriate for optimal prediction but now are legally forbidden. The challenge for employers is to use measures that without any score adjustment provide sufficient screening and valid prediction but do not cause disparate impact. An unexpected dilemma has also developed in the use of personality tests for selection because these tests have commonly been scored differently for women and men (Saad and Sackett, 2002).

Finally, Title II of the 1991 Civil Rights Act called attention to the relative absence of women and minorities at higher levels of organizations and set up a commission to study this "Glass Ceiling." The 21-member bipartisan commission was charged with studying business policies for advancement and employee development, compensation and reward systems, and existing law, and with making recommendations for increasing the advancement of minorities and women in business and government organizations. After preparing its final report published in 1996, the commission was disbanded (US Department of Labor, 1996).

Affirmative action

Perhaps the most contentious and misunderstood aspect of the legal context for diversity management is the policy of affirmative action. Most employment-related affirmative action stems from Executive Order 11246, signed by President Johnson in 1965, and later extended by other executive orders. This policy requires federal contractors above a certain size to develop plans that will ensure that no one is discriminated against on the basis of sex or race.

Affirmative action was originally intended to be a remedial procedure to overcome the lingering effects of past discrimination. A simple prohibition of future discrimination was thought to be ineffective in reversing the effects of many years of explicit exclusion and differential treatment. Therefore, "affirmative" or proactive steps were recommended or required of those who wished to contract with the federal government. Affirmative action requires that a contractor examine its workforce and the relevant labor market to determine if the proportion of qualified people from gender and ethnic groups roughly matches their availability in the workforce. If discrepancies occur, the employer must develop a plan for moving toward a workforce that is demographically representative of those qualified for employment. Goals or targets should be set and steps should be articulated for moving toward them. Underrepresented groups may be targeted for recruitment, and discriminatory obstacles (such as lack of transportation or childcare or word-of-mouth job advertising) may be reduced or removed. When two equally qualified applicants are being considered for a job or a promotion, a relative lack in the numbers of women or people of color may be used to justify the preferential selection of the woman or the person of color.

Some people have confused affirmative action with quotas, and many believe that affirmative action requires hiring "unqualified" women or minorities. In fact, preferential treatment and quotas are generally prohibited as disparate treatment under Title VII. They are legal *only* when a company loses or agrees to a settlement in a lawsuit, and a judge imposes this action as a penalty or consent decree. Otherwise quotas and preferential treatment are not permitted.

In some cases, "voluntary" affirmative action may be undertaken by a company that has not (yet) been sued. The Supreme Court in *United Steelworkers v. Weber* (1979) set forth a four-part test for a voluntary affirmative action plan: (1) its purpose must be remedial in nature; (2) it must not unnecessarily trammel the interests of other employees; (3) it must not bar absolutely members of the majority group as a class; and (4) it must be "reasonable," usually understood to mean temporary (Kleiman and Faley, 1988).

The complexities of affirmative action have been the subject of numerous books and articles (e.g., Blanchard and Crosby, 1989; Crosby and VanDeVeer, 2000; Skedsvold and Mann, 1996) and a full discussion here is beyond the scope of this chapter. In a nutshell, it is relevant for the management of diversity because it provides one process by which previously homogeneous or internally segregated organizations become more demographically diverse. To the extent that affirmative action succeeds in increasing diversity, it provides the context in which the effective management of diversity becomes critical to the health of the organization and the productivity and satisfaction of its members.

The Age Discrimination in Employment Act (ADEA) of 1967

Employees and potential employees 40 years of age or older are protected from age discrimination in employment such as hiring, discharge, forced retirement, layoffs, training, wages, or benefits. In its current form, the ADEA contains no maximum age limit, and covers private and public employers as well as overseas subsidiaries of American companies with 20 or more employees. Three exemptions exist for mandatory retirement: certain executives at age 65, law enforcement officers and firefighters, and elected or appointed high-level public officials (Gutman, 2000).

Most ADEA cases involve allegations of age discrimination in layoffs or retirement; older employees are likely to have higher salaries and thus companies' salary costs will be reduced more when they leave the rolls. Employers are permitted to provide financial retirement incentives to employees in return for voluntary waiver of the right to sue under ADEA. However, the rules for this provision are technical and specific, and programs must be carefully crafted to comply with the law. Most ADEA cases involve elements of intentional discrimination. For example, hostile environment claims (modeled on sexual harassment claims that the work environment is abusive) have also been supported under ADEA (e.g., *EEOC v. Massey*, 1997). Adverse or disparate impact arguments were made successfully in early ADEA cases, but the increasingly conservative Supreme Court stated in *Hazen v. Biggins* (1993) that it had never decided that disparate impact analysis could be applied in ADEA cases. Lower courts since that time have generally rejected adverse impact ADEA claims (Gutman, 2000). The Supreme Court has also recently (in *Kimel v. FL BOR*, 2000) restricted the application of the ADEA when the employer is a state government.

With the aging of the US workforce, the protections of the ADEA will continue to grow in significance (Judy and D'Amico, 1997). Casual age-based stereotypic or prejudicial comments may provide the basis for intentional discrimination or hostile environment suits. According to Gutman (2000), Congress perceived age discrimination to be the result of mistaken beliefs about the capabilities of older workers. The ADEA may encourage us to judge individuals on the basis of their individual characteristics rather than our stereotypes. This is a significant accomplishment in the context of diversity management.

The Americans with Disabilities Act (ADA) of 1990

Another important law for those concerned with diversity is the ADA. The Rehabilitation Act of 1973 provided for affirmative action and non-discrimination on the basis of disability for federal employees. In contrast, Title I of the ADA covers the private sector and the non-federal public sector, protecting qualified individuals with disabilities from discrimination in employment but not requiring affirmative action. Under the ADA, disability refers to a current and relatively permanent condition of physical or mental impairment that substantially limits the individual in an important activity such as seeing, walking, or working. Protections extend to those perceived to be disabled, such as the caretaker of an AIDS patient or a person in remission from a serious illness, and to those with a record of impairment, such as past drug abusers. Specific provisions cover AIDS/HIV patients (who are protected by the law) and current drug abusers or those whose conditions pose a threat to the safety of others (who are not protected). Sexual preference is excluded, as well as transvestism, transsexualism, and other sexual behavior or gender identity disorders, compulsive gambling, kleptomania, and pyromania (Gutman, 2000).

Employers are not permitted to inquire about disabilities – it is up to the applicant or employee to suggest what accommodation in testing, equipment, or other conditions will be suitable or necessary. The level of accommodation that is reasonable is determined on a case-by-case basis considering factors such as the cost, feasibility, and size of the company. Accommodations might include special testing conditions, physical alterations of working space or equipment, or restructuring of non-essential aspects of the job or the work schedule. To prevent discrimination, medical examinations cannot be required prior to a hiring offer and cannot be required only of a disabled individual. Pre-employment drug testing is not considered a "medical exam," but the more clinical forms of psychological testing, if used, cannot be required before an offer is made.

In the early 1990s many employers worried that the ADA had too broad a reach. Their early concerns have been tempered by developing case law. To gain redress under ADA the plaintiff must show two things: that she or he is disabled, and that he or she is qualified, with or without accommodation, to perform the essential functions of the job in question (Gutman, 2000). It has proven to be surprisingly difficult to show these two things in court. Especially limiting have been some recent Supreme Court decisions about correctable conditions (e.g., myopia in *Sutton v. United Airlines*, 1999) and regarding suits against state governments (*University of Alabama v. Garrett*, 2001), causing some to wonder about the effectiveness of the ADA in protecting the employment rights of the disabled. A 1999 study by the American Bar Association revealed that court decisions favored employers in over 95 percent of cases ("Employers win," 2000).

What are the implications of the ADA for those interested in the more effective management of diversity? First, it calls attention to the need to base hiring decisions on demonstrated qualifications rather than stereotypic notions of suitability, and for accommodation by the employment setting – not just by the individual – on a case-by-case basis. The ADA also raises difficult questions about perceptions of fairness when objective methods, such as validated employment tests, are altered for some individuals but not for others. The broad definition of disability invites controversy. Although the courts have to date favored employers, some fear that individuals will attempt to use ADA law and the threat of litigation to gain unfair advantage. Recent court decisions have raised the possibility that other federal statutes may be lost as the basis for challenges to discrimination by state agencies, but have extended the Title VII theory of hostile environment discrimination to cases under the ADA (Clark, 2001).

Sexual harassment

The legal prohibition against sexual harassment dates from EEOC regulations written in 1980 that defined sexual harassment as a form of sex discrimination prohibited by Title VII. In 1986 in the case of *Meritor Savings Bank v. Vinson*, the court distinguished between two types of sexual harassment: *quid pro quo*, in which sexual favors are required in exchange for employment-related consequences; and hostile environment, in which the perpetrator's "severe or pervasive" behavior changes the employment conditions into abusive ones, and the victim indicates that the conduct is "unwelcome." In later cases, the court has ruled that the victim need not prove serious psychological damage in order for harassment to be considered unlawful (*Harris v. Forklift*, 1993); and that same-sex heterosexual harassment violates the law (*Oncale v. Sundowner*, 1998). In addition, employers may be held liable for harassment if they "knew or should have known" about the behavior and did nothing to stop it. These and two other cases (*Burlington v. Ellerth*, 1998, and *Faragher v. Boca Raton*, 1998) have led to the conclusion that employers *will* be held liable in *quid pro quo* harassment, *may* be held liable in hostile environment harassment by supervisors, and probably will not be liable in cases of harassment by non-supervisory co-workers, unless supervisors knew or should have known of the harassment but did not act to address it (Gutman, 2000).

Finally, in hostile environment cases, the courts have not been consistent in their evaluations of the alleged offensive behavior. Some courts (e.g., the Sixth Circuit in *Rabidue v. Osceola*, 1986) have considered behavior to be harassing if it rises to the level that a "reasonable person" would find offensive. Other courts (e.g., the Ninth Circuit in *Ellison v. Brady*, 1991), believing that men and women differ in their opinions about what is considered harassing, have judged on the basis of what would be seen as offensive by a "reasonable woman." Gutek and O'Connor (1995) reviewed the legal and psychological evidence about the reasonable woman standard and concluded that although women define sexual harassment "more broadly and inclusively" (p. 151) than men, this difference is not large.

Sexual harassment provides a microcosm of what makes diversity management so complex and difficult, and so important and rewarding. Power differentials, variations in normative expectations by different groups whose social interactions are constrained by experience and convention, misinterpretation and misunderstanding, unwillingness to confront and engage in honest communication, ambiguity and avoidance, victim blame, and shifting standards for appropriate behavior are some of the diversity themes that can be seen in scenarios involving sexual harassment. Despite all the problems, however, people of good will can use the law to change behavioral norms.

THE BUSINESS CASE FOR DIVERSITY: PROTECTING THE BOTTOM LINE

As the diversity movement has matured, some proponents have articulated rationales for managing diversity that are thought to be persuasive to those "powerful stakeholders" who control organizational resources (Linnehan and Konrad, 1999). The "business case" for diversity management essentially states that good diversity management leads to increased profitability for a company.

The trends reviewed in this chapter have been used to support this argument. Some believe that as our economy becomes more complex, businesses must become more innovative and creative in order to survive and thrive (Cox and Blake, 1991; Robinson and Dechant, 1997). Diversification of the workforce is thought to be one way to increase innovation and creativity (e.g., McLeod, Lobel, and Cox, 1996). It has also been argued that effective management of diversity will result in lower costs to the organization in terms of grievances, lawsuits, employee turnover, and ineffectiveness due to poor communication and dissatisfaction (Cox, 1997). Finally, many companies recognize the consumer dollars that are controlled by members of ethnic minority groups, and believe that by hiring employees who come from growing sectors of the economy they will better appeal to these increasingly profitable markets.

The "business case" for diversity management has gained a great deal of credibility in the business community. According to Bowl (2001), a survey of HR professionals conducted by SHRM and *Fortune* magazine reported that a majority believed their diversity initiatives had improved the organization's culture, employee recruitment, and relations with clients, as well as creativity and productivity. Reduced interpersonal conflict was also reported. Although social scientists might criticize the study's low response rate and targeted sample, the survey's report does indicate that some stakeholders are reinforcing the argument that good diversity management is good for business.

SUMMARY AND CONCLUSIONS

This introductory chapter began by distinguishing two different ways of defining diversity, one in terms of group membership and the other a more inclusive definition that considers many dimensions of difference among people in organizations. The rationale and implications of each were explored. Among the factors that have made diversity a popular topic in psychology and in business are the demographic changes occurring in the labor force, which in perception may appear more extreme than they are in reality. Several changes in the socioeconomic context and the very nature of work were reviewed. Global influences and increases in the service sector have been accompanied by dramatic increases in the use of electronic communication. Work is more often performed in team environments, mergers have become more common, and many more workers are temporary, part-time, or moving more rapidly through a series of jobs. The fair employment legislation and regulation of the last 40 years, in particular Title VII of the 1964 Civil Rights Act and affirmative action, have succeeded in increasing the workforce diversity of many employment settings.

As contemporary organizations acknowledge the importance of effective diversity management, it becomes increasingly necessary to understand the processes that operate when organizations become more diverse. While businesses are interested in profits, scholars are invested in knowledge. Scholarly researchers want to understand the processes by which differences among people have their beneficial or deleterious effects. The following chapters move us toward a greater understanding of these processes.

2

THE ARGUMENTS AGAINST DIVERSITY: ARE THEY VALID?

Kecia M. Thomas, Dan A. Mack, and Amelie Montagliani

This chapter examines five major anti-diversity arguments that target women and the disabled, as well as the aged. In addition, we expose arguments against diversity that present diversity efforts (especially racial diversity) as barriers to organizational effectiveness, and we highlight those arguments that present diversity as merely a politically correct code word for affirmative action. For each argument we examine the biases within them and ask if there is an alternative way to frame the issue. Where possible these anti-diversity arguments are examined in light of empirical data. Furthermore, we question the prevalence of these myths by turning to larger societal beliefs in meritocracy, colorblindness, and a national melting pot that likely sustains and reinforces the diversity myths exposed. Lastly, we highlight broad lessons for successfully managing diversity and avoiding the costs of mismanaged diversity efforts.

Efforts to manage racial and gender diversity in both the public and private sectors sometimes meet with skepticism or resistance. Some individuals question whether diversity can be achieved in the workplace without substantial costs. Business people are accustomed to conducting cost-benefit analyses. Even beneficial programs are discarded if their costs exceed their benefits.

We have identified five major arguments about the high costs of diversity efforts that are used to dismiss efforts to promote diversity in the workplace. The first argument is that diversity offers little to organizational effectiveness and well-being. The second argument is that the cost of women-centered efforts are too high because women are more likely than men to let family responsibilities interfere with job loyalty and performance. The third argument is that disabled workers are thought to come with high costs to productivity and to impose a financial burden on organizations. The fourth argument is that there is less "payback potential" for hiring, training, and retaining older workers as compared to their younger counterparts. The fifth argument is that "diversity" is simply a politically correct term for affirmative action.

This chapter examines each of these arguments in turn. For each of them we ask if there are alternative ways to frame the issues. We look for the biases within the arguments and attempt to extend the same critical approach to counter-arguments in favor of diversity. Where possible, we look at the arguments in light of empirical data.

Our examination leads us to believe that the arguments are, by and large, without much merit. Having found the arguments to be weak, we then turn to the question of why they have been given such credence. Some scholars note that the anti-diversity agenda represents a contemporary form of racism or sexism, and we review the concepts articulated by such scholars. Whether or not the anti-diversity agenda is a form of covert prejudice, the agenda does seem to be in keeping with some national metaphors and myths. The chapter ends by looking at these myths, specifically the meritocracy myth, the colorblind ideal, and the melting pot metaphor, all of which appear to support diversity on the surface, yet each may distort and deny diversity at a deeper level.

ANTI-DIVERSITY ARGUMENTS

Argument 1: Diversity impairs organizational effectiveness

An often heard argument is that diversity, especially in regards to the minority labor force, offers very little to the organization as a whole in terms of knowledge, skills, and abilities. Making the workplace look different, according to this argument, adds little to organizational effectiveness. In fact, according to this argument, diversity may actually threaten effectiveness:

> My conclusion is that "managing diversity" is an ideological movement masquerading as a booster of corporate performance. While its advocates are right to point to the need for companies to adapt their rules to changing conditions, many of the recommendations of the diversity activists are illogical and counterproductive. Many companies which uncritically embrace these precepts are likely to experience more conflict between employees and weaker performance. (**D'Souza, 1995: 335**)

Many anti-diversity arguments appear to rest upon the belief that diversity, especially due to race, will create negative interpersonal dynamics among workers and thus threaten their productivity, or that workers of color themselves lack the ability to contribute meaningfully to workplace productivity. Hacker (1995) suggests that some organizations avoid diversity in order to ensure that employees, patrons, and clients remain comfortable with one another and in order to avoid the inevitable conflict that putting people of different races together will bring. Likewise, Kirschenman and Neckerman's (1991) qualitative study of employer perceptions of an inner-city workforce demonstrated that Black and Hispanic workers were perceived to be inferior to more recent immigrants, especially in regards to a work ethic. The employers in this sample also believed that a more homogeneous workplace helped to foster positive relationships among staff that would benefit the organization, and that diversity would not do this. D'Souza (1995: 334) shares a similar belief: "Advocates of 'managing diversity' never seem to consider the possibility that many ethnic traits may be liabilities for the effective functioning of most organizations." It is also suggested that to embrace diversity through developing diversity-sensitive human resource systems may threaten employee satisfaction and organizational productivity, as well as compromise the nation's principles of merit and fairness (Gottfredson, 1992).

Pro-diversity researchers take a different view. They see the effects of diversity as being contingent upon the level of commitment of the organization to the principles of diversity. Harvard Business School scholars David Thomas and Robin Ely (1996) argue that organizations address diversity from different perspectives, which result in different organizational outcomes. These authors label these diversity perspectives as *discrimination and fairness, access and legitimacy,* and *learning and effectiveness.*

Discrimination and fairness organizations are those that are concerned with fairness upon organizational entry and recruiting diversity. These organizations may look diverse – especially at the lowest levels of the company – but they have difficulty creating a positive climate for diversity and thus retaining talented people of color and White women because diversity of thought, experience, knowledge, and skills is not truly valued and utilized. The presence of minority members is unfortunately their only gauge of a "successful" diversity effort. Ultimately, discrimination and fairness organizations end up spending additional funds on recruiting, selecting, and training new workers because of their high turnover rates.

Access and legitimacy organizations do a better job at retaining diversity and typically use their diversity as a source of niche knowledge. That is, ethnic and gender diversity among employees may be used to understand the diverse markets that these employees represent. Although addressing the needs of these markets adds to the profitability of organizations, access and legitimacy organizations lose out in incorporating that knowledge throughout the entire company. Such niche knowledge is contained within a small segment of the company and is not allowed to challenge and enhance the thinking, learning, and creativity of other functions. Furthermore, the valuing of ethnic minority workers solely for their niche knowledge may lead to feelings of alienation, exploitation, and possibly "ghettoization" that may promote higher turnover. Given that their insights have not been infused throughout the organization, their higher turnover costs the organization in terms of both lost knowledge and lost personnel.

Learning and effectiveness organizations encourage fairness throughout all organizational systems and reap the benefits of niche knowledge that diversity may offer. They also use diversity as an opportunity for all organizational members (Whites included) to contribute to the organization in new and different ways. A good example of a learning and effectiveness organization is a small, non-profit public-interest law firm included by Ely and Thomas (2001) in a study of three organizations that addressed diversity from the discrimination and fairness, access and legitimacy, and learning and effectiveness paradigms. The law firm measured its progress related to diversity by considering two questions: (1) to what degree do newly represented diverse groups have the power to change the organization? and (2) to what degree are traditionally represented groups willing to change? In the case of this small law firm, the drastic change in the demographic composition of staff, and the changing focus on various lines of clients and business initiated by newly represented group members, were clear indications that the organization was utilizing the knowledge, experiences, and skills of its diverse employees to guide its strategy and future growth .

Dass and Parker (1999) identify IBM as another example of an organization that reflects the learning and effectiveness paradigm of diversity. IBM's motto of "none of us is as strong as all of us" reflects its diversity and learning motivation. Like other learning and effectiveness organizations, "Its focus is on identifying important similarities and differences and managing them in the interests of long-term learning" (p. 72).

Like Ely and Thomas (2001), Harrison, Price, and Bell (1998) conceptualized the costs of diversity as being contingent on the ways that diversity is viewed and implemented. They distinguished between surface-level diversity and deep-level diversity. Surface-level diversity focuses on visible markers such as race and gender. In contrast, deep-level diversity refers to diversity of thought and attitudes. When organizations solely attend to surface diversity, they can incur diversity-related costs; with deep-level diversity, they reap the benefits of diversity.

Attending to surface-level diversity alone may result in emotional conflict within work teams (Pelled, Eisenhardt, and Xin, 1999). In a paper that introduced the concept of "faultlines," Lau and Murnighan (1998) proposed ways in which the surface-level diversity attributes within a group (i.e., faultlines) can impact the dynamics and political processes of the group. Specifically, strong faultlines often develop when one or more diversity attributes are aligned; for example, when the most tenured members of a work team are male and White and the least tenured and most recent members are female and ethnic minority. In this case, a strong faultline is produced in which subgroups based upon race, gender, and tenure can form, thus increasing the probability of conflict between two subgroups – especially in regards to issues salient to the demographic attributes that result in the faultline developing.

Lau and Murnighan (1998) suggest that whereas general diversity has potential for performance gains due to increased creativity, faultlines may lead to losses in group performance because of increased subgroup conflict. The reason why demographically focused faultlines tend to form immediately within a group setting is because they are the most easily noted when a new group forms. Group members may implicitly categorize themselves into subgroups (based on demographic faultlines) and this may limit cross-demographic communication and severely hinder group cohesion. Ultimately, the lack of communication and cohesion, coupled with the emergence of subgroups (based on faultlines), can lead to conflict, depending on how pronounced the faultlines are within the group.

With deep diversity – when surface-level diversity is appreciated for the diversity of perspective it can offer – it is plausible that organizations can minimize the occurrence of emotional conflict (Joplin and Daus, 1997). It is also suggested that truly diverse organizations can make good use of emotional conflict, especially by using it as a way to arrive at a clarification of values and foster honest communication (McDaniel and Walls, 1997).

In order to reap the benefits of deep-level diversity, organizations must promote equal employment opportunity by attending to the surface characteristics of their human resource management (HRM) practices. Konrad and Linnehan (1995a) found in their study of formal HRM systems that an organization's use of identity-conscious structures, as opposed to identity-blind structures, is positively associated with indicators of the employment status of women and people of color. In other words, it appears that paying attention to surface characteristics through the use of identity-conscious structures is necessary in order to avoid the biases of decision-makers within an organization. Once demographically diverse newcomers are brought into an organization, systems must be put in place that reflect the organization's appreciation of the deep-level diversity that a diverse workforce can offer. Furthermore, Kossek, Zonnia, and Young (1995; cited in Richard, 2000) found that organizational demographic approaches focused on increasing diversity were necessary but insufficient for reaping the benefits of diversity. A two-pronged diversity strategy is needed for diversity to contribute to organizational success.

How can an organization adopt a strategic perspective that allows diversity to be an opportunity for learning and effectiveness? Thomas (1996, 1998) argues that multicultural leadership is key. Leaders who manage multicultural organizations must develop a new set of competencies, such as becoming bicultural boundary spanners, rejecting ethnocentrism, and working toward a higher level of awareness of their own racial or ethnic identity (see chapter 8, this volume).

A bicultural boundary spanner is able to negotiate and navigate multiple identity groups. For example, Bell (1990) found that career-oriented Black women used both their Black social networks and predominantly White professional associations to acquire the social support and professional and career-related information they needed to succeed. Multicultural leaders must also resist ethnocentrism. That is, they must resist the natural urge and temptation to perceive and evaluate from within their own cultural frame of reference. Ethnocentric leaders give the benefit of the doubt to people like themselves and miss out on the knowledge, skills, and abilities that culturally different people can offer. By working toward a higher level of racial or ethnic self-actualization, leaders come to appreciate not only the culture of others, but also their own culture. By being culturally secure, multicultural leaders are open to diversity and they serve as an important and influential role model to others in the organization by engaging in efforts to support diversity rather than resist it. Chapter 5 of this volume provides an in-depth discussion of multicultural leadership.

What is the empirical evidence relevant to the different arguments about the bottom-line value of diversity? There are a number of ways to answer this question, such as focusing on the costs of mismanaging diversity and attending to the productivity indicators of organizations and their financial statements. Effectively managing diversity can reduce costs by lowering the risk of legal challenges to existing work practices. For example, in their study of diversity-related HRM practices, Konrad and Linnehan (1995a) found that organizations undergoing EEO-related lawsuits had fewer people of color among their employees than organizations that were not facing such lawsuits. These authors suggest that organizations with the worst employment statistics regarding diversity were the most likely to be subjected to lawsuits.

Litigation costs associated with discrimination claims within organizations create a huge financial liability for many companies. For example, the Rand Corporation estimates that a company will spend at least $100,000 defending itself in a wrongful termination lawsuit (Risser, 1993). The US Equal Employment Opportunity Commission reported that in 2001, 80,840 individual charges of discrimination were filed with their office. Almost 36 percent of these involved racial discrimination, and approximately 30 percent were due to sex discrimination. Discrimination cases can be extremely costly, regardless of the outcome for the organization. Even if a company wins a lawsuit, the legal fees alone can average between $100,000 and $500,000, not counting the intangible costs from productivity losses when employees are spending time with attorneys instead of performing their duties. If the company loses, there may be additional financial burdens of awards to the plaintiff, including back pay, compensatory damages, punitive or liquidated damages, front pay, the plaintiff's attorney fees, pre- and post-judgment interest, and appeal costs, all of which can range from tens of thousands of dollars to over a million ("What is this going to cost me?" 2002).

The Denny's restaurant chain is an example of an organization that has overcome many of the costs of mismanaging its diversity. During 1993, two highly publicized class-action lawsuits were filed against it, charging the company with racism and discrimination. However, through the far-reaching and focused efforts of James Adamson, the chairman and CEO of Advantica Restaurant Group, Inc. (the parent company of Denny's), the company is now hailed as a prime example of workplace diversity. In less than a decade, Denny's has transformed itself from the "poster child of discrimination" to the winner of several prestigious awards, including Fortune's "50 Best Companies for Asians, Blacks and Hispanics," the NAACP's "Fair Share Corporate Award for Minority Business

Development," and Working Woman's "Top 25 Companies for Women Executives" (Adamson, 1998).

There is convincing research that suggests that diversity can improve organizational effectiveness by influencing processes such as innovation and creativity, and that diversity can also influence an organization's bottom line (Kuczynski, 1999). Ng and Tung (1998) found that compared to branches of a bank that were culturally homogeneous, culturally heterogeneous branches experienced lower levels of absenteeism and achieved higher levels of productivity and financial profitability, despite their employees having lower scores on job satisfaction, organizational commitment, and workplace coherence, and higher rates of turnover.

Richard (2000) examined how employee productivity, return on equity, and performance in the areas of marketing, sales growth, profitability, and market share were related to the diversity variability within an organization's workforce and it's growth strategy. Using 63 banks from three different states in the US, Richard found that the relationship between cultural diversity and organizational performance is not properly examined unless context factors such as the business growth strategy of the organization are considered. Organizations with racial diversity and a growth strategy experienced higher levels of employee productivity, return on equity, and organizational performance (operationalized as marketing, sales growth, profitability, and market share) than firms with the same level of diversity and no growth or a downsizing strategy. In other words, racial diversity, when combined with a growth strategy, will enhance productivity, and this relationship increases as strategic growth increases. Richard cautioned that if we ignore an organization's strategic context we may not detect a positive relationship between effectiveness and diversity, and perhaps even conclude that there is a negative relationship.

Does diversity impair organizational performance? It depends on the organization under study. For those organizations that lack multicultural leadership and fail to attend to diversity and use it as an opportunity for learning about new markets and new ways of working, there may well be costs associated with emotional conflict among workers and fighting lawsuits. However, for those organizations that use surface-level diversity as an opportunity to learn about and form deeper-level diversity, and that have a strategic perspective and context in which diversity is reinforced, there are many financial and productivity benefits.

Argument 2: Women lack commitment to employment

Despite laws and regulations protecting the individual choices of women in the workplace, female employees are still eyed with a degree of suspicion. Women of childbearing age are often regarded as more likely to leave their jobs than their male counterparts. In addition, women are often seen as poor economic risks because they are ill more frequently than men and they tend to quit their jobs once they marry and/or have children (Biles and Pryatel, 1978; Korabik and Rosin, 1995; Morrison, 1994). People who offer this argument against diversity note that women face more work–family conflict than men.

Some research appears to support the argument that female workers cost companies more than male workers because women have higher rates of turnover (Lawlor, 1994). At all phases in their careers, women leave their jobs more frequently than men. One can gain the impression that women may have different work motivations and less commitment to work than men.

In-depth research, however, shows that initial appearances can be deceiving. Researchers have found few, if any, differences between men and women in personality, response to work, and overall effectiveness (Dipboye, 1987; Morrison, White, and Van Velsor, 1992; Powell, 1980). Indeed, women and men seem very similar in terms of psychological attitudes and reactions to their workplaces. Kelley and Streeter's (1992) review of the gender and organizations literature revealed very few differences between men and women's responses to work. There *are* a few small gender differences, but they indicate that women are more involved in their jobs than are men. Kelley and Streeter conclude that, for the most part, it is the work context itself that drives employees' reactions to work, not gender.

Surveys show that only a tiny percentage of executive women leave their jobs because of family responsibilities (Morrison, 1994). So, why do women leave jobs? The main reason is to escape the oppressive effects of the glass ceiling or other forms of sex discrimination. In a survey of over 300 female managers, respondents who felt their expectations had not been met, who described their jobs as limited in leadership potential, responsibility, variety, time flexibility, and autonomy, or who were subjected to treacherous office politics in male-dominated work environments, reported higher intentions to quit (Rosin and Korabik, 1991). A separate survey of more than 500 top female executives revealed very similar findings. Many of the executive women claimed to be disgusted with the combination of family-unfriendly policies and other forms of sexism (Lawlor, 1994).

Women may be more aware of the barriers they face than are their employers. One recent study compared the perspectives of CEOs and female executives on career barriers for women (Ragins, Townsend, and Mattis, 1998). The CEOs blamed women's lack of experience for why they were not reaching executive levels; executive women, however, reported a male-dominated corporate culture as the most significant obstacle to women's advancement.

Systematically collected social science evidence shows that women are more accurate in their perceptions than the CEOs. Of the 40–90 percent of working women who have been the victim of some form of sexual harassment on the job (Oppenheimer, 1995), almost two-thirds of complaints were brought against a woman's immediate supervisor or another person of greater power ("Sexual harassment in the Fortune 500," 1988). In fact, one poll found that half of all sexual harassers are direct supervisors of their targets (Gutek, 1985), while another more recent poll found that 70 percent of harassers were supervisors or more senior employees than their female targets ("Statistics on sexual harassment," 1994). With numbers such as these, it appears that women do indeed experience discrimination in the workplace by higher-ranking males.

Although sexual harassment in the workplace is a serious concern for working women, it is not the only form of discrimination they face. Women are also subjected to more subtle forms of discrimination that are more difficult to detect. In a longitudinal study comparing the turnover rates for women and men and Fortune 500 companies, Stroh, Brett, and Reilly (1996) found that women do, indeed, have higher turnover rates than men, albeit for reasons other than familial obligations. The women who left their jobs cited such reasons as lack of career opportunities, job dissatisfaction, and disloyalty to the organization.

Plenty of research exists supporting the notion that women receive different developmental opportunities than men (Van Velsor and Hughes, 1990). In a study comparing the developmental experiences of male and female managers, men were found to experience greater task-related developmental challenges, whereas women experienced greater developmental challenges stemming from obstacles they faced in their jobs (Ohlott, Ruderman, and McCauley, 1994). Although both genders received equal opportunities to handle new responsibilities and to start new ventures and turn around businesses in trouble, men and women at identical levels in organizations differed in terms of the criticality, visibility, and breadth of their responsibilities and in the degree to which they interacted with others outside their organizations. In particular, women did not get key assignments involving international responsibilities, negotiation roles, managing multiple functions, and key business units, and experienced a greater degree of influencing without authority than men. In other words, women were being given stereotypical challenges that subsequently limited their career development. (See panel 2.1 for a case study on an organization that is ensuring equal developmental opportunities for both men and women.)

In an attempt to explain why women may not receive some of the same opportunities as men in the workplace, Glick and Fiske (2001) outlined the concept of "benevolent sexism" that appears to work against the career progression of women. According to these authors, the term "benevolent sexism" refers to sexism that, to the person initiating the behavior, seems benevolent because he or she views women as people who need to be protected, supported, and adored. However, this view ultimately concludes that women are weak and best suited for conventional gender roles in the workplace. Benevolent sexists view themselves positively, as gallantly carrying the burden or being protectors and providers for women, which appears legitimate given their greater amounts of responsibility and privileged roles. However, further research needs to be conducted to fully understand the role of benevolent sexism in the workplace (Begany and Milburn, 2002).

In sum, when people argue that women are a "poor risk" because they quit their jobs more often than men, they are seeing the problem from the wrong

2.1 *Best practice: The role of diversity*
in Proctor & Gamble's organization[1]

Over the last several decades within the United States, both women and minorities have been eyed with suspicion with regards to their potential contributions and commitment to organizations. Although these suspicions have been grounded within a larger societal perspective on women and minorities, some companies have "gone against the grain" and have changed their own perspectives on these groups, ultimately leading to positive results for these diverse groups and the organizations for which they work. One such organization is Proctor & Gamble.

Proctor & Gamble launched several diversity initiatives in the early 1990s, one being the Advancement of Women Task Force, aimed at the advancement of women throughout the organization. One of the most effective programs has been the "Mentor Up" program, which assigns junior-level employees, including women, as mentors to senior leaders on issues such as diversity, IT, and biotechnology. One such mentor–protégé relationship has been between Steve David, Proctor & Gamble's chief information officer (CIO), and Lois Lehman-McKeeman, a PhD in toxicology. Although the purpose of the mentoring relationship between Lehman-McKeeman and David was to teach the senior leader about biotechnology, the experience has had a greater impact than expected on them both.

David and Lehman-McKeeman came from two different fields and business perspectives within the company and were thus challenged to try different strategies for learning from each other. Getting to know the other person in a way that fosters trust also presents a challenge to any mentor–protégé relationship. Both participants have to be willing to try new ways of presenting or learning information, including meeting each other on each other's own turf.

In part because of her academic background, Lehman-McKeeman originally viewed her role as that of an instructor and set out an informal course of instruction. However, her approach adapted quickly as she got to know David. When interviewed about their overall experience of working together, both David and Lehman-McKeeman considered that learning how to communicate and work with others in the organization across levels, functions, and even gender was valuable to them as individuals. The benefits gained by Lehman-McKeeman and David as individuals will undoubtedly be translated into benefits for the business, by helping each individual to better understand the relevance of the other's work to their own work and to the mission of the organization as a whole.

In addition to the business advantages, programs such as these at Proctor & Gamble have translated into real results for women and other minority groups. By the late 1990s, Proctor & Gamble was seeing the fruits of its labors in several areas, including the job-level representation and retention rates of both women and women of color.

Due to the success of its domestic diversity efforts, Proctor & Gamble has focused on diversity when developing its new business plan for the global reorganization of its structure and culture. For example, Proctor & Gamble is making a "considered judgment" that in both Japan and the United Kingdom the company wants to be the "company of choice" for women who are interested in growth, development, contribution, and ultimately leadership. An example of Proctor & Gamble's commitment to diversity, including that related to geography, is the way the company has addressed the fact that, in South Africa, there is no real public education. As part of the contract negotiation process the company agreed to include an "educational stipend" for employees, to enable their children to go to school.

Allowing women and other minorities the opportunities to be creative, to think outside the box, to contribute, and to feel valued, has translated into win-win situations for companies such as Proctor & Gamble. By providing such opportunities, Proctor & Gamble has shown that changes within the workforce do and can occur, thus nullifying the work-related myths associated with women and minorities.

However, one cannot deny that such results would not have been possible without a change in thinking within the executive ranks of Proctor & Gamble. As the CEO and President, Durk Jager, stated: "Unless you have diversity in thinking, you will never get real diversity – racial or gender or national diversity."

Discussion questions

1 Why do mentoring relationships result in beneficial outcomes for the individuals involved, as well as the organization? Why don't more organizations sponsor mentoring programs?
2 What might be some differences in outcomes between "mentoring up" programs and traditional mentoring programs?
3 How do you think Proctor & Gamble's "Mentor Up" program would be received in other countries? What types of diversity-related efforts would be most successful in other countries?
5 Discuss the advantages and disadvantages, if any, for individuals who participate in diversity-related organizational programs.
6 What types of diversity-related programs would you like to see in your current organization?

angle. Women leave jobs not because they have different values or motivations than men, but because their opportunities are blocked. The way to solve the problem is not to refuse to hire women, but to keep opportunities open for women.

Argument 3: The disabled drive up employment costs

Although the Americans with Disabilities Act of 1991 protects workers with physical and/or mental disabilities from discrimination, beliefs and stigmas about the effect of a disability on one's ability to contribute to organizational life still exist (Stone, Stone, and Dipboye, 1992). One common assumption about physically disabled workers is the belief that physical limitations cause them to miss more work than do non-disabled workers, produce poorer quality work, and drive up the costs of healthcare premiums. Cox (1994: 90) elaborates by suggesting that "employers have traditionally resisted hiring persons with disabilities partly because of the belief that they pose safety risks, increase health care costs, have higher absence, and lower productive capacity than non-disabled workers."

In actuality, disabled workers can be a major asset to an organization's workforce. Workers with disabilities are often the most loyal to their employers, thus saving organizations money from turnover costs (Hughes and Kleiner, 1995; Mergenhagen, 1997). For example, Pizza Hut plans to increase the more than 3,000 disabled workers it currently has on staff primarily because the turnover rate for these employees is one fifth of that for its remaining 68,000 workers. In addition, workers with disabilities are often as productive or more productive than their non-disabled colleagues (Cox, 1994). DuPont found that employees with disabilities equal or exceed co-workers without disabilities in job performance levels, attendance rates, and attention to safety issues (Mergenhagen, 1997). The surprising conclusion is that, due to worker loyalty, disabled workers can actually cost an organization less than able-bodied workers.

Those still concerned about the potential costs of medical benefits for disabled workers may consider hiring employees through agencies such as the United Cerebral Palsy Association (Hughes and Kleiner, 1995). Employers do not pay health benefits if disabled workers are brought in through these agencies. In addition, tax credits are often available for companies that hire workers with cognitive disabilities. Moreover, ADA measures to accommodate workers with disabilities are minor and usually inexpensive (Mergenhagen, 1997). For example, a minor and inexpensive accommodation for a job candidate with a vision disability may involve making a required written test available in a larger font.

Argument 4: Older workers have little potential for payback

Many arguments against a diverse workforce of old and young workers involve the perceived payback potential of older employees. For example, many organizations are concerned that the cost associated with hiring and training older workers will outweigh the benefits of their employment, either because older workers are perceived as producing lower quality work or because they will simply not be in their jobs long enough to make a substantial impact or contribution to the organization (Cox, 1994; Greller, 1997). Cox and Nkomo's (1992) study of low-level managers discovered that a worker's age had a negative effect on promotability ratings even after controlling for education, tenure, and job performance.

Argument 4 does not appear to conform to what we know from empirical studies. Age has not been found to be strongly related to competence (Pasupathi, Carstensen, and Tsai, 1995), and learning capacity generally does not noticeably decline before the age of 70 (Kauffman, 1987). Moreover, one meta-analysis conducted by McEvoy and Cascio (1989) revealed that age and job performance are generally unrelated.

One important consideration, which is often overlooked, is that older workers are as diverse a group in terms of abilities and motivation as are younger workers. Just like young people, some older workers are interested in lifelong learning, while others are not. Unlike younger workers, however, older workers already possess a lifetime of experiences to build upon and apply to novel situations (Cox, 1994).

Some companies are starting to reconsider early retirement options for older workers. Such companies fear the premature organizational loss of history, experience, and problem solving abilities (Greller, 1997). Arrangements are being made to retain the benefits of an older workforce while also providing additional career opportunities for mid-career workers whose careers have plateaued (Minehan, 1997). Potential programs for senior workers include job sharing, phased retirement, part-time employment, job redesign, and job transfers (Tracy, 1996). Such programs allow employers to attract and retain experienced and productive employees approaching retirement age, while improving morale, enhancing the sense of purpose, increasing employment flexibility, and producing greater income for older workers.

Argument 5: Diversity is just the politically correct term for affirmative action

Early and formal organizational attempts at the diversification of America's workforce focused on affirmative action programs designed to include members of underrepresented groups in the corporate sector. Affirmative action, as we know it today, originated in Executive Order 11246, signed in 1965 by President Johnson. Executive Order 11246 required government contractors and subcontractors to emphasize recruitment and training of qualified individuals from underrepresented groups in the workforce (Gutman, 1993). It is a two-step process and is required only of organizations that are government contractors or are the government itself (although most organizations have volunteer affirmative action plans). The first step is to collect statistics, using conventional procedures that allow for comparisons between the numbers of qualified individuals in designated categories and the numbers employed. When a discrepancy appears (e.g., many qualified women available and only a few employed), sensible corrective actions must be taken.

Although the "classical" type of affirmative action instituted by Executive Order 11246 has provoked some backlash, other forms have provoked much more (Steeh and Krysan, 1996). Unfortunately, some confuse affirmative action with quotas. Some critics believe (incorrectly) that affirmative action programs require the selection of unqualified personnel based only upon minority status (Rosen and Jerdee, 1979). Many resent the selection of a woman or an ethnic minority over a White man in the event of a tiebreak.

Although affirmative action has enjoyed great success in allowing minorities and women entry into lower levels of many organizations, some argue these programs are not progressive enough in building support systems for newly hired minorities (Thomas, 1990). Going beyond affirmative action, diversity programs aim to ensure that all employees have access to equal opportunity in training and development and to organizational support systems, both formal and informal.

The argument that diversity is just another word for affirmative action is thus wrong on two counts. First, diversity management should go far beyond affirmative action in changing the climate within organizations. Second, diversity programs cannot be said to "replace" affirmative action because the numbers-crunching hard-nosed business approach of affirmative action – which operates much like any other form of accountability in business – will continue to be needed to help organizations feel sure that they are in fact as fair-minded as they hope to be (Crosby and Clayton, 2001).

Is Diversity Resistance the New Prejudice?

Given that the arguments against diversity seem to be neither well considered nor supported by empirical data, several scholars have expressed suspicion about their origins. Could it be that some people resist organizational efforts at diversity because they harbor prejudices against others who are not in the old mold? Certainly, the rampant bigotry of the US has declined sharply, at least in response to opinion polls (Gallup Organization, 2002). Perhaps today's resistance is simply the socially acceptable and legitimized contemporary form of old fashioned animosities.

Social psychologists have identified three forms of subtle prejudice that help us understand resistance to diversity efforts. *Aversive racists* engage in subtle, rationalized prejudice due to their feelings of ambivalence. At the root of this conflict is the need of Whites to balance the values of egalitarianism and fairness with their early-learned anti-Black sentiments (Gaertner and Dovidio, 1986). Similarly, *modern racists* engage in subtle prejudice due to their ambivalence towards Blacks brought about by a conflict between negative beliefs and attitudes about Blacks and the need to not perceive themselves as racist (McConahay, 1983). Aversive racist tendencies are most likely exhibited by political liberals (Dovidio and Gaertner, 2000). *Modern and symbolic racists* are likely more conservative politically (Dovidio and Gaertner, 2000), and they manifest their racism toward programs and policies that represent or symbolize ethnic groups such as Blacks, and which they believe will give Blacks an unfair advantage. Symbolic racists resist changing the racial status quo, since they believe that doing so (especially through policies, laws, and programs) would violate American values of individualism, self-reliance, and hard work (Nelson, 2001).

Aversive, modern, and symbolic racism are very similar explanations for the contemporary forms of prejudice that pervade society and organizations. Each of these explanations for contemporary prejudice points to the nature of anti-Black sentiments as being learned early in one's development. In addition, aversive, modern, or symbolic racists are unaware of their prejudice, unlike the racism of previous eras, which was overt and in some cases a point of pride. Each of these three forms of subtle prejudice involves individuals' struggles with racial ambivalence and the need to see themselves as upholding positive egalitarian value systems (see panel 2.2 for an additional discussion of this topic).

OTHER AMERICAN MYTHS

Several scholars have looked at the hold of the anti-diversity arguments on the American psyche and linked them to some dearly held values, which are associated with their own sets of myths (Sniderman and Tetlock, 1986), that may or may not be linked to racist and sexist prejudices (Lott and Maluso, 1995).

2.2 *Racism in today's workplace*[2]

Imagine a situation facing three hiring managers (Rex, Tim, and Mark) in a predominantly White engineering firm. Three mid-level engineering positions have been created and six applicants, three Blacks and three Whites, have applied for the position. Two applicants (one White and one Black) are clearly qualified and are hired. Two other applicants (one White and one Black) are clearly not qualified and are not hired. The remaining two applicants are not strong candidates, but neither are they totally unqualified to perform the duties of the position. To make matters more confusing, the credentials for both applicants are virtually identical.

Rex, Tim, and Mark are meeting to decide which applicant to hire. The following excerpts were taken from their discussion:

"We should be glad that the company is not subject to affirmative action policies. Because both candidates are equally qualified, it would not be fair to give one applicant the job for a reason not under his or her control, such as race. That might be seen as reverse discrimination. Whatever the choice, we must make sure the candidate is selected based on qualifications, not on an unfair 'shortcut.' I say we ask someone in the organization to help make the decision." (**Rex, Architecture Software Manager**)

"Although it is not 'politically correct' to admit, one does not have to go much further than the daily newspaper or nightly news to see evidence that Blacks, as a group, are less committed and less achievement-oriented than Whites. We should consider the facts and choose the White candidate. Even though it might be a hard pill to swallow, the odds are in favor of the organization being better served in the long run by hiring the White candidate." (**Tim, Systems Support**)

"Regardless of their qualifications, the good of the company is ultimately at stake. Look at the big picture. The company is predominantly White and our clients are predominantly White. Hiring the Black candidate would actually be a disservice, both to our company and clients, but also to the Black candidate. This inherent 'lack of fit' with our current workforce and clients would put undue hardship on all parties involved. For the sake of the organization *as a business*, I would recommend hiring the White candidate." (**Mark, Technology Supervisor**)

Based on these responses, recent diversity researchers would say the following about each manager:

(1) Rex: *modern racist*. Modern racists believe racism and discrimination are wrong; therefore, the issue isn't whether Blacks should be equal, but how that equality should be implemented in policy, law, and employment. They have a problem giving "special treatment" to Blacks because they believe it violates the work ethic that says that one only advances in life based on one's own achievements and hard work, not on "unfair" shortcuts. They believe discrimination is a thing of the past; that Blacks are too pushy, trying to get into places where they are not welcome; that the demands of Blacks are unfair; that their gains (due to social programs that provide economic, housing, and other opportunities) are undeserved and unfair. The first four tenets, they believe, do not constitute racism because they are empirical facts. They believe racism is bad.

(2) Tim: *symbolic racist*. Symbolic racism has been defined as a "blend of anti-Black affect and traditional American moral values embodied in the

Protestant Ethic." According to this view, Whites who would be classified as symbolic racists tend to resist changing the racial status quo in all areas of life – economically, socially, and politically. The term "symbolic" is used to describe this resistance, which originates not out of self-interest, but out of the general belief that Blacks violate traditional American values (such as self-reliance, individualism, hard work, obedience). Although some have challenged the uniqueness of this form of racism from other forms (e.g., overt racism), the importance of this theory is in the link between values and racial attitudes.

(3) Mark: *aversive racist*. Aversive racism is hypothesized to characterize the racial attitudes of many Whites who endorse egalitarian values, who regard themselves as non-prejudiced, but who discriminate in subtle, rationalizable ways. Aversive racists experience ambivalence between their egalitarian beliefs and their negative feelings toward Blacks. Biases related to normal cognitive, motivational, and sociocultural processes may predispose a person to develop negative racial feelings. However, egalitarian traditions and norms promote racial equality; as a consequence, aversive racists do not discriminate in situations in which they recognize that discrimination would be obvious to others or themselves. Instead, discrimination occurs when bias is not obvious or can be rationalized on the basis of some factor other than race.

As a society, we need to re-examine the reasons for which we make decisions, and be open to the idea that racism is still alive and well – it has just taken a different form, one we call *modern racism*.

> Like a virus that has mutated, racism has also evolved into different forms that not only are more difficult to recognize but also to combat. This subtle process underlying discrimination can be identified and isolated under the controlled conditions of the laboratory. In organizational decision-making, however, in which controlled conditions of an experiment are rarely possible, this process represents a substantial challenge to the equitable treatment of members of disadvantaged groups. (**Dovidio and Gaertner, 1998: 25**)

Discussion questions

1 Where have you seen or heard of examples of symbolic, aversive, or modern racism?
2 In your opinion, what have been the most important factors for the emergence of these new forms of racism?
3 How would a person know if she or he followed one of these forms of racism? What signs would they look for? How would they behave? What obstacles would they face in admitting their beliefs?
4 In your opinion, what can be done to reduce or eliminate these three forms of racism?

Heydebrand (1978) supports a critical analysis of organizational life in order to reveal the historically embedded, partial, and ideological nature of organizations which are part of a larger sociohistorical context. That is, critical theorists support the close examination of organizations in order to understand the ways in which society influences what goes on within them and how organizations reflect the times in which they exist. Critical theorists also want to understand how the beliefs, practices, customs, and behaviors of organizations (i.e., culture) benefit some individuals and disadvantage others. Therefore the practices, assumptions, and beliefs and myths that occur within organizations are not neutral, but rather they are part of a larger social and political struggle for power.

According to Schreiber (1983), critical theory takes no assumption or argument as certain and considers organizational beliefs and organizational practices as features of a historical, social, and political context, relevant to a particular time and place. Schreiber argues that viewing organizational life from a critical perspective is important because,

> Practices and assumptions that have gained such status handicap us in a number of ways. First, by not questioning their contemporary applicability, we direct our attention away from the current environment. Second, if an assumption is not up for question, then we do not focus on it and its utility and we continue to believe in its relevance. In not questioning, we divert attention from the assumption, from the current environment, and from the match between the assumption and from the current environment. (**Schreiber, 1983: 243**)

Arguments and myths, like other cultural artifacts such as organizational legends and heroes, aid in establishing and maintaining an organization's culture (Smircich and Stubbart, 1985). They also sustain the values of the larger society in which the organization operates. Three national metaphors and myths that we argue resist diversity both inside and outside of organizations are the myth of meritocracy, the colorblind ideal, and the melting pot metaphor.

The myth of meritocracy

The myth of meritocracy posits that anyone can succeed if they work hard enough. In other words, stations in life are perceived to be simply a function of the amount of effort we invest in our jobs. The underlying assumption is that the only requirement for success is effort. Thus, failure is due to a lack of ability or effort. This myth is often used as a bludgeon against minorities and women because their lower positions in organizations are assumed to be logical extensions of their abilities and/or effort. This myth does not recognize the impact of histories of exploitation and exclusion that operate within and outside of organizations.

The myth of meritocracy is dependent upon a societal culture that values individualism (Tatum, 1999) and protects dominant groups' privilege (McIntosh,

1993). By embracing individualism, those who embrace the myth of meritocracy are able to see themselves as credible, deserving, and worthy. It also allows them the belief that achieving their goals in life is solely dependent upon their innate ability and hard work. Those who adopt the meritocracy myth deny the existence of systems of oppression and privilege that stifle or provide opportunities based upon color, gender, and/or sexuality. McIntosh (1993) eloquently defines privilege as an invisible knapsack of provisions that is taken for granted and is supposed to remain unseen. To acknowledge the benefits that dominant group membership – and thus privilege – offers to one's well-being, job opportunities, and career mobility, would threaten these individuals' sense of self and self-worth.

Myth of the colorblind ideal

According to the myth of the colorblind ideal, individual differences such as race should be ignored because they are irrelevant, implying that the color of some-one's skin is meaningless and that the treatment of people of color in history can be ignored (Cox and Nkomo, 1990). The problem with this is that one cannot separate a person's race from his or her identity, because it is impossible *not* to notice race or color. Moreover, the colorblind approach does not recognize the authentic differences that are the defining features of identity (Fowers and Richardson, 1996), nor does it recognize power differentials that can hamper minority achievement. As a result, while the colorblind premise is a positive one, the reality of ignoring individual identity, culture, and minority status often has very negative consequences for minority groups. The underlying hypocrisy of the colorblind perspective is that its perpetuation tends to encourage subtle and even overt forms of discrimination against minority groups (see Shofeld, 1986). When individuals are not allowed to recognize and appreciate differences be-tween themselves and others, there is instead a reliance upon ethnocentric stand-ards and on stereotypes for explanations of differences that inevitably perpetuates rather than ends discriminatory behaviors. The result is increased tension and segregation and the positioning of race as taboo (Shofeld, 1986). The colorblind approach resists diversity and makes the mention or discussion of race taboo, thus silencing it. It also provides a shelter for aversive racists. When race doesn't matter, individuals are allowed to engage in racism without fear of being identi-fied or suffering repercussions. The colorblind perspective privileges dominant groups by reinforcing the message that "we're all the same and that differences don't matter." Shofeld (1986: 250) concludes:

> The colorblind perspective is not without some subtle dangers. It may ease initial tensions and minimize the frequency of overt conflict. Nonetheless, it can also foster phenomena like the taboo against ever mentioning race or connected issues and the refusal to recognize and deal with the existence of intergroup tensions. Thus, it fosters an environment in which aversive racists, who are basically well-intentioned,

are prone to act in a discriminatory manner. Further, it makes it unlikely that the opportunities inherent in a pluralistic institution will be fully realized and that the challenges facing such an institution will be dealt with effectively.

In organizations, the adoption of the colorblind perspective leads to a failure to capitalize on diversity. As discussed earlier, by recognizing the existence of diversity and gaining an understanding of the important contributions diverse groups can make to organizations, many aspects of organizational life can be enhanced. The colorblind perspective in contrast silences the mere recognition of differences (the surface-level diversity) and subsequently the valuing and implementation of the benefits that diversity can offer (the deeper-level diversity).

The melting pot myth

Parallel to the colorblind perspective is the metaphor of America as the great melting pot, where individuals from any country, nationality, race, creed, color, religion, or culture can come and live together in harmony. This belief automatically assumes that everyone sheds their original identities equally in favor of the "American" identity; that we are a national identity devoid of race or color. One underlying requirement not often recognized is that minorities are expected to assimilate to the dominant US culture (e.g., White, male), without retaining any vestige of their own cultures. Thus, little attention is given to how this assimilation may affect individuals who are forced to conform to a foreign culture while at the same time experiencing the distortion, marginalization, or omission of their home culture in the classes, textbooks, newscasts, newspapers, and magazines of the culture in which they reside (Hacker, 1995). In addition, the melting pot myth implies that all people have been readily accepted into this American identity, which has not always been the case. Consequently, when individuals are unable to completely assimilate, they are kept distant, excluded, and considered deficient in some manner by the majority culture (the myth of meritocracy, for example), which subsequently leads to the same devaluing and underutilization of resources (i.e., minorities) discussed throughout this chapter.

In discussing the melting pot metaphor and its resulting cycle of exclusion, Wildman (1996: 113) suggests, "In our culture, the image of the melting pot is forceful; it speaks to the powerful positive image that assimilation carries. The message to those outside the mainstream dominant culture is 'Melt in with us, be like us, or fail to do so at your peril'." This narrow-mindedness can lead to dissatisfied and unproductive employees, high turnover, and low overall organizational performance (Thomas and Ely, 1996). "Rather than as a cauldron, many commentators today prefer to see America as a mosaic or even a lumpy stew. At best, the pot still contains plenty of unmelted pieces" (Hacker, 1995: 8). Diversity is inherently more beneficial to our society than the assimilation depicted in the melting pot metaphor, since it includes a recognition and appreciation of the contributions of all members of society. We must recognize that not all of us have melted together into one identity, nor should we (Wildman, 1996).

CONCLUSION

The meritocracy myth, colorblind ideal, and melting pot metaphor have created a societal climate that discourages diversity and privileges homogeneity and the defined norm of the dominant group (Wildman and Davis, 1996). These systems of beliefs help to make the existence and maintenance of diversity myths socially acceptable. That is, diversity efforts can be opposed in socially acceptable ways by positioning diversity efforts as unfair, inequitable, and inconsistent with these societal ideals. Yet it is these ideals themselves that must be challenged. Organizations are microcosms of society. Individuals who work within organizations bring their attitudes, beliefs, and stereotypes into the workplace. Although what goes on in society is often reflected in the workplace, organizational leaders can create a different climate for diversity that does not reinforce privilege or discrimination (subtle or overt).

An important lesson offered by this analysis of the arguments against diversity is that organizational context matters. Repeatedly, it was demonstrated that diversity due to race, gender, disability, or age can be an asset for organizations whose values and strategy are open to diversity. Powell (1998) supports this conclusion and argues that organizations can simultaneously pursue a workplace that is both cohesive in its values *and* which is diverse in order to enhance creativity, innovation, productivity, and subsequently organizational effectiveness. Leadership support for diversity as a learning opportunity rather than a detriment is foremost in establishing an organizational context that can recruit and retain diversity in order to reap its organizational rewards (Chrobot-Mason and Thomas, 2002; Thomas, 1998).

Notes

1 To learn more about diversity efforts at Proctor & Gamble, see "Organization 2005: New strategies at P&G, *Diversity Factor*, fall 1999, and "Coaching the boss," *Computerworld*, January 29, 2001.
2 Based on research by John F. Dovidio (Colgate University) and Samuel L. Gaertner (University of Delaware).

Part II

MODELS AND PROCESS

Issues concerning diversity potentially impact every dimension of organizational behavior. Students and practitioners of OB are wise to consider how diversity in culture and worldviews affect fundamental social processes in the workplace, such as communicating expectations about role behavior and leading and working in a team. Moreover, the study of workplace diversity is inextricably tied to social justice concerns, in that members of non-dominant social identity groups continue to face barriers to receiving equal benefits or equal protection from harm in the workplace. Thus, the chapters in this section outline key processes that are important for understanding how these inequalities are maintained, and how they can be mitigated.

Chapter 3 moves us in the direction of theory building. Janet Kottke and Mark Agars describe existing models that help explain why and how organizations should progress toward multicultural inclusion, and then articulate their own model of multicultural inclusion in the workplace. Furthermore, the authors evaluate the empirical research that has examined various tenets of these models. Chapter 4 discusses the process of role-taking in organizations – a set of fundamental social processes that explains how we convey and interpret information about what roles we each are expected to fulfill on the job. After discussing several cultural factors that differentially shape people's behaviors, values, and expectations, Dianna Stone and Eugene Stone-Romero purposely complicate the traditional role-taking model by imputing these cultural dimensions in the psychological and social processes that occur during role-taking episodes.

Chapter 5 examines the process of leadership in organizations and provides valuable advice for leaders in diverse environments. Donna Chrobot-Mason and Marian Ruderman review many of the challenges faced by members who are not part of the dominant majority in being fully integrated in the workplace, in order to provide leaders with a thorough understanding of their task in effectively managing diversity. The authors conclude with a discussion of the skills leaders need to be multiculturally competent – an increasingly requisite skill set for today's leaders.

Chapter 6 examines the intersection between occupational health and diversity, especially race and gender. Important international conferences and new journals on occupational health have helped to raise scholars' awareness of the costs of ignoring stress and health, and well-being concerns in the workplace have grown rapidly in the past two decades. Lynda Sagrestano documents how non-Whites and women face particular risks of stress and injury due to structural and informal sources of bias and discrimination that continue to plague their workplace experiences.

Together, these chapters discuss the basic elements needed to grasp the general challenges and opportunities of understanding and managing workplace diversity.

3

MODELS AND PRACTICE OF DIVERSITY MANAGEMENT: A HISTORICAL REVIEW AND PRESENTATION OF A NEW INTEGRATION THEORY

Mark D. Agars and Janet L. Kottke

In this chapter we review existing theoretical models and research related to managing diversity. A common theme of early models is their description of reactions to the changing demographics of the workforce, with each model having as its end goal the successful management of a diverse workforce. Later models attend to the processes by which an organization achieves a diverse workforce. We also present the development of an encompassing multi-level model to guide future research and theory development. A brief overview of the research of individual, group, and organizational outcomes related to diversity training and interventions is also presented. Initial research indicates positive outcomes for diversity interventions at all three levels, revealing that recent attention to diversity management has been fruitful, but that more work is needed.

Workforce diversity is an issue that all contemporary organizations face (see chapter 1, this volume). Although the level of diversity may differ depending on industry or geographic location, no organization is free of the impact of demographic changes and globalization. Consequently, organizational leaders and scholars must give serious thought to how best to approach diversity management.

American corporations have by and large recognized the imperative. By 2001, 75 percent of the Fortune 1000 companies had invested in diversity initiatives of some kind (Daniels, 2001). Substantial numbers of large corporations have chief diversity officers at the top management levels. Sometimes the recognition has developed internally, as with the case of the Bank of Montreal, which won the Catalyst Award in 1994 for its attention to gender equity. Sometimes the recognition has been forced on a corporation, as was the case for Texaco in 1996. In response to evidence of company-wide prejudice and discrimination for ethnic minorities, Texaco was ordered to pay $140 million in damages. Texaco then spent 1 billion dollars developing a five-year plan for workforce diversity initiatives.

The cost to organizations that fail to manage diversity effectively is high (Cox, 2001; Kandola, 1995). However, organizations that have failed to address diversity, and suffered the consequences, may still turn themselves around through the implementation of sound diversity management initiatives. For an example, see panel 3.1, which describes the case of Denny's restaurant.

In response to the demographic changes in America's workforce, organizational psychologists and management scholars have attempted to understand diversity and to study diversity management. According to Ivancevich and Gilbert (2000: 77), diversity management can be defined "as the commitment on the part of the organization to recruit, retain, reward, and promote a heterogeneous mix of productive, motivated, and committed workers including people of color, whites, females, and the physically challenged." Some of these scholarly efforts have centered on the development of models of diversity and of diversity management.

This chapter describes several models that have been developed to guide practitioners and researchers in the field. Models and their close relatives, theories, provide an underlying rationale for why certain relationships exist, and why others do not, and they provide researchers with guidance about what to study. Models and theories outline relationships between hypothetical constructs, from which we derive testable hypotheses. Using a model or theory as a basis for testing hypotheses requires us to think in terms of systems, which conveniently mirror the nature of the organizations we often wish to study. When we have sound theory and models to guide our research and practice, we advance the field of organizational psychology and, ultimately, provide useful solutions to organizations.

Below, we outline the published models of diversity management that look at phenomena at a group level, and note contributions from areas outside organizational psychology. We then articulate our own model, which incorporates but also moves beyond the features of several existing conceptualizations. After laying out our own model, we review some relevant empirical research.

3.1 *The turnaround at Denny's*

Managing diversity badly can lead to significant trouble, as Denny's restaurants discovered in the 1990s. Black customers had been forced to wait longer than other patrons, asked to pay in advance, or were turned away at some restaurants. Soon, Denny's was in the midst of a media nightmare. Advantica, the parent company of Denny's, paid $54 million in legal settlements. No estimate can be made of the millions of dollars lost in business. Advantica, which also owns Carrow's and Coco's restaurants, found itself in a public relations quagmire over its failure to effectively manage diversity.

To right itself, Advantica introduced several initiatives to address the diversity of its workforce, its governing board, and its customer base. When Jim Adamson was hired as CEO in 1995, he made dramatic changes in the way business was done at Denny's. One of Adamson's first announcements was that he was "going to do everything possible to provide better jobs for women and minorities. And, I will fire you if you discriminate." Denny's instituted a hiring program that attempts to screen out potential discriminators. Diversity became a performance criterion for managers. *All* 70,000 employees of the parent company and its Denny's franchises were required to undergo diversity training that emphasized respect for differences among people. Finally, Denny's created management training programs and underwrote loans to encourage more minority ownership of Denny's franchises.

The turnaround from a hostile to a friendly environment for women and minorities at Denny's is evident in the numbers. In 1993, when the first lawsuit was filed, only one Denny's was owned by an African American; now 64 (14 percent) are owned by African Americans, and 119 (42 percent) by minorities; 36 percent of the board of directors are women and minorities (there were none in 1993); 43 percent of top management is women and minorities; 32 percent of management consists of women and minorities; and 48 percent of Advantica's employees are minorities.

In 2000 and 2001, *Fortune* magazine rated Advantica number one among the "50 Best Companies for Minorities." Other awards have rolled in, too. *Working Woman* ranked Advantica twelfth among the top 25 companies in 2001 for women executives, and *Latina Style* magazine placed Advantica in its top 50 as a place for Hispanic women to work. Other recognition has come from *Asian Enterprise* magazine, the Center for Responsibility in Business, and the National Association for the Advancement of Colored People.

Discussion questions (read the entire chapter before answering these questions)

1 Explain how the history of Denny's emulates the stages presented by the early models of diversity management described in this chapter.
2 How has Denny's used the concepts of unfreezing and freezing in its transition from diversity unfriendly to diversity friendly?

THEORY AND MODEL DEVELOPMENT IN DIVERSITY MANAGEMENT

Existing organizational models of diversity and diversity management

We outline the models in rough chronological order, starting with those first published. The early models of diversity management might best be characterized as attempts to understand organizational reactions to changing demographics, political environments, and the consequences of affirmative action. These models take an organizational perspective and propose how an organization should accept and take advantage of a changing, more diverse workforce. A common thread to these earlier models is that they describe organizational states. In these models the goal is to move the organization from one state to the next and toward progressively better approaches to addressing diversity, with the last state being the prototypical or desired goal. Although these models provide broad recommendations as to how organizations might progress from one state to the next, they also describe conditions under which such change would be necessary as well as the characteristics of organizations that achieve such change.

Gary Powell's model

One of the earliest models (Powell, 1993) characterizes diversity management in terms of how organizations respond to equal employment opportunity issues. According to Powell, organizations may be proactive, reactive, or benignly neglectful. In Powell's model, the most desirable attitude an organization may take is proactive. A proactive organization acts on its own without the prompt of anti-discriminatory laws to recruit women and minorities to the workplace, recognizing the value of a multicultural workforce. In contrast, a reactive organization accepts the responsibility of recruiting and hiring women and minorities because the organization wishes to be in compliance with existing law. Finally, an organization can choose to do nothing (benign neglect). However, such organizations risk lawsuits, boycotts of their products and services, and loss of public goodwill.

Taylor Cox's early model

Like Powell, Cox (1991) describes three types of organizations (monolithic, pluralistic, multicultural) that represent stages of receptivity of an organizational climate for valuing diversity. What differentiates organizations into these three types is the approach to acculturation of minorities and women to the organizational culture, the level of integration of minorities and women within the organizational structure, the amount of prejudice and bias, and the prevalence of intergroup conflict. The monolithic organization is accepting of women and minorities as long as these entrants to the workplace accept the majority culture. A pluralistic organization recognizes that women and minorities can contribute unique value to an organization, but the structure of the organization itself does not change. Rather, the organization promotes some carefully selected tokens with high visibility to convince people that they are active in addressing diversity. Not until an organization progresses to the multicultural state does it truly manage diversity, according to Cox. In a multicultural organization, women and minorities are not only contributing, valued members of the workforce, but, also, the organization has modified its structure to acknowledge that substantial change is necessary to take full advantage of its diverse workforce.

Roosevelt Thomas's model

Comparably, Thomas (1991, 1996) categorizes organizations into one of three types on the basis of their responses to the changing face of the workforce: affirmative action, valuing differences, or managing diversity. Organizations who respond to the changing realities of the labor market with affirmative action are seeking ways to increase the representation of minorities and women in their organizations. Affirmative action, as Thomas (1990, 1991) and others (see Crosby, in press) have noted, has limitations for the organization and for minorities and women. Organizations implementing valuing difference initiatives strive to improve the relationships among their employees by encouraging acceptance and understanding of diversity. However, as Thomas asserts, to take advantage of the potential of a diverse workforce, the organization must change its core cultures and systems to sustain the coordinated efforts of a diverse workforce (i.e., managing diversity).

Thomas (1996) outlined eight possible, but not necessarily desirable, actions that organizations may take for responding to the growing diversity in human resources:

1 Include a greater variety and number of minorities and women.
2 Deny that differences exist.
3 Assimilate minorities and women into the dominant culture.
4 Suppress differences for the sake of the organization's overall goals.
5 Isolate people who are different into special functional units, projects, or geographical operations.
6 Tolerate the coexistence of people with differences.
7 Build relationships among people to overcome differences.
8 Foster mutual adaptation, which may require changes to the organizational structure and the organization's policies.

The first five actions (include, deny, assimilate, suppress, isolate) are attempts to set aside the voices of those different from the majority and are most evident in organizations that are responding within the affirmative action paradigm. The next two (tolerate and build relationships) are seen as accommodations and are typical responses by organizations that take a "valuing differences" approach.

Only the eighth option (foster mutual adaptation) represents acceptance and management of diversity.

Robert Golembiewski's model

Using broader social history as a backdrop, Golembiewski (1995) described organizational reactions to changing demographics. He labeled five approaches to diversity as diversity under duress, equal opportunity, augmented affirmative action, valuing differences, and managing diversity. He further described the mechanisms that drive these five approaches to diversity. Diversity under duress is driven by a need to solve a problem. Both equal opportunity and augmented affirmative action are reactions to legal requirements. Valuing differences by the organization is an acknowledgment by the organization that understanding differences may lead to less conflict within the organization. Finally, in managing diversity, the organization changes structures, policies, and reward systems to achieve organizational goals and encourages employees to develop fully their differences within the organizational setting.

Intermediate models

The models described so far have some aspects in common with each other. In each of these models, organizations progress from a less desired state to a more desired state. In the early stages, organizations are reacting to environmental conditions; in the later stages they are proactive, attempting to manage the environment. In all four models the authors' change strategies acknowledge the importance of organizational characteristics in creating the desired end state. For example, to move an organization toward a proactive position, Powell (1993) recommends that the organization set goals that are consistent with the organization's mission and purpose, enlist the support of top management, diagnose the current organizational climate, and develop a coherent management system. Cox (1994) and R. Thomas (1991, 1996) also emphasize the importance of diagnosing the current organizational climate before undertaking an initiative. Golembiewski (1995), consistent with these authors' recommendations, argues persuasively for the need to overhaul the organizational structure from top to bottom so diversity can effectively be managed. Finally, the first models to be published say little about the processes by which change happens. They make very clear which end states are desirable, but they leave some ambiguity about how to reach the desired end states.

Building on the stage models, Dass and Parker (1999) and Thomas and Ely (1996) integrate process into their models of diversity management; specifically, they advocate a learning orientation. Slocum, McGill, and Lei (1994) identified a "learning organization" as adapting, accepting, and encouraging of change, and focused on continuous improvement in work processes and in continued development of the workforce. The "learning organization" concept integrates well with diversity management. Employees of learning organizations are open to change; consequently, they provide the kind of workforce that is likely to be accepting of diversity efforts. Similarly, organizations that support these characteristics are more likely than others to be receptive and accommodating of diversity.

The addition of a learning orientation to earlier thinking about diversity management represents an important step toward explaining underlying processes. Organizations that have adapted a learning effectiveness approach to diversity management, as described by Thomas and Ely (1996), are characterized by having leaders that value and build on the multiple perspectives offered by a diverse workforce. Furthermore, they see such perspectives as learning opportunities. They also support an open culture, which stimulates the growth and development of all employees while maintaining high standards of performance. However, taking a learning orientation is not equivalent to diversity management. For example, we do not know whether an adaptive perspective that proves functional for developing new job skills will be equally effective in developing interpersonal relationships with dissimilar others. In addition, the learning orientation represents only a partial explanation of underlying processes leading to effective diversity management. Although these intermediate models advance the field, further development is necessary, particularly in describing the underlying processes.

Taylor Cox's revised model: Model for work on diversity

In 2001, Taylor Cox published his "Change Model for Work on Diversity," which represents a substantial development from his earlier model (e.g., Cox, 1991; Cox and Blake, 1991). In his 2001 model, Cox builds on his earlier ideas and argues that the change to a multicultural organization involves activities in each of five components. The model is a detailed explication of the changes to organizational practices and policies that must occur for an organization to become multicultural (as described in Cox, 1991). The five components outlined by Cox include leadership, research and measurement, education, alignment of management systems, and follow-up. As can be seen in figure 3.1, there are multiple activities representing each component. The leadership component includes both broad activities, such as the need to establish management philosophy and vision that support diversity, and more specific elements, such as developing a strategy for communicating this vision throughout the organization. Cox's model also incorporates important processes such as the need to assess organizational diversity competence (research and measurement), develop internal expertise and systems to enhance the learning process (education), ensure alignment of systems within the organization with management vision (alignment of management systems), and accountability to the process (follow-up). In defense of these components as choices for his model, Cox presents multiple examples from his experience as a diversity change consultant that illustrate the importance of each. According to Cox, success at diversity management can be assessed by examining an organization's

Figure 3.1 Cox's (2001) model for work on diversity

progress within each of the five components. He suggests that progress is likely to be uneven, such that an organization may be advanced in the leadership component, but only beginning to develop education processes. To become a multicultural organization requires a systematic approach to diversity management, which necessitates advances in each of the five components.

Richard Allen and Kendyl Montgomery's model for creating diversity

Whereas Cox's revised conceptualization offers excellent tips to practitioners, another recent model developed by Allen and Montgomery (2001) emphasizes

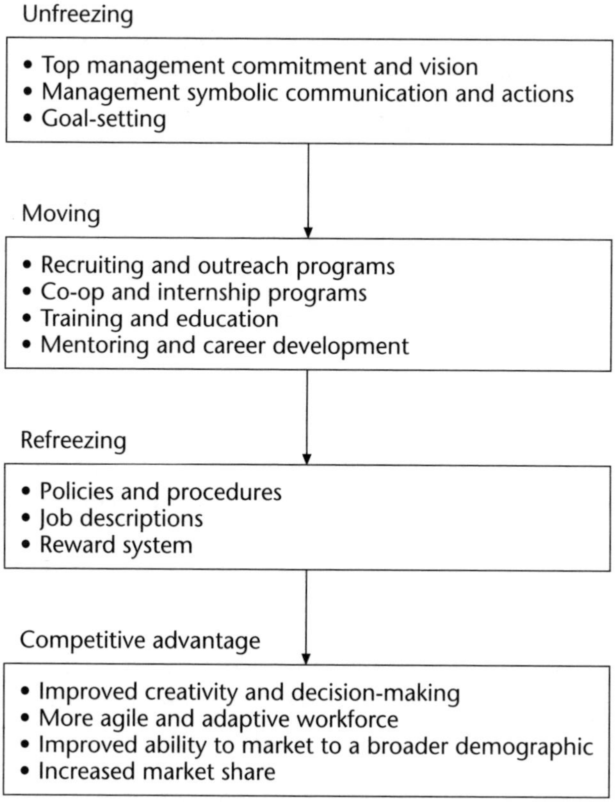

Unfreezing

> • Top management commitment and vision
> • Management symbolic communication and actions
> • Goal-setting

Moving

> • Recruiting and outreach programs
> • Co-op and internship programs
> • Training and education
> • Mentoring and career development

Refreezing

> • Policies and procedures
> • Job descriptions
> • Reward system

Competitive advantage

> • Improved creativity and decision-making
> • More agile and adaptive workforce
> • Improved ability to market to a broader demographic
> • Increased market share

Figure 3.2 Allen and Montgomery's (2001) model for creating diversity

theory over practice. Their model for creating diversity is an advance over earlier models in that it conceptualizes the diversity management process in terms of a change model. Allen and Montgomery argue that managing diversity is first about managing the change process; consequently, direction is available from existing knowledge of organizational change. Specifically, as can be seen in figure 3.2, Allen and Montgomery argue that effective diversity management is an organization-development and change process targeting diversity-related competencies. Their model bases diversity change on Schein's (1992) adaptation of Lewin's (1951) model of organizational development and change, in which organizations unfreeze from their current state, move to a new state, and refreeze at a desired end state. Allen and Montgomery identify several organizational practices at each state that are the focus of this developmental process, and necessary for effective change. Examples of these practices include top management commitment and vision at the unfreezing stage, development and training programs during the moving stage, and the establishment of appropriate diversity policies and procedures during refreezing. Their model also describes the competitive advantage achieved by organizations that effectively create diversity. Such organizations are characterized by improved creativity for decision-making, a more adaptive workforce, a broader marketing capability, and an overall increased market share.

The field of organizational behavior has seen the development of several models attempting to help organizations address emerging changes in the demographics of the workplace. Individually and collectively these models represent important advances in our understanding of diversity management. Other advances have come from related disciplines, and these developments warrant our attention.

Insights from related fields

Kandola (1995) noted that scholars would be much further along in their understanding of diversity management if they simply paid attention to existing research in other areas of organizational psychology. "By ignoring such research, the writers on diversity fail to make the linkage between the ideas they are discussing and the more central concepts of managerial effectiveness and organizational culture" (p. 161). Although these concerns are not unique to the diversity management literature, if we are to build a coherent science of diversity management, attention must be paid to incorporation of existing theory and prior research. A few examples of such insights relevant to the study of diversity management will be introduced.

One rather insightful commentary on the diversity management field is presented by Jordan (1995). Jordan argues that the lack of cross-discipline communication is a primary obstacle to advances in diversity management. She asserts that increased communication between disciplines, for example between anthropology and organizational studies, would foster an integration of ideas and understanding of diversity management in advanced of what either perspective can achieve independently. Jordan also illustrates the merits of considering diversity management from an anthropological perspective, citing, among other differences, anthropologists' more comprehensive and complex conceptualization of culture, and their consideration of organizations from both an etic (looking for cross-organizational generalities) and an emic (focusing on the uniqueness of each organization) approach. Jordan's contributions include her recognition of the lack of cross-discipline communication, and the identification of another perspective that offers valuable insights into diversity management.

Others (Chen and Eastman, 1997; Mor-Barak, 2000) provide similar insights when they suggest that effective diversity management requires an ecosystems approach. Coming from a social work perspective, Mor-Barak argues that true diversity management requires that an organization incorporate community responsibility into its actions regarding diversity. More specifically, organizations need to become active in supporting their surrounding communities (e.g., sponsor educational programs in local schools), invest in former welfare recipients to increase the job skills and standards of living of this disenfranchised group, and consider that the new global economy requires thinking beyond national boundaries in diversity initiatives. The most important implication of an ecosystem perspective on model development is to force us to think in terms of open, instead of closed, organizational systems.

Yet other developments that have implications for diversity management examine individual processes. Several researchers (Berry, 1984; Cox and Finley-Nickelson, 1991; LaFromboise, Coleman, and Gerton, 1993) discuss the individual acculturation process, which describes the adaptation of an individual within a social culture. Berry (1984) suggests that an individual progresses through one of four modes of acculturation, which he calls assimilation, separation, deculturation, and integration. According to Berry, with assimilation, the culture of the dominant group becomes the standard of behavior, and individuals seek to assume that standard. With separation, minority cultures do not merge with majority cultures. Instead, individuals from minority cultures remain isolated from the majority. With deculturation, minority group members value neither the minority culture nor the majority culture; thus, individuals lack strong ties to either group. Lastly, integration refers to a situation in which members from each culture change to some degree in order to accommodate common norms. There are negative and positive outcomes associated with each process, and the consequences of each have important implications for the organization. Cox and Finley-Nickelson (1991) argue that the organizational context, specifically its receptivity to diversity, will influence the extent to which individuals will engage in one acculturation process over others.

LaFromboise, Coleman, and Gerton (1993) present an additional acculturation process, the "alternation" model, which suggests that minority individuals need not be forced to practice one culture over the other, or to adapt their own culture. Instead, these authors argue that individuals become competent in multiple cultures and alternate the expression of each as a function of the context. This alternating is the cultural parallel of what linguists refer to as "code-switching," when multilingual individuals speak the language best suited to the context. Although an in-depth discussion of acculturation is beyond the scope of this chapter, the ideas advanced by each of these authors represent important considerations for researchers and practitioners of diversity management. Much like the alternative perspective presented by Jordan (1995) and Mor-Barak (2000), the acculturation research sheds light on relevant phenomena that have been underrepresented in the diversity management field.

In another example, Austin (1997) argues that to understand the impact of diversity, we must consider cognitive processes such as schemas, scripts, or group stereotypes that accompany demographic differences. Specifically, Austin proposes that it is not simple demographic differences that lead to effective or ineffective group performance. Instead, the level of group diversity and an individual's threshold for new experiences will determine the extent to which diversity

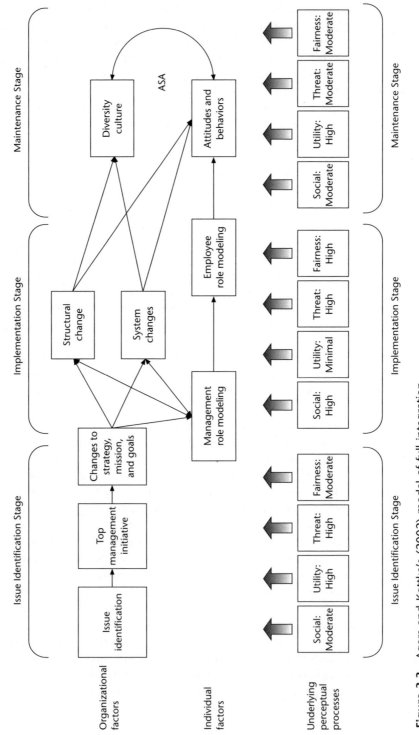

Figure 3.3 Agars and Kottke's (2002) model of full integration

impacts cognitive processing, which ultimately leads to positive or negative performance.

A final example of advancement in the diversity management field is presented by Schneider and Northcraft (1999). Schneider and Northcraft integrate social identity theory (Tajfel and Turner, 1986), which emphasizes the importance of individual identification with multiple social groups, and the theory of social dilemmas (Messick and Brewer, 1983), which posits that individuals must consider multiple and potentially conflicting outcomes of the same decision. Taken together, these theories illustrate that decisions made in the face of dilemmas will be influenced by an individual's social identities. This understanding helps identify obstacles to diversity management and provide solutions to potential resistance. By consideration of both social identity theory and the theory of social dilemmas, Schneider and Northcraft articulate theoretical explanations for why diversity management has been so difficult to accomplish.

FULL INTEGRATION THEORY

Returning our focus to models, our own "Full Integration Theory" (for a more complete discussion, see Agars and Kottke, 2002) identifies the characteristics indicative of an organization that effectively manages diversity. In our model, the "fully integrated" organization is similar to Cox's "multicultural" and Thomas's "managing diversity" organization. All such organizations have developed policies, practice, and culture to support diversity. Where our model differs from others is in explicating the processes by which organizational change occurs. The specifics of the model have been developed to address gender diversity; many of the principal elements, however, are fundamental to any diversity management effort.

The core of the model is presented in figure 3.3. It identifies diversity change management as a multi-level, systems-based, three-stage process. The model considers a number of factors related to the success or failure of an organization in its effort to become fully integrated. According to the model, organizations progress through three stages in their efforts to effectively manage diversity. These stages are (1) issue identification, during which organizations make diversity management a priority; (2) implementation, during which existing practices are adapted and new policies are implemented that support a diverse workforce; and (3) maintenance, during which formal and informal processes are established that encourage and facilitate an organizational culture supportive of diversity.

Throughout the three-stage process, the Full Integration Theory identifies four fundamental perceptual processes, which, depending on how they are managed, represent either the primary obstacles or primary facilitators of full integration. These processes include (1) social perceptions such as gender stereotypes (Deaux and Kite, 1985) and social identities (Tajfel and Turner, 1986), which influence our thoughts, attitudes, and actions; (2) perceptions of threat, which often lead to rigidity of action that results in narrowed views, performance of dominant responses, and reduced risk taking (Staw, Sandelands, and Dutton, 1981); (3) perceptions of justice (Greenberg, 1987), which is whether or not diversity management efforts are perceived as fair; and (4) perceptions of utility (Boudreau, 1991), which is the demonstration (or failure to demonstrate) the financial bene-fits of diversity management. These fundamental processes drive the success or failure of diversity management efforts.

During the issue identification stage, organizations become aware of the need for diversity management. The impetus for such awareness will be somewhat different for each organization. Consequently, any one organization's progress towards integration will be individualized. This individualization would be evidenced in the pace (sense of urgency) with which the organization addresses diversity. Nevertheless, the model proposes that each organization will follow the same path to integration.

Once awareness has occurred (issue identification), top management must support diversity efforts through the initiation of formal action such as structure change or changes to mission and goals, as well as informal actions in their interactions with organizational members. The greatest obstacle at this stage is creating awareness and convincing top management that diversity management initiatives have value to the organization. Consequently, utility is the most important process at this stage. Other processes are relevant at this time as well. For example, social cognitions are important because "full integration" may be categorized as a "women's" or a "minority" issue, not a "company" concern, and may not be taken seriously by top management. In fact, such categorization may be the result of the impetus for top management awareness (e.g., a sexual harass-ment case).

Perceived threat may also be an issue during this stage. At the organizational level, if the threat of a lawsuit has raised the diversity management agenda, it is likely to initially create rigid responses, less innovative solutions, which will be less functional for diversity management. The threat–rigidity response on the part of individual employees must also be considered by management when developing plans for diversity management initiatives. Fairness issues are less critical during the issue identification stage, although for efforts to be successful they must have an element of fairness or they are likely to fail. Organizations that implemented affirmative action policies with little regard for fairness perceptions quickly found themselves in the position of being perceived as supporting pre-ferential treatment (Konrad and Linnehan, 1999). These programs failed not be-cause they were not well intended, but because they did not consider fairness from all perspectives. Conversely, diversity management initiatives that are based entirely on fairness, with little or no consideration of other factors, namely utility, are not likely to get the needed support from top management. Successful pro-gression through the issue identification stage requires that leaders become aware of diversity concerns and that they are motivated to take action. Furthermore, leaders must attend to concerns of fairness, utility, and social perception, while demonstrating a willingness to initiate changes, both formal and informal, to the organization's mission and goals. Without awareness (issue identification), motivation (top management initiative), and action (changes to mission and goals), organizations will remain stagnated. Conversely, successful navigation through the issue identification stage leads to action necessary to implement diversity initiatives.

Stage 2 is characterized by the implementation of structural and social practices, policies, and procedures intended to support the integration of diversity. These include formal changes to organizational structure, as well as the implementation of development systems and reward systems that emphasize integration. This stage also requires behavioral changes and role modeling that exemplify new intentions.

As an organization moves into the implementation stage, the relative importance of each of the four underlying processes begins to shift. During the implementation stage, utility processes remain an issue, in that cost-benefit concerns remain important to the organization, but little emphasis is placed, at this time, on financial outcomes. As a result, utility has only minimal importance at this stage. The implementation stage is marked by the development and implementation of formal and informal organizational policies and practices that support gender diversity. Formal activities may include (1) the institution of reward systems that incorporate diversity and are bias free; (2) recruitment and selection practices that target broader, more inclusive populations; (3) harassment policies; and (4) greater diversity in leadership positions. Less formal practices are primarily centered on role modeling of pro-diversity behaviors that begins at the top level, and flows down through levels of management so that behaviors are modeled by employees throughout an organization. These aspects of implementation are easy to identify, but not so easy to accomplish. For one, social perceptions, specifically gender-role expectations, make bias-free practices and evaluations difficult. Group conflict, driven by social identities that develop along demographic lines, can also inhibit efforts. In addition, substantial changes in reward policies, recruitment and selection policies, and demographics can quickly lead to perceptions of threat by existing organizational members, and perceptions of unfairness by all. These negative outcomes are not necessary, but the Full Integration Theory details the management of social perceptions, perceptions of threat, and justice perceptions as critical to successfully managing the implementation stage of diversity management. Just as failure to manage utility will stagnate diversity management efforts in Stage 1, failure to manage the three remaining processes at Stage 2 will be equally defeating.

Ultimately, successful transition through the implementation stage requires formal and informal change throughout the organization. The result is an alignment of organizational structure and systems with the behaviors of leaders and, ultimately, employees, in support of integration. Once such changes begin, meaningful changes to organizational culture and individual attitudes can occur. Such events are the focus of the final stage, maintenance.

Stage 3, the maintenance stage, is a time of increasing stability. After diversity management policies and practices have been established, the primary goal is that they come to represent the organizational culture. Once implemented, natural processes, such as those suggested in Schneider's (1987) Attraction–Selection–Attrition (ASA) theory, work to strengthen a diversity management culture. This outcome is counterintuitive, in that Schneider's theory predicts greater homogeneity over time, not heterogeneity. However, if organizations guide the development of culture that values and supports a diversity-accepting workforce, then the ASA process will result in a workforce comprised of like employees. In addition, underlying processes of fairness and utility once again become critical.

In sum, the Full Integration Theory recognizes the change-based nature of diversity management, recognizes that relevant factors exist at multiple levels, and recognizes that such efforts require a systems perspective. Furthermore, the model informs practitioners and researchers about how to proceed with efforts directed at diversity management, by providing recommendations based on the four fundamental processes that either hinder or facilitate diversity management.

EMPIRICAL EVIDENCE RELATING TO DIVERSITY MANAGEMENT MODELS

Before presenting research findings, a few caveats are necessary. For the purposes of this chapter, we have broadly defined diversity in the workplace. However, the research to date has generally limited itself to relatively few variables. Many researchers have collected data on gender and race/ethnicity. Age has also been widely researched as a factor affecting the effectiveness of top management teams and leadership here (cf., Knight et al., 1999; Tsui, Egan, and Xin, 1995; Tsui and Gutek, 1999), but researchers interested in age do not always identify age as a diversity variable in the manner it has been used in our discussion. Research on the experiences of the physically challenged (Woodhams and Danieli, 2000) and those of different sexual orientation (Button, 2001) has been scant. In fact, we would argue that these forms of diversity may be substantially different in their character, and thus their implications for organizations may be different than the prevailing assumptions underlying ethnic, gender, and age diversity.

Researchers interested in diversity within organizations have considered different *levels of analysis* (individual, group, organization), different *methods* (case studies, field studies, archival data analyses, laboratory experiments), different *outcomes* (employee perceptions, stock prices, head counts of non-traditional employees), and have employed different *definitions of diversity* (surface- or deep-level variables). To organize the next section, type of outcome will be used to present an illustrative overview of these studies with an emphasis on the most current research.

Individual-level data: Employee perceptions, attitudes, awareness, and behavior

Diversity training is the most common organizational intervention directed at the individual. Unfortunately, diversity programs are hard to evaluate (Comer and Soliman, 1996; Ivancevich and Gilbert, 2000) except through case reviews, of which there are many examples (e.g., Alderfer, 1992; Danto, 2000; Fulkerson and Schuler, 1992; Gowing and Payne, 1992; Hudson and Hines-Hudson, 1996; Morrison and Herlihy, 1992; Roberson and Gutierrez, 1992; Schweiger, Ridley, and Marini, 1992; Sessa, 1992; Walker and Hanson, 1992; Zintz, 1997). As diversity programs are often introduced organization-wide, no controlled comparison can be made of their effects, hence the preponderance of case studies in the literature. Attempts to qualitatively review case studies have been limited (Kiselica and Maben, 1999), but they offer a more advanced form of critical evaluation not provided in single case studies.

Though few experimental studies exist (Hanover and Cellar, 1998; Roberson, Kulik, and Pepper, 2001), the results of diversity training generally have been positive on individual attitudes (cf., Kiselica and Maben, 1999; Rynes and Rosen, 1995). In the Hanover and Cellar (1998) study, middle managers of a Fortune 500 company were assigned to either a diversity training workshop or to a control group. The attitudes and self-reported behaviors of both groups were collected four months before and two months after training. Participants who had received diversity training had improved attitudes about diversity. In Roberson, Kulik, and Pepper's (2001) study, business students were assigned to heterogeneous and homogeneous groups and all participants received diversity training. Their results indicate that homogeneous groups may be more beneficial in cementing diversity values in individuals who have had previous exposure to diversity training, suggesting that future diversity programs may be more beneficial if previous experience is considered in composing groups for the purpose of diversity training.

A myriad of studies has been conducted that address other aspects of individual-level diversity outcomes. Most studies have focused on attitudes. A sampling of the results for affective outcomes shows the value of valuing diversity. Relational values, such as empathy, equality, and fairness, are seen as more important to diverse organizations (Chen and Eastman, 1997). Employee commitment rises as organizations show increasing commitment to diversity (Hopkins, Hopkins, and Mallette, 2001; Mattis, 2001). At least one study showed that behavioral outcomes accompanied attitude changes. Hanover and Cellar (1998) found that after training, middle managers displayed more diversity-friendly supervisory practices, such as discouraging stereotypic comments or jokes at work, or encouraging discussions about how diversity might affect work productivity or group cohesion.

The support for diversity programs may rely upon the justification given for the programs. Richard and Kirby (1997, 1999) conducted two analog lab studies in which they constructed hiring scenarios with different justifications for hiring decisions. In the earlier study (Richard and Kirby, 1997), White males who had not been hired rated the hiring decision more favorably and as having more procedural fairness when the scenario provided a political/legal justification than when no justification was given. In the second study (Richard and Kirby, 1999), African-American men who were told that they had been hired instead of a comparably qualified White peer also rated a hiring decision more favorably under a justified diversity program than a non-justified diversity program. In sum, both majority and minority group members preferred logical explanations for a diversity initiative.

Another focus has been on how members of the majority group, traditionally identified as White men, may differ in their support for diversity programs relative to women and minorities. White men tend to hold different attitudes than women and minorities about the concept of diversity and diversity initiatives (Konrad and Linnehan, 1995b; Mor-Barak, Cherin, and Berkman, 1998; Parker, Baltes, and Christiansen, 1997); however, these differences may not mean that organizations need to retreat from diversity initiatives for fear of offending a portion of their workforce. For example, White men's commitment to the organization for which they work may not be dependent on the organization's diversity goals. That is, White men may disagree with the goals of the bureaucracy (Naff, 1998) but remain committed to the organization (Hopkins, Hopkins, and Mallette, 2001). In contrast, women and people of color may be more committed, as evidenced by their intention to stay, when the organization for which they work expresses commitment to diversity goals and objectives (Mattis, 2001). Further, there is evidence from a large-scale study of government workers (Parker, Baltes, and Christiansen, 1997) that White men who see their organization as promoting diversity are not less satisfied with the organization, or their job opportunities, nor are they less loyal to the organization. Taken together, these results would seem to indicate that although a diversity initiative could lead to different perceptions by demographic group, the outcomes might still have acceptable consequences for the organization.

The models noted earlier in the chapter consider diversity at the organizational level of analysis and as such have not been frequently used as a basis for research at the individual-level outcome in diversity. The only model mentioned previously for which research could be located is the Cox (1991) model of an organization's level of diversity acceptance. In a study by Kirby and Richard (2000), organizational employees were queried for the reasons that their organizations were undertaking diversity programs. Specifically, Kirby and Richard were attempting to evaluate Cox and Blake's (1991) proposition that organizations can gain competitive advantage through diversity. When employees were asked to rank the importance of the six arguments for diversity initiatives, resource acquisition (or competitive advantage) was the top explanation. Another study, done with college students (Gilbert and Stead, 1999), also found support for the competitive advantage argument.

Summary of individual-level outcomes

Relatively few conclusions can be drawn from the individual outcome research. Diversity training programs do lead to more positive attitudes about people from diverse backgrounds. Also, different demographic groups display different attitudes towards organizations that implement diversity initiatives. However, these different attitudes may not lead to great differences in job involvement or organizational commitment. That is, White men remain despite less attachment to an organization, and women and minorities become more loyal to an organization that implements diversity programs.

Group-level outcomes

Unlike the research on individual-level outcomes, the group-level research clusters about specific theories or models and much of the research is experimental (laboratory based) and longitudinal (conducted over time). The group research tests specific models of group development or process using group diversity as a group composition variable and some aspect of group performance or affect as an outcome variable.

As is true with the individual-level outcome research, the research on demographically diverse work groups yields inconsistent results (Williams and O'Reilly, 1998). A few general conclusions can be stated, however: diverse groups are less cohesive (Lichtenstein et al., 1997), are characterized by more task and emotional conflict (Pelled, Eisenhardt, and Xin, 1999), are more likely to suffer withdrawal behaviors from its members (O'Reilly, Caldwell, and Barnett, 1989), but are more creative in solutions (Priem, Harrison, and Muir, 1995).

Because of the mixed results, researchers have taken two, non-contradictory approaches to explain the differential group processes inherent in diverse groups. One approach has been to investigate possible moderator variables. A moderator variable is a third variable that affects the relationship of two other variables. For example, Pelled and her associates (Pelled, 1996; Pelled, Eisenhardt, and Xin, 1999) have found that group conflict can moderate the relationship between demographic diversity and group performance. The diversity of a group can lead to affective or emotional conflict within the group; diversity can also promote task-related conflict. The latter type of conflict can enhance group performance; the former type of conflict can reduce group performance.

The other approach taken in the group research has been to deepen the definition of diversity. Whereas in the research discussed within the individual-level outcome literature, where diversity usually refers to demographic variables *only*, diversity in the group research may include different cognitive styles, values, personalities, and beliefs. Readily observable demographic differences may be important factors in group formation, but more deeply held beliefs may be the critical factors operating in group processes that lead to group outcome.

To further investigate group composition, Harrison, Price, and Bell (1998) differentiated between surface- and deep-level diversity. Surface-level diversity is defined as differences in overt biological characteristics such as age, sex, and race/ethnicity; deep-level diversity refers to differences in attitudes, beliefs, and values that require extensive interaction for one to become aware of them. In a comparable differentiation, Shaw and Barrett-Power (1998) refer to Type I, the more readily detectable characteristics such as cultural values, personality characteristics, and task-related knowledge, and Type II, the underlying attributes that include socioeconomic status, education, functional specialization, human capital assets, and work experiences. Both types may affect the development of a group and, in turn, the performance of that group.

Using the concepts of surface- and deep-level diversity as the means to categorize studies, Webber and Donahue (2001) conducted a meta-analysis of 24 group studies. Surprisingly, they found no relationship between group composition and group outcome (performance or cohesion). However, one variable, longevity of group, was not evaluated. Most studies did not report the duration of their groups and thus it could not be evaluated as a potential moderator. Studies done by Watson and associates (Watson, Johnson, Kumar, and Critelli, 1998; Watson, Johnson, and Merritt, 1998) and Harrison, Price, and Bell (1998) have demonstrated that group outcomes vary at each stage of group development. The benefits of diversity, therefore, may not appear until well into a group's functional life.

Summary of group outcome research

The value of the laboratory research is that definitive statements can be made about the effects of diversity on group outcome. Caution must be exercised in interpreting these studies, as most have been on artificially constructed groups in classroom settings. These researchers have come the farthest, however, in attempting to understand the underlying processes that may support diversity initiatives within organizations, as well as the factors that lead to failure.

Organizational-level outcomes

As Comer and Soliman (1996) noted, very few organizations have evaluated their diversity initiatives. The majority of research conducted at the organizational level has comprised case studies that have examined the implementation of diversity programs (e.g., Dobbs, 1998; Iannuzzi, 1997; Jackson and Associates, 1992; Ross, 1999; Witherspoon and Wohlert, 1996) and characteristics of organizations that have done so (e.g., Wentling and Palma-Rivas, 2000). We are fortunate these organizations are willing to share the lessons they learned in implementing diversity initiatives, but if we are to understand the bottom-line implications of diversity, multiple firm studies are necessary. No doubt the difficulty in conducting organizational-level research has also contributed to the paucity of research that examines organizational-level outcomes.

The research beyond the popular case study has examined organizational-level data by comparing the composition of an organization's workforce and its financial performance. This line of research is sensible, as it is consistent with some of the tenets of the advantages of diversity, that diversity can help an organization gain competitive advantage (e.g., Agars and Kottke, 2002; Allen and Montgomery, 2001; Cox, 1991; R. R. Thomas, 1996). One of the earliest empirical studies, investigating whether or not the effective management of diverse human resources within a firm can lead to financial success, was reported by Wright et al. (1995). Wright et al. examined the stock prices of firms that had been awarded the Department of Labor's Exemplary Voluntary Efforts (EVE) award for affirmative action programs or had been the defendants in discrimination lawsuits. Wright et al. (1995) reasoned that high quality affirmative action programs were indicators of effective management of diversity and discrimination suits could serve as proxies for ineffective diversity management. Stock prices increased for firms that had been awarded the best practices awards and decreased for firms that had the outcomes of discrimination suits made public. These results, however, cannot be taken as conclusive because Bierman (2001), who attempted a replication and extension of the Wright et al. study, failed to find the same results. For both the data of firms used by Wright et al. and a more complete dataset, Bierman found negative stock returns for EVE award winners.

Research conducted by another group of researchers (Bellinger and Hillman, 2000; Hillman et al., 1998) found support for the competitive advantage of diversity. Hillman and her colleagues compared the demographic composition of corporate boards of directors from Standard and Poor's 500 stock index to their investor returns (based on stock prices). Companies with the most women and minority directors had investor returns that were appreciably higher than those companies with no women or minority directors. These results could be due to increased access to information about their diverse consumers and employees. A diversity-minded organization may also attract more, larger investors, although alternative explanations are possible.

Summary of organizational-level outcomes

Despite the equivocal results from the Wright et al. and Bierman studies, the strategy of studying firm performance to verify the theoretical arguments that diversity can lead to competitive advantage is valuable. The Hillman et al. (1998) and Richard (2000) studies suggest that organizations committed to diversity may reap financial benefits as a result of their more diverse workforces.

CONCLUSION

As this chapter has illustrated, the last ten years have seen considerable progress in the development of models to manage diversity. For one, there is strong consensus about which characteristics organizations have that value diversity

The Catalyst organization has been making a difference in the field of diversity for 40 years. Founded in 1963, Catalyst is a non-profit applied research organization that follows and studies organizational practices related to the advancement of women in organizations. Catalyst identifies "Best Practices" in diversity management and provides guidance to organizations in their efforts.

Since 1987, Catalyst has recognized organizations that demonstrate innovative efforts related to the advancement of women, through their announcement of the Catalyst award. Each year, companies considered by Catalyst to be innovators in the development of diversity management approaches, and who can demonstrate meaningful results, receive the award. Catalyst evaluates each approach on such criteria as measurable results, senior-level leadership and support, accountability, originality, replicability, effective communication of the approach, and the integration of an approach with business strategy. Examples of past successes include 2002 winners Marriott, International, Inc., for its program "Women and Marriott: Partners for the Future"; Bayer Corporation, for its initiative "Bayer Women: Leaders for the Global Market Place"; and Fannie May, for its development of programs that support its approach to embracing diversity. Other winners include Corning International in 1999, Sara Lee Corporation in 1998, and Hewlett-Packard Company in 1992. These organizations, and other companies that have won the award, should be recognized for their advances in addressing gender and diversity management issues. They are exemplars of what effective diversity management can be, and they serve as models for other companies. They also are a rich source of information for researchers interested in studying diversity management.

To advance the field of diversity management, we need to learn from those who are successful. The Catalyst award brings attention to these successes, which means other organizations will become aware of what can be done, and some will begin their own efforts. The attention also means that researchers can look to these organizations for information. The Catalyst award highlights the fact that effective diversity management requires a consideration of the entire organization. By recognizing that effective efforts take a systematic approach, Catalyst helps raise awareness that a comprehensive perspective is critical to successful diversity management.

Discussion questions

1 In what ways does the Catalyst award contribute to our efforts to identify and understand what is successful diversity management?
2 How do the criteria for the Catalyst award winners relate to the models of diversity management and the evidence for successful diversity initiatives presented in this chapter?

management, although greater consideration of processes related to why diversity management succeeds or fails is needed. Researchers and theorists from a variety of disciplines have valuable contributions to make, and we have only just begun collaborative efforts.

Overall, there are positive outcomes to the diversity management process and diversity training. Diversity training programs support the view that changes in attitudes are possible and that the change is positive. There is also evidence that the group-process research further advances our understanding of the long-term implications of diversity. There is also initial evidence that organizations may experience financial benefit from effective diversity management.

Final thoughts

Efforts to improve diversity management and to implement effective models of diversity management are often slow to develop on their own. As discussed throughout this chapter, the benefits of effective diversity management take time to emerge, and are sometimes difficult to articulate to organizational leaders in a way that leads to serious commitment on the part of organizations. How can organizations be made aware of the value that comes when diversity management approaches are effective? Unfortunately, those individuals who believe in the value of diversity management face many obstacles in their attempts to raise organizational awareness and, more importantly, to actually initiate diversity management efforts. One organization that has helped in this regard is Catalyst, and we describe their efforts in panel 3.2.

As more diversity management practices are recognized for their effectiveness, and organizations are held accountable for making sure such initiatives work, other organizations can learn from these examples, and the practice of diversity management will advance. The field includes researchers, consultants, and organizational members, all striving to further our understanding of diversity management. By building on previous work, collaborating across disciplines, developing sound theoretical models, and recognizing successful efforts, the field of diversity management will continue to move forward.

4

THE INFLUENCE OF CULTURE ON ROLE-TAKING IN CULTURALLY DIVERSE ORGANIZATIONS

Dianna L. Stone and Eugene F. Stone-Romero

With few exceptions, currently popular models in the fields of Industrial and Organizational Psychology, Organizational Behavior, and Human Resources Management fail to consider the influence of culture on behavior in organizational settings. Thus, we review literature on several dimensions of culture (e.g., individualism versus collectivism, achievement orientation versus ascription orientation, universalism versus particularism) that are relevant to organizational behavior. In addition, we describe Katz and Kahn's (1978) seminal model of role-taking in organizational settings. We present a revised version of the same model that specifies how culture influences the role-taking process. Finally, we offer several practical implications of our revised role-taking model.

For several centuries, individuals of European (e.g., Anglo-Saxon) ancestry have made up the overwhelming majority of individuals in the US workforce. However, as Hays-Thomas (chapter 1, this volume) notes, in recent years the workforce has become considerably more diverse in terms of race, sex, ethnicity, and a host of other factors. One very important implication of these trends is that workers in US work organizations are often the products of many different cultural and subcultural backgrounds. As we detail below, there are a number of important consequences of this cultural heterogeneity for behavior in organizational settings. Of particular interest to us is the way in which culture influences the role-taking process.

RELATIVE NEGLECT OF CULTURAL DIVERSITY ISSUES IN THE LITERATURE ON WORK ORGANIZATIONS

A review of relevant literature shows that relatively little research in Industrial and Organizational Psychology and related disciplines (e.g., Human Resources Management, Organizational Behavior) has focused on the effects of cultural diversity on organizational behavior (Betancourt and Lopez, 1993; Earley and Erez, 1997; Erez and Earley, 1993; Stone-Romero, Stone, and Salas, in press; Triandis, 1994). Because of this, Triandis (1994) and others (e.g., Erez and Earley, 1993) have argued that many organizational theories are underdeveloped, failing to consider the critical role that subjective culture plays in organizational behavior. *Subjective culture* (referred to hereinafter as *culture*) has been defined in terms of such variables as social norms, roles, beliefs, values, communication patterns, affective styles, and orientations toward time (e.g., Hofstede, 1980, 1991; Triandis, 1980).

Consistent with the views of Triandis (1994) and others, we believe that it is critical to gain an understanding of the issues faced by organizations that employ workers from different cultures. Thus, the primary purposes of this chapter are to (a) describe one of the key frameworks that have been used to explain organizational behavior, i.e., the Role-Taking Model (RTM) of Katz and Kahn (1978); (b) review literature concerned with several cultural dimensions that are relevant to organizational behavior; (c) describe how individuals from different ethnic groups differ from one another in terms of the same cultural dimensions; (d) specify how culture influences the scripts (Shank and Abelson, 1977) that are available to individuals, and how these influence organizational behavior; (e) present a Revised Role-Taking Model (RRTM) that incorporates the notions of culture and scripts; and (f) discuss the practical implications of the RRTM.

THE ROLE-TAKING MODEL

Katz and Kahn (1978) characterized organizations as systems of interrelated roles. Given the typically high level of interdependence between incumbents in such roles, members of any given person's *role set* (e.g., the person's supervisors, peers, and subordinates) depend upon the focal person to exhibit appropriate and dependable role behavior. We use the term *focal person* to describe an individual who is the focus of attention in an analysis of role-taking.

The role-taking process

In any given organization, role set members develop beliefs about what the focal person should and should not do in his or her role. They then communicate

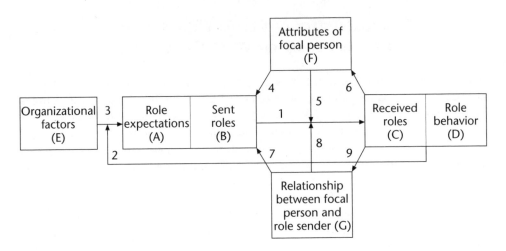

Figure 4.1   The Katz and Kahn (1978) Role-Taking Model

corresponding expectations to the focal person in the hopes of motivating appropriate role behavior.

Figure 4.1 shows the elements associated with the role-taking process. Elements in the model and hypothesized causal connections between them are indicated by capital letters and numbers, respectively. In the paragraphs that follow, we describe the elements and explain the role-taking process. In doing so, we illustrate important concepts using a hypothetical example involving John, one of 12 salespeople in the men's clothing department of a large, up-scale department store, and Mary, his direct supervisor. John has worked at the store for about three years. He took the salesperson job two months after finishing high school. Mary, who recently earned a BS in Business Administration from a prestigious university, was hired two months ago to manage the men's department.

Role expectations

Role expectations (A) are beliefs that role set members have about the types and amounts of various behaviors that are appropriate for a focal person (i.e., role incumbent) in a given role. For example, Mary expected John to do a number of things in his salesperson role, including assisting customers to find merchandise, stocking shelves and clothing racks, returning clothing from fitting rooms to racks and shelves, and operating the cash register.

Sent roles

Sent roles (B) are the expectations that are actually communicated to the focal person in the hopes of influencing his or her behavior. Typically, they reflect only a subset of the role sender's expectations about the focal person's behavior. For instance, when Mary first met John, she told him that he was "responsible for the smooth operation of the men's clothing department," assuming that she and John had similar conceptions of the salesperson role.

Received roles

Received roles (C) are the focal person's beliefs about the role that is to be enacted. They are a function of three major factors, i.e., sent roles (B), the focal person's attributes (F), and the relationships between the focal person and his or her role senders (G). We consider the latter two factors below.

Attributes of focal person

As a result of the influences of (1) culture-based anticipatory socialization for roles (Porter, Lawler, and Hackman, 1975), (2) role-related training, (3) personality, (4) role-related knowledge, skills, and abilities, and (5) a number of other factors (all of which are represented by element F), each focal person has a unique conception concerning the amounts and types of behaviors that are appropriate for his or her role. As indicated by arrow 5 of the RTM, attributes of the focal person influence the degree of correspondence between the sent role and the received role, and thus affect role behavior. For example, because of John's beliefs about his job-related "strengths," he assumed that being responsible for the men's clothing department meant waiting on customers and operating the cash register, assuming that "menial tasks" (e.g., returning clothes to racks) would be handled by the "less capable" salespeople in the department.

Arrow 4 of the RTM indicates that the focal person is more than a passive recipient of sent roles. He or she often attempts to influence the roles that are communicated to him or her by role senders. Thus, for example, in the hopes of avoiding what he considered to be work that was "beneath him" (e.g., returning clothing to shelves and racks), John frequently told Mary that his time was best spent attending to customers and ringing-up sales.

Relationship between focal person and role senders

The focal person's willingness to behave in accordance with sent roles is influenced (arrow 8) by the interpersonal relationships (G) that he or she has with role set members. The more amicable the interpersonal relationship between the focal person and a given role sender, the greater the likelihood that the focal person will receive sent roles in an accurate manner and comply with them. For instance, John and Mary did not get along with one another very well because he resented the fact that she was chosen to be the manager of the men's clothing department. As a result, John frequently ignored or misinterpreted roles sent by Mary.

Arrow 7 of the RTM indicates that the relationship between the role sender and the focal person affects sent roles. Thus, for example, because John and Mary had a strained interpersonal relationship, she frequently communicated expectations to him in an officious manner.

As Arrow 9 of the RTM indicates, received roles and role behavior influence the interpersonal relationship between the focal person and the role sender. For instance, because Mary viewed John as a poor worker, she found every interaction with him to be unpleasant, and did nothing to hide her feelings toward him during their interactions.

Role behavior

Role behavior consists of the specific acts of the focal person in his or her role, including the expression of attitudes and opinions. It deserves stressing that it is the received role (C), as opposed to the sent role (B), that serves to directly influence the focal person's role behavior (D). Thus, role senders are often perplexed by discrepancies between their role expectations and the behavior of the focal person. For instance, Mary was constantly puzzled by John's seeming unwillingness to comply with her role expectations.

Organizational factors

The RTM specifies that the expectations of role senders are affected by such organizational factors as their size, structure, technology, policies, procedures, and reward systems (arrow 3). Thus, for example, because the duties of salespeople were well-specified in the job description for the salesperson position, Mary expected all incumbents in this role to perform all of the duties that were detailed in it.

Performance feedback

Arrow 2 of the RTM indicates that information about the focal person's behavior feeds back to influence the expectations developed by role set members. If a focal person fails to perform successfully in his or her role, role set members may take action to correct the person's behavior. Thus, for example, upon sensing that John was not helping others to return clothing to shelves and racks, Mary gave him explicit instructions to do his fair share of this type of work or face disciplinary action, including possible dismissal.

In the next section, we digress to discuss cultural dimensions that affect behavior in the workplace. We then return to this discussion of the RTM to describe how cultural factors influence the role-taking process.

CULTURE AND WORK BEHAVIOR

Research has shown that culture-based values and other dimensions of culture influence individuals' work-related attitudes, intentions, and behaviors (Hofstede, 1980, 1991; Katz and Kahn, 1978; Stone and Stone-Romero, 2002; Stone-Romero

Table 4.1   Relative standing of several subcultures on cultural dimensions

Cultural dimension	Anglo-American	Hispanic American	African American	Asian American	Native American
Individualism versus collectivism	Individualistic	Collectivistic	Collectivistic	Collectivistic	Collectivistic
Power distance	Low	High	Low	High	Low
Achievement versus ascription	Achievement	Ascriptive	Neutral	Ascriptive	Ascriptive
Universalistic versus particularistic	Universalistic	Particularistic	Particularistic	Particularistic	Particularistic
Time orientation	Future	Present	Present	Past	Past informs present
Communication directness	Direct	Indirect	Direct	Indirect	Indirect
Displayed emotionality	Low	High	High	Low	Low
Credible sources	Experts, accomplished persons	Older males, family, high-status persons	Family, high-status persons	Older males, family, high-status persons	Elders

and Stone, 1998, in press). In view of this, we next consider research on selected dimensions of culture that are of relevance to organizational behavior (Bond, 1988; Hofstede, 1980, 1991; Marin and Marin, 1991; Triandis, 1994; Trompenaars and Hampden-Turner, 1998). Table 4.1 lists the dimensions and shows the standing of five representative US subcultures (i.e., Anglo-Americans, Hispanic Americans, African Americans, Asian Americans, Native Americans) on them.

Some caveats about making generalizations based on culture

Prior to considering the characteristics of the above subcultures, it should be noted that although subcultural groups may, on average, differ from one another on one or more culture-based dimensions (e.g., individualism versus collectivism), there may be considerable within-subculture variability on the same dimensions. For instance, research by Triandis (1994) has shown that individual differences in gender, socioeconomic status, historical background, and religion often influence the values of individuals within a given culture or subculture. More specifically, the research revealed that regardless of national culture (e.g., Asian versus non-Asian), men and individuals from high socioeconomic backgrounds tend to be more individualistic than women and individuals from low socioeconomic backgrounds. Furthermore, research on acculturation (Berry, 1990) has shown that individuals within a specific subculture often differ from one another considerably in terms of their degree of acculturation to a dominant culture's norms and values. The important implication of the foregoing is that inferences about individuals should not be based on knowledge of their ethnicity or nationality alone. Instead, they should consider the degree to which individuals subscribe to the values of a given culture or subculture (Betancourt and Lopez, 1993). Thus, for example, the orientations (e.g., values, beliefs, customs) of individuals who have emigrated to the US from other nations are often a function of their socialization experiences in both their country of origin (e.g., China, Mexico, Europe) and the US.

Cultural orientations of subcultures

In the paragraphs that follow, we consider the ways in which cultural and subcultural groups differ from one another in terms of the above-noted dimensions. In addition, we consider selected research on such differences.

Individualism versus collectivism

Individualism is a value having to do with the strength of ties that should exist between individuals. Individualists believe that such ties should be loose, and that individuals should look after themselves and their immediate family (Hofstede, 1980, 1991). In contrast, collectivists believe that people should belong to in-groups or collectives, which should look after them in exchange for their unconditional loyalty. In collective cultures (e.g., those of the Japanese and Native Americans) people are integrated into strong, cohesive social systems throughout their lives.

Research shows that there are major differences between nations in terms of the degree to which people value individualism versus collectivism (Hofstede, 1980, 1991). Whereas individuals in the US with Anglo-Saxon (also referred to as Anglo or Anglo-American) backgrounds tend to be highly individualistic, individuals from other subcultures in the US (e.g., Hispanic Americans, Asian Americans, African Americans, and Native Americans) tend to be collectivistic (Okun, Fried, and Okun, 1999).

Power distance

Power distance is a value that reflects the degree to which the less powerful members of a social system (e.g., a work organization) believe that power should be distributed in an unequal manner in the system and accept this distribution (Hofstede, 1980, 1991). The more that there is power inequality in a culture, the greater the belief that there should be superior–subordinate differences in power

(Hofstede, 1980, 1991). In low power distance cultures (e.g., Anglo-American) there is limited dependence of subordinates on supervisors, and there is a preference for consultation or participation in decision-making. In high power distance cultures (e.g., Hispanic Americans, Asian Americans) there is often a great deal of dependence of subordinates on supervisors, and there is a clear hierarchy of authority in organizations.

Achievement orientation versus ascriptive orientation

Numerous analysts (e.g., McClelland, 1961; Trompenaars and Hampden-Turner, 1998; Weber, 1958) have argued that achievement orientation versus ascriptive orientation is an important dimension of culture. In *achievement-oriented* cultures, accomplishment serves as the basis for an individual's identity and the status he or she is accorded by others. Moreover, accomplishment is often indexed by economic wealth or material possessions.

In contrast, in *ascriptive-oriented* cultures, people tend to attribute status to others on the basis of factors that are not controlled by them, including gender, family connections, and inherited wealth or title (McClelland, 1961). In addition, in such cultures, respect for superiors is important and often the wisdom of age is highly valued. Research shows that many Anglo-Americans have an achievement orientation and base their identity on their accomplishments, acquired wealth, and material possessions (e.g., Trice and Beyer, 1993). In contrast, research shows that members of other US subcultures (e.g., African Americans, Hispanic Americans, Asian Americans, Native Americans) are much less likely than Anglo-Americans to base their identities on achievement. Instead, they often place considerable emphasis on ascription and relationships (Okun, Fried, and Okun, 1999). As a result, their identities are a function of their primary group memberships (e.g., family, clan, work group). For example, Native Americans often base their identities on the extent to which they have worked in the interest of other tribal members (Deloria, 1994). As a result, the process used in selecting chiefs in the Mohawk tribe places considerable emphasis on a number of qualities of individuals being considered for this role, including the degree to which they have shown a consistent pattern of altruistic and benevolent behavior toward other members of the tribe. Moreover, many African Americans base their identities on such factors as style, expression, spontaneity, and spirituality (Kochman, 1974, 1981).

Universalistic versus particularistic orientation

Another dimension along which cultures vary is universalism versus particularism (Trompenaars and Hampden-Turner, 1998). Cultures that subscribe to a universalistic orientation (e.g., European Americans) tend to follow a set of universal codes of practice and rules that are applied uniformly to all people (Weber, 1947). In addition, they value literal adherence to contracts, and favor rational decision-making. In contrast, cultures that subscribe to a particularistic orientation (e.g., Hispanic Americans, African Americans, Asian Americans) place more emphasis on relationships, and are willing to "bend the rules" to accommodate particular circumstances and individual needs (Imai, 1986; Morishima, 1982; Ouchi, 1981). In addition, they feel that decisions about others should take into account friendships with them. For example, a manager may elect to hire Person A over Person B, because Person A is a friend. It deserves adding that if a friendship-based hiring decision is influenced by such factors as the race, age or sex of job applicants and neglects criteria that should have been used to make a valid selection decision, it may represent a violation of extant law (e.g., the Civil Rights Act of 1974).

Interestingly, research shows that many Western cultures subscribe to a universalistic orientation, and believe that organizational rules or policies are fair only when they are applied in a standardized fashion (Stone and Stone-Romero, 2002; Weber, 1947). However, many Eastern cultures subscribe to a particularistic orientation, and believe that policies are fair when they consider the specific needs of individuals (Stone and Stone-Romero, 2002). For example, a universalist manager would work towards consistency in the treatment of subordinates. In contrast, a particularist would establish unique relationships with each subordinate, often reaching private understandings with them about work-related matters (Trompenaars and Hampden-Turner, 1998).

It deserves adding that the universalistic versus particularistic orientation is not equivalent to Triandis's (1994) notion of low versus high context cultures. Cultural context has to do with the degree to which communication involves touching, expressions of emotion, and eye contact. In high context cultures (e.g., Mexican-American) people value implicit, often unspoken, communication, whereas in low context cultures (e.g., Anglo-American) people value only things that are said explicitly, often based upon facts and expertise.

Time orientation

Cultures differ in terms of their orientation toward time (e.g., Bond, 1988; Triandis, 1994). Time orientation refers to a culture's views about time, and the emphasis placed on the past, the present, and the future. Some cultures (e.g., Anglo-Americans) view time as linear and place a great deal of emphasis on efficiency and punctuality (Okun, Fried, and Okun, 1999). Within these cultures punctuality is associated with success and likeableness, and the view that time should not be wasted is evidenced by Benjamin Franklin's well-known admonition that "time is money."

However, other US subcultures (e.g., Hispanic Americans, African Americans, Native Americans) have relatively flexible views about time, and use fairly large intervals in judging lateness. Individuals are considered to be "on time" even if they arrive well beyond an expected arrival time. In addition, the quality of interpersonal relationships is considered to be more important than punctuality.

As noted above, another aspect of time orientation is the extent to which cultures have a past, present, or future time orientation. Research shows that Anglo-Americans often place a great deal of emphasis on planning for the future and being able to delay gratification (Marin and Marin, 1991; Weber, 1958). In addition, compared to other subcultures in the US, they believe that the future will be better than the past or the present (Taylor and Brown, 1988; Okun, Fried, and Okun, 1999). Moreover, they divide the day into arbitrary blocks of time to encourage efficiency, and schedule personal and work lives around the clock.

Anglo-Americans are said to be *monochronic* because they tend to focus on one task at a time, and often feel compelled to complete it before beginning work on another (Okun, Fried, and Okun, 1999). Similarly, they are often more concerned with the outcomes of work rather than work processes. In addition, they tend to work very quickly to accomplish tasks, and expect their efforts to produce short-term payoffs quickly (Stone-Romero and Stone, 1998). As a result, researchers have argued that Anglo-Americans have a short-term, "bottom-line" perspective (Imai, 1986; Morishima, 1982; Stone-Romero and Stone, 1998).

In contrast, members of other US subcultures (e.g., Hispanic Americans, Native Americans, African Americans) have a more present-oriented time perspective, viewing the present as more important than the future (Okun, Fried, and Okun, 1999). As a result, relative to Anglo-Americans, members of these other subcultures tend to engage in relatively less planning for the future, are less likely to delay gratification, and have a more relaxed and spontaneous lifestyle (Marin and Marin, 1991). Furthermore, members of these subcultures are said to be *polychronic* because people within the culture tend to engage in multitasking and are more concerned with processes than with outcomes (Okun, Fried, and Okun, 1999). Moreover, as noted above, members of the same ethnic groups also stress that a primary part of the work process is developing positive interpersonal relationships with others. As a consequence, they often work more slowly than Anglo-Americans (ibid).

In contrast to members of some other US subcultures Asian Americans often stress the past (e.g., tradition) in their orientations toward time (Bond, 1988; Imai, 1986; Morishima, 1982; Okun, Fried, and Okun, 1999; Ouchi, 1981; Stone-Romero and Stone, 1998). In addition, they stress persistence in working toward goals, recognizing that it often takes sustained effort to reach goals.

Bond (1988) labeled the Asian cultural view of time *Confucian dynamism*. His research showed that people from Asian cultures tend to have a long-term time perspective. In addition, they tend to view relations between individuals in terms of their relative status, show sensitivity in personal relationships, and value education, frugality, patience, tradition, and perseverance. As a result, Asian Americans who subscribe to the Confucian dynamism philosophy often focus on producing high quality work, and stress continuous improvement in work processes (Imai, 1986; Morishima, 1982; Ouchi, 1981; Stone-Romero and Stone, 1998).

Communication style

Subcultures vary considerably in terms of several aspects of communication style, and these differences often result in misunderstandings in work organizations and other social systems. Communication style can be viewed in terms of four basic elements: (1) the goals of communication, (2) the directness of communication, (3) the level of emotion conveyed by communication, and (4) the basis of imputing credibility to communication sources. Each of these notions is explained below.

There are cultural and subcultural differences in the goals associated with communication. In collective cultures (e.g., those of the Japanese, Native Americans, and many Hispanic Americans), maintaining harmony and saving face are important goals of communication. For instance, members of Hispanic-American subcultures (see table 4.1) often stress *simpatia* (i.e., congeniality), and value individuals who promote smooth or pleasant social relationships by showing empathy and respect for the feelings of others (Marin and Marin, 1991). Likewise, individuals from Asian-American and Native-American subcultures view the maintenance of in-group harmony as a primary goal of communication (Witherspoon, 1977). In contrast, members of individualistic cultures (e.g., Anglo-Americans) are more concerned with communicating the truth and with basing their arguments on facts and rational arguments. Interestingly, although African Americans are considered to be collective, some research shows that they are similar to Anglo-Americans in terms of communication style, stressing the truth in communication and emphasizing it over maintaining harmony in interpersonal relationships (Kochman, 1974). As Kochman noted, Blacks often use a "non-fronting" communication style in which "a person speaks his mind openly and sincerely, not holding back or 'concealing' what he thinks and feels, and if one gets loud, heated and emotional in the process of such expression, all the better, because within the oral Black view that would be interpreted as lending 'conviction' to what one says" (p. 102).

Cultures also vary in terms of the directness of communication. In particular, people in collective cultures often use indirect forms of communication, and tend to "beat around the bush" rather than getting directly to the point. They also place a great deal of value on silence or the unspoken work (e.g., non-verbal communication). However, people in individualistic cultures (e.g., Anglo-Americans) typically emphasize verbal communication, and are direct in their communication style. In addition, they prefer to talk about tasks and other non-personal issues. As a consequence, members of collective cultures often consider individuals from individualistic cultures to be rude or impolite because of their direct communication style and disregard of social courtesy (e.g., saying "good morning").

In addition, cultures and subcultures differ in terms of the value placed on emotion or neutrality (i.e., detachment) in communication (Trompenaars and Hampden-Turner, 1998). People from individualistic cultures (e.g., Anglo-Americans) often emphasize calm, unemotional forms of communication, even when there are disagreements about issues. However, members of several collective cultures (e.g., Hispanic Americans, African Americans) often display their emotions freely when communicating with others, and exhibit considerable passion when discussing issues. Interestingly, the use of emotional communication is *not* common across all collective cultures. For example, Asian Americans and Native Americans have a relatively reserved interpersonal style.

There also are cultural and subcultural differences in terms of the basis used for imputing (i.e., attributing) credibility to communication sources. Because members of collective cultures accept high power distance relationships, relative to members of individualistic cultures, they impute greater credibility to elders, family members, and high status persons. In contrast, because members of individualistic cultures value achievement and accomplishment, relative to people from collective cultures, they are more likely to impute credibility to sources that are expert, intelligent, and have a record of high achievement.

CULTURE-BASED SCRIPTS AND ORGANIZATIONAL BEHAVIOR

In order to achieve their goals, organizations require dependable role behavior on the part of their members (Katz and Kahn, 1978). However, it is virtually impossible for organizations to inform role incumbents of all of the prescriptions and proscriptions associated with their roles. Thus, most organizations rely upon the anticipatory socialization (Porter, Lawler, and Hackman, 1975) of workers for jobs, including the learning of general scripts for work behavior. A *script* is a plan or structure that describes the sequences of behaviors that should be enacted in a particular context (Shank and Abelson, 1977). For example, teachers have scripts for delivering lectures, servers have scripts for waiting on tables, and police officers have scripts for making felony arrests. Scripts enable a person to organize knowledge and infer the patterns of behavior (i.e., behavioral sequences) that are appropriate in particular contexts (e.g., work organizations). They also allow a person to "fill in the gaps" when information about appropriate behaviors is unavailable. When a script is called for use, individuals enact the roles and behaviors associated with it (Shank and Abelson, 1977). Thus, for example, a manager need not tell a server in a restaurant to ask for a customer's food or drink order, because the server knows that taking a customer's order is part of the server script.

Interestingly, when workers come from different cultures or subcultures, they often have experienced different types of prior socialization. As a result, they are prone to enact different types of scripted behavior. This behavior can be both verbal and/or non-verbal in nature. For example, as noted above, in the Anglo-American subculture, punctuality is part of the typical work script. People are expected to arrive on time for meetings, and lateness is regarded as disrespectful and wasteful of the time of others. Furthermore, Anglo-American work-related scripts stress efficiency and the rapid completion of tasks. In contrast, members of other subcultures (e.g., Hispanic Americans, African Americans, Native Americans) have work-related scripts that place a relatively low level of emphasis on punctuality. Instead, for example, the scripts of Hispanic Americans dictate that a person should spend time forming relationships and being a *buena gente* (i.e., a nice person; Okun, Fried, and Okun, 1999). Likewise, several non-Anglo subcultures (e.g., Japanese Americans) stress that workers should take their time on tasks, and focus on work processes rather than short-term outcomes.

Not surprisingly, time-conscious Anglo-Americans are often perceived to be impolite by members of several subcultures (e.g., Hispanic Americans, Native Americans). In addition, Anglo-Americans often view Hispanics or Native Americans as frivolous because they are late or waste time on relationship formation. Furthermore, as noted above, Asian Americans often have a work script that emphasizes respect for others (e.g., they arrive early to show respect for others), long-term time perspectives, and the continual improvement of work processes.

Because members of different cultures or subcultures often work in accordance with very different scripts, a number of negative consequences may ensue, including (a) conflict between individuals from different subcultures, (b) inaccurate perceptions about the work performance of individuals from different subcultures (e.g., working slowly is interpreted as a sign of laziness), (c) individuals from non-dominant cultures being accorded out-group status, and (d) reduced overall organizational efficiency and effectiveness.

In view of the above, it is clear that culture must be taken into account in understanding the behavior of role incumbents who come from different cultures. Thus, we developed a revised version of Katz and Kahn's (1978) seminal RTM. We now describe this modified model.

THE REVISED ROLE-TAKING MODEL

Figure 4.2 presents a Revised Role-Taking Model (RRTM). Rectangles in the figure represent elements that were part of the RTM, whereas ovals represent elements that we added to take cultural influences into account. Note that each element in the RRTM is identified by an upper-case letter (A–L), and assumed causal connections between the elements are identified by numbered arrows (1–17).

As the RRTM specifies, culture influences the attributes of the focal person (arrow 17), the scripts that are available to role senders (arrow 11) and the effect of such scripts on role expectations and sent roles (arrow 12), organizational factors (arrow 10), the scripts that are available to the focal person (arrow 13) and the effect of such scripts on received roles and role behavior (arrow 14), and the relationships between the focal person and role senders (arrows 15 and 16). Several examples of these effects are provided below. Note, however, that we contrast role relationships in Anglo-style organizations with such relationships in Japanese-style organizations. (For the defining characteristics of these two types

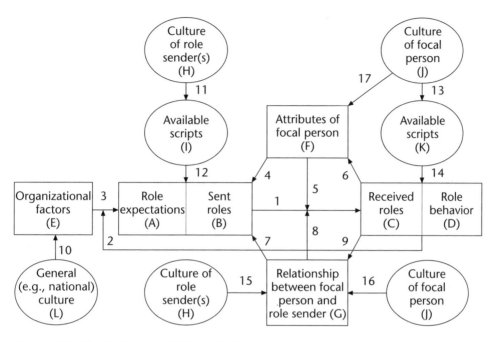

Figure 4.2 The Revised Role-Taking Model

of organizations, see Imai, 1986; Morishima, 1982; Ouchi, 1981; and Stone-Romero and Stone, 1998). The principal reason for doing so is that the effects of culture are clearer for these organizational types than they are for an organization in a specific culture that has workers from different subcultures.

Influence of culture on role expectations

The RRTM specifies that culture influences both work-related scripts and role expectations. For example, because Anglo-style organizations stress universalistic values, work-related scripts and role expectations in such organizations tend to emphasize clearly defined roles and standard work procedures (Weber, 1947; Katz and Kahn, 1978). As a result, in Anglo-style organizations, roles are often based upon job analysis procedures and their adjuncts. Such procedures involve the detailed specification of not only the content of a job, but also the knowledge, skills, and abilities needed to perform it. In addition, in Anglo-style organizations, efficiency and competitive achievement tend to be valued more than relationship formation. In contrast, in Japanese-style organizations, work roles tend to be defined in general terms (Imai, 1986; Morishima, 1982; Ouchi, 1981; Stone-Romero and Stone, 1998). Furthermore, compared to Anglo-style organizations, Japanese-style organizations place considerably more emphasis on relationships among work-group members and the continuous improvement of work processes, rather than on the immediate completion of tasks. These and other differences in work-related values and orientations often have a marked effect on role expectations (A) and sent roles (B).

Influence of culture on the sent role

As noted above, culture influences communication processes. Therefore, it affects how roles are communicated to role incumbents. For example, in Anglo-style organizations, role senders are likely to use a direct communication style, and to communicate role expectations explicitly. In addition, because Anglos are more individualistic than the Japanese (Hofstede, 1980, 1991), in Anglo-style organizations, sent roles are more likely to provide information on the contingencies (rewards and punishments) associated with meeting or failing to meet role expectations. In contrast, relative to Anglos, the communication style of the Japanese is typically more indirect. Thus, in Japanese-style organizations, roles are more likely to be communicated in a general fashion. Furthermore, because the Japanese tend to be collective, in Japanese-style organizations there is little need for supervisors to communicate role expectations in specific terms. One reason for this is that group norms play a key role in motivating role-consistent behavior (Imai, 1986; Morishima, 1982; Ouchi, 1981; Stone-Romero and Stone, 1998).

Influence of culture on the received role

We hypothesize that culture affects the roles received by individuals. For instance, because Anglos are individualistic, they are more likely than the Japanese to ask the question of "What's in it for me if I comply with sent roles?" As a result, we posit that Anglo role incumbents will be more likely than Japanese role incumbents to reinterpret or change role expectations to make them consistent with actions that result in personal gain. Consequently, in Anglo-style organizations, supervisors often resort to using contingent reward systems (e.g., piece-rate pay plans) and close supervision to ensure that incumbents comply with role expectations and sent roles (Katz and Kahn, 1978; Weber, 1947). However, because the Japanese have collective values, relative to Anglos, incumbents in Japanese-style organizations will be more likely to receive the roles communicated by role senders in an accurate fashion, less likely to modify such roles in ways that promote personal gain, and less likely to need close supervision in order to behave in ways that are consistent with role expectations and sent roles (Imai, 1986; Morishima, 1982; Ouchi, 1981; Stone-Romero and Stone, 1998). One important reason for this is that complying with the expectations of others is a way of showing good will toward the collective and maintaining group harmony.

Influence of culture on role behavior

As the RRTM model indicates, culture-based scripts (K) influence a focal person's propensity to exhibit different types and amounts of role behavior (arrow 14). For example, we hypothesize that because Anglos value individualism, relative to the Japanese, their role behavior will be more dependent on reward contingencies and, therefore, more variable. The consistency in role behavior for workers in Japanese-style organizations stems from two factors: a collective value orientation that stresses that individual success is linked to group success, and a recognition that consistent role behavior is vital to group success (Markus and Kitayama, 1991a, 1991b).

Influence of culture on organizational factors

As the RRTM suggests, national culture influences organizational factors (arrow 10) and, thus, the expectations developed by a focal person's role set members. This position is consistent with the views of organizational theorists (e.g., Hofstede, 1980, 1991; Imai, 1986; Morishima, 1982; Ouchi, 1981; Trice and Beyer, 1993) who have argued that the cultures of work organizations are influenced and framed by the dominant national culture within which organizations operate. Thus, national culture provides an ideological context for organizations, and has a direct impact on such organizational factors as their structure, design, use of technology, formalization of policies, standardization of procedures, and reward systems (Imai, 1986; Katz and Kahn, 1978; Morishima, 1982; Ouchi, 1981; Stone-Romero and Stone, 1998; Trice and Beyer, 1993). In addition, as noted above, organizational factors have a direct influence on role expectations (arrow 3). For example, diversity theorists (e.g., Cox, 1994) have argued that the structures, policies, and practices of most US organizations are consistent with Western European values and ideologies, and that these aspects of culture dictate the types of behaviors that are appropriate in such organizations. Thus, many US organizations set up systems that stress science and rationality, efficiency and practicality, individualism, and competitive achievement (McClelland, 1961; Trice and Beyer, 1993; Weber, 1947). Examples of each of these values and their impact on organizational factors are offered below.

First, as a result of the value placed on science and rationality, Anglo-style organizations emphasize rationality in decision-making, including a reliance on impersonal, objective standards for making decisions (Trice and Beyer, 1993). In fact, Anglo-style organizations tend to formalize rules and procedures in organizations in an effort to avoid favoritism and partiality in decision-making (e.g., personnel selection decisions). Second, because Anglo culture values efficiency and practicality, Anglo-style organizations often use scientific management practices and bureaucratic principles as a means of structuring work and controlling employee behavior (Taylor, 1911; Weber, 1947). For example, in such organizations, jobs are studied to determine the most efficient methods of doing work, elaborate systems are set up for regulating employee behavior, and technology is used to increase worker efficiency and effectiveness. Third, because Anglos tend to be highly individualistic and competitive (Deloria, 1994; Hofstede, 1980, 1991; McClelland, 1961; Spence, 1985), Anglo-style organizations tend to use reward systems that foster inter-individual competition (e.g., merit pay, piece-rate pay). In addition, because of the Anglo emphasis on competitive achievement (McClelland, 1961; Spence, 1985), Anglo managers are often intolerant of poor performance, and workers are only guaranteed employment for as long as they meet or exceed extant performance standards. Fourth, workers in Anglo-style organizations in the US have been generally supportive of egalitarianism, freedom, and democracy, and many Anglo workers believe they have a right to be part of any control system that affects them (Trice and Beyer, 1993). Thus, workers in many Anglo-style organizations support systems that allow employees to participate in decision-making, and the reduction of hierarchical control systems (Erez and Earley, 1993). However, it deserves adding that the move toward participation in decision-making in US organizations may very well be attributable to the influx of Japanese-style management practices to the US. Traditionally, the structure of US organizations has been guided by the bureaucratic model of Weber (1947), which emphasizes hierarchical control and centralized decision-making (Katz and Kahn, 1978). In contrast, in Japanese-style organizations, decisions are typically made through the *ringi* process in which every individual who will be affected by a decision evaluates its merits and provides his or her "stamp of approval" (Ouchi, 1981; Stone-Romero and Stone, 1998).

As should be evident from the above, the dominant culture of a nation (or a region within it) is a key determinant of organizational factors, and, therefore, influences the types of role expectations that are developed and sent to role incumbents. In turn, organizational factors influence organizational standards (e.g., performance criteria), thus dictating the types and levels of role behavior that are viewed as appropriate. One dysfunctional consequence of this culturally based organizational control is that individuals from non-dominant cultures may often be at a disadvantage when their performance is evaluated (Cox, 1994). For instance, we posit that Japanese Americans, Native Americans, and individuals from several other non-Anglo subcultures will experience considerable role conflict and role ambiguity in US organizations because their culture-based work scripts and self-generated role expectations are often inconsistent with the standards for role behavior that are present in Anglo-style organizations. For example, a study by Hosoda, Chen, and Stone (2001) found that relative to Anglo-Americans, Asian Americans are more likely to report dissatisfaction with their jobs and are less likely to be promoted in US-owned organizations.

Asian Americans may also experience problems in Anglo-oriented organizations because such organizations typically have reward systems that emphasize inter-individual competition, and Japanese Americans may view such competition as

inappropriate. In addition, although Japanese culture values indirect communication styles and close, supportive interpersonal relationships, Anglo-oriented
organizations do not generally value these orientations (Imai, 1986; Morishima,
1982; Ouchi, 1981; Stone-Romero and Stone, 1998).

It should be clear from the foregoing that a host of problems may arise
when the values of the dominant culture in an organization conflict with those of
role incumbents from non-dominant cultures. Note also that although the above
examples involve contrasts between Anglo-style organizations and Japanese-style
organizations, problems stemming from cultural clashes can arise in many other
situations (e.g., Anglo workers in Native-American organizations).

Influence of culture on interpersonal factors

As our RRTM makes clear, the cultural backgrounds of role incumbents (J) and
role senders (H) influence the quality of their interpersonal relationship (arrows
15 and 16), which, in turn, affects role expectations (A), sent roles (B), received
roles (C), role behavior (D), and the degree to which sent roles are consistent
with received roles (arrow 8). Thus, for example, we hypothesize that the focal
person will be more likely to have good interpersonal relationships with role set
members and to comply with their expectations when the focal person and the
role set members come from similar (as opposed to dissimilar) cultures or subcultures. Likewise, when a focal person's role set members come from a different
culture or subculture than that of the focal person, he or she is likely to experience considerable threat, role ambiguity, and role conflict (see Katz and Kahn,
1978, and chapter 6, this volume, for definitions of these concepts). As a result,
relative to focal persons from the dominant cultural group, focal persons from
non-dominant subcultural groups may be less likely to comply with role expectations, and more likely to experience a host of negative consequences (e.g., low
performance ratings, role conflict, relegation to out-group status, low pay, less
mentoring, and diminished advancement opportunities). Furthermore, in such
situations, the entire organization is likely to experience lowered levels of productivity. In support of this view, research on African Americans and Hispanic
Americans has shown that members of non-dominant subcultures typically have
fewer developmental opportunities, fewer mentoring opportunities, and lower
salary levels than Anglo-Americans (Dreher and Cox, 1996; Stone, Stone, and
Dipboye, 1992).

It deserves adding that there is considerable evidence in social psychology
that attitude similarity between an individual and a target has a positive impact
on the individual's affective reactions to the target, attraction to the target, and
willingness to help the target (Byrne, 1971). Likewise, research in organizational
psychology suggests that similarity between individuals has a positive effect on
such outcomes as hiring recommendations (Peters and Terborg, 1975) and performance ratings (Pulakos and Wexley, 1983). Furthermore, there is evidence that

the greater the discrepancy between an individual's values and those of a target, the less positively the target is viewed by the individual (Moe, Nacoste, and Insko, 1981).

A recently developed social psychological theory, namely Terror Management Theory (Solomon, Greenberg, and Pyszczynski, 1991), provides an intriguing explanation of the just-noted findings. The theory posits that when an individual interacts with a person who does not share his or her culture-based worldviews (e.g., beliefs, attitudes, values, standards), the individual's esteem will be threatened and anxiety will be evoked. One reason for this is that the cultural standards associated with a person's worldview often serve as buffers of anxiety. When an individual is confronted with worldviews that differ from his or her own, his or her anxiety buffer is likely to break down. Thus, we posit that when individuals from different subcultures work together in organizations, threats to self-esteem and the resultant anxiety will lead to strained interpersonal relationships (arrows 15 and 16).

REACTIONS TO CULTURAL HETEROGENEITY IN ORGANIZATIONS

When individuals are faced with threats to their worldviews, they are likely to use a number of strategies to deal with such threats, including avoiding further contact with people who have discrepant worldviews, and working toward the assimilation or acculturation of such people. Schneider's (1987) Attraction–Selection–Attrition (ASA) model suggests how this process operates in work organizations. More specifically, in work organizations efforts are made to *attract* job applicants who share the worldview of existing organizational members, *select* (i.e., offer jobs to and hire) individuals who most share the extant worldview, and encourage the *attrition* of individuals who fail to adopt the same worldview. Not surprisingly, research supports the ASA model. For example, it indicates that members of several non-Anglo ethnic groups (e.g., African Americans, Hispanic Americans) often have higher turnover rates and experience greater stress levels in US organizations than do Anglos (Cox, 1994).

To the extent that organizations operate in accordance with the ASA model, their members will tend to show high levels of homogeneity with respect to their values, attitudes, beliefs, ideologies, and a number of other culture-related variables. One positive consequence of this will be better interpersonal relationships between role incumbents and members of their role sets. However, cultural homogeneity will also lead to a host of problems. One is that in a multicultural society, such as that of the US, it will become increasingly difficult for organizations to maintain the cultural homogeneity of their members. For example, it may prove difficult to bring about the assimilation of all new entrants to organizations. Second, because the customers or clients of many US firms are often quite diverse (in terms of such variables as race, age, sex, socioeconomic status, and religion), a diverse workforce is often quite functional in terms of meeting the needs of clients or customers who have different cultural backgrounds (Cox, 1994). Third, research shows that a multicultural (rather than monocultural) perspective on hiring can help organizations to attract and retain talented members of diverse ethnic groups. These individuals can develop creative solutions to problems, and respond more quickly to the forces that are present in an increasingly multicultural society (Cox, 1994). In view of these considerations, we strongly support efforts aimed at increasing the cultural diversity of workers in US organizations. In addition, we believe that the RRTM can be instrumental in promoting such diversity.

4.1   *El Caballo Blanco Restaurant*

Gilberto Rodriguez is the owner and manager of El Caballo Blanco, a Mexican restaurant in Fairfax, Virginia. He moved to the US from Mexico in 1988, and learned the restaurant business while working as a cook in an Anglo-American restaurant in Washington, DC. When he opened El Caballo Blanco in 1998, he decided to hire all Mexican-American servers and manage the restaurant in the style used in Mexico, rather than the US. One of the primary differences in these styles is that in Mexico all servers treat customers as special guests and greet them very warmly (e.g., they often say "Estas en es su casa," which translates to "You are in your house"). Another difference between the two styles is that in Mexico servers are not assigned specific tables, but work as part of a team that collectively attends to the needs of all customers. Team members work together to greet and seat customers, take their orders, serve food and beverages, and clean tables. In addition, they share tips equally at the end of a shift. As a result of the teamwork among servers and the warm and friendly way in which customers were treated by the employees of El Caballo Blanco, customer satisfaction was very high. In addition, the employees worked well together and seemed to truly enjoy their work. Thus, El Caballo Blanco became a favorite restaurant in the area, and its business grew rapidly.

As business grew, Gilberto decided to hire an additional server. However, when he attempted to hire a Mexican American, he found that none was available. He therefore hired an Anglo-American named Chris Donovan, who had experience as a server in two Anglo-American national restaurant chains. Given Chris's previous work experience, Gilberto felt that he needed very little training. So, Gilberto just introduced Chris to the other employees and gave him a brief orientation on the menu and kitchen. However, once Chris began work, he refused to cooperate with the Mexican-American servers. In fact, he often competed with them for tables (especially large groups) and chastised them when they assisted customers at "his" tables.

By the end of his first week on the job, Chris complained to Gilberto and the other servers that although he worked harder and faster than other servers, he had to share all of "his" tips with them. As a consequence, the Mexican-American servers became unhappy, and their team efforts began to break down. In addition, some arguments erupted between Chris and the other servers. Within a month of Chris's presence at El Caballo Blanco, customers began to sense that the "atmosphere" of the restaurant had changed for the worse, and some regular customers stopped eating there. Moreover, in light of the interpersonal problems caused by Chris and the decline in customer satisfaction, the Mexican-American servers met with Gilberto and recommended that he fire Chris.

Discussion questions

1   Based on the Revised Role-Taking Model presented in this chapter, what are the likely causes of the problems in this case?
2   What cultural factors influenced Chris's behavior?
3   What cultural factors influenced the Mexican-American servers' behavior?
4   How did the dominant culture of the restaurant determine the kinds of scripts and associated server behaviors that were appropriate or inappropriate?
5   Based on the Revised Role-Taking Model, what steps would you take as a manager to resolve the problems noted in the case?
6   What strategies can managers use to avert cross-cultural problems in the workplace?

IMPLICATIONS OF CULTURAL HETEROGENEITY FOR PRACTICE

As US work organizations become more culturally heterogeneous, management practices will have to show greater flexibility. There are at least three reasons for this. First, managers (and other organizational members) need to recognize that their own values are not necessarily shared by all of their subordinates. Thus, for example, reward systems will need to take into account the differing valences (i.e., perceived reward or punishment values) that individuals from different sub-cultures attach to various outcomes (e.g., pay, fringe benefits, day care facilities for children, paid and unpaid leave). Second, in developing role expectations and communicating them to role incumbents, role senders will need to take into account the fact that the work-related scripts of individuals from different sub-cultures may differ from one another in important ways. Thus, for instance, managers will need to communicate sent roles in ways that are sensitive to the communication styles of focal people. Third, the criteria used in evaluating the performance of workers will need to take into account the fact that individuals from different subcultures often use different strategies for accomplishing tasks. For example, a focus on quantity of production in evaluating performance may penalize individuals who are concerned with quality and the improvement of work processes. In the long run, such a focus may prove quite dysfunctional to an organization (Stone-Romero and Stone, 1998).

CONCLUSION

As should be clear from the foregoing, appropriate role behavior is vital to organizational efficiency and effectiveness (Katz and Kahn, 1978). However, in multicultural organizations, the managerial practices that have long been used in US organizations may not promote such behavior. Thus, it is critical to understand how culture affects the behavior of role incumbents. We hope that our RRTM proves to be of value for this purpose. In addition, we hope that the same model helps organizations and their members to reap the rich rewards of diversity that are articulated in other chapters of this book, and to minimize or avert the dysfunctional consequences that stem from the failure to consider the implications of cultural diversity in organizations.

5

LEADERSHIP IN A DIVERSE WORKPLACE

Donna Chrobot-Mason and Marian N. Ruderman

Workforce diversity brings significant challenges to organizational leaders who must attempt to minimize intergroup conflict and foster cooperation among heterogeneous work group members. In this chapter, implications of diversity for key leadership processes are discussed, including assembling a team, developing the talent of individuals on the team, and enhancing teamwork. The development of critical leadership skills in contemporary diversified organizations is also examined.

Although organizations in the United States and elsewhere are more diverse than in the past, the old hierarchies and traditional practices have not given way to completely new ones. Most organizational leaders continue to be White males, and the few women and people of color who find themselves in leadership positions face significant barriers as they bump against or break through the glass ceiling. Previous research has shown that women in leadership roles face several challenges, such as perceptions that women are unsuited for management, discrimination, and exclusion from informal networks (Catalyst, 1998). Furthermore, Black women have to deal with the additional obstacles of racism, pressure to make race invisible, and challenges to their authority (Bell and Nkomo, 2001). In a roundtable discussion with ten senior managers of color, Thomas (1997) reported that minority leaders believe they must work harder to be accepted, yet still feel as if they are outsiders who continually fight an uphill battle for inclusion and acceptance.

In addition to struggling against institutional bias and exclusion in the workplace, minority leaders also must overcome strong stereotypes that the most effective leader is White and male. Implicit leadership theory suggests that followers hold specific stereotypes about leaders and these stereotypes can affect follower perceptions of leader effectiveness and power to influence (Ayman, 1993). Research has demonstrated consistent findings that, when asked to describe a "good manager," most respondents describe someone possessing masculine characteristics (Powell and Butterfield, 1989). Furthermore, research suggests that although female perceptions of the characteristics required to be successful in management may be changing (Brenner, Tomkiewicz, and Schein, 1989; Schein, Mueller, and Jacobson, 1989), male perceptions have changed very little since the 1970s and men still subscribe to a masculine stereotype of successful managers (Heilman et al., 1989). Similarly, a recent study by Chung and Lankau (2001) examining Caucasians' perceptions of a successful manager revealed that Caucasian managers are perceived as nearer to the stereotype of a successful manager than members of other racial groups.

Whereas one area of research has focused on documenting the obstacles and challenges faced by minority leaders, another area of inquiry has focused on identifying the changing role of majority leaders as they attempt to foster teamwork and cooperation among an increasingly heterogeneous workforce. The fact that diversity brings both opportunity and challenge to the workplace has been well documented. On one hand, research has shown that diverse perspectives and ideas may lead to greater creativity and innovation (Jackson, 1992). On the other hand, an increase in diversity has been linked to greater conflict, lower job satisfaction, and increased turnover (Riordan, 2000). In this chapter we argue that leaders play a pivotal role in determining whether a diverse workforce represents a competitive advantage or an organizational cost.

This chapter examines issues of leadership in diverse work organizations when the leader is part of the majority group. We assume that leaders want their groups and organizations to function well, and we base our discussion on that assumption. We also recognize that effectiveness is hard work. The aim of the chapter is to help leaders become as effective as possible in diverse organizations. This aim dictates the structure of the chapter. After outlining some views of leadership, we discuss the implications of diversity for key leadership processes, including assembling a team, developing the talent of individuals on the team, and enhancing teamwork. We conclude by considering the skills a leader may need to develop in order to be effective in contemporary diversified organizations.

THE CHANGING VIEWS OF LEADERS

As projections of an increasingly diverse labor force began to materialize during the early 1990s, organizational researchers and scholars warned of the immense changes that leaders would encounter as a result of a more heterogeneous workforce (House, 1995; Joplin and Daus, 1997; Morrison, 1992). Loden and Rosener (1991) wrote of the need for leaders of diversity to serve as role models within their organization to initiate a change in the organizational culture that ensures collaboration among minority and majority employees. In 1991, Roosevelt Thomas challenged organizational leaders to view diversity management as a comprehensive process for developing an environment that works for all employees. In general, this literature argued that changes in workforce demographics meant that leaders must actively initiate and engage in widespread organizational change in order to create a work environment that supports diverse employees.

Although we wholeheartedly agree with this perspective, we suggest that for the most part, leaders have failed to actively manage diversity and that organizational barriers and bias against minority employees remain widespread problems. Perhaps one of the reasons for this is a widely held belief that the best way for managers to approach demographic differences among employees is to ignore differences and treat everyone in the same way. This belief is known as the colorblind perspective. Recent research by Neville et al. (2000) has shown that individuals who hold colorblind racial attitudes, defined as the belief that race should not and does not matter, are more likely to hold racial and gender prejudices. A second approach some leaders take toward managing diversity is to adopt the "Golden Rule" that many Christians in America are taught as children from the Bible (Morrison, 1992). The rule states "Do unto others as you would have them do unto you."

The problem with adopting either of these approaches to managing diversity in the workplace is that both perspectives attempt to minimize or ignore differences and treat everyone as if they were alike. Indeed, the Golden Rule suggests that we treat everyone as if they were just like us. Even if it were realistic to believe that we could ignore such visible differences as gender and race, research on Social Identity Theory (SIT) suggests that leaders who ignore differences will likely be sending the message that their employees are not valued members of the organization (Cox, 1994). That is because SIT argues that the social groups we belong to help us define our place in society and contribute significantly to our self-esteem (Tajfel, 1981). For example, a Hispanic employee who reports to a leader that adopts a colorblind perspective may feel that her Hispanic heritage, a very important part of how she defines herself, is not valued by the organization. Additionally, if her manager attempts to treat everyone in the work group exactly the same way, he will likely fail to recognize the unique contributions she may make to the work group, in part because of her Hispanic heritage. Leaders who adopt this perspective run the risk of mismanaging diversity. This may be detrimental to the functioning of the work group not only because the value of employee differences becomes a missed opportunity, but also because mismanagement or no management of diversity can lead to negative work outcomes. Research has shown that simply increasing diversity within a work group is associated with less frequent communication (Zenger and Lawrence, 1989), lower psychological attachment (Tsui, Egan, and O'Reilly, 1992), and increased turnover (O'Reilly, Caldwell, and Barnett, 1989).

In contrast, leaders who understand both the potential advantages and disadvantages of a diverse workforce will be better equipped to take a more active role in managing diversity. They will take steps to encourage and reward creative and innovative ideas and support alternative work styles and approaches to

problem solving. Leaders who effectively manage diversity will attempt to minimize the conflict and power struggles that are likely to occur when the workforce
becomes more diverse. Finally, they will treat employees as individuals, with
sensitivity toward diversity issues and conflicts. Such an individualistic leadership
approach is rooted in contemporary leadership theories, such as leader–member
exchange, which will be discussed below.

Leadership theories and diversity

The earliest leadership theories attempted to identify the specific traits and
attributes that made an effective leader. The goal of leadership trait theories was
to identify *who* would make a successful leader. Subsequently, more complex
theories of leadership, such as the Ohio State leadership studies during the late
1940s and early 1950s, attempted to identify the pattern of leadership behaviors
that result in maximum performance, in an attempt to define *what* leaders do that
contributes to success. Results of this program of research suggested that leaders
who engage in behaviors that involve both high concern for production and high
concern for people will be most effective. It was not until the 1970s, when path–
goal theory emerged, that leadership theorists began to consider the idea that
a particular leadership style may not be equally effective for every situation
or every employee. Developed by Martin Evans and Robert House, path–goal
theory identified four leadership styles: directive, supportive, participative, and
achievement-oriented (House and Mitchell, 1997). The theory presumes that leaders
can engage in any or all of the leadership styles and that the most appropriate
style or combination of styles depends on a number of situational variables.

Traditional leadership theories, for the most part, considered leadership under
the assumption that followers were a homogeneous group. Today, with the growing force of diversity in organizations, leadership theories developed in earlier
years are now recognized to be flawed (Chen and Van Velsor, 1996; DiTomaso
and Hooijberg, 1996; Hooijberg and DiTomaso, 1996). There is a movement to
look at leadership behavior in organizations from a more pluralistic perspective
in order to take into account different beliefs, values, needs, and experiences.

Contemporary theories, such as leader–member exchange, take a more individualistic approach to leadership that is consistent with the challenges of a
diverse workforce (Chen and Van Velsor, 1996; Scandura and Lankau, 1996).
Leader–Member Exchange Theory (LMX) focuses on the work relationships that
develop between leaders and work group members (see Graen and Uhl-Bien, 1995,
for a review). Supervisor–subordinate relationships defined as low exchange are
characterized by highly formalized interactions, limited to that which is defined
by the employment contract. High exchange relationships between a supervisor
and subordinate go beyond that which is specified in formal job descriptions and
involve interactions regarding both material and non-material goods. Essentially,
LMX theory suggests that each superior–subordinate dyad involves a unique

relationship in which both members contribute to the quality of that relationship. Gerstner and Day (1997) reviewed findings on LMX research and reported that high quality relationships (characterized by higher trust, interaction, and support) were related to positive work outcomes such as higher performance and lower turnover. Consistent with LMX theory, we suggest that leaders of diverse work groups must take the initiative to develop unique interpersonal relationships with each employee to foster high quality relationships.

Although contemporary leadership theories such as LMX hold promise for redefining effective leadership within the context of diversity, additional work is clearly needed in this area. What we currently consider to be theories of leadership are really theories of a Western form of leadership based on White American males (Hooijberg and DiTomaso, 1996). For theories of leadership to be truly descriptive and useful it is important that they take into account the preferences and needs of a broader group of employees and leaders, so that they better reflect the experience of the workforce of the new millennium.

IMPLICATIONS OF DIVERSITY FOR KEY LEADERSHIP PROCESSES

Leader processes: Assembling a team

One of the key functions of leaders is the recruitment and selection of new employees into the work team. Despite the large number of legal cases, as well as empirical research, during the last three decades that have documented the prevalence of minority discrimination in hiring practices (Cox, Welch, and Nkomo, 2001), recent research suggests bias in selection remains a problem today. Huffcutt and Roth (1998) empirically summarized research on racial group differences in employment interviews and found that Black and Hispanic applicants received significantly lower ratings by White male interviewers than White applicants. Selection procedures such as interviews hold great potential for bias. One reason for discrimination in subjective hiring practices is something known as "homophily bias" (Kanter, 1977) or the "similarity-attraction paradigm" (Byrne, 1971). These terms refer to the natural bias and preference individuals have for interactions with others who are similar. In general, we tend to be attracted to people with whom we share certain personal characteristics, such as race, gender, age, and attitudes. We also find interactions with people who are similar to be easier and more desirable. Schneider (1987) argued that organizations become increasingly homogeneous through the process of attraction, selection, and attrition. First, individuals are attracted to organizations where they believe they will "fit in" with other employees and the organizational values and culture are consistent with individuals' belief systems. Second, current organizational members are most likely to feel comfortable with applicants who are similar and thus are likely to hire new employees who hold similar characteristics. Third, Schneider (1987) argued that perceived similarity impacts retention, as employees are more likely to be satisfied and remain with an organization when they feel that they "fit in." Thus, because most organizational leaders continue to be White males, there is a natural bias for such leaders to attract and select other White males.

Research supports the homophily bias in workplace practices. Kraiger and Ford (1985) found that raters tended to give higher performance ratings to persons of the same race. Research also suggests that minority employees will be more attracted to organizations and more likely to apply when recruitment advertisements portray diverse workers (Perkins, Thomas, and Taylor, 2000) and when the recruiter is a member of a minority group (Thomas and Wise, 1999). In general, then, organizational leaders will feel more comfortable with individuals who are similar in demographic characteristics, and thus be more likely to select those individuals for the work team. In addition, minority employees will be more attracted to organizations where minorities are represented.

Another reason for the continuance of discrimination in subjective hiring practices is that even though blatant forms of racism in the workplace are no longer considered acceptable, a more subtle form of racism has emerged, called "modern" or "aversive racism" (see chapter 2, this volume, for a discussion of the subtle differences between these concepts). Individuals who hold modern racist views believe that racism is no longer a problem and that minorities are receiving undeserved gains in society (McConahay, 1986). In their program of research, Dovidio and Gaertner (1998) have demonstrated that many White Americans still hold negative attitudes toward Blacks. Unlike the overt hostility that was often expressed toward Blacks prior to the civil rights movement, Whites' negative attitudes toward Blacks today involve discomfort, uneasiness, sometimes fear, and may often be unconscious. In fact, they argue that many majority members do not believe they are prejudiced, but yet are unaware of the negative attitudes they hold toward minority members. Brief et al. (1997) suggest that this new form of racism is expressed in the workplace only when a discriminatory action can somehow be justified as non-racist. Because most people do not want to be seen as racist, they will not act upon negative attitudes toward others when their behavior will surely be viewed by others as racist. However, in more ambiguous situations, such as when hiring, individuals may act in a discriminatory manner and justify their decision by saying they hired the White applicant because he can be more responsive to the needs of White customers.

For example, Brief et al. (2000) demonstrated that prejudiced individuals who are provided with a business justification from a legitimate authority figure to discriminate against Black job applicants were likely to do so. Non-prejudiced research participants did not discriminate under any circumstances. Since the 1970s, social psychologists have studied non-verbal behaviors (e.g., eye contact, speech patterns, interpersonal distance) as indications of underlying prejudice in work contexts such as a job interview. Word, Zanna, and Cooper (1974) found that Black and White applicants were treated very differently by White interviewers; Black applicants were met with less eye contact, greater interpersonal distance, more speech errors, and shorter interviews. Similar findings have been replicated a number of times (see Dovidio and Gaertner, 1998, for a review of the literature) in which researchers have demonstrated the results of subtle, subconscious bias within the hiring context.

What can leaders do about the natural bias and unconscious negative attitudes they may hold against others who are dissimilar? Chrobot-Mason and Quiñones (2001) argued that awareness of biases, stereotypes, and negative attitudes is an important first step in working to eliminate workplace discrimination. Leaders who are aware of the personal biases they hold and are conscious of the potential for discrimination in recruitment and hiring practices may be less likely to rely on stereotypes when making selection decisions. Leaders may also take steps to increase their knowledge and comfort level with members of diverse groups. Research has shown that positive interactions with dissimilar others can lead to more positive attitudes, when the interaction is between members of equal status and the interaction is cooperative rather than competitive (Brewer and Brown, 1998).

Leaders may also reduce the risk of discrimination during hiring practices by utilizing standardized selection procedures so that all applicants are treated in the same way and evaluated according to the same objective and job-relevant criteria. Fernandez (1999) advocates the use of structured interviews in which all applicants are asked a standard set of questions, to employ the use of diverse recruiters and interviewers, and to utilize a diverse team of raters to evaluate a candidate's performance. He also argues for the importance of establishing clear and specific criteria to be used by all involved in the selection process.

Leader processes: Developing others

One of the primary leadership responsibilities is developing the talents and abilities of others. Challenging job assignments, training experiences, feedback, mentoring programs, and role models are all used to help employees refine their capabilities and skills. Developing others is important both in order to ensure work group effectiveness and preparation of staff for future assignments.

Leaders use four primary strategies for developing others: challenge, assessment, recognition, and support (Ruderman and Hughes-James, 1998). These four strategies combine Morrison's (1992) model of development for non-traditional managers and the Van Velsor, McCauley, and Moxley (1998) general model of development. These strategies work in concert to promote growth and learning. Leaders who understand these forces can use them to enhance the capabilities of their workforce. Below, we consider each component of development in light of workforce diversity.

Challenge refers to experiences that push people to do something new or to behave or think differently. Much of our learning at work occurs through challenging experiences – be they demanding relationships, difficult job assignments, hardships, or training programs (McCall, Lombardo, and Morrison, 1988). Challenging experiences are developmental because they offer both the motivation and the opportunity to learn new and different skills (McCauley et al., 1994). Executives of different demographic groups attribute much of their success to challenging experiences (Lyness and Thompson, 2000).

There are, however, differences in how challenges occur in different demographic groups. There is evidence that women are not exposed to the highly developmental task-related leadership challenges with the same frequency as men (Ohlott, Ruderman, and McCauley, 1994). Similarly, a recent study by Catalyst (2000) revealed that although women are swelling the managerial ranks, only 13 percent achieve expatriate roles. Lyness and Thompson (2000) also found that fewer women than men are getting overseas experiences. Although women and men may be promoted to similar organizational levels, they are not receiving the same developmental value of those experiences.

Further, women experience additional challenges that men do not. Adler, Brody, and Osland (2001), for example, describe the added challenge women face of developing a style that men are comfortable with. According to a survey of top men and women at Best Foods, more than ten times as many women as men believed that it was critical for women to develop a style men were comfortable with.

There is also evidence that challenges are differentially distributed according to race. One study found that African-American managers of both genders obtain proportionally fewer key job assignments than White managers (Ruderman and Hughes-James, 1998). Further, there is evidence that African Americans experience challenges that Whites do not face. In particular, they experience race-related obstacles that the other managers do not. They have to deal with being tokens and being stereotyped. These add extra challenges to the already demanding managerial responsibilities.

When a leader is developing members of the team, attention should be paid to the level of challenge each team member experiences. Any specific challenge should be considered in light of the other forces bearing on team members. A challenge can be a potent developmental force in some situations and the proverbial straw that breaks the camel's back in others.

Assessment and feedback are critical developmental tools as well. Assessment has to do with helping an employee understand where he or she is with regard to a particular set of challenges or behaviors linked to effectiveness. Assessment and feedback can be given either informally or formally. Informal feedback takes the form of casual conversations that deal with actions and their associated strengths and weaknesses. This is important because it allows employees to see themselves as others do. However, one complexity associated with informal feedback is that White men tend to have greater access to it than do people of color or White women (Morrison, 1992). Thus, members of non-dominant groups have limited access to a key source of development.

To counteract the limited distribution of informal feedback, most organizations also use a variety of formal feedback tools. These include performance appraisals and 360-degree feedback instruments. The term "360-degree feedback" refers to the systematic collection of opinions about someone's performance from a wide range of people for the purposes of development. The feedback may come from the boss, peers, direct reports, or even customers, in addition to the individual involved. The benefit of 360-degree feedback is that the employee gets to see how a range of others view him or her against a specific set of standards.

Regardless of the method of feedback used, the possibility of bias complicates giving feedback across the lines of gender, race, culture, or ethnicity. Both leaders and followers can make errors in interpreting the behaviors or styles of others (Triandis, Kurowski, and Gelfand, 1994). For feedback to be helpful it is important that it be seen as credible. The expected feedback dynamic is that positive feedback should reinforce certain behaviors and constructive feedback should suggest areas for improvement. The process may go awry if the recipient of the feedback perceives suggestions for improvement coming from a biased or prejudiced individual. If the feedback recipient believes that the feedback giver is biased due to race, gender, or ethnicity, he or she may tend to reject the feedback. Cox (1994) calls the process of trying to figure out the validity of a piece of feedback "interpretative confusion." Whenever feedback is given across demographic groups the possibility for this additional source of error and discomfort is increased. This can happen both in the case of informal feedback and more formal feedback. Thus it becomes particularly important that leaders in diverse work groups learn how to give direct, specific, behavioral feedback and to do so in ways that can be heard by people from cultures who prefer indirect communication. It also becomes important for workers in diverse work groups to seek feedback from as wide a group of people as possible so that the possibility of bias from any one person is reduced. (For a discussion of how African Americans' responsiveness to feedback may be related to their level or stage of racial identity, see chapter 8.)

Support comes from many sources and refers to relationships that enhance learning and development. Supportive relationships can provide advice, encouragement, information, and friendship and can be extremely useful to employees who are in the midst of a challenging experience. In terms of development there are three key relationships to pay attention to: (1) dyadic relationships between the leader and the follower, (2) mentoring relationships, and (3) networks.

Dyadic relationships between leaders and followers are best explained through the Leader–Member Exchange Model (LMX). As mentioned before, the LMX model suggests that leaders and followers develop work relationships that may be characterized as high or low quality. Research has shown that employees who are demographically different than their supervisor are more likely to have a lower quality work relationship, characterized by lower trust, interaction, respect, and support (Tsui, Egan, and Xin, 1995). Tsui and O'Reilly (1989) examined the effects of demographic dissimilarity on the relationship between 272 superior–subordinate dyads. They found that employees who were dissimilar from their supervisors on traits such as gender and race were perceived as less effective by their supervisors. They also found that employees in mixed gender and mixed race dyads reported higher levels of role ambiguity and role conflict. Based on these findings, it seems that diverse work relationships between dissimilar leaders and followers tend to pose special problems. Fortunately, Scandura and Graen (1984) found evidence that supervisory training in active listening skills and one-on-one conversations intended to increase reciprocal understanding can improve work relationships, especially those that were initially low quality relationships.

Mentoring relationships, another form of support, can be either informal or formal. Informal relationships occur naturally between junior and senior members of an organization. They are unstructured and can form on the basis of a natural affinity between two people. For a variety of reasons, African Americans report fewer mentoring relationships than Whites (Cox and Nkomo, 1991; Davidson, 1997; Bell and Nkomo, 2001). This may be because Whites simply prefer to associate with others like themselves (Dickens and Dickens, 1991; Bell and Nkomo, 2001) or because White men may worry that supporting a person of color may pose an obstacle to their own career advancement (Kram and Hall, 1996). O'Neill, Horton, and Crosby (1999) found that while women report no fewer mentors than men, women protégés have more cross-sex mentoring relationships than men. Further, Ragins and Cotton (1991) report that women experience significant barriers in finding a mentor that stem from a fear on the part of male mentors that the relationship could be misconstrued as romantic.

Thomas (1989) suggests that taboos regarding race and sex significantly shape the dynamics of mentoring relationships. According to Thomas (2001), issues that make such relationship tricky include negative stereotypes, skepticism about intimacy, public scrutiny, and peer resentment. White women in a cross-sex mentoring relationship or people of color in a cross-race relationship may be at a disadvantage when it comes to acquiring support. They may miss out on the psychosocial components of mentoring, such as friendship, confirmation of identity, and access to informal feedback.

Networking is another form of support that can occur formally as well as informally. Ibarra (1993, 1995) suggests that different demographic groups may have differential access to networking relationships. Networks provide support and validation for managers who share similar experiences in addition to access to information, resources, advice, and powerful people. In most organizations, managerial networks are likely to be heavily White, American, and male because these are the majority of people who populate the managerial ranks. However, this may not be the best arrangement for all employees. Because a basic human need is to be with similar others, members of non-dominant groups also desire to seek out members of their own kind for friendship, validation, and role modeling. Because members of non-dominant groups are not as prevalent in organizations, these managers must reach far and wide into the organization to create rich network relationships (Ibarra, 1993, 1995). As a result, members of non-dominant groups have more heterogeneous networks with greater contact outside the immediate work group and fewer relationships with people in powerful positions. The implication of this difference is that White women and people of color have differential access to the social and political benefits of networking. Thus, in developing members of a heterogeneous workforce, it is important to realize that different employees have different networking needs. For members of non-dominant groups, the most effective relationships appear to be strong psychosocial relationships with similar others and strong instrumental relationships with different others (McCambley, 1999; Murrell and Tangri, 1999). In both cases trust is an essential component of the relationship, but the level of personal disclosure differs, as do expectations about political capital.

Recognition is important because it reinforces learning and risk-taking. It also sends signals of value and worth. This can in turn enhance self-esteem and increase an employee's commitment to the job. Recognition is critical when it comes to rewarding learning from challenging assignments. However, in many organizations there is a perception that people of color and White women do not get the same level of recognition as White men do. Organizational reward systems tend to value the qualities of the majority, thereby overlooking the qualities intrinsic to other groups (Acker, 1990). In a review of research on race and ethnicity in organizations, Cox, Welch, and Nkomo (2001) point out that an outcome of this difference is that with few exceptions, the highest positions in organizations still go to White men.

Recognition may take many forms beyond promotion and salary. It can include credit, praise, invitations, and awards. It is very important that recognition is distributed appropriately. A bias or tendency on the part of leaders to limit recognition to similar others could inadvertently hamper development of employees from non-dominant groups.

Development of others is never easy and there is no simplistic recipe. Each of these strategies contributes to the development of others; however, their real power is in combination. Challenges open up the employee to new ways of thinking and behaving. Assessment and feedback provide information as to how the employee is doing. Support cushions the challenge and reinforcement rewards learning and risk-taking.

However, sometimes these forces don't work the way they are supposed to. Morrison (1992) points out that for White women and people of color, an imbalance often occurs so that challenge exceeds the other components of the model. Barriers such as subtle and overt discrimination, prejudice, extra scrutiny, isolation, tokenism, and discomfort with dissimilar others create additional challenges for some members of the workforce. These additional challenges may mean that workers from non-dominant groups get overloaded on challenge and assessment and short-changed on support and recognition. This can lead to an overwhelming situation rather than a developmental one.

There are, however, some steps that can be taken to achieve balance among these forces. Leaders can take steps to enhance their ability to develop others:

- Carefully use challenging assignments when matching employees with tasks. It is important to ensure that all employees with potential are given access to challenging assignments. It is also important to take into account the extra challenges experienced by members of minority groups. Too little challenge can result in little growth; too much can be overwhelming.

- Learn how to initiate and develop relationships with people who are different from you. Learn how to connect with people who may come from a different background or perspective. Expose yourself to different sources of diversity so that you can appreciate the views of others.
- Understand the concept of interpretive bias. Try to use as objective methods as possible when evaluating others. Don't be afraid to give feedback to someone dissimilar from you. Feedback is an essential tool for learning.
- Review the level and types of rewards distributed to group members. Assess whether or not there are disparities due to immigration status, race, gender, or ethnicity. Look at both formal rewards such as pay and promotions as well as informal rewards such as praise, honors, credit, and invitations. Monitoring the concrete results of one's good intentions is certainly as or more important than perpetually questioning one's own intentions.

Leader processes: Enhancing teamwork

Perhaps the most significant role leaders may play in facilitating teamwork in a diverse work group is to improve interpersonal communication. The best way to foster good interpersonal communication is, in turn, to ensure that minority members have voice. That is, leaders must take steps to foster a work environment where minority employees feel that they can express their opinions and ideas, and that others will listen. Leaders have the opportunity to facilitate positive communication among diverse employees in three sets of situations: (1) when managing work groups, (2) when intergroup conflict arises, and (3) when interacting with subordinates interpersonally or on a one-on-one basis. Each of these will be discussed below.

In managing work teams, leaders spend a significant amount of time facilitating meetings which serve as a forum to delegate tasks, generate ideas, solve problems, and make decisions about how and when work will be accomplished. Research by Jackson (1992) and others has demonstrated that diversity in work groups can be associated with increased creativity and better quality decisions. Greater diversity leads to the consideration of a greater range of perspectives and opinions, which can enhance creativity and innovation (Milliken and Martins, 1996). Yet many work groups fail to provide an environment where diverse perspectives and opinions are heard, thus forfeiting the potential value that diversity may bring. Barker et al. (2000) summarized the research in this area by stating that because minorities are more often in positions of lower status and power, they often feel ostracized, contribute less to decision-making, are less committed to the group, and are confronted with negative expectations.

In general, research supports the notion that minority members in work groups are often overlooked or marginalized, and their ideas tend to be devalued. Greenhaus, Parasuraman, and Wormley (1990) reported that Blacks perceived less discretion and autonomy on their jobs than Whites. Ibarra (1995) found that minority managers had fewer intimate relationships within their career network than White managers, suggesting that minorities are often socially isolated in the workplace as well. Cox (1994) suggests that cultural differences in communication style may affect diverse work group interactions. For example, modesty in the presence of one's superiors is a cultural norm in Asian and Pacific Americans that is often manifested in behaviors such as reluctance to speak out at meetings or ask questions. Such behavior is often misinterpreted as incompetence or lack of interest. Leaders may foster a more supportive forum for open discussion during work group meetings by employing a variety of strategies that may serve to encourage a variety of perspectives and ideas. One such example is the nominal group technique discussed in panel 5.1.

5.1   *The nominal group technique: Giving voice to a variety of opinions*

One strategy that leaders may use to ensure that minority opinions and ideas are voiced during work group meetings is called the nominal group technique (NGT). This technique is similar to brainstorming, in that one of the goals is to generate a long list of creative ideas and suggestions. However, NGT has been shown to be more effective than brainstorming in generating creative and high quality ideas (Gratias and Hills, 1997), perhaps because NGT solicits greater expectations for individual performance than brainstorming. NGT involves the following five steps (Callanan, 1984):

1 Each group member lists suggestions for solving a specific problem on a sheet of paper, without speaking to the other group members.
2 The group leader asks each member to present one idea at a time, which is recorded on a master sheet. The group leader proceeds in a clockwise fashion and asks all group members to present an idea, until all new ideas have been recorded.
3 After some discussion to clarify ideas, group members anonymously rank the best ideas on the list. Results are tabulated and those ideas with the highest scores are presented.
4 Each idea is then deliberately discussed and modified, based on group member input.
5 Each group member once again anonymously ranks each idea and the highest scoring ideas are then submitted for action.

By seeking input from each team member individually prior to group discussion, the leader can ensure that all team members have equal opportunity to contribute ideas. Additionally, the anonymous ranking of ideas by all group members provides a forum in which each person's vote is weighted equally in the final decision-making process.

Along with diversity comes the possibility of conflict. Although conflict in the workplace is generally viewed as negative and something to be avoided, recent research suggests that some types of conflict can lead to positive work outcomes. Pelled, Eisenhardt, and Xin (1999) found that diversity in functional background (e.g., a background in engineering versus human resources) leads to increased conflict when group members are working on a specific task. However, this type of conflict actually had favorable effects on measures of performance. The authors argue that task conflict may enhance task performance because such conflict fosters a deeper understanding of task issues. In working through such issues, group members engage in a free exchange of information that facilitates problem solving, decision-making, and generation of ideas. Likewise, Jehn, Northcraft, and Neale (1999) found that informational diversity was likely to lead to improved performance when tasks were non-routine. Additionally, they found that diversity based on social categories such as age and gender led to greater satisfaction and commitment when group members work interdependently or cooperatively on tasks.

The results of these studies again suggest that leaders should encourage and foster a work environment where alternative perspectives and ideas are encouraged and rewarded. At times, some degree of conflict about how to complete the work or how to resolve an issue may actually be essential to evoke new opinions and strategies within the work group. Task conflict, however, should be distinguished from emotional conflict, which results from stereotyping and involves interpersonal clashes (Pelled, Eisenhardt, and Xin, 1999). Unlike task conflict, emotional conflict does not lead to higher performance and is something to be avoided. Leaders should be extremely diligent to minimize conflict due to negative behaviors based on stereotypes and prejudices against diverse members of the work team. However, leaders should allow and perhaps even encourage some level of conflict to emerge among the work team to facilitate the free exchange of ideas, at least as it pertains to the task itself and does not involve personal issues or debates about individual differences.

Finally, leaders should consider the significant role they play in establishing effective one-on-one communication with their subordinates. Lawler and Finegold (2000) argue that given the increased diversity of the workforce, organizations need to move toward individualizing employment relationships. This involves personalized interactions with employees, recognizing that each employee has unique needs, experiences, values, strengths, and developmental opportunities. In communicating with diverse employees one-on-one, leaders should consider individual preferences in communication strategies. For example, in his work on mixed race mentoring relationships, Thomas (1993) identified two types of strategies used for dealing with racial differences. Some prefer a direct style in which racial differences are openly discussed. Others tend to deny and suppress race-related issues. Although he found that both types of strategies could be effective for mentoring relationships if the superior and the subordinate both prefer the same strategy, he also reported that the type of strategy selected was unanimously the strategy preferred by the superior. Thus, we recommend that leaders of diversity attempt to become comfortable with both communication strategies and use that which is preferred by the individual employee.

DEVELOPING MULTICULTURAL COMPETENCE

How can leaders, especially those from hegemonic groups, cope with the challenges of diverse work groups? Many diversity researchers have argued that leaders of diversity must develop new skills to manage a heterogeneous workforce and that most leaders are ill-prepared for tackling the issues and conflicts that often arise from diversity in the workplace (Chemers and Murphy, 1995; Morrison, 1992). "No longer will good leadership skills be sufficient. Excellence across a broader range of skills will be a baseline requirement for successful leadership in a diverse workforce" (Joplin and Daus, 1997: 32).

Although the need for leaders to develop diversity skills may be apparent, a clear definition of what such skills are and how they should be acquired remains elusive. Cox and Beale (1997) define diversity competency as an ability to respond to the challenges and opportunities created by diversity in the workplace. Offermann and Phan (2002: 188) define cultural intelligence as "the ability to function effectively in a diverse context where the assumptions, values, and traditions of one's upbringing are not uniformly shared with those with whom one needs to work." Furthermore, they suggest that cultural intelligence is context dependent. That is, effective leader behaviors vary across situations and people and there is no one right answer or single response that a leader may take to manage diversity successfully each time. Although research and theory in the area of diversity skill development is in its infancy, we wish to propose a more specific definition and examples of the skills leaders need to effectively manage a diverse workforce.

We contend that future leaders must develop "multicultural competence." We define multicultural competence as proficiency in diagnosing diversity issues and resolving diversity-related conflicts and organizational problems by reaching a mutually satisfying solution for all parties involved. It is our view that to become multiculturally competent, leaders need to increase their knowledge of cultural differences, develop greater self-awareness, and acquire four general skills.

Knowledge of cultural differences

Effective leaders of diversity must understand differences in values, customs, beliefs, and norms across various cultures. Global leaders, those who work overseas or who manage employees from different countries, must be aware of the extent to which people from different cultures vary in the way they conduct business. In their work on project GLOBE involving data from 18,000 middle managers from 62 countries, Javidan and House (2001) found that people from different cultures vary in the way they value assertive work behaviors, adhere to established gender roles, rely on procedures and policies, view authority figures, emphasize group affiliations, and emphasize performance, among others. For example, in countries such as Russia, Thailand, and Spain, there is a strong expectation of obedience toward supervisors and clear distinctions between those with status and power and those without. In contrast, countries like the US and Denmark tend to be more egalitarian and value broader employee participation in decision-making. Global leaders must consider differences in expectations and norms when conducting business with members of another culture or when working overseas. Research on cross-cultural training intended to prepare leaders for working overseas has shown that increased knowledge of the host culture tends to be effective when trainees are provided with opportunities to practice appropriate behaviors and are provided positive reinforcement (Bhawuk and Brislin, 2000; Black and Mendenhall, 1990).

Leaders who manage a group of employees who reside and/or were born in the same country will still likely need to be aware of the existence of important differences based on cultural variations. Strong subcultures exist even within the US (e.g., Hispanic, African-American, and American-Indian subcultures), reflecting differences in values, beliefs, customs, and behavioral norms that exist between various cultures even within the same country (see chapter 4, this volume, for a fuller discussion). For example, in the African-American culture, direct confrontation and forthrightness are the preferred methods for resolving conflicts. This preference is often viewed as highly assertive or bold by Anglo standards (Cox, 1994). Leaders must also be sensitive to power and status differences among groups within any one culture.

Knowledge of cultural differences is important because it helps to create an organizational climate of respect for different perspectives. Workplace clashes which stem from negative behaviors based on stereotypes can be ignited by a disrespectful act. Sometimes the disrespect is intentional, but often times the disrespect stems from ignorance. Helping organizational members better understand different perspectives and cultural orientations can create a climate in which organizational members are better equipped to respect one another.

Increased self-awareness

Although knowledge of cultural differences is important to the development of multicultural competence, it is not enough. Even if one could amass enough knowledge about all the different cultures, it is important to keep in mind that individuals within a culture vary in their values, beliefs, and expectations as well. Therefore, as we mentioned earlier, it is critical that leaders of diversity engage in personalized interactions. In order to accomplish this, leaders must become more aware of their own biases, prejudices, and attitudes toward dissimilar others. As McIntosh (1993) argues, it is important to examine the "cultural baggage" we each bring to a relationship in order to understand how interpersonal interactions may be affected by such things as stereotypes, past negative experiences with certain groups, and a lack of understanding about the barriers members of minority groups face each day. Goleman (1998) suggests that understanding our own emotions and their influence on our relationships is critical to effective behavior in organizations and becomes even more important in the context of managing diversity.

Offermann and Phan (2002) also recommend that leaders make an effort to understand the assumptions and expectations they hold based on their own cultural heritage. Furthermore, they believe that this is a more difficult task than understanding foreign cultures because many of the beliefs and values we hold are taken for granted and not immediately apparent to us. Research by Devine and colleagues (Devine and Monteith, 1993; Devine and Vasquez, 1998) has shown that becoming more aware of our own biases and prejudices can serve as motivation to monitor and change our reactions toward others. They asked research participants both about how they *would* respond to an intergroup encounter and how they think they *should* respond. Those individuals who reported themselves as having lower prejudiced attitudes experienced guilt when they failed to live up to their own personal standards. The researchers also found that awareness of prejudice and guilt associated with such attitudes can be a strong motivational force for learning how to avoid prejudice in the future and reduce the effects of prejudice on judgments (Devine and Monteith, 1993).

Multicultural skills

Beyond increased knowledge of cultural differences and self-awareness, leaders will likely need to develop additional skills, or broaden existing ones within the context of diversity, to effectively manage a heterogeneous workforce. Although empirical work is still needed to establish a skill set that can be linked to positive diversity outcomes (i.e., minority retention and satisfaction), we propose a short list of general skills that we believe are related to multicultural competence for leaders. This list is not intended to be exhaustive; rather, it is an attempt to initiate discussion about what we see as the four most important skills: conflict management, interpersonal communication, feedback seeking, and role modeling.

Conflict management

Inherent in many diversity conflicts are issues related to group differences in power and status (Linnehan and Konrad, 1999). Leaders of diversity may play an important role in reducing intergroup inequality and creating perceptions of justice and fairness. Haslam (2000) argues that leaders will be most effective in resolving conflicts when they understand and attend to the interests and values of both groups. Thus, leaders must develop a high level of trust with members of both parties involved in a diversity conflict, and rely on conflict resolution skills, such as negotiation and compromise, to reach a solution that is perceived as fair for both groups·involved. One example of this is portrayed in panel 5.2.

5.2   *The racial insult: What should the leader do?*

Joseph Andrew's 50th birthday celebration took place on a Saturday night at a lush country club in Michigan. His sister, who made the elaborate dinner party, invited Joseph's entire department. Joseph worked at a medium sized county government agency. Born and bred in Michigan, Joseph is White and often described by others as a "good ole boy." Joseph has worked for the department for eight years and by all accounts has always had good relationships with his co-workers. His department consists of 20 people: 11 White men, 1 Asian American, 3 White women, 4 African-American men, and 2 African-American women, in addition to the supervisor, who is a White man. This department has demographics similar to the larger agency, itself composed of 120 people and led by Nick, a 52-year-old White male.

Everyone was having a good time at the party, which included Joseph's friends and family in addition to his co-workers. When Joseph went to talk to his co-workers after drinks and hors-d'oeuvres, he made a comment to Ralph, a Black colleague, which stopped the festivities for Ralph. Attempting a joke, Joseph said, "I didn't know they let 'you people' in a place like this." Joseph was laughing and seemed to be joking as he said this. Ralph's response was to say "You can't talk to me like this" and leave.

Monday morning, everyone is back at work. Nick, the agency chief, who was away for the weekend, found a letter from Ralph on his desk. In addition to describing the incident, the letter demanded an apology from Joseph before Ralph would work with him again. Further, the letter was sent to the local TV stations, local newspapers, the *Detroit Free Press*, and the *New York Times*. Before Nick can put the letter down, the phone rings with a call from a reporter asking for his comment. He tells them he is looking into the incident. Nick next checks his email and realizes the letter was also emailed to the entire staff of 120 in the agency. His inbox is filled with opinions about the incident.

Midpoint discussion questions

1 As someone in a position of leadership, what should Nick do?
2 Does it make any difference that the incident happened after hours and offsite?
3 What role do you think the media plays in such an incident?

In order to work effectively on the same crew, Joseph and Ralph need to get along. Nick realized this situation was problematic and volatile as soon as he read the letter. His first response was to notify his boss, the human resource department, and the department of public relations. Next, he got in touch with the diversity trainers who had led mandatory diversity training earlier in the year. Nick's next step was to talk with both Joseph and Ralph separately and find out what happened. He then checked with others at the party. Nick's assessment was that Ralph was deeply hurt by Joseph's comment, but that Joseph really felt he had been kidding. Joseph claimed that he and Ralph were buddies and could kid around like this. Ralph saw this completely differently and felt he shouldn't have to work side by side with someone like Joseph.

While Nick was meeting with Joseph and Ralph, the entire agency was busy discussing the incident and the emails were flying. Everyone wanted to know what happened. The party incident was replayed over and over again. There were informal discussions about other racial incidents in the agency.

Nick brought Ralph and Joseph together in a meeting. They were each able to bring someone for support. Both the director of the human resource department and the diversity training facilitator attended. Joseph reluctantly apologized to Ralph. Ralph requested that Joseph apologize publicly since the statement was made publicly. Joseph refused. Nick then privately spoke with Joseph and asked him to think about this for one day and the implications of not apologizing. He told him how important he felt it was for both the department and Joseph's personal development that he apologize publicly. After the day of reflection, Joseph came back and agreed to the public apology. He wrote a letter of apology to Ralph and the department as a whole that was emailed to the entire agency.

In addition to this, Joseph apologized to Ralph in a series of meetings arranged to have a dialogue about the incident. Joseph and Ralph's immediate boss and the diversity facilitator led these meetings. Everyone in the agency had the chance to process both the event and the subsequent apology in a meeting. Joseph and Ralph walked out of the meetings able to work with each other again.

Discussion questions

1 What do you think of Nick's response? What would you have done differently?
2 Do you think this would have played out differently in a private corporation?
3 What do you think Joseph and Ralph learned from this incident?
4 What advice would you give Nick for the future?
5 Would you leave Joseph and Ralph on the same crew?
6 How appropriate was Ralph's response to Joseph's behavior?

Interpersonal communication

One of the themes throughout this chapter is the need for leaders of diversity to engage in personalized interactions with followers. As a result, leaders must become proficient in the use of communication strategies that encourage trust, honesty, and openness. As mentioned previously, one of the biggest challenges leaders of diversity face is finding ways to encourage and facilitate the open exchange of ideas and opinions in order to fully benefit from a diverse workforce. Therefore, multiculturally competent leaders will have knowledge and make use of a variety of strategies for ensuring that minority employees have voice. The nominal group technique is one strategy outlined in panel 5.1, but there are many other techniques that leaders of diversity should rely on to facilitate effective communication. Listening skills will also prove to be critical for understanding the unique problems and barriers that minority employees encounter in the workplace. Although it is easier to understand and empathize with people who are similar, multiculturally competent leaders will listen to dissimilar others with an open mind and attempt to understand the issues that minority members face in the workplace, even if they have never shared or witnessed this experience.

Feedback seeking

Multiculturally competent leaders will constantly seek feedback from external sources to evaluate their own behavior as well as the fairness of organizational practices and policies. Because traditional leaders managing a non-traditional work group may not be fully aware of the barriers that non-traditional employees face, they must actively seek feedback from diverse perspectives to uncover diversity issues and problems. Leaders of diversity should engage in a variety of strategies to gather information about their ability to manage diversity effectively. These strategies should include both formal and informal mechanisms for gathering critical feedback, such as surveys, focus groups, and one-on-one conversations with influential members of minority groups. Even the best-intentioned leaders of diversity are bound to make mistakes or offend certain groups at times. However, multiculturally competent leaders will seek ongoing feedback that makes them aware when this occurs and then take steps to correct the misunderstanding and learn from that experience.

Role modeling

Finally, leaders who effectively manage diversity must send a strong message that they are committed to increasing diversity and improving the work environment so that all employees may reach their full potential. Behaviorally, this means that leaders must serve as role models within the organization by setting goals and communicating a vision that involves the hiring and retention of a diverse workforce (Cox, 2001). It also means being personally involved with diversity initiatives and demonstrating a commitment to change. As mentioned earlier, multiculturally competent leaders must learn how to initiate and develop relationships with people who are different and expose themselves to people who come from different backgrounds and perspectives. This requires personal growth and development as well as taking some risks. Leaders should seek to expand their "comfort zone" by placing themselves in situations where they become the minority.

Developing proficiency in these four skill areas (conflict management, interpersonal communication, feedback seeking, and role modeling) is not an easy task. Leaders who strive to become multiculturally competent must understand that this is a long-term process that involves both patience and commitment. A one-day training seminar on diversity will simply not be enough. Chrobot-Mason and Quiñones (2001) propose that development of diversity skills involves three stages: (1) awareness, (2) skill building, and (3) action planning. Awareness involves developing a greater understanding of cultural differences as well as greater awareness of one's own stereotypes and biases. Skill building involves opportunities to practice behaviors supportive of diversity objectives, such as the use of conflict management strategies to facilitate collaboration among dissimilar others. The third stage of development, action planning, involves setting both organizational and personal goals for change. Organizational goals might involve changes in organizational practices, such as increasing the number of minority applicants. Personal goals might include becoming involved with diverse community groups. Again, leaders committed to improving their multicultural competence should consider all three stages when developing proficiency in diversity skills.

SUMMARY

Throughout this chapter, we have argued the need to re-examine traditional beliefs and theories regarding what constitutes effective leadership. There is substantial evidence that non-traditional leaders (women and people of color) still face considerable challenges in the workplace that serve to undermine their ability to have an impact and achieve career success. Organizations, therefore, must continue to examine practices and policies that inhibit the selection, development, and success of minority leaders.

We have also argued that organizational leaders should play a critical role in bringing diverse employees together to accomplish work. Although leading a more heterogeneous work team presents additional and unique challenges, it also presents unique opportunities for organizational leaders. Rather than adopt a colorblind approach, we believe that leaders must be cognizant of the impact that organizational practices and policies, as well as their own behaviors, may have on assembling, developing, and motivating a diverse work group. Additionally, organizations should provide opportunities for multicultural competency development and reward leaders who take advantage of such opportunities. Developing the skills needed to effectively manage a diverse work group will not only be a benefit to leaders in the new millennium, but will likely become a necessity as the workplace continues to diversify.

6

HEALTH IMPLICATIONS OF WORKPLACE DIVERSITY

Lynda M. Sagrestano

In 1990, the National Institute of Occupational Safety and Health (NIOSH) (Sauter, Murphy, and Hurrell, 1990) outlined six psychosocial risk factors in the workplace, including (1) work load and work pace, (2) work schedule, (3) role stressors, (4) career security factors, (5) interpersonal relations, and (6) job content. This chapter examines the joint influence of physical, social, and environmental factors as they relate to these psychosocial risk factors in the workplace, and the potential for these factors to influence physical health. Specifically, each of these factors has the potential to interact with gender and/or race/ethnicity in specific ways, leading to unique stressors experienced by women and minorities in the workplace, which may be related to adverse health outcomes. The NIOSH framework is used to discuss several stressors experienced by women and minorities that arise due to the specific challenges these groups face in the workplace. In addition, potential interventions to reduce stress and adverse health outcomes related to the workplace are discussed.

Occupational stress is the subject of increased attention. Workers' compensation rates and large-scale studies show that stress in the workplace is on the rise, especially among women (Galinsky, Bond, and Friedman, 1993; Northwestern National Life, 1991; Swanson et al., 1997). Research has focused primarily on the causes and consequences of occupational stress, and its relation to psychological distress and adverse health outcomes. In 1990 the National Institute for Occupational Safety and Health (NIOSH) (Sauter, Murphy, and Hurrell, 1990) outlined six psychosocial risk factors in the workplace: (1) workload and work pace, (2) job content, (3) work schedule, (4) role stressors, (5) career security and advancement, and (6) interpersonal relations. This chapter examines each of these psychosocial risk factors in the workplace, and their potential to influence physical health. Specifically, each of these factors has the potential to interact with gender and/or race/ethnicity in specific ways, leading to unique stressors experienced by women and minorities in the workplace, which may be related to adverse health outcomes. The NIOSH framework is used to discuss several stressors experienced by women and minorities that arise due to the specific challenges these groups face in the workplace.

OCCUPATIONAL STRESS AND ADVERSE HEALTH OUTCOMES: AN OVERVIEW

Occupational stress research and advocacy has focused primarily on the causes and consequences of occupational stress, most notably psychological distress. Within the area of occupational health, associations between stress and physical health outcomes have received little attention. However, this association has been the focus of much research in the area of health psychology more generally. For this reason, the basic processes linking stress to adverse health outcomes will be briefly reviewed.

Stress has been defined as a negative emotional experience accompanied by predictable biochemical, physiological, cognitive, and behavioral changes that are directed toward altering the stressful event or accommodating to its effects (Taylor, 1999). It can be conceptualized as a negative state of arousal that arises when the demands of a situation exceed the resources available to cope with that situation. The stress and coping process are interactive and ongoing. When faced with a taxing situation, individuals first engage in "primary appraisal," when they evaluate the situation and the potential for harm. They then engage in "secondary appraisal," when they evaluate their resources for coping with the stressor. Because stress is by definition related to an appraisal of resources, it is determined by the person–environment fit (Lazarus and Folkman, 1984). According to social psychologist Kurt Lewin, behavior is a function of the interaction between the person and the situation, including the extent to which the person fits with the situation (Pervin, 1968). For example, if a person possesses the skills needed to complete a job, fit will be high and stress will presumably be low. If a person does not possess the needed skills, fit will be low and stress will be high. Similarly, when resources are adequate to deal with a stressor, the objective experience of stress is low, but when resources are inadequate, the objective experience of stress is high.

The processes by which stress affects physical health are many and varied. Although the physiological processes are beyond the scope of this chapter, it is important to note that stress has direct physiological effects on humans, including elevated lipids, elevated blood pressure, decreased immunity, and increased hormonal activity. In addition, stress has a direct impact on health habits, including smoking, alcohol and drug use, nutrition, and sleep. Stress may also interfere with treatment and the use of services by decreasing compliance with medical advice, decreasing the likelihood of seeking care, and delaying the time until seeking care (Baum, 1994; Baum and Posluszny, 1999).

How, then, is stress related to illness? To the extent that stress affects each of the pathways outlined above, it can produce physiological, psychological, and behavioral changes that are conducive to the development of illness. Yet not all people under stress develop illness. Instead, preexisting vulnerabilities, both physical and psychological, play an important role in this process. For those who have an initial vulnerability, stress may lead to illness. Research suggests that the association between stress and illness is strongest for cardiovascular disease, infectious diseases, and pregnancy complications (Adler and Matthews, 1994).

The workplace is one of the major sources of stress in the lives of Americans. Although many studies report no differences in the number of job stressors between men and women, recent research suggests that differences exist in the frequency and perceived severity of specific stressors (Spielberger and Reheiser, 1994). Understanding the source of gender differences, in general, is complex. Some researchers come from an individual differences approach, in which characteristics of the individual, such as biological sex, are examined as explanations of group differences. Others come from a social structural approach, in which characteristics of the social context, both at the situational level and the broader social–cultural level, are examined to understand the behavior of women and men in situations. An individual differences approach focuses on between-group variability (e.g., the difference between men and women), typically neglecting within-group variability (e.g., the differences among women), which is often much greater. A social structural approach focuses on within-group variability, but may neglect between-group differences (Feingold, 1995; Hare-Mustin and Marecek, 1990). Nonetheless, it is likely that gender differences emerge from a complex interaction of individual-level factors in the context of specific situations, such as power differentials and unequal access to resources, rather than resulting from inherent biological differences between men and women (Sagrestano, Heavey, and Christensen, 1998). A similar argument could be made for the emergence of racial and ethnic differences in behavior. The following sections detail six psychosocial risk factors in the workplace outlined by NIOSH (Sauter, Murphy, and Hurrell, 1990), specifically with respect to how they interact with gender and race/ethnicity, and the potential for these factors to influence physical health.

REVIEW OF SPECIFIC PSYCHOSOCIAL RISK FACTORS IN THE WORKPLACE

Workload and work pace

The first psychosocial risk factor identified by NIOSH has to do with workload and work pace. Karasek (1979; Karasek et al., 1988) developed the job strain model to explain the attributes of the job environment that are conducive to stress.

The model is two-dimensional, with two key attributes interacting to create four conditions of job strain. The first dimension, "job demands," is characterized by the psychological demands of the job, such as time pressure, deadline stress, heavy workloads, and conflicting demands. The second dimension, "job decision latitude," reflects the amount of control over decisions concerning the way work is accomplished and the skills used to cope with demands (e.g., control over variety, content, and pace of work). The job strain model suggests that those jobs with similar levels of job demands can be differentially stressful depending on the amount of decision latitude or control afforded to the individual (Karasek, 1979; Karasek et al., 1988; LaCroix and Haynes, 1987; Piltch et al., 1994). Specifically, jobs high in psychological demands will produce job strain when the worker has a low level of control over decisions as to how to cope with those demands. In contrast, jobs high in demands coupled with a high degree of decision latitude can be motivating, leading the worker to meet new challenges, and ultimately may be health enhancing (Karasek, Russell, and Theorell, 1982; LaCroix and Haynes, 1987).

For women and men, higher levels of job demands are associated with higher levels of distress, and higher levels of perceived job stress are associated with reporting more physical symptoms and symptoms of mental distress (Ganster, Fox, and Dwyer, 2001; Heaney, 1993; Piltch et al., 1994; Sauter, Hurrell, and Cooper, 1989; Wallerstein, 1992). Research using the job strain model suggests that job strain is a risk factor for cardiovascular disease, both directly and indirectly through elevated blood pressure, cholesterol, and cortisol levels, and increased cigarette smoking (Fox, Dwyer, and Ganster, 1993; Ganster, Fox, and Dwyer, 2001; Karasek et al., 1988; Theorell and Karasek, 1996). Recent research suggests that the association between job demands and physical outcomes is significant for those with low job control, but not those with high job control (Melamed et al., 1998). For example, physical responsivity (i.e., blood pressure) was tested for male workers in an industrial plant with varying workloads. Blood pressure increased with increasing workload for those with low job control, but not those with high job control (Melamed et al., 1998). In addition, job situations of high demand and low control may place women at particularly high risk for coronary heart disease (LaCroix and Haynes, 1987).

Research has documented that women are overrepresented in jobs with high demand and low levels of decision latitude, whereas men in high demand jobs tend to have high levels of decision latitude (Hall, 1989; Haynes, 1991; Heaney, 1993; Karasek and Theorell, 1990; Spielberger and Reheiser, 1994). High strain seems to be especially pronounced among women in secretarial positions, who often experience high job pressure, low levels of responsibility, under-utilization of skills, and lack of autonomy (Haynes, 1991; Narayanan, Menon, and Spector, 1999; Spielberger and Reheiser, 1994). Increases in technology have resulted in greater job segregation for men and women, with men engaging in more technical work and women engaging in end-user occupations such as data entry and clerical work (Haynes, 1991).

With respect to race and ethnicity, Latino Americans and African Americans are much less likely than European Americans to be in managerial and professional occupations. Specifically, at the time of the 1990 census, 12 percent of Hispanic males held managerial positions, as compared to 19 percent of non-Hispanic males (del Pinal, 1993). Although African Americans are increasingly moving into such occupations, they tend to be at lower levels within job categories. For example, 45 percent of African-American men in service jobs are janitors, cleaners, and cooks, and 30 percent of African-American women employed in technical/sales/administrative support positions are cashiers, secretaries, and typists (Bennett, 1993). Among Latino Americans, 16 percent of men and 39 percent of women work in service occupations and 28 percent of men and 15 percent of women work as laborers and operators. Among non-Hispanic Whites, in contrast, 21 percent of men and 45 percent of women work in service occupations and 19 percent of men and 7 percent of women work as laborers and operators (del Pinal, 1993). In general, the overall labor market remains sharply segregated by sex, and women continue to be overrepresented in clerical and service occupations, and underrepresented in production, craft, repair, and labor occupations (Smith, 1993). The overrepresentation of women and people of color in jobs with low levels of responsibility, under-utilization of skills, and lack of autonomy suggests that they are at greater risk for job strain than men and European Americans.

Job content

In addition to workload and work pace, characteristics specific to the content of the job itself can lead to stress. That is, the nature of tasks performed (e.g., fragmented, invariant, short-cycled tasks) have been found to be associated with adverse mental health outcomes, especially to the extent that they provide low levels of stimulation or use of creativity (Sauter, Murphy, and Hurrell, 1990). Lack of variety (e.g., monotony), in particular, has been associated with increased psychological distress and absenteeism due to illness (Korunka, Weiss, and Karetta, 1993; Melamed et al., 1995a; Xie and Johns, 1996). Monotony had the highest impact in distress when the task was short-cycle, repetitive work (Melamed et al., 1995a). Furthermore, short-cycle, repetitive work is associated with several risk factors for coronary heart disease, including elevated blood pressure and serum lipid levels (Melamed et al., 1995b). With respect to sex differences, research by Melamed et al. (1995a) suggests that subjective monotony (the perception that work is monotonous) is related to absenteeism due to illness for women, but not men. Specifically, in a study of blue collar workers in manufacturing plants in Israel, although men and women were equally likely to rate their jobs as monotonous, work conditions were related to sickness absence for women, but not men. In a second study using the same sample, short-cycle, repetitive work conditions (e.g., jobs in which the same discrete set of behaviors is repeated over and over quickly) were found to be related to risk factors for coronary heart disease more consistently among women than men (Melamed et al., 1995b).

The physical conditions of the workplace (e.g., poor air quality, poor ergonomic designs of offices, noise exposure, use of hazardous materials or machinery) can also have an effect on health (Melamed, Fried, and Froom, 2001; Stokols, Pelletier, and Fielding, 1996; Wegman, 1992). In the United States, there were 5.9 million work-related injuries and illnesses in 1998, or 6.7 cases per every 100 full-time workers (US Bureau of Labor Statistics, 2001b). A worker is injured on the job every five seconds, and each day 17 workers die of work-related injuries (DHHS, 2000). Minorities have a higher likelihood of sustaining work-related injuries and dying than do European-American workers, in part because they are overrepresented in positions with the highest occupational risks. In addition to physical injuries and death, the perception of risk leads to increased stress levels for individuals in such occupations, which likely leads to additional negative health outcomes (Keita and Jones, 1990).

With respect to gender, epidemiological data indicates that women are at much lower risk of occupational injury and death than men (Bell, 1991). However, homicide is the leading cause of death for women in the workplace, accounting for 40 percent of workplace-related deaths (NIOSH, 1996), and the second leading cause of workplace-related death for men and women combined (DHHS, 2000). Furthermore, although men and Whites account for the largest number of homicide victims, non-White workers have the highest rates of work-related homicide (NIOSH, 1996). The majority of workplace homicides are robbery-related, often occurring in grocery or convenience stores, restaurants, and gas service stations. In addition, over 25 percent of women victims of workplace homicide are assaulted by people they know, including co-workers, customers, spouses, and friends. Non-fatal assaults are also disproportionately directed at women, with women sustaining approximately two thirds of assault injuries. The majority of female victims of assault (70 percent) are employed in service occupations such as healthcare, and an additional 20 percent take place in retail locations (e.g., restaurants, grocery stores) (NIOSH, 1996, 2001).

Work schedule

The third psychosocial risk factor identified by NIOSH relates to the work schedule. Specifically, research suggests that the temporal arrangement of work, and in particular rotating shifts and permanent night shifts, can have an adverse effect on psychological, social, and physical well-being (Martens et al., 1999; Sauter, Murphy, and Hurrell, 1990). Flexible hours and telecommuting can relieve some of the stress experienced by people who juggle competing roles (Nelson and Hitt, 1992).

Shift work

Research suggests that working rotating shifts, compressed weeks, and changing hours is associated with health complaints, loss of appetite, sleep disruption, substance abuse, and problems related to psychological performance (e.g., decreased energy, decreased alertness, increased apathy) (Cervinka, 1993; Folkard et al., 1993; Healy, Minors, and Waterhouse, 1993; Hossain and Shapiro, 1999; Kandolin, 1993; Martens et al., 1999). Interestingly, shift work in and of itself may have less of an impact on health outcomes than the extent to which workers have control over scheduling (Fenwick and Taussig, 2001; Taussig and Fenwick, 2001).

Research suggests that women who work shifts report more physical and psychological problems than men (Kandolin, 1993). For both men and women with children, working night shifts is associated with an increased likelihood of divorce within five years. Among men this threat to marital stability is most severe in the first five years of marriage, whereas among women the threat is most severe later in marriage (Presser, 2000).

Flextime

Although more than a quarter of the US workforce has some ability to adjust its daily work start and end times, many more employees would like access to such flexible scheduling (Golden, 2001). Research on flexible schedules suggests that flextime is associated with lower levels of depression and somatic complaints, reduced use of sick days, reduced absenteeism, and reduced work–family conflict (Baltes et al., 1999; Lobel, 1999; Thomas and Ganster, 1995; Winett, Neale, and Williams, 1982). Disparity exists in access to flextime, such that women, people of color, and those who are less educated are less likely to have access to it. In 1997, 28.7 percent of male workers and 26.2 percent of female workers used flextime (Golden, 2001). However, the inability to deal effectively with unexpected domestic situations is a burden that tends to fall on women rather than men, and as such, issues related to flexible time may have more of an impact on women than men (Nelson and Hitt, 1992).

Based on the literature, Lobel (1999) proposed several flexibility initiatives, including part-time work, job sharing, working at home, short increments of time off, phased retirement, phased-in work schedule following leave, compressed work week, and flexible benefits. She notes that changes such as this will reduce company turnover and improve the recruitment and retention of women and minorities.

Telecommuting

Telecommuting (or teleworking), an arrangement in which individuals perform some or all of their job away from the office, is a relatively new phenomenon that emerged as a viable alternative to the traditional workplace during the gas crisis of the 1970s (Ellison, 1999; Hill, Hawkins, and Miller, 1996). With advances in information and communication technology, the number of workers in the US who are relying on telecommuting for all or part of their work has increased substantially (Ellison, 1999). Telecommuting provides many advantages, including increased ability of workers to meet family responsibilities, and increased ability of employers to accommodate people with disabilities (Ellison, 1999; Hill,

Hawkins, and Miller, 1996; Mirchandani, 1999). Telecommuting, however, also has several disadvantages, including increased social isolation, disruptions to career development, and the perpetuation of traditional sex roles due to the highly gendered reasons for telecommuting (Ellison, 1999; Mirchandani, 1999).

The primary motivations for telecommuting may be different for men and women. Whereas men often telecommute to increase flexibility and productivity by reducing commuting time, the majority of women who telecommute do so to help balance work and family responsibilities. Because women and men telecommute for different reasons, their experiences of telecommuting may be different. Specifically, one important issue for telecommuters has to do with maintaining boundaries between work and family (Ellison, 1999; Hill, Hawkins, and Miller, 1996; Mirchandani, 1999). Research suggests that many telecommuters engage in ritualistic behaviors to transition from work to non-work in an attempt to set and maintain boundaries. Maintaining boundaries may be more difficult for women than men because women take primary responsibility for housework and childcare responsibilities in their families. Additionally, although many women who telecommute do so for childcare purposes, there is little evidence that individuals can work effectively while caring for small children, as small children demand attention, often preventing sustained and effective work (Ellison, 1999; Mirchandani, 1999).

Of particular concern with respect to health outcomes is the loss of links to social networks (Ellison, 1999; Hill, Hawkins, and Miller, 1996). Specifically, individuals engaging in telecommuting may experience isolation from important social networks that can be vital to career development. Telecommuters often forgo social support from co-workers, which may lead to increased stress and other psychological problems. In addition, by not developing informal networks, telecommuters are less likely to develop mentoring relationships, which in turn can affect their ability to obtain raises and promotions. Issues of career security are associated with increased stress (see below).

Role stressors

The fourth psychosocial risk factor identified by NIOSH relates to role stressors. These are stressors that arise from the different tasks and expectations one has as they relate to various types of obligations. The issues of role ambiguity and role conflict have been important constructs in organizational psychology since the 1950s. Role ambiguity arises when information about role behaviors is unavailable or uncertain, either due to environmental factors or internal factors. Sources of role ambiguity may include rapid growth in the organization, increases in technological innovation, and poor communication, including contradictory messages (Kahn et al., 1964; King and King, 1990).

Role conflict refers to the dissonance arising from a situation in which two or more sets of pressures are simultaneously imposed, such that compliance with one undermines compliance with the other. The pressures can be either external (e.g., incongruent expectations from one person, incongruent expectations from two or more others), or internal (e.g., incongruent expectations between the self and another), and role overload can occur when incongruent demands from multiple sources emerge (Kahn et al., 1964; King and King, 1990). One area of role conflict that is especially pertinent to issues of gender and health outcomes is work–family conflict, discussed below. In general, role conflict and ambiguity have been linked to decreased self-confidence, increased job tension, decreased job satisfaction, and adverse mental health (e.g., depression, anxiety, and lowered life satisfaction) and physical health (e.g., increased heart rate and blood pressure) outcomes (Caplan and Jones, 1975; French and Caplan, 1970; Frone, Russell, and Cooper, 1995; Jackson and Schuler, 1985; Kahn et al., 1964; Rhoads, Singh, and Goodell, 1994).

Work–family conflict

For individuals who simultaneously work and have families, the issue of role conflict, arising from managing multiple roles (e.g., worker, spouse, parent, adult, child), can have profound effects on mental health, physical health, and quality of family relationships (Frone, Russell, and Cooper, 1997; Jex, 1998; Perry-Jenkins, Repetti, and Crouter, 2000). Roles may be organized hierarchically (e.g., some roles are assigned more importance than others) or non-hierarchically (e.g., balance is maintained across a series of roles, or full engagement occurs in aspects of every role. Research by Marks and MacDermid (1996) indicates that those who organize their roles in a more balanced fashion experience less role strain and depression, and higher self-esteem.

Two perspectives on role conflict have emerged in the literature. One perspective emphasizes the problems, especially for women, of attempting to combine work and family. The other perspective concentrates on the advantages of combining work and family, for women as well as men.

There are several reasons why women and men might find it hard to combine paid work and family responsibilities (Kossek and Ozeki, 1998; Perry-Jenkins, Repetti, and Crouter, 2000). Role conflict can occur when people do not have enough time or other resources (e.g., money) to meet the demands of all their roles, or when the actions demanded by a role are in opposition to those demanded by another role. Role conflict, like other forms of stress, is thought to affect people's mental and physical health (Caplan and Jones, 1975; French and Caplan, 1970; Frone, Russell, and Cooper, 1995; Jackson and Schuler, 1985; Kahn et al., 1964; Rhoads, Singh, and Goodell, 1994).

Women may experience more work–family role conflict than men. More and more women are sharing in the provider role historically performed by men, but men are not entering into domestic roles in equal measure (Barnett and Marshall, 1991; Crosby, 1991; Gutek, 1993; Hochschild, 1989; Matuszek, Nelson, and Quick, 1995; Nelson and Hitt, 1992; Wortman, Biernat, and Lang, 1991). Especially among young families, mothers have very little discretionary time to do whatever they want. Indeed, the data suggest that the majority of young mothers spend the vast majority of their time either working or sleeping (Frankenhauser, in Hochschild, 1989; Matuszek, Nelson, and Quick, 1995).

Increasingly, women are in the position of trying to care for their children and their elderly parents, especially as elder care tends to fall on daughters rather than sons. Women in this "sandwich generation" experience adverse mental and physical health outcomes (Brody et al., 1987; Nelson and Hitt, 1992; Voydanoff and Donnelly, 1999). Specifically, research suggests that women caring for an older person are more likely to interrupt their work to handle caregiving respons-ibilities than are men, and as a result they experience higher levels of stress and absenteeism (Chapman, Ingersoll-Dayton, and Neal, 1994).

Because women continue to bear the major responsibility for childcare, the negative psychological consequences of role overload tend to affect women more than men (Ozer, 1995; Ozer et al., 1998; Phillips and Imhoff, 1997; Ross and Mirowsky, 1989; Steil and Turetsky, 1987). Lack of discretionary time may impair mental and physical health by decreasing opportunities for relaxation, recupera-tion, and exercise.

Not only can roles compete with each other for time and other scarce resources, but also they can contaminate each other. Specifically, negative events in one role can have a distressing influence on life in other roles (Kossek and Ozeki, 1998; Perry-Jenkins, Repetti, and Crouter, 2000). More research has been conducted on work-to-family spillover than on family-to-work spillover (Kossek and Ozeki, 1998). For example, research by Repetti indicates that stress at work is associated with withdrawal from interactions with spouse and children for both men and women (Repetti, 1989, 1994; Repetti and Wood, 1997), including more marital tension and negative mood at home (Hughes and Galinsky, 1994b; Repetti, 1993; Santos, Bohon, and Sanchez-Sosa, 1998). Furthermore, increased work pressure is associated with increased conflict with adolescent offspring and increased behavior problems among younger children (Crouter et al., 1999; MacDermid and Williams, 1997). There is some evidence that the spillover effect is stronger for men than women (Eagle et al., 1998; Larson and Almeida, 1999). For example, Eagle et al. (1998) found that men reported more work-to-family and strain-based family-to-work conflict than women. They suggest that in recent generations men have experienced increasing pressure to devote more time to family responsibilities and spend more time with their children; however, employers have not offered solutions to help men balance these demands.

Much less attention has been paid to the issue of family-to-work spillover (Kossek and Ozeki, 1998; Perry-Jenkins, Repetti, and Crouter, 2000). Nonetheless, the research suggests that family conflict negatively impacts job performance and is associated with withdrawal from work (Frone, Yardley, and Markel, 1997; MacEwen and Barling, 1994). Furthermore, family conflict is associated with reduced productivity and increased absenteeism (Forthofer et al., 1996).

Not all scholars concentrate on the negative consequences of multiple roles. The "expansion theory" (Barnett and Baruch, 1985; Barnett and Hyde, 2001; Baruch, Biener, and Barnett, 1987), in contrast to the spillover perspective, emphasizes that

Lynda M. Sagrestano

multiple roles are associated with positive outcomes (e.g., higher income, increased self-esteem, challenge), which can be energizing. Barnett and Hyde (2001) recently reviewed the literature supporting the expansion theory, outlining three major conclusions relevant to work and family roles pertinent to mental and physical health.

Their first major conclusion is that multiple roles benefit both women and men by leading to enhanced mental, physical, and relationship health. They note that individuals can have a strong commitment to more than one role. Research suggests that women who hold a positive attitude toward employment have better mental and physical health (Hughes and Galinsky, 1994a; Kandel, Davies, and Raveis, 1985; Repetti, Matthews, and Waldron, 1989). Those who juggle multiple roles report less depression and more positive well-being and physical health (Crosby, 1991; Repetti, Matthews, and Waldron, 1989; Ruderman et al., 2002; Russo and Zierk, 1992). Similarly, men who engage in multiple roles experience more positive well-being and fewer physical symptoms of distress than those with fewer roles (e.g., those who are not fathers) (Barnett, Marshall, and Pleck, 1992; Gore and Mangione, 1983).

Another major conclusion outlined by Barnett and Hyde is that the association between multiple roles and health outcomes is due to several factors. First, research suggests that roles may be interactive, such that relationships and experiences in one domain may buffer or mitigate the effects of stress in another domain (Barnett, Marshall, and Pleck, 1992; Barnett, Marshall, and Sayer, 1992). For example, the negative effects of job stressors may be buffered by a supportive marriage (Repetti, 1998). However, research also suggests that stressors related to juggling multiple roles may not be buffered by satisfaction with the parental role (Voydanoff and Donnelly, 1999). Second, the added income of a dual-earner family decreases economic hardship and its associated distress (Ross and Huber, 1985). Third, engaging in multiple roles provides multiple opportunities to develop supportive relationships, which, in turn, lead to more positive well-being. For example, social support from co-workers is associated with reduced anxiety and depression (Polasky and Holahan, 1998). This effect is stronger for wives than husbands, as husbands tend to derive their social support from their wives (Greenberger and O'Neil, 1993).

A third major conclusion outlined by Barnett and Hyde is that multiple roles are most beneficial when the quantity and quality of the roles are optimal, for beyond certain limits, individuals will experience overload and distress. For example, research suggests that five roles are optimal for well-being for most people (Thoits, 1986). Furthermore, research on time demands indicates that time spent in a role decreases psychological distress up to a point, but when the time demands become excessive, distress increases (Klein et al., 1998; Voydanoff and Donnelly, 1999). In general, however, role quality, rather than number of roles or time spent in roles, is associated with mental, physical, and relationship health (Barnett, Marshall, and Pleck, 1992; Hyde et al., 1995; Klein et al., 1998). For example, satisfaction with parental, marital, and work roles is associated with low levels of depression and anxiety among individuals in dual earner couples; this association is stronger for women than for men (Greenberger and O'Neil, 1993). Finally, it should be noted that the causal direction is not clear. That is, it may be that healthier women seek out multiple roles, rather than multiple roles lead to better health (Nelson and Hitt, 1992).

Employer's role

Recently employers have begun offering employee-sponsored childcare, either onsite or nearby, as a fringe benefit for employees with young children, in an effort to decrease absenteeism due to childcare issues (Kossek and Nichol, 1992; Milkovich and Gomez, 1976). Evidence suggests that onsite day care facilities help employers with recruitment and retention of new employees who have young children (Kossek and Nichol, 1992). Furthermore, organizational commitment is higher among those employees whose employers provide assistance with day care than those whose employers do not provide day care (Grover and Crooker, 1995). Studies of onsite childcare programs suggest that they increase job satisfaction and decrease stress, although the evidence that they reduce absenteeism has been equivocal (Goff, Mount, and Jamison, 1990; Johnson, 1991; Kossek and Nichol, 1992; Raber, 1994; Zedeck and Mosier, 1990). Currently, approximately 9 percent of employers offer onsite childcare, and the likelihood is much greater among companies with women in top positions (Fassinger, 2002).

In addition to caring for children, many middle-aged workers are also involved in caring for their elderly parents. Similarly to childcare, the burden of responsibility for elder care tends to fall disproportionately on women. Although research suggests that employees who care for young children have higher rates of absenteeism than employees who care for elderly parents (Boise and Neal, 1996), the financial and emotional strain associated with caring for an elderly parent may have an impact on productivity and stress. To help with this problem, some employers are now offering onsite care for dependents of all ages, as well as in-house counseling programs and long-term care insurance (Schultz and Schultz, 2002). This issue is becoming more salient as the general population ages and more workers are confronting the challenges of balancing work and elder care.

Career security and advancement factors

The fifth psychosocial risk factor identified by NIOSH relates to career security and advancement. With the changing economy and restructuring of corporations in the 1990s, the notion of job security has changed dramatically. Individuals no longer spend their whole career with one company, but rather develop skills that will make them employable or "portable" (Cascio, 1995; Nelson, Quick, and Simmons, 2001). Whereas previous generations have built entire careers working their way up in one corporation, individuals now may move from company to company, with very little loyalty on the part of employers or employees. In addition, a segment of workers has shifted to temporary or contract status, eroding their access to health insurance and other employment benefits (Stokols, Pelletier, and Fielding, 1996). Women and minorities are more likely than men and non-

Hispanic Whites to be contract workers or part-time workers (US Bureau of Labor Statistics, 2001a; Graham, 1993), putting them at particular disadvantage with respect to insurance and benefits.

Technological advances have also changed the nature of the workplace. Cascio (1995) notes that the economy is changing to one where fewer people are employed, but they perform at a higher level with new technology and new ways of organizing work. This requires a workforce that is technologically literate. The competing goals of increased production and smaller workforce result in work overload (Nelson, Quick, and Simmons, 2001). One consequence of these historical changes in the workforce is lack of job security. Research suggests that lack of job security, under- or over-promotion, and fear of job obsolescence are associated with adverse psychological outcomes (Kasl and Cobb, 1982; Sutherland and Cooper, 1988). For example, longitudinal research over five years found that individuals who experienced threatened employment security after the study had begun reported increased levels of morbidity (i.e., illness) as compared to levels prior to the threat, including ischemia (restricted blood flow to the heart) and higher cholesterol levels for men and women, and increased blood pressure among women only, although reports of health behaviors did not change during the five-year time period (Ferrie et al., 1998). Because women and minorities tend to be at the lower levels of each job category (Bennett, 1993; Martin, 1992), they likely experience more stress due to lack of job security.

The last few decades have seen a shift from a production-oriented economy to a service-oriented economy (Nelson, Quick, and Simmons, 2001). Jobs in the service sector often include an interactive component, where employees must provide services to customers who may be demanding or irate (Singh, Goolsby, and Rhoads, 1994). Providing high quality services in this environment requires managing emotions, most notably masking frustration, which is likely highly stressful. This management of emotions has been termed emotional labor (Hochschild, 1983), and has subsequently been classified into demands to express positive emotions and demands to suppress negative emotions. Demands to express positive emotions, in particular, have been associated with health symptoms, especially among individuals with lower identification with the organization and lower job involvement (Schaubroeck and Jones, 2000). Interestingly, whereas the emotional labor of women often involves creating an emotional display that is friendly or ingratiating, the emotional labor of men is often characterized by being demanding or authoritative (Hochschild, 1983). Regardless, the stress associated with emotional labor has been linked with substance use, headaches, and other forms of psychological distress (Adelman, 1995). Women and minorities are more likely to be represented at the point of interface with clients, and are therefore more prone to such stressors (Carr-Ruffino, 2002).

Glass ceiling

According to the United States Department of Labor, the glass ceiling can be defined as "those artificial barriers based on attitudinal or organizational bias that prevent qualified individuals from advancing upward in their organization into management level positions" (Martin, 1991). The term "glass ceiling" has been used as an analogy for "a barrier so subtle that it is transparent, yet so strong that it prevents women and minorities from moving up the management hierarchy" (Morrison and Von Glinow, 1990: 200). The underlying assumption of the concept of the glass ceiling is that women and minorities have the motivation, ambition, and capacity for positions of power and prestige, but invisible barriers keep them from reaching the top (see chapter 7, this volume, for a complete discussion of the glass ceiling).

Martin (1991) suggests that the glass ceiling is lower than expected. Women remain clustered on lower levels of the organizational decision-making hierarchy, occupying less than 15 percent of senior management positions (Nelson and Hitt, 1992). Members of disadvantaged groups are even less likely than European-American women to be promoted to top positions. For example, African-American women occupy jobs that are less secure, have fewer benefits, and pay less than those held by European-American women (Mays, 1995). The highest levels of organizations are almost completely impenetrable to women and people of color (Martin, 1991).

Although women experience a greater degree of occupational mobility than men (i.e., they change jobs more often), such mobility is more likely to be lateral, not involving promotions or increases in income or status. This limited career advancement has been associated with high levels of stress, as well as the departure of women from organizations to go into business for themselves, where they have more control. In addition to stress, limited career advancement has been associated with adverse physical health outcomes (Haynes and Feinleib, 1980; Moore and Buttner, 1997).

Interpersonal relations

The sixth psychosocial risk factor identified by NIOSH relates to interpersonal relations, including poor relationships with colleagues, supervisors, and subordinates, ranging from racism and discrimination to sexual harassment.

Sexual harassment

The definition of sexual harassment encompasses several different types of unwanted or uninvited sex-related behavior, which can be organized into three distinct categories: gender harassment, unwanted sexual attention, and sexual coercion. Gender harassment refers to sexually inappropriate behavior, including insulting, misogynistic, and degrading remarks that reflect hostility and offensive attitudes about women. These can be classified into remarks that reflect sexist hostility (e.g., sexist comments, such as women do not belong in the workplace) and remarks that reflect sexual hostility (e.g., sexualized animosity, such as using degrading names for female body parts). Unwanted sexual attention can be described as sexual behavior that is uninvited, unwanted, and unreciprocated, but that is not a contingency to a reward or threat of punishment. Sexual coercion is the implicit or explicit threat of punishment or promise of job-related rewards contingent upon sexual cooperation (Fitzgerald and Hesson-McInnis, 1989; Fitzgerald, Hulin, and Drasgow, 1994; Gelfand, Fitzgerald, and Drasgow, 1995).

From a legal perspective, sexual harassment includes two categories: *quid pro quo* and hostile environment (EEOC, 1980a, 1980b). The legal definition developed by the Equal Employment Opportunity Commission is as follows:

> Unwelcome sexual advances, requests for sexual favors, and other verbal or physical conduct of a sexual nature constitute sexual harassment when (1) submission to such conduct is made either explicitly or implicitly a term or condition of an individual's employment, (2) submission to or rejection of such conduct by an individual is used as the basis for employment decisions affecting such individual, or (3) such conduct has the purpose or effect of substantially interfering with an individual's work performance or creating an intimidating, hostile, or offensive working environment. (**EEOC, 1980b**)

The first two conditions are termed *quid pro quo* and refer to situations in which the promise of job-related rewards or the avoidance of punishment is contingent on sexual cooperation. The third condition is termed a *hostile environment*, and describes the situation in which unwanted sexual advances and offensive verbal behavior become severe enough to affect employment (Fitzgerald and Hesson-McInnis, 1989; Fitzgerald, Hulin, and Drasgow, 1994; Gelfand, Fitzgerald, and Drasgow, 1995).

Although it can be difficult to determine reliably the prevalence of sexual harassment (Arvey and Cavanaugh, 1995), evidence suggests that behaviors that could potentially be construed as sexual harassment are widespread in the public and private sectors, with estimates ranging from 28 percent to 90 percent of women who have had such experiences (Fitzgerald, Hulin, and Drasgow, 1994; Gelfand, Fitzgerald, and Drasgow, 1995; Gutek and Koss, 1993; Koss et al., 1994). A review of several studies suggests that, on average, 42 percent of women report harassment (Gruber, 1990). Gender harassment is the most widespread form of harassment in the workplace, with estimates as high as 60–70 percent of women reporting this type of hostility (Piotrkowski, 1998; Vaux, 1993). Evidence suggests similar rates of gender harassment for European-American and minority women (Piotrkowski, 1998), although it is possible that existing measures of sexual harassment do not adequately account for the types of incidents that women of color are likely to experience. Rates of sexual coercion and unwanted sexual attention are much lower, with the smallest percentage of women reporting sexual coercion (Fitzgerald, Hulin, and Drasgow, 1994).

Individual responses to harassment are varied, but have been classified into a fourfold typology along two dimensions: self-focused v. initiator focused and self-response v. supported response (Knapp et al., 1997). The majority of women respond by avoiding the initiator and ignoring the situation (i.e., self-focused, self-response), although this strategy may be the least effective. Taking formal action or involving others (e.g., a boss) in the response (i.e., supported responses) is much less prevalent. Although taking action may be more effective in ending the harassment, it is also associated with increases in negative job consequences, especially for male targets of sexual harassment (Bowes-Sperry and Tata, 1999; Gutek and Koss, 1993; Stockdale, 1998). Approximately 10 percent of women who are harassed leave their jobs (Gutek and Koss, 1993). How one responds to harassment can moderate the consequences of harassment, including psychological and health-related outcomes (Fitzgerald et al., 1997).

Exposure to harassment has been associated not only with adverse job-related outcomes (e.g., job dissatisfaction, absenteeism, turnover), but also with psychological and physical health outcomes. Specifically, harassment has been associated with increased headaches, sleep disturbances, stress, anxiety, depression, anger, and fear. These effects can be manifested even when the types of harassment are relatively low-level or infrequent (Fitzgerald et al., 1997; Gutek and Koss, 1993; Koss et al., 1994; Loy and Stewart, 1984; Piotrkowski, 1998; Schneider, Swan, and Fitzgerald, 1997).

Research on sexual harassment of women of color is sparse, with few studies specifically examining the issue, or even reporting the racial/ethnic breakdown of the sample studied. However, the evidence available suggests that sexual harassment of women of color is not solely an issue of sex-based discrimination, but also reflects sexual racism, and these dual sources of marginality may put women of color at greater risk of sexual harassment than white women (Murrell, 1996).

6.1 *Gloria Storges v. UWI and Joe Tarnett*[1]

Gloria Storges began work a few years ago as one of the tool clerks in the tool shop in Building 1 of UWI, a large manufacturing company. The tool shop contained all but the most basic of tools, and handled all of the tool repairs and maintenance on the shop floor as needed. She had her own tool cart, and spent most of her time pushing her tool cart between the tool shop and the shop floor. Gloria knew pretty much what to expect at UWI because some of her relatives worked there; she hoped to get into the apprentice program, which would lead to a skilled, relatively high-paying job.

Gloria was one of the few women at UWI who worked on the shop floor. Traditionally, the men on the shop floor were a pretty rowdy bunch, joking and kidding around. Employees were allowed to decorate their own work areas. Some had pictures of themselves or their families posted in their work areas. Many of the shop workers hung pictures of nude girls and centerfolds; one showed a naked woman cut up like a side of beef – rump roast, breast, and shoulder roast. Another poster showed a horse standing over a naked woman licking her genital area. Above the Ladies Room was a big picture of a beaver in water and a sign, "Beaver Pond." The workers tended to use pretty crude language on the shop floor.

About eight months after Gloria began working at UWI, Joe Tarnett became the supervisor of the tool shop and, therefore, Gloria's direct supervisor. As the supervisor, Joe was in charge of Gloria's work assignments, work schedule, disciplinary actions, and of course her performance evaluations. After Joe had been in the tool shop for a few weeks, Gloria felt as though he was following her around too much. He said he checked up on all the workers by watching them on the shop floor because they did not spend much time in the tool shop itself. One day, Joe asked Gloria to lunch, but she declined. He said he was trying to build teamwork. Then one day he said to her, "Ya know, if you were nice to me, it would make your job a lot easier." Gloria interpreted this statement as a sexual proposition. Joe explained that he was just encouraging her to be more sociable and to get along with people at work. He said Gloria was snobbish and not very friendly. Several weeks later, Joe issued Gloria a yellow slip – a disciplinary action, which stated she was excessively out of her work area. Gloria acknowledged that she was out of her work area, but claimed that lots of people were out of their work areas some of the time and she was in her work area when there was work to do. Joe said that she was not in her work area when she was supposed to be working. Having a yellow slip in her file would jeopardize Gloria's chances for transfers and access to the apprenticeship program.

Gloria went through the process of filing a formal complaint against Joe. She complained of his comment and behavior toward her, believing that the yellow slip was related to her unwillingness to have a relationship with him. Joe said that was nonsense. He was not interested in a relationship with her, and it was his job as supervisor to see that his employees were doing their jobs. Gloria spent too much time out of her work area and not enough time doing her work.

Shortly thereafter, a sign was displayed in the lunchroom that stated, "Gloria Storges is a bitch." Gloria left work and went to see a doctor because she wasn't feeling well, and he said that she seemed to be under a great deal of stress. He recommended that she take a leave of absence from her job, and UWI granted a one-month paid leave. It was not possible to prove who put up the sign, but Gloria thought Joe did it. He strongly denied that he had anything to do with it.

Soon after her return from the leave of absence, Gloria said she found dirty pictures on her work cart, a condom filled with lotion in her coat, egg on her car, and dog excrement on her car door handle. There was no proof as to who committed these acts. Gloria believed Joe was behind them. Joe strongly denied it, and said that other workers resented her being able to take a month off with pay. Also, Gloria claimed that someone stole her umbrella, but it later turned up in her locker. Some workers thought Joe might have been involved in these things, but others did not think he was involved and thought that Gloria made some of it up.

Gloria first complained verbally to the EEO rep about 14 months after she started working at UWI, and she later signed a formal complaint. Since she did not get any information from them, she wasn't sure if they did any kind of an investigation. UWI maintained that they did an investigation but could find no proof that any UWI employee did any of the things that Gloria alleged.

Finally, Gloria was out of work for some minor surgery. Her doctor sent a note to UWI saying that Gloria should be placed in a different, less stressful department when she returned. UWI would only agree to consider a transfer if Gloria returned to the tool shop first. Gloria never returned to UWI and was eventually fired for failure to return to work. Soon after Gloria was terminated, she filed a lawsuit against UWI and Joe Tarnett, alleging that she had been sexually harassed while working at UWI. UWI contended that she had not been sexually harassed at all and given that Gloria's performance appraisals during her tenure at UWI were average or a little below average, they had gone out of their way to accommodate her. The performance appraisals were not surprising, explained Gloria, since Joe Tarnett wrote some of them.

Discussion questions

1 In your view, was Gloria Storges sexually harassed?
2 If you do think she was harassed, which type or types of harassment do you think she experienced? Gender harassment? Unwanted sexual attention? Sexual coercion?
3 Do you think Gloria met the legal criteria for *quid pro quo* or for hostile environment?
4 How would you describe Gloria's response to her own belief that she was harassed? Was she self-focused or initiator focused? Was she self-responsive or supported? If the things that happened to Gloria had happened to you, how would you have responded?
5 To what extent do you think the physical symptoms Gloria experienced were due to her belief that she was harassed?
6 Was UWI justified in firing Gloria for not returning to work in the tool shop? Why or why not? What other alternatives did they have?
7 What sorts of things could UWI do to help make the workplace less hostile for female employees and prevent further complaints of sexual harassment?

Racism and discrimination

The term "prejudice" has typically been defined as the negative feelings people have about others based on their membership in or connection to a social group. In contrast, "discrimination" is typically used to describe behavior directed against individuals based on group membership (Allport, 1954). "Racism" and "sexism" refer to prejudice and discrimination based on race or sex, respectively. Although overt forms of prejudice have declined since the Civil Rights Act (Schuman et al., 1997), discrimination is still prevalent and affects women and people of color (Hacker, 1995).

The discrepancy between conscious attitudes, on one hand, and behaviors, on the other, may be explained, in part, by unacknowledged and more subtle forms of prejudice, which tend to be expressed in more indirect ways (Dovidio and Gaertner, 1998; Fernandez, 1981; Sears et al., 1997). Specifically, the theory of "aversive racism" (Gaertner and Dovidio, 1986) suggests that many individuals who consider themselves to be egalitarian and non-prejudiced have negative feelings and beliefs about African Americans and other groups. These negative feelings lead to dissonance for those who view themselves as egalitarian. As a result, aversive racism leads to discrimination that is subtle and can be rationalized, and yet has consequences that are as significant as overt racism. For example, recent research on aversive racism suggests that from 1989 to 1999, self-reported overt prejudice decreased, and European-American research participants did not discriminate between African Americans and European Americans in situations when the qualifications of the candidate were clearly strong or weak; however, when the qualifications were not clear, European-American participants did discriminate (Dovidio and Gaertner, 2000). Because so many of the examples of aversive racism can be explained by other, non-racial factors, European Americans often remain unconvinced of what is going on, whereas people of color, with a large pool of examples to draw on, are accused of being overly sensitive to the issue of racism (Pettigrew and Martin, 1987).

According to Pettigrew and Martin (1987), people of color often experience "triple jeopardy." That is, they experience stress due to negative racial stereotypes, the solo role (i.e., being the only representative of their demographic group), and the token role (i.e., being perceived by European-American co-workers as incompetent because they were hired via affirmative action). This constellation may lead to several outcomes, including biased recruitment practices, verbal insults, proximity avoidance, feelings of isolation, fewer social interactions, and less social support, any of which may lead to disempowerment and create barriers to advancement. Ultimately, triple jeopardy results in increased stress and decreased job satisfaction (Holder and Vaux, 1998).

Recent research suggests that for African Americans and Latinos, stressors related to race explain job satisfaction levels over and above routine work-related stressors (Gutierres, Saenz, and Green, 1994; Holder and Vaux, 1998; Mays,

Coleman, and Jackson, 1996; Sanchez and Brock, 1996). That is, people of color must cope with the same work stressors as everyone else, and in addition must manage race-related stressors. For African-American women, race-related employment discrimination is directly associated with stress. Specifically, discrimination once on the job (e.g., activities toward advancement, skill development) rather than discrimination blocking entry into the labor market, is associated with stress for this group of women (Mays, Coleman, and Jackson, 1996).

Solo status and tokenism may pose special difficulties. Specifically, solo status and numerical rarity are associated with increased token stress for racial minorities, leading to adverse mental health outcomes (Jackson, Thoits, and Taylor, 1995; James, 1994; Saenz, 1994). For example, in a study of 167 elite black leaders in the US (e.g., executives, political leaders, military leaders, academics), numerical rarity by race was associated with increased depression and token stress (e.g., loss of black identity, multiple demands of being black, isolation). Among the black women leaders in this sample, numerical rarity by gender was significantly associated with gender tokenism and increases in role overload, leading to adverse mental health outcomes such as anxiety (Jackson, Thoits, and Taylor, 1995). Furthermore, women in male-dominated occupations feel more pressure from discrimination than women in balanced or female-dominated professions, and they experience more adverse mental health outcomes when they do not conform to masculine interpersonal styles (Gardiner and Tiggemann, 1999).

With respect to tokenism, three sources of stress have emerged from the literature: performance pressures, boundary heightening, and role entrapment (Kanter, 1977). Performance pressures result from high visibility, which leads tokens to believe they are subject to high levels of scrutiny, and feel pressure to perform well as representatives of their demographic group. Boundary heightening (also referred to as the out-group homogeneity effect) results from the exaggeration of similarities among members of a group and differences between members of different groups. That is, group members tend to exaggerate both the commonalities of members of their own group as well as their differences from members of the other group. The differences can become the subject of jokes and other behaviors that lead to social isolation for tokens. Role entrapment refers to typecasting tokens according to dominant stereotypes. The more skewed (i.e., the less balance there is between dominant and minority group membership) the work environment, the more likely one is to experience each of these stressors (Jackson, Thoits, and Taylor, 1995; Kanter, 1977). For example, research with elite African-American leaders suggests that the stress associated with token status is linked with depression and psychological symptoms (Jackson, Thoits, and Taylor, 1995). Finally, people sometimes assume that minorities are hired simply in order to meet affirmative action quotas, and are otherwise incompetent. This may lead minorities to question their own abilities, increasing stress (Gutierres, Saenz, and Green, 1994; Heilman, 1996).

INTERVENTIONS TO REDUCE THE ADVERSE EFFECTS OF WORKPLACE STRESSORS

The stressors outlined in this chapter are many and complex, and thus no single intervention will effectively address them all. Instead, it makes sense to consider interventions at three levels: the work environment, the individual, and at the interface of work and family (Quick, 1999).

Work environment interventions

Changes in the work environment and organizational culture are perhaps the easiest to make, and can include activities such as job design, redesign, or enlargement; participative decision-making; building social supports in the workplace; team building; task revision; implementing employee assistance programs; promoting equity in pay and benefits; eliminating occupational segregation; promoting bias-free job evaluation programs; promoting equal pay for equal work; developing sexual harassment policies and diversity training initiatives, and supporting educational and skill development opportunities (Lobel, 1999; Nelson and Hitt, 1992; Quick, 1999; Swanson et al., 1997).

Individual interventions

Interventions at the individual level are most common, typically classified as stress management programs. Such interventions are designed to help employees positively reframe workplace demands and stressors, helping to minimize distress. This might include working with employees to learn to use negative feedback as a catalyst for change in behavior or attitude so as to prevent further negative feedback. Other techniques include time management, promoting physical fitness, muscle relaxation training, meditation, cognitive-behavioral skills, biofeedback, psychotherapy, education, and career counseling (Nelson, Quick, and Simmons, 2001; Quick, 1999).

Work–family interface interventions

Several changes that can be implemented at the organizational level can serve to ameliorate stressors associated with the interface of work and family. These include programs such as flextime, telecommuting, dependant-care provisions, family and leave policies, family support systems, health insurance, and family-level counseling. For example, for employees who travel often, development of extended family support systems, socially constructed support systems (e.g., spouse clubs for military families), or other sources of support can help ease the effects of work stress on family relations (Quick, 1999).

Summary

Although stress in the workplace affects everyone, there are many factors and situations that affect women and people of color in ways that are different than men and people of European-American descent. In particular, NIOSH's identification of the six factors discussed throughout this chapter may have particular consequences for women and people of color. To the extent that individuals in the workplace, their managers or supervisors, and individuals in positions of power, work to alleviate such stressors, we will see a healthier workforce, which will ultimately benefit both employees and employers.

Note

1 This scenario has not been published in full. However, it is the basis for research reported in Gutek et al. (1999) and Stockdale et al. (2002). It is used by permission of Barbara Gutek and Maureen O'Connor.

Part III

DIVERSE GROUPS

The previous six chapters articulated the essential grammars of workplace diversity by describing issues that are important to understanding diversity, no matter what its form. However, different diverse groups have their unique concerns. The five chapters in this section take a closer look at some of the history and background to a wide array of groups that have been disadvantaged in the workplace. In addition to providing an overview of relevant issues, the authors include literature reviews of extant research and recommendations for future directions.

Chapter 7 concerns gender issues in the workplace, especially those affecting the advancement of women into the upper echelons of business.

Chapter 8 examines the status of African Americans in the workplace, with attention paid to forces that perpetuate discrimination and segregation, factors that inhibit or facilitate career success, and the role of racial identity theory in helping to broaden our understanding of African-Americans' reactions to workplace issues. Chapter 9 looks at three related but distinct groups – based on the "physical" issues of age, disability, and obesity – who continue to be targets of both subtle and blatant discrimination and misunderstanding. Chapter 10 provides an overview of issues concerning one of the most blatantly (yet, in many places, legally) mistreated groups in the workplace: gays, lesbians, and bisexuals. The authors include fascinating case studies of two leading firms that have worked to make sexual minorities central to their workplace diversity initiatives, and one major organization, the US military, that serves as a striking contrast. Chapter 11 provides a rare and thorough treatment of class diversity.

Of course, this section cannot deal directly with all those groups that could be considered by a volume devoted to workplace diversity. Separate chapters on Hispanic Americans, Asian Americans, Native Americans, religious minorities, other racial–ethnic groups, and groups that have been politically and economically disadvantaged in the workplace, were not developed, simply for lack of space (see chapter 4 for a discussion of cultural issues that pertain to many of these groups). We hope readers will glean themes and trends from the chapters presented here, apply them to help form a broader understanding of all diversity groups, and promote research and development on these and other important groups.

SHATTERING THE GLASS CEILING IN THE NEW MILLENNIUM

Linda K. Stroh, Christine L. Langlands, and Patricia A. Simpson

This chapter reviews the status of women in management today and includes a discussion of what we have learned over the past decade about barriers to women's successful careers. The chapter includes a real-life case study of one organization's attempt to become an employer of choice and provides examples of the way this organization began to break down those barriers. The chapter concludes by identifying ways other companies can break down the barriers to women's success.

What makes a corporation an employer of choice – that is, what do current and potential employees deem desirable in an employer? This question has been discussed extensively in both the popular and academic press, but reaching a consensus has been difficult. Identifying what it is that makes an organization an employer of choice for women is even more of a challenge. What distinguishes a company that is able to attract and retain women who rise through the ranks to the highest levels?

This chapter begins with a review of the status of women in management today. It then discusses what we have learned over the past decade about the obstacles that prevent women managers from succeeding in their careers. The chapter concludes by identifying ways companies can break down the barriers impeding women's success.

How Far Have Women Come?

Much has been written in the last 15 to 20 years about the glass ceiling women encounter as they try to rise up the ranks of corporate America. The *Wall Street*

Journal's Corporate Woman column first introduced the term in the mid-1980s by describing the glass ceiling as "a puzzling new phenomenon." "There seemed to be an invisible – but impenetrable – barrier," the writer said, "between women and the executive suite, preventing them from reaching the highest levels of the business world regardless of their accomplishments and merits" (US Bureau of National Affairs, 1995).

Does a glass ceiling still exist? How far have women actually come in the labor force today? To answer these questions, it helps to look at a few statistics.

Presence of women in management and executive positions

As recently as 1972, women held only 17 percent of managerial positions. By 1995, however, the figure had jumped to an impressive 42.7 percent (US Department of Labor, 1996). In addition, as shown in table 7.1, from 1995 to 2000, women held an increasing percentage of the senior positions in Fortune 500 companies.

Employers should be proud of the progress they have made toward gender equity. Data show that when it comes to deciding who should be promoted, the gap between men and women seems to be closing over time. In 1990, 32.8 percent of male workers reported that they had been promoted at some time in their careers, versus 31 percent of women. By 1996, however, women had slightly surpassed men in this regard: 26 percent had been promoted, versus 25.6 percent of the men (Cobb-Clark and Dunlop, 1999).

Problems remain, however. A great disparity is revealed when one compares the numbers of women in the general labor force with the numbers of women in top management. The following list shows that there is still much work to be done before women and men will be equally represented in high-level positions in Fortune 500 companies. In 2000, according to Catalyst (2000), women comprised:

- 46.5 percent of the US labor force
- 49.5 percent of managerial and professional specialty positions
- 12.5 percent of corporate officers (up from 11.9 percent in 1999)

Table 7.1 Senior management positions held by women in Fortune 500 companies, 1995–2000

Position	1995 (%)	2000 (%)	Percentage change
Women board directors	9.5	11.7	+2.2
Women corporate officers	8.7	12.5	+3.8
Women CEOs (number)	1	2	+100

Source: Catalyst (2000)

- 11.7 percent of board directors
- 6.2 percent of highest titles (up from 5.1 percent in 1999)
- two Fortune 500 CEOs

One study of the financial services industry has shown that many of the promotions of women take place beneath management levels (Lyness and Judiesch, 1999). The profiles of those organizations in which women and men are promoted may explain some of the reasons why the glass ceiling persists. From 1990 to 1996, women were more likely to be promoted in medium-sized firms, defined as those with 100–500 employees (Cobb-Clark and Dunlop, 1999). Men were more likely to be promoted in companies with more than 500 employees. Another statistic is equally revealing: men with children are more than 3 percent more likely to be promoted than women with children (27.9 percent versus 24.7 percent).

Despite these facts, Catalyst, a New York-based advocacy group, says there is reason for hope. According to its projections, the percentage of women corporate officers will be considerably higher in the near future: 16.5 percent in 2005, 20.1 percent in 2010, and 27.4 percent in 2020 (Catalyst, 2000).

Male–female differences in salary

Another critical issue that must be examined when evaluating how far women have come in the last couple of decades is how well women in corporate America are compensated compared to men. What progress, if any, has been made in closing the salary gap between men and women?

Not surprisingly, given women's overall progress in the workforce, there is cause for both excitement and disappointment. Since 1979, women's earnings in general have increased by 14 percent, and men's have decreased by 7 percent. However, on average, women still earn significantly less than men: only 76 percent of what men earn (Bowler, 1999). Figure 7.1 illustrates these trends. Contrary to what one might expect, women with college degrees have been no more successful than women without degrees at closing the salary gap. Although it is true that the salaries of women with college degrees increased by almost 22 percent over the past 20 years, female college graduates can expect, on average, to earn only $707 per week, whereas male college graduates can expect to earn $939 per week – a differential of 25 percent.

Other statistics are more heartening. Data from the US Department of Labor, for example, show that from 1981 to 1996 there was a 7 percent increase – from 16 percent to 23 percent – in the number of married couples in which the wife earned more than the husband (Winkler, 1998). This shows not only that women are gaining in compensation in the workplace, but also that they are gaining bargaining power at home, as they have more say on where to allocate the family income.

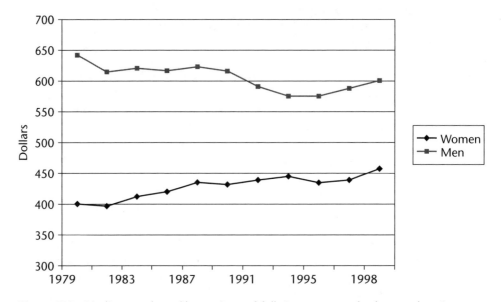

Figure 7.1   Median usual weekly earnings of full-time wage and salary workers in constant (1998) dollars by sex, 1979–98 annual averages (Bowler, 1999)

Great strides have also occurred in specific fields, such as information techno-logy (IT). According to research by *Information Week*, the median salary for women IT staff in 1999 was $50,000 – only 9 percent less than the salary for men in IT. This promising trend is also seen in managerial positions in IT. In 1999 the median salary for women IT managers was $68,000, versus $72,000 for men – only a 6 percent difference (Mateyaschuk, 1999).

Interestingly, researchers have found that women are not necessarily upset when they make less than their male counterparts. Graham and Welbourne (1999), for instance, found some evidence that women have equal or higher salary satis-faction than men in similar positions, even though the women have lower salaries. They suggest that women's lower salary expectations may account for this complacency.

EXPLAINING THE GAPS

Explaining the salary gap

Several anecdotal explanations have been given for why women generally earn less than men. Some commentators, like the right-wing agitator Diana Furchtgott-Roth (Furchtgott-Roth and Stolba 1999), see differences as caused by women's own behaviors and choices. Other analysts, like economists Barbara Bergmann

(1986) and Heidi Hartmann (Shaw et al., 1993) and sociologist Barbara Reskin (1998), outline the attitudinal and structural barriers to gender equity.

Bergmann, Hartmann, and Reskin base their conclusions on studies like the one conducted among 20 companies selected from the Fortune 500. Data were collected on samples of male and female managers, all of whom had similar levels of education, worked in similar industries, and earned similar percentages of their family incomes, and had similar career ambitions. Despite having done "all the right stuff," the women earned an average of 11 percent less than the men (Stroh, Brett, and Reilly, 1992). A follow-up study showed that the women still earned significantly less than the men even when the women looked to the external labor market to close the salary gap (Brett and Stroh, 1998).

Other studies also found strong evidence of sex discrimination. Lyness and Thompson (1997) found that although women and men in their sample had comparable attitudes toward work, women were given positions with less authority and received fewer stock options. The differences were more pronounced for women in top management than for women in lower positions. Along the same lines, Hultin and Szulkin (1999) discovered that women's salaries are affected by the structure and power relations in the organizations in which they work. Specifically, women who work in organizations with mostly male managers are more likely to have lower salaries than women in organizations with more women at the top. Other recent research by Varma and Stroh (2001) further illuminates the issue. They found that male supervisors tended to rate their male subordinates higher than their female subordinates, while female supervisors rated their female subordinates higher than the males. Given that most women have male supervisors, women are more likely to receive lower performance evaluations and thus smaller raises than the men.

Do women, then, bear none of the blame for the salary differences? Hardly. Some of the reasons for women's lower salaries can be traced back to women's behaviors. At least one laboratory study has revealed that men are somewhat better than women at negotiating good compensation packages (Stuhlmacher and Walters, 1999). Presumably, the same gender difference exists outside the artificial laboratory. If women are not as assertive as men when it comes to annual wage and salary negotiations, they certainly limit their long-term salary potential.

Another factor influencing gender gaps in salaries concerns hours worked. Data from the US Department of Labor, shown in table 7.2, reveal that on average women and men work approximately the same number of hours. Yet, among high-level jobs, differences emerge. The difference in the percentages of men and women who worked 45–54 hours is significant: 33 percent versus 24 percent. Men clearly have the upper hand if earning higher salaries is a reward, at least in part, for working extra hours.

Two recent studies confirm the suspicion that hours at the desk help explain the gender gap among those earning very high salaries. First, a study of MBAs, from their first jobs through mid-career, found that women worked fewer hours

Table 7.2 Hours worked per week by men and women managers, executives, and officers, 1997

Weekly hours	Women (%)	Men (%)
35–44	67	47
45–54	24	33
55–99	8	20
Average	44	47

Source: Hecker (1998)

than men. Although the women were no less satisfied with their careers than were the men, significant gender gaps occurred in earnings (Schneer and Reitman, 1995). Second, a study by Brett and Stroh (under review) showed that among men and women who work extremely long hours (61+ per week), men are likely to "overwork" more hours than women. That is, those working extremely long hours are more likely to be men. Brett and Stroh's study also revealed pernicious discrimination. Men who worked more than 60 hours a week earned an average of $162,285 a year, while women who worked the same number of hours in the same types of jobs earned $114,881.

The major explanation offered by many researchers for gender differences in compensation is that women tend to congregate at lower levels of management. If women are in lower-level occupations, it is natural for them to earn less money than men. The question then becomes why don't more women make it to the ranks of upper management? Why don't more women make it to executive positions?

Explaining gaps in promotions

In 1996 Catalyst published a major study about the glass ceiling. Its sample included CEOs in 1,000 multinational companies and the most successful women in their companies. Catalyst asked the CEOs and the women to account for why relatively few women make it to the top ranks. The women in the study identified the following three barriers as the most important:

- Male stereotyping and preconceptions of women (52 percent).
- Exclusion from informal networks of communication (49 percent).
- Lack of significant general management/line experience (47 percent).

And what, meanwhile, did the CEOs say was holding the women back?

- Lack of significant general management/line experience (82 percent).
- Lack of time in the pipeline (64 percent).

One CEO said, "I think that, without question, some women have chosen not to pursue certain tracks that, for one reason or another, might be more attractive to men." Another noted that "many women have been held back because they haven't been prepared to make the same sacrifices as perhaps men are. They're not apt to move or relocate."

The gulf in attitudes between the CEOs and the successful women did not escape comment. In general, the CEOs thought that the main reason why the women in their organizations were not advancing was because of individual characteristics of the women, whereas the women pointed to their companies' cultures and practices. Also, the CEOs were twice as likely as the women to say that opportunities for women had increased in the past five years.

Where does the truth lie? Might the women be looking around to justify their own lack of success? Might the CEOs be "blaming the victims" as they seek to deny significant problems in their own companies? One way to determine what credence to place in both sets of explanations is to look at data systematically collected by social scientists in carefully conducted studies.

Stereotypes about women

Despite the advances women have made in the labor force in the last two decades, stereotypes still surround many discussions about women. A study by Coltrane and Adams (1997) documented how stereotypes are reflected and perpetuated in the media. These researchers examined the roles of men and women in 1,699 television commercials aired during the 1990s. They found that women characters were more likely than men to be shown with their families, shown in service/clerical occupations, and treated as sex objects. Women were less likely than men to be shown in positions of authority or in professional occupations, or indeed in any job at all.

Ely (1995) has examined the impact of sex stereotypes in business organizations. She found that women who said they performed stereotypical female roles were the most likely to work in firms with few women in positions of power. The women in such firms characterized men, in general, as more masculine than feminine; saw female attributes as less favorable to career success; had difficulty enacting gender roles that were satisfying to them personally while enabling them to fit in with their firms' norms and expectations for success; and perceived that men in management focused on women's sexuality. By contrast, Ely also found that women in firms with more sex integration at the top more easily integrated masculine and feminine traits; viewed feminine attributes as sources of competence and strength; found their firms to be more accepting of non-sexual aspects of women; and felt less frustration and anger about requirements to act stereotypically masculine at work.

Ely's research gives us a greater understanding of the barriers women face in trying to attain top management positions. Given that the majority of corporate executives are men, most organizations have low sex integration at the top. It is no wonder then, according to Ely's findings, that women in these organizations have trouble breaking free from stereotypical female roles in the workplace.

Sex discrimination in the workplace

Sometimes – but not always – stereotypes result in discriminatory behavior. Although Title VII of the Civil Rights Act of 1964 forbids discrimination based on someone's gender, sex discrimination is still a problem in corporations across America. In 2000 alone, 25,194 sex-based charges were filed with the Equal Employment Opportunity Commission (EEOC, 2002a).

One study points out how stereotypes can lead to discrimination. Davison and Burke (2000) found that both women and men received lower ratings in the application process when they applied for jobs that were stereotypically thought of as better suited for someone of the opposite sex – that is, women who applied for upper-management positions and men who applied for positions as executive assistants. The study also found that women applicants were discriminated against more than male applicants when less job-relevant information was provided about the applicants. This may be because, with limited information, interviewers may base their decisions on superficial factors, such as the sex of the applicant, which places women at a disadvantage.

Often structural barriers are subtle. In individual instances they may be hard to recognize, yet the cumulative effect may be quite dramatic. The impact of a male managerial hierarchy on women's advancement to management-level positions is detrimental, yet fosters men's attainment of managerial roles (Tharenou, Latimer, and Conroy, 1994). Career encouragement leading to training and development plays an integral role in the advancement of both women and men to managerial positions, but it is of greater significance for women. Tharenou, Latimer, and Conroy (1994) found that career encouragement for women leads to increased take-up of training and development, thus helping them achieve more managerial roles, whereas career encouragement for men is less of a factor for them to seek training opportunities. Women need more training opportunities than men because they are given fewer on-the-job responsibilities and experience; they therefore need to supplement their experience with training to reach the managerial level.

Research also supports the hypothesis that the glass ceiling isn't just keeping women out of top management positions. It also exists at lower levels of organizations, keeping women out of supervisory management positions as well (Hurley, Fagenson-Eland, and Sonnefeld, 1997). Dalton and Daily (1998) claim that due to the lack of experience caused by the glass ceiling, women are not as frequently asked to take on inside director positions that usually lead to CEO appointments. Even though women are increasingly asked to be outside directors (such as "resource" directors), these positions do not signal women's movement into the higher ranks of corporate America. It seems that at all levels within the organization, men continue to have greater opportunities than women.

What is the effect of gender discrimination on women's job satisfaction? The greater the discrimination, the less women feel satisfied with and committed to their jobs. The greater the discrimination, the more women plan to leave their jobs and also the more life stress they experience (Shaffer et al., 2000).

Apparently, even young women – juniors and seniors in high school – are aware of the sexual discrimination they may encounter in their future workplaces, as well as the barriers to post-secondary education (McWhirter, 1997). At the same time, young men and women are equally sure that they can overcome any barriers they may encounter in meeting their career goals.

A severe form of sex discrimination is sexual harassment. The US Equal Employment Opportunity Commission defines sexual harassment as sexual attention, sexual coercion and gender harassment, and it reports that 5,849 charges of sexual harassment were filed with the EEOC in 1980–9; and a whopping 37,725 charges from 1990–9 (EEOC, 2002b). Some of the increase is undoubtedly due to the greater attention given to this issue in the popular press and other forums. But whatever the reason, the statistics are still alarming.

What are the effects of sexual harassment in the workplace? Studies have shown negative correlations between even small amounts of unwanted attention and women's advancement in their careers (Schneider, Fitzgerald, and Swan, 1997). Over time, sexual harassment also negatively affects women's overall sense of satisfaction with their lives and sense of psychological well-being (Glomb et al., 1999). And whether the women label the behavior as sexual harassment or not, they are likely to experience similar negative consequences (Magley et al., 1999). Chapter 6 of this volume provides more information about sexual harassment and its effects on women's health.

Women's contribution to their own lack of career achievement

Not all barriers reside in the organizations. Women often contribute to their own lack of mobility. According to a study of 900 female and male managers conducted by the Management Research Group of Portland, Maine, women and men differ somewhat in their orientation to work. The study found that women were results oriented, whereas men engaged in more strategic planning and business analysis. Research also points to the fact that women are no less risk adverse than men when confronted with the same choices (Drew, 1999).

Among women and men at varying levels of the organizational hierarchy, differences are also detectable. Melamed (1995), for example, showed that, compared to men, women succeed based on their own merits, hard work, and limited domestic responsibilities, primarily in organizations that recognize well-educated, highly skilled individuals. Men succeed because they have a certain personality profile: they tend to be independent, dominant, and extroverted.

Although women are no less risk averse than men, women's relative refusal to strategize and their relative lack of extroversion may make them less likely than men to seize opportunities for training and education. Although some recent research has found that women are actually receiving more on-the-job and off-the-job training than men of similar age in similar job situations (Simpson and Stroh, 2002), other data indicate that women may not seek or be given the same educational benefits as men (Keaveny and Inderrieden, 1999).

Another very real constraint on women's ability to progress into the boardroom may be their family responsibilities. Despite a dramatic increase in the number of annual hours worked by married women with children less than 6 years old – from 583 hours in 1978 to 1,094 hours in 1998 (Cohen and Bianchi, 1999) – most women still assume the majority of domestic responsibilities (Wirth, 1998). Home responsibilities sometimes are, or are believed to be, incongruent with the responsibilities of upper management.

Research has proven that taking a leave of absence, regardless of the reason or the gender of the employee, results in fewer subsequent promotions and smaller salary increases. Other research has shown that the more leaves of absence are taken, the greater are the penalties for the employee. And because women tend to take more leaves of absence – especially to care for newborns – they tend to be offered fewer promotions and increases in salary (Judiesch and Lyness, 1999).

MEASURES WOMEN CAN TAKE TO SHATTER THE GLASS CEILING

Although there is no question that the glass ceiling can have dramatic effects on women's careers (see table 7.3 for a list of the barriers women face), the good news is there are steps women can take to lessen those effects. Action is only possible, however, when women feel they have the support of their organizations and a trusting relationship with decision-makers, and do not feel that their image is at risk (Ashford et al., 1998).

A study of the highest-ranking women in corporate America revealed four critical behaviors women must engage in to break through the glass ceiling in their organizations (Catalyst, 1996):

- Consistently exceed expectations (77 percent).
- Develop a style with which male managers are comfortable (61 percent).
- Seek out difficult or highly visible assignments (50 percent).
- Have an influential mentor (37 percent).

Exceed expectations

Among the recommendations top women made to other women was to "do the best you possibly can at every assignment no matter how trivial. Always go the

Table 7.3 Barriers to shattering the glass ceiling

1 Lack of lateral movement (glass walls) deprives women of experience in line supervision needed for vertical advancement.
2 Male executives tend to support people like themselves.
3 Reluctance to admit women into informal office networks.
4 Recruitment practices involve reliance on word-of-mouth and employee referral networking.
5 Developmental practices and credential-building experiences, including advanced education and assignments to corporate committees, task forces, and special projects, are often not as available to minorities and women.
6 Monitoring for equal access and opportunity was almost never considered a corporate responsibility or part of the planning for developmental programs or policies.
7 Women's participative management leadership style is seen by men as a lack of authority and confidence.
8 Human resource officers believe that women are less committed to careers, have less initiative, and are less willing to take risks.
9 Many boardrooms remain cozy clubs, where CEOs interact collegially with peers.
10 Some CEOs fear that women won't know or observe the unspoken rules – such as saving sticky questions for private conversations.

Source: Eyring and Stead (1998)

extra mile. It's not enough to be willing, you have to do it, even if no one is looking." Another suggested that women need to "be willing to work much harder than your male peers" (Catalyst, 1996). Some may think that always needing to exceed expectations may create the "superwoman" phenomenon (whereby women must push themselves to constantly outperform others), thus perpetuating the masculine culture of management. Perhaps, once we see more women represented in top management, the use of this tactic will become unnecessary. In the meantime, it appears to women at the top to be a necessary evil.

Develop a style with which male managers are comfortable

Some suggest that women need to learn how to adapt to a predominantly male culture and, more specifically, the "male managerial model." Underlying this model is the assumption that successful managers follow a masculine management style and display male characteristics. When women are viewed as showing female managerial styles, they are often regarded as less effective than their male counterparts. If they adopt male styles, they are viewed as unfeminine (Ragins, Townsend, and Mattis, 1998).

There is a fine line between figuring out how much of a masculine management style women should adopt, and losing touch with feminine characteristics in the workplace. Women need to access their own business environment and decide if a masculine management style will help them obtain top positions. Women then have to make the decision as to whether adopting management styles uncharacteristic of their own nature is worth the trade-off. Recent research suggests that women, more often than men, have to make these emotional-labor trade-offs in the workplace in order to get ahead (Simpson and Stroh, under review). Obviously, men do not need to alter their behavior as much as women in order to portray the male characteristics of a masculine management style. Therefore, men do not need to trade off between their own nature and adapting characteristics foreign to them in order to succeed.

International management is one area of management that disputes this claim, however. Some studies suggest that a stereotypical "women's style of management" (obtaining greater group consensus, being a better listener, more democratic as opposed to autocratic in decision-making) is in fact more, not less, successful in the workplace (Stroh, Varma, and Valy-Durbin, 2000). By using this style of management, women managers are often seen as more effective by their subordinates because of the confidence they gain by making decisions that comply with their subordinates' expectations. Although the consultative style of management may lead to positive results, female managers might not be given their due credit and thus may not progress in the organizational hierarchy. As noted by Eagly and Johannesen-Schmidt (2001), women using this progressive style of management may pose a threat to those older managers who use a more traditional approach to management and are fearful of change.

Seek out difficult or highly visible assignments

Difficult or highly visible assignments lead to professional growth and present learning challenges. They serve as "grooming" for executive positions. Such assignments also provide critical access to key decision-makers and influential mentors in the company. Women must take the initiative in finding key assignments and must convince others that they are capable of undertaking them (Ragins, Townsend, and Mattis, 1998). Top management does not generally approach women about taking on a high-risk assignment. It is therefore critical that women express their interest in taking on such challenges. Most women agree that working with senior people gives them the opportunity to develop trust and confidence and to prove that they can get the job done.

Have influential mentors

Many people in corporations believe that mentors are an extremely important element in career success. Some research substantiates this claim. Individuals with mentors generally have greater career mobility, receive more promotions, and advance at a faster rate than their counterparts in the company (Dreher and Ash, 1990). Women who do not have mentors have lower expectations with respect to advancement opportunities and less likelihood of securing employment outside their organizations (Baugh, Lankau, and Scandura, 1996).

Other research is more cautious on the subject. Burke and McKeen (1997) found that mentoring relationships among managerial and professional women were only moderately and inconsistently related to income, career advancement, and job satisfaction. Similarly, Kram (1985), who originated the research on mentoring, has cautioned against the complexities that arise when mentoring relationships become overly intimate.

Whether to select a male or a female mentor is a matter of some debate. Among the possible advantages of a male mentor is that he has established networks and credibility, as well as information usually given only to those in the "old boy network" (Ragins, Townsend, and Mattis, 1998). One frequently cited study suggests that White male mentors confer benefit while other mentors do not. Using a sample of graduates of MBA programs, Dreher and Cox (1996) found that those graduates who established a mentoring relationship with White males earned an average of $16,840 more in annual compensation than those graduates with mentors with other demographic profiles.

Establishing an informal relationship with a mentor also seems to be important to the success of the relationship. Ragins and Cotton (1999) found that employees with informal mentors viewed their mentors as more effective, received greater cash compensations, and received better career outcomes than those employees whose relationships with their mentors were selected or assigned by the organization and in general were structured more formally. Most revealing, this study found no difference between those employees who were not mentored and those with formal mentoring relationships. Formal mentoring programs may serve as a springboard to informal mentoring relationships, but women should not stop the quest to find an informal mentor simply because they are assigned a formal mentor by their company.

Start your own organization

Another option available to women is to strike out on their own. A study conducted by Catalyst (1999a) showed that 29 percent of women noted that they started their own businesses because their former employers had glass ceilings that could not be shattered: 47 percent of the respondents said that they felt that their accomplishments were not recognized at their former employers; 34 percent felt they were not taken seriously; 29 percent felt isolated; and 27 percent saw others promoted ahead of them.

Many women who go it alone have shown they can develop careers beyond typical corporate boundaries (Brush, Wong-MingJi, and Sullivan, 1999). As a result, women now own companies that generate a whopping $3.6 trillion in revenue and represent 40 percent of US businesses (Freeman, 2000). One should caution, however, that there are great risks in starting one's own business, as the failure rate of new ventures, whether they're owned by men or women, is extremely high.

What Organizations Can Do to Shatter the Glass Ceiling

Company initiatives

Sensible companies realize that the onus for change cannot fall primarily on women employees. Many companies have already taken steps to make their practices fair to women and men. To combat problems of subtle bias in the selection of employees, for example, many corporations have turned away from informal recruiting. They see that it is to an organization's advantage to conduct structured interviews and to use other selection criteria (e.g., paper and pencil testing) that are not gender biased (Davison and Burke, 2000). Similarly, many companies have sought to improve the environment for women and men by offering sexual harassment training. Such training is especially useful in combating unwanted sexual behavior toward women managers, who are often resented by their male subordinates, by their peers, and by higher-level managers (Wirth, 1998).

A study of 1,000 companies in the Houston, Texas area, each with 200 or more employees, showed that all employees, not just women, took pride in their company's efforts to shatter the glass ceiling (Eyring and Stead, 1998). Although only 15 percent of those questioned thought their companies had been very successful, 80 percent of the managers interviewed felt their companies were doing better than their competitors and 68 percent felt they were doing better than other companies in general. The researchers concluded that most progressive companies were likely to do one or more of the following:

- Have a task force in place to address issues important to women.
- Clearly communicate goals for the movement of women to the managers in the organization.
- Have women represented on special task forces that address issues important to women.
- Explicitly include women of color in programs targeted toward women.
- Include issues important to women on their regular employee survey.
- Have minority networks to provide support for women of color.
- Hold managers accountable for the development of women through the performance appraisal process.
- Have systems in place for identifying high-potential women.
- Facilitate the movement of women into line positions with profit/loss responsibility.
- Provide diversity awareness training for managers.

Another study conducted in 1995 by the Glass Ceiling Commission reported the following characteristics as common to all successful glass ceiling initiatives (US Bureau of National Affairs, 1995):

- They have CEO support.
- They are part of the strategic business plan.
- They are specific to the organization.
- They are inclusive.
- They address preconceptions and stereotypes.
- They emphasize and require accountability up and down the line.
- They are comprehensive.
- They track progress.

Three types of glass ceiling initiative have received special attention. First, a great deal of research suggests that one way to increase the percentage of women advancing into upper management is to institute programs aimed at helping employees better balance work and family responsibilities. Maternity leave, family leave, parental leave, childcare facilities or services, flexible work arrangements, flextime, job sharing, compressed work weeks, and telecommuting are all positive examples of viable organizational initiatives aimed at shattering the glass ceiling. The majority of these programs are implemented to attract and maintain female workers. However, it is important to encourage men to take advantage of these benefits as well. If they don't, women may be pegged as not being committed to their careers and further hindered in their chances of advancement (Wirth, 1998).

A second type of initiative concerns women's networks. As discussed in greater detail in panel 7.1, both formal and informal networks are essential for providing women with visibility, contacts, information, and support for obtaining higher positions in companies (Wirth, 1998). Women's networks have also been shown to have significant impact on a male-dominated corporate culture (see panel 7.1). McCambley (1999) writes of her experience with the mentoring program established for women at NYNEX. Through this program, an "old boy's network among girls" was created and all of the men and women, along with the corporation as a whole, profited from the experience.

7.1 *Becoming an employer of choice*

A major Fortune 500 company in the consumer products industry – a very traditional, male-dominated sector of the economy – was concerned because the percentage of women managers in its workforce was especially low. Management in the company recognized that, with its predominately male, White workforce, the organization was unable to compete adequately in the global labor marketplace. Management also knew that it had made hiring, promotion, and development mistakes in the past. As part of its plan to improve its competitive strength, the company determined that it had to become an employer of choice for women, both inside and outside the organization.

The beginning

In 1996 the company CEO created a task force to discuss women's advancement opportunities within the organization and how to overcome some of the barriers impeding women. One of the key suggestions was to establish a women's network. In 1998 a consultant was hired to work with the organization to formalize the process. Subsequently, a mission statement, goals, and objectives were developed.

Mission

To assist [the company] in becoming a leading food company in attracting, retaining, developing, and promoting an inclusive workforce and to support [the company's] key strategies, including becoming an employer of choice.

Goals and objectives

- Provide formal and informal networking opportunities for women in management.
- Sponsor events that focus on career development for women in management.
- Promote recruitment efforts that include women and people of color.
- Assist in developing a positive learning culture.
- Provide feedback from exempt, professional women to the officers' group.
- Hold focus group meetings with members/officers to discuss and address female employees' concerns.
- Increase representation of women and people of color at top and middle-management levels.
- Partner strategically with human resources department to identify training and development opportunities.
- Partner with senior management and business unit leaders to raise awareness within the organization of problem and proposed solutions.
- Provide quarterly developmental meetings for the women in the network.
- Undertake annual surveys to assess change in women's perceptions of the glass ceiling.

The network

The women's network included 104 women in the management group of the organization. Their average age was 39.1 years, and 79 percent were White. Fifty-five percent were married, and 72 percent had no children. Somewhat surprisingly, 28 percent did not have bachelor's degrees. They had been in the workforce for an average of 18 years and for 8.1 years at this company. Thirty-eight percent considered themselves to be in lower management, while 57 percent considered themselves middle or upper managers. (For the purposes of the study, these categories were combined, since only one woman was in upper management.) Five percent of the women were lawyers or in other professional categories. On average, the women earned 74 percent of their families' income, attesting to the importance of their work to the quality of their families' lives.

Network accomplishments
Through focus group meetings, surveys, and gentle nudging, the women's network shared responsibility for the development of several initiatives:

- Succession planning process that included women.
- Implementation of performance evaluations.
- Posting of all positions.
- Development of systematic promotion and hiring practices to include all possible candidates.
- Reassessment of the education reimbursement program and its implementation.
- Ability to monitor all new hires/promotions within the organization.

Changes in perceptions
A survey of the members of the women's network was conducted to assess challenges to women's career success and to determine members' perceptions of the strength of the glass ceiling in the organization. A year later, another survey was conducted to determine whether positive changes in perceptions had occurred. The findings of the two surveys are summarized in the table below.

Summary of the findings of the surveys

Question	Survey 1	Survey 2
1 Is there a glass ceiling at this company?	90% yes	81% yes
2 Your level of management?	46% mid/upper	57% mid/upper
3 What percent of your skills and abilities are you using on this job?	46% utilization	57% utilization
4 Are the following barriers to your success?		
(a) Upper management	78% yes	76% yes
(b) Your sex	72% yes	71% yes
(c) Your immediate supervisor	61% yes	58% yes
(d) Your level of education	25% yes	42% yes

Additional surveys were conducted of the women in the network at the end of each quarterly development session. These surveys suggested the following:

- In every instance, the career development meetings were perceived as excellent, averaging almost 5 on a five-point scale.
- Over time, the women in the organization had come to view the meetings as excellent networking opportunities (78 percent, 80 percent, 91 percent, and 98 percent, respectively, agreed).
- Quantitative feedback showed significant support for the sessions. Members of the network thought the meeting content had helped them advance their careers in the organization (average rating 4.5 on a five-point scale). This finding was especially noteworthy, given that members of the women's network were from a variety of functional areas with significantly different needs.

Finally, there were changes not only in the women's perceptions of the organization, but also in the organization itself. Over the three years the network was in existence, one woman was hired into one of the top five positions in the company, three women were promoted to the next level of the company, and several women were hired into the next level of the organization. Further, these changes occurred in a relatively short time.

Implications of findings
Not only did the women in management regard the network as beneficial to their development, but also senior management responded positively to the network's recommendations and suggestions, as demonstrated by the number of initiatives that were supported. Clearly, the network positively influenced company culture and had an impact in effecting change (one year).

Implications for other organizations
As the findings from this case study demonstrate, women's networks can be positive forces for change for women themselves and result in significant changes in organizational culture. Research by Catalyst and others suggests similar positive results. The creation of women's networks is not without problems, however.

Some of the biggest hurdles encountered in the development of the women's network discussed in the case study involved the administrative assistants in the organization. They did not understand why they could not be part of the network, and their mostly male supervisors did not either. It seems that the women in this company were classified by their gender, not their level of skill and expertise. What was regarded as a lack of "inclusion" was a constant problem for the network. As a possible solution to this problem, management should have considered creating a network for the female administrative assistants (and/or for members of other minority groups), as other companies have done.

Other companies have had problems getting senior management to support the idea of creating a women's network. In the company discussed here, female employees spent hours with senior and middle managers (in individual and group settings) to increase their awareness of the need for the network and to gain their support. Although senior management made huge strides in this area, much work still remains to be done before all the men in the organization are aware of the barriers standing in the way of women in this company.

Discussion questions

1 Why is hiring women an important component to becoming an employer of choice?
2 What role do women play in an organization that works to maintain the status quo and limit women's careers?
3 What role do men play?
4 Given that women have babies, is it inevitable that they will and should be less successful in their careers?

Closely related to the above is a third type of initiative: career tracking. Career tracking "identifies women with high potential, as helping them gain visibility and experience through challenging and high-profile assignments" (Wirth, 1998). Many companies have targeted high-potential women early in their careers and provided special leadership development opportunities that groom women for positions higher up in the organization. Most organizations with more women at the top have systematically developed succession planning programs that have strategic career development opportunities for women. These companies have been careful to include women in succession planning activities and discussions. Companies that have been successful in retaining and attracting talented women have had programs that the women regarded as helpful to them in advancing their careers.

Changing the culture of an organization so that it recognizes the barriers faced by women and institutes programs to eliminate those barriers must start at the top. At Corning, the CEO and top executives are encouraged to use what they have learned at gender training programs in their daily work (Eyring and Stead, 1998). A three-year follow-up program ensures that initiatives learned at the training program will be incorporated as standard business practice, thus changing the overall culture so that it becomes more inclusive.

Results for companies

Companies have reaped rewards from their investments in family friendly initiatives. Supportive practices such as flexible scheduling have generally had positive effects on employees' control over family and work matters. This control, in turn, is associated with less work–family conflict, depression, job dissatisfaction, somatic complaints, and high cholesterol levels (Thomas and Ganster, 1995), which leads to happier and more productive workers. The availability of work–family benefits and a supportive work–family culture has also been shown to positively affect organizational commitment and to negatively affect intentions to leave organizations (Thompson, Beauvais, and Lyness, 1999).

Introducing work–life benefits has helped organizations in other ways as well. Lambert (2000) found that the more workers believed their companies' work–life benefits helped them and their families, the more likely they were to submit improvement suggestions, voluntarily attend meetings, and assist others with job duties.

In-depth analysis of the accounting firm Deloitte and Touche has shown the economic benefits that a company can derive from a commitment to gender fairness. Deloitte and Touche have reaped the rewards of its glass ceiling initiatives – but only after suffering the consequences of paying little or no attention to the issue. In June 1992 a study found that more than 80 percent of the women who had left the organization were still employed, working for other organizations (Trimberger, 1998). Deloitte's turnover rate for female managers, female senior managers, and female senior professionals was 33 percent, and the main reason cited for leaving was the lack of opportunities for women at the company. Recognizing this problem, Deloitte instituted several programs aimed at enhancing working relationships between men and women. It created mentoring programs, established networking and career-planning programs, devised measurable criteria for career advancement, and increased communication efforts within the company. Since making these efforts, Deloitte has tripled the number of women in key leadership positions and the number who have been made partners. In addition, the turnover rate for senior female employees has dropped by 18 percent. Equally impressive, through its flexible work program it has retained more than 176 client service professionals and saved the company an estimated $13 million in turnover costs.

WHAT DOES THE FUTURE HOLD?

Overcoming the barriers to women's rise to the top of corporate America is not easy for the women striving to shatter the glass ceiling, or the organizations working to become employers of choice for women. After all, as the discussion in this chapter has made clear, there are many barriers, and organizational cultures and behaviors are steadfastly ingrained. At the same time, companies are increasingly recognizing that to succeed in today's competitive climate, they need the best people for key positions, and often those people are women. Equally important, as this chapter has also made clear, researchers are identifying specific strategies and practices women can employ to increase their chances of advancing. As these findings are more widely disseminated, more women are beginning to employ the recommendations.

In the meantime, much work remains to be done. It will take time and concerted, serious effort for organizations to become employers of choice for women, and thereby increase their competitive strength. In the words of Meyerson and Fletcher (2000: 136), organizations will need to "ferret out the hidden barriers to equality and effectiveness one by one. This approach asks leaders to act as thoughtful architects and to reconstruct buildings beam by beam, room by room, rebuilding with practices that are stronger and more equitable, not just for women but for all people."

8

TOWARD THE INCLUSIVENESS AND CAREER SUCCESS OF AFRICAN AMERICANS IN THE WORKPLACE

Kevin Cokley, George F. Dreher, and Margaret S. Stockdale

This chapter examines the status of African Americans in the workplace and pays particular attention to the barriers that African Americans face, both to achieving full structural and informal inclusiveness in organizations, and to subsequent career success. After reviewing the evidence of occupational and job segregation and their consequences for career mobility and earnings, evidence of problems in gaining access to influential networks and mentoring relationships is discussed. This is followed by a fuller discussion of the career attainment process and the various ways that race affects the pathways to career success. The chapter concludes by examining the role that racial identity may play in affecting how African Americans negotiate their careers and organizational experiences in settings that may be more or less responsive to the value of diversity.

African Americans are not at the top of the corporate heap. Among large employers, very few African Americans make it to the rank of corporate officer. In fact, African Americans tend to cluster closer to the bottom than the top of the American economy.

What accounts for the relative lack of economic success among Black Americans? One could take a very simplistic approach and blame the disadvantage of African Americans entirely on White prejudice and discrimination. Some commentators have claimed that Whites have a deep and primitive fear of Blacks and that, consciously or unconsciously, Whites attempt at every turn to suppress Black people (Horne, 1992). At the other extreme, some scholars have laid the blame for the remaining gap between Whites and Blacks exclusively at the feet of African Americans. In their bestselling book *America in Black and White*, for example, Harvard educators Stephan and Abigail Thernstrom (1997) document how far African Americans have advanced since the days of Jim Crow laws which legalized segregation, and then cast about for explanations of the remaining disparities. They attribute the disadvantaged position of African Americans to low cognitive ability (for which they blame educational institutions for "dumbing down" educational standards), inadequate family structure, and a tendency toward crime and violence on the part of Blacks.

Such simplistic accounts are probably not very helpful in explaining the dynamics of race relations in the United States generally. Certainly, they do little to explicate the position of Blacks in corporate America. Yet, if the situation is to change, understanding is crucial.

Explicating the situation of African Americans in corporate America is the goal of this chapter. After a brief look at some of the statistics on differential outcomes for Blacks and Whites, we lay out two very different models, each of which can help us to comprehend why African Americans have not advanced further. One of the models emphasizes systemic factors, while the other looks at how interpersonal and intrapsychic factors can accelerate or retard the advancement of African Americans. The chapter closes by noting some of the implications of the different models.

THE STATUS OF ETHNIC MINORITIES IN THE AMERICAN WORKPLACE

Real advances toward workplace equality for individuals from any racial/ethnic background have been made since the Civil Rights Act of 1964. Yet, great disparities still exist. Blacks earn less than Whites. Occupational and job segregation are still widespread. So is prejudicial thinking. The experiences of African Americans also differ from those of White employees in many aspects of employment, such as access to mentors of one's own race.

Earnings

Black earnings are lower than White earnings. In 2000 there were over twice as many non-Hispanic Whites working full-time who earn $50,000 (27.5 percent) than there were Blacks who earn such high salaries (13.6 percent) (US Census Bureau, 2001a). In the same year, the median income for White male, full-time, year-round workers was $42,224, compared to $30,886 for Black men and $25,042 for Hispanic men. For female full-time, year-round workers, the disparities across race are not as dramatic, but nonetheless apparent. White women earn $30,777 compared to $25,736 for Black women and $21,025 for Hispanic women (US Census Bureau, 2002).

People who work in predominantly "black" jobs – whether or not they are Black themselves – are paid less than others. Tomoskovic-Devey (1993) found that the more Blacks there are in a job, the lower are the wages. This was true even when the levels of education and job experience (called human capital variables) of participants were taken into account. Blacks tended to be clustered in low-paying, low-prestige jobs that held little hope for occupational advancement. In their study of New York State government employees, Durr and Logan (1997) also found that African-American managers were disproportionately relegated to "minority job markets" – jobs that were specifically designed for minority occupants, such as "Affirmative Action Officer" or "Supervisor of the Educationally Disadvantaged." Holding a "minority job" was associated with a $4,900 annual income deficit compared to holding a job in the "mainstream" market, after accounting for age and education.

Occupational and job segregation by race

Occupational segregation refers to the extent to which individuals of various racial/ethnic backgrounds are disproportionately represented in various occupational groupings. The US Equal Employment Opportunity Commission (EEOC) keeps records on how many Whites, African Americans, Hispanics, Asians, etc., are represented in nine major occupational groups: officials and managers, professionals, technicians, sales workers, office and clerical workers, craft workers, operatives, laborers, and service workers. This is notably a very broad classification scheme and critics argue that it grossly simplifies the degree to which occupations and jobs are segregated by race (and gender) (see Tomoskovic-Devey, 1993). Nonetheless, according to recent EEOC statistics (EEOC, 2000), White men are overrepresented in the occupations of officer/manager (16.2 percent of White men are officers/managers compared to 10.7 percent of the population in general), professionals (16.8 percent v. 15.9 percent), technicians (6.8 percent v. 6.1 percent), crafts (14.3 percent v. 7.9 percent), and operatives (17 percent v. 13.7 percent). Black men, in contrast, are sharply *underrepresented* in the occupations of officer/manager (5.8 percent), professional (5.9 percent), and technician (4.6 percent), and *overrepresented* in comparison to White males as well as to the population generally in laborer (15.2 percent v. 7.8 percent of the population in general and 7 percent of White men) and service worker (17.3 percent v. 11.3 percent v. 6.4 percent).

Racial segregation in occupations exists for women as well. According to data from the 1999 Current Population Survey (collected by the US Census Bureau), 35 percent of non-Hispanic White women are in managerial or professional occupations, compared to 24 percent of Black women (which is considerably higher than the percent of Black men in such jobs). White women are also more likely than Black women to hold technical, sales, and administrative support jobs (41 percent v. 38 percent, respectively). Black women, however, are more likely than

White women to hold service jobs (27 percent v. 15 percent, respectively), and to hold jobs as operators, fabricators, and laborers (9 percent v. 6 percent, respectively) (McKinnon and Humes, 1999). Differences in occupational representation by race/ethnicity are found with other ethnic identity groups as well. Although it glosses over the substantial gender differences, figure 8.1 graphically depicts the ethnic disparities in occupational positions.

Slightly different than occupational segregation is job segregation. Job segregation is the extent to which a given job is disproportionately composed of same-race/ethnicity individuals within an organization. A peek at job segregation shows that strong forces operate to keep Blacks and Whites (as well as other racial/ethnic groups) separate. Sociologist Donald Tomoskovic-Devey (1993) has examined data from a random state-wide survey of employed North Carolinians. The survey asked participants to indicate, among other things, the percent of employees holding the same job as themselves in their organization who are of the same race (and gender). When the survey was conducted (1989), Blacks composed 22 percent of the population of North Carolina. Thus, a racially balanced job, according to Tomoskovic-Devey, would be one in which between 11 and 33 percent of job occupants are Black. Only 2 percent of jobs were considered racially balanced, however. Tomoskovic-Devey also noted that approximately 54 percent of either Blacks or Whites would have to change jobs in order to achieve racial balance.

Looking at job segregation, psychologist Joel Lefkowitz (1994) documented a phenomenon labeled *ethnic drift*. He found that a substantial proportion of new job incumbents who had initially been assigned to supervisors of a different race were reassigned to same-race supervisors within five months of employment. This reassignment was unrelated to employees' initial job test scores, recruiters' expectations for advancement, or the extent to which their initial supervisors liked (or disliked) them. These data suggest that *homophily*, or the tendency for same-race or same-sex individuals to group together, maintains and possibly reinforces workplace segregation.

Race disparities in employment decisions

It is known that employment decisions depend on both the race/ethnicity of the decision-maker and the race/ethnicity of the person about whom employment decisions are made. This holds true for employment interview ratings, performance evaluation ratings (see Kraiger and Ford, 1985), and other similar decisions. For example, Landau (1995) found in her survey of over 1,200 moderate- and high-potential managers in a large Fortune 500 company that even after accounting for differences in age, education, organizational tenure, type of job, and satisfaction with career support (a topic we will return to later), Blacks were rated as having significantly less promotion potential than Whites.

Landau's findings are not isolated. Kraiger and Ford (1985) conducted a meta-analysis of the extant literature reporting race of ratee (employee) and race of

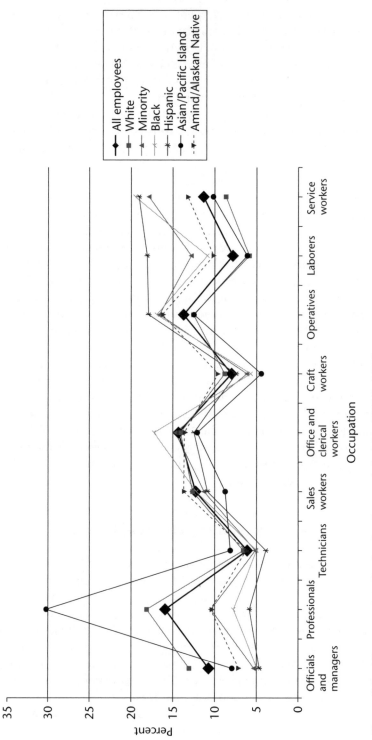

Figure 8.1 US occupation distribution by race/ethnicity (EEOC, 2000)

rater (supervisor) and found that White raters gave higher ratings to White ratees whereas Black raters gave higher ratings to Black ratees. Among studies of White raters (of which there were substantially more than studies of Black raters), the pro-White bias was larger in field studies than in laboratory studies, suggesting that under controlled circumstances, raters provide more socially desirable evaluations. More recently, Huffcutt and Roth (1998) conducted a meta-analysis of all the research on employment interview evaluations and found that, on average, evaluations of Blacks were one-fourth of a standard deviation lower than evaluations of Whites. Although the magnitude of this bias toward White applicants varied under different types of interview situation, the difference was always in favor of Whites – with one exception. When interviewing for jobs that were considered to be highly complex and thus the applicants in the pool were considered elite, there was no race difference in evaluations (in fact, it slightly favored Blacks).

Racial disparities in access to informal networks and mentoring

Blacks appear to have different experiences at work than do Whites. Greenhaus, Parasuraman, and Wormley (1990) surveyed over 900 managers and their supervisors in three large organizations. Forty-five percent of the managers in their sample were Black. Black managers reported being less accepted than White managers. Blacks also reported lower career satisfaction, and were rated lower by their supervisors compared to Whites. These findings led other researchers to wonder about what goes on within organizations to lead to such feelings and outcomes.

Having an influential mentor and/or network of influential relationships is critical to career success (e.g., Dreher and Ash, 1990; Dreher and Cox, 1996). People tend to form close relationships, such as mentor–protégé relationships, with others who are similar to them. Because the most influential people in organizations tend to be White men, Blacks are often at a disadvantage in securing such relationships.

In a study of 63 middle-level managers, Ibarra (1995) found that social networks of Black and White professionals differed. Furthermore, such differences related in complex ways to career outcomes. Not surprisingly, given that few Blacks are in positions of authority and influence in organizations, Blacks were more likely than Whites to have cross-race mentors. Interestingly, Blacks who were considered to be "high potential" were relatively likely to form network ties with both Blacks and Whites, whereas low-potential Blacks tended to form networks only with Whites.

McGuire (1999, 2000) conducted a comprehensive survey of over 1,000 managers in a large financial services firm to investigate race and gender differences in influential social networks within the company. She found that the social networks of minorities and women were of lower status than those of White men.

Furthermore, she found that the race (and gender) differences in network status were merely due to hierarchically based job segregation within the organization. Black managers who did attain top-level management positions had social networks that were as influential as top-level White managers' networks. Yet, all in all, the social networks of Blacks were not as influential as Whites' because Blacks held lower-status positions and were physically separated from influential Whites.

McGuire's findings echoed Dreher and Cox's (1996) findings that Blacks who developed cross-race mentoring relationships with Whites tended to have significantly higher salaries than those who developed same-race relationships. Furthermore, Thomas (1993) found that cross-race mentor–protégé pairs who agreed to deal with race issues openly were more likely than pairs who disagreed about how to handle race issues to develop supportive, enduring mentoring relationships. Thomas (1999) also explained how Blacks can help facilitate and make the most out of cross-race mentoring relationships. Blacks, especially those in influential positions, can (a) help break down White managers' resistance to mentoring junior Black colleagues; (b) help Whites understand the appropriateness of sponsoring and promoting Black employees; (c) make the benefits of mentoring Black protégés more salient to Whites; and (d) make the benefits of being mentored by White managers salient to potential Black protégés.

Together, these findings suggest that access to influential people is important for all aspiring employees but, due to structural isolation, Blacks may have more difficulty than Whites in creating such relationships. In addition, managing such relationships may well depend on a host of interpersonal processes, including racial identity and mutuality of perspectives.

Stereotypes and prejudice against Black employees

Stereotypes are automatic trait associations that are applied to members of social categories, i.e., the assumption that if person is from group X (e.g., a Black person or a White person) then they possess characteristic Y. Psychologist Virginia Schein (1973, 1975) found that both men and women tended to view the stereotypes of men to be consistent with the stereotype of a manager, whereas the stereotype of women was not associated with the stereotype of managers. Tomkiewicz, Brenner, and Adeyemi-Bello (1998) applied Schein's methodology to ethnic stereotypes among White employed adults. The researchers found that the correspondence between stereotypes of Whites and managers was quite high (r', an intraclass correlation coefficient measuring the strength of association between two sets of ratings, = .54, p < .05), whereas the correspondence between stereotypes of African Americans and managers was quite low (r' = .17, ns). In essence, these findings show that to "think manager" is to "think White."

The extent to which employers or raters hold prejudicial attitudes toward African Americans may compound the problems of negative stereotypes about

African Americans in judging their suitability for central positions in organizations, such as management. As noted in chapter 2 of this volume, the nature of prejudice against African Americans has changed from an overt, explicit form to a subtler, implicit form (e.g., modern racism, aversive racism, or symbolic racism; see Dovidio and Gaertner, 1991, and McConahay, 1983). Most people understand that it is socially unacceptable to openly express negative attitudes toward African Americans, yet many people still make unconscious stereotypical associations with African Americans or believe that racism is a thing of the past and that current disparities between Blacks and Whites are deserved.

If modern prejudice is subtle, so too is the form of discrimination that derives from it. Arthur Brief and his colleagues (Brief et al., 2000) conducted research in a simulated business setting by having non-Black undergraduate students review materials from applicants for a marketing job. Half of the research participants read a memo from the president of the company stating that the job was in an all-White teamwork environment and that the company wanted to keep such marketing teams homogeneous. The other half of the participants read no such memo. The researchers found that, when there was a stated business justification, modern racists were more likely than others to discriminate against qualified Black applicants. When the racism was implicitly condoned by the company, modern racists chose to interview a less qualified White applicant rather than a qualified Black applicant. In the absence of a business justification, modern racists were no more likely than others to discriminate.

Sometimes blatant prejudices operate in a subtle way. Stewart and Perlow (2001) administered a measure of *overt* prejudice to 181 undergraduate students and later asked them to choose between a Black or White applicant for either a low-status (janitor) or high-status (architect) position. Although this sample tended to possess non-racist attitudes, those who demonstrated particularly prejudicial attitudes placed more confidence than non-racist individuals in their decision to hire the Black applicant for the low-status position and to hire a White applicant for the high-status position.

RACE AND THE CAREER ATTAINMENT PROCESS

How are we to make sense of the statistics on earnings, segregation, access to mentors, and prejudice? A general model of the career attainment process may be helpful. Such a model or conceptual map contains linkages among components. Our job is to identify the components most susceptible to the influence of race (and their associated mechanisms).

A general framework of the determinants of career attainment is shown in figure 8.2. It represents a very traditional approach to the topic. Building upon the ideas originally presented by Campbell et al. (1970), the career attainment process is shown to be a function of ability, motivation, and opportunity. That is, these three constructs are shown to interact in accounting for attainment. Ability

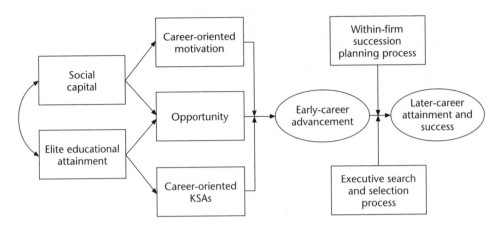

Figure 8.2 A traditional framework of the career-attainment process (adapted from Campbell et al., 1970)

relates to the possession of career-oriented knowledge, skill, and ability. Motivation relates to desire and effort level, or how much energy one puts into career attainment. Motivation also relates to the concept of career aspiration. Opportunity is a distinct construct and includes interrelated dimensions that provide organization members with the chance to acquire and display attributes related to role competencies and effectiveness (see chapter 4, this volume, for a more complete treatment of the role-taking process). Such factors as access to information about how to complete task assignments, access to information about organizational culture and reward systems, access to training and development experiences, being designated a "high potential" employee, and having access to senior-level role models or mentors, all comprise the sub-dimensions of opportunity (Dreher and Dougherty, 2002).

Components of the model

Social capital

Adler and Kwon (2002) point out that social capital research is based on the notion that the goodwill others have toward us is a valuable resource. Further, they state that if "goodwill is the *substance* of social capital, its *effects* flow from the information, influence, and solidarity such goodwill makes available" (p. 18) to us. The belief that social capital (as conceptualized in terms of social network structures and social resources) directly influences career attainment is not new. Popular advice for advancing one's career almost always mentions the importance of networking (e.g., Bolles, 1992; Kanter, 1977). What is new is that organizational researchers have begun to integrate theories of social capital with empirical research on career success. For example, Seibert, Kraimer, and Liden

(2001) integrated three different conceptualizations of social capital – weak tie theory (Granovetter, 1973), structural hole theory (Burt, 1992), and social resource theory (Lin, 1990) – and used this integrated framework to account for career attainment and success among a diverse sample of business and engineering school alumni. Their results showed that the structural properties of social networks were related to social resources (e.g., the number of contacts at higher organizational levels), and that social resources were related to multiple measures of career success. The positive effects of social resources on career success were fully explained by access to information, access to resources, and career sponsorship (a form of mentoring assistance).

Educational capital

The positive relationship between elite educational attainment (educational capital) and career success has been studied extensively and supported by numerous research findings (Becker, 1964; Blau and Ferber, 1992; Judge et al., 1995). Corporate elites in the US (comprised of highly paid managers and professionals) are overrepresented by White males who attended prestigious colleges and universities ("The Corporate Elite," 1991; Hillier, 1990; Kotter, 1995a). In their seminal work on the determinants of economic success, Jencks (1979) and his colleagues clearly documented the strong positive relationship between schooling level and career attainment. They reasoned that schooling effects may represent an arbitrary rationing device for allocating scarce jobs; or that schooling imparts (or at least signals the presence of) skills, knowledge, attitudes, or aspirations that are valued by employers. An analysis of their data clearly reveals that only part of the association between schooling and career success is due to what students actually learn in school. Thus, much of what accounts for later career attainment takes place at the time admission decisions are made at elite undergraduate, graduate, and professional schools. Although other factors can be taken into account, admission tests like the Scholastic Aptitude Test (SAT), the Graduate Record Exam (GRE), the Medical College Admission Test (MCAT), and the Law School Admission Test (LSAT), play a central role in determining career attainment and success in the US.

Timing

Our model also has a temporal component. We posit that to advance far in an organization one needs early career success. A review of the ages of corporate officers for many of the world's largest corporations reveals that it is very common to be promoted into executive roles early in one's forties.

One educational path that can lead to becoming a corporate officer is the Master of Business Administration (MBA) degree. Over the last ten years it has become increasingly common for top MBA programs to admit only students who have four or five years of post-undergraduate degree work experience (Dreher

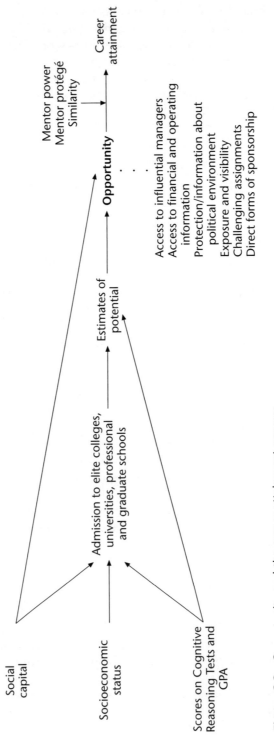

Figure 8.3 Opportunity and the career attainment process

and Ryan, 2000). Thus, it is now common for MBA program graduates to complete their degrees when they are well into their late twenties or early thirties. Therefore, individuals must be able rapidly to acquire the competencies needed to be competitive for senior management positions. People must be placed in accelerated developmental career paths if they are to be ready for admission into an executive talent pool. Anything that slows down the acquisition of requisite skills will likely interfere with movement into executive positions.

One noted management theorist, Elliot Jacques (1989), has even developed a framework for predicting who has the capability to reach executive status that explicitly takes into account both age and current capability. According to this theory, individuals predicted to reach the top must display high capability very early in their careers. Jacques's ideas fit nicely with the notion of "sponsored" mobility, as developed by Rosenbaum (1984) and observed by Kanter (1977).

Moderators

Our framework also shows that two processes act as key moderator variables – that is, as variables affecting relations between other variables. In this case, the succession planning process and the executive search and selection process both affect the relation between early career attainment and later career success. Primary antecedents of career success are two forms of human capital – referred to here as social and educational capital. Turning first to the two moderator variables, we speculate that race is likely to be related to both processes. Regarding the executive search process, very little is known about the way executive search firms conduct business. It is clear that changing companies at mid-career is common, and that executive search firms play a central role in this type of market exchange. There is also evidence that, at least for White male managers and professionals, taking advantage of opportunities in the external labor market provides a sizable compensation premium. People who change jobs *and* organizations earn substantially more money than people who change jobs but stay with the same organization (Brett and Stroh, 1998; Dreher and Cox, 2000).

Race and opportunity

Access to information, access to resources, and career sponsorship are central to the concept of opportunity. Figure 8.3 illustrates our model. The model makes clear how it is that Blacks with the same qualifications as Whites have less career attainment, even in the absence of conscious or unconscious racial prejudice.

Race and social capital

People who share core identities like gender and race are likely to form stronger informal ties than those lacking such commonality (D. A. Thomas, 1990; Tsui and

O'Reilly, 1989), and they are known to have greater spontaneous interpersonal trust (D. A. Thomas, 1990). Hence, White males are more likely than members of other identity groups to form social contacts with the predominantly White male network of people with the power to hire and negotiate salaries in US organizations. This conclusion has been reinforced by researchers who have directly studied race effects in social networks (Brass, 1985; Ibarra, 1995).

The connection between race and social capital starts before people join the organization that employs them. Figure 8.3 shows that social capital can influence career progress and attainment through its effects on admissions decisions in elite colleges, universities, and graduate and professional schools. This is because many schools use what is known as the "presumptive admissions" model (Sacks, 2001). Using this approach, schools mechanically select those with top admission test scores (and GPAs), automatically rejecting those at the bottom. However, for applicants in the middle, a more complete and full review is provided. It is here that social capital effects are likely to be present. For example, because most letters of reference are favorable, particular attention may be paid to letters from alumni and others who are part of the social networks of decisions-makers.

Race and educational capital

Just as the connection between race and social capital within an organization starts before one even joins the organization, so the connection between race and educational capital starts before one even sets foot into kindergarten. Parental education and wealth (socioeconomic status – SES) are powerful predictors of admission test scores (Sacks, 1999). On average, test takers from high SES families or from families in which a parent holds a graduate or professional degree will outperform their counterparts from families with lower educational or SES levels. Because race is a powerful predictor of SES and educational attainment in the US and many other parts of the world, understanding how race can affect career progress and attainment is, in large part, a function of understanding the role of college and university admissions policies in exacerbating racial inequalities in our society.

Also, we suspect that race affects estimates of potential in another way via its influence on cognitive reasoning test scores. As shown in figure 8.3, test scores can directly influence estimates of potential in managerial and professional roles. An illustration of how this process operates comes from an experience of one of the authors. While visiting the campus of a highly ranked liberal arts college (Carleton College), one of us observed a recruiting poster provided by the management consulting firm McKinsey and Company (one of the world's leading firms of this type). The poster made it clear that the company was looking for (among other things) people with high SAT scores. A review of the McKinsey and Company's web page states that, when hiring from undergraduate programs, a critical competency is intellectual ability – defined in terms of "logical reasoning, curiosity, creativity, business judgment, tolerance for ambiguity, and an intuitive feel for numbers." The company appears to be using SAT scores to help estimate levels of this competency. This is a curious approach, given that the SAT was designed to predict likely success in college. Measures of success in college (e.g., GPA) are "achievement," not "aptitude" measures. Carleton College is highly selective (average SAT scores among incoming students are very high) and known to use stringent grading standards. Thus, instead of focusing on a person's direct record of achievement (GPA), McKinsey and Company appears to be focusing on a measure that is an imperfect predictor of achievement. High SAT scores are being equated with high potential.

There is strong reason to suspect that African Americans obtain scores on standardized tests that underestimate their true abilities. As panel 8.1 explains, Black test takers may be especially prone to "stereotype threat" (Steele and Aronson, 1995). Through stereotype threat the prejudice of Black mental inferiority can become a self-fulfilling prophecy.

Race and the moderator variables

Because Blacks and other minorities have less access to influential social networks and less access to information compared to Whites, they may have a distinct disadvantage during salary negotiations, which ultimately result in lower salary offers when changing jobs. If it is the case that the external labor market for experienced managers is largely brokered by a relatively small number of managerial search firms, that these search firms are largely staffed by White male professionals, and that the databases of these firms underrepresent women and racial minorities, the basis for the moderator effects could be established. This is an area of inquiry that clearly calls for empirical investigation. Finally, we speculate that the same social networking processes that operate in the external labor

---

8.1 *Stereotype threat and performance on cognitive ability tests*

Many minority group members must contend with negative stereotypes about their group's intellectual ability and competence. These experiences have been highlighted by the publication and public debate associated with books like *The Bell Curve* by Herrnstein and Murray (1994). For those minorities who strongly identify with academic and intellectual pursuits, a process called *stereotype threat* (more recently labeled *social identity threat*) has been shown to depress performance on standardized cognitive ability tests (Steele and Aronson, 1995). Steele and his colleagues see this as a social-psychological predicament that can beset the members of any group about whom negative stereotypes exist. Building upon an earlier literature, Steele and Aronson argued that these negative stereotypes load the testing situation with a degree of self-threat not borne by people not stereotyped in this way. This additional threat can interfere with test performance in a variety of ways. For example, it can divert attention onto task-irrelevant worries by causing over-cautiousness and self-consciousness. Or, because it can lower performance expectations, test takers may withdraw effort.

Using Black and White Stanford University students as subjects (subjects likely to be highly identified with academic and intellectual pursuits), Steele and Aronson conducted a series of studies designed to test the stereotype threat hypothesis. These studies used experimental research designs – with subjects being randomly assigned to conditions that varied the degree to which a difficult cognitive ability test was depicted as either *ability-diagnostic* or as *ability non-diagnostic*. For instance, in one ability-diagnostic condition, subjects were told that the study was concerned with "various personal factors involved in performance on problems requiring reading and verbal reasoning abilities" (Steele and Aronson, 1995: 799). These subjects also were told that after the test was completed, they would receive feedback to familiarize them with their strengths and weaknesses in verbal problem solving. In the typical non-diagnostic condition, the descriptions of the study made no reference to the diagnosis of verbal ability and feedback was justified as a way to familiarize subjects with the types of tests they may encounter in the future. The tests used consisted of 30 verbal items, 27 of which were difficult items taken from Graduate Record Examination (GRE) study guides.

After controlling for previous performance on the Scholastic Aptitude Test (SAT), results consistently showed that Black participants in the diagnostic condition performed significantly worse than Black participants in the non-diagnostic condition. These differences were not observed among White test takers.

Discussion questions

1 Why do you think that reminding a person that he or she is a member of a social identity group about which negative stereotypes exist would cause such a person to perform poorly on a test?
2 African-American participants in the Steele and Aronson study were reminded of their social identity by telling them that the test they were to take was diagnostic of verbal problem solving. Why was this a threat to their social identity? What types of cues might provoke a stereotype threat for women? For older workers? For poor people?
3 To what extent to do you think that stereotype threat can account for Euro-American v. African American differences in educational capital? Why? Using this knowledge about stereotype threat, what could we do to help eliminate such disparities?

market (getting a job in a new organization) may operate in internal labor markets (advancing within an organization).

Summary

In summary, we have provided a general "opportunity-oriented" framework to map out the determinants of career success. As a review of figures 8.2 and 8.3 makes clear, the influence of race on career attainment begins very early in life. Access to influential mentors, coaches, and sponsors is likely to be reserved for individuals who have distinguished themselves by finishing degrees at elite colleges, universities, and graduate schools and by developing a high degree of social capital. These are typically not accomplishments that come late in life. Thus, because race can have a marked effect upon the early life acquisition of educational and social capital, it can have a particularly profound affect upon subsequent career attainment.

AFRICAN-AMERICAN RACIAL IDENTITY

Much as social systems matter, African Americans are not inanimate pawns in the social structure. A complete explanation of the arrested attainments of Blacks must restore to Blacks the agency that some models of covert racism deny them. African Americans, in other words, are not simply buffeted by the forces around them. To complete the model of career opportunity, it is necessary to consider how African Americans experience the situations in which they find themselves.

Racial identity theory is an extremely useful tool to help us understand how people, racial minorities in particular, shape and are shaped by their environment. Racial identity is yet another dimension that can influence opportunities for career advancement and full inclusion. We think it is possible that many African Americans have unwittingly contributed to the current situation, not through a lack of competence or investment in their education or careers, but rather through an inability to engage in effective, collective protest.

In its most basic conceptualization, racial identity theory posits that all individuals in this country are socialized as racial beings. This socialization results in the development of a racial identity, which operates as a significant part of a cultural worldview. This worldview is subtle yet omnipresent. It influences all aspects of life, including life at work.

The model of William Cross

When he was a psychology graduate student at Princeton University during the turbulent civil rights and Black Power movements, William Cross observed changes in the identity of many Black people. In a classic article, Cross (1971) described what appeared to be five stages of Nigrescence, or the process of "becoming Black." The first stage, *Pre-encounter*, described Blacks who were more identified with White culture than Black culture, and who were very critical of Black people. Individuals in this stage were anti-Black and pro-White. The second stage, *Encounter*, was characterized by a jolting experience the Black person had which forced her to deal with the reality that race matters, whether she acknowledged it or not. For many Blacks who came of age in the 1960s, their encounter experience came when Martin Luther King, Jr. was assassinated. This encounter thrust the individual into the third stage, *Immersion-Emersion*, where the individual is totally immersed into Blackness. Individuals in this stage viewed everything that was associated with Black as good, and everything associated with White as evil and bad. However, this stage has an emotional toll, and individuals eventually began to emerge from this into the fourth stage, *Internalization*, where Blacks internalized a healthy Black identity, which did not rely on the denigration of Whites. Individuals in this stage could interact and be friends with Whites and other non-Black individuals without losing their sense of Blackness. The fifth and final stage, *Internalization-Commitment*, described individuals who were committed to a plan of action and were actively involved in fighting discrimination and prejudice.

After 25-plus years of research and criticism, Cross (1991, 1995) revised his model. The pre-encounter stage is no longer simply seen as consisting of anti-Black attitudes. Instead, individuals may hold one or more of three types of pre-encounter attitudes. Pre-encounter Blacks may hold *assimilationist* attitudes; that is, race may not be salient for them, but being American and assimilating to White American culture is more important because it opens more doors of opportunity. Pre-encounter Blacks may hold *miseducated attitudes*, where they hold stereotypical views about Blacks (i.e., Black people would rather take a handout than work hard for something). Finally, pre-encounter Blacks may hold *self-hatred attitudes*, where they hold extremely negative views about being Black (e.g., hating their Black skin). The immersion-emersion stage remained the same. The internalization stage consists of at least two identities, Black Nationalist and Multiculturalist. Individuals who hold Black Nationalist attitudes emphasize Black self-determination and Black self-empowerment, whereas Multiculturalist Blacks strongly identify with other social identities (i.e., gender, sexual orientation, etc.) as well as their Black identity. In short, individuals can have positive, internalized Black identities with different ideologies about race and sociopolitical allegiances.

William Cross's work has had a great impact on psychologists and sociologists. One aspect of that impact is the way in which other psychologists have developed their own models based on Cross's work. One such psychologist is Robert Sellers (Sellers et al., 1997).

Sellers has developed the Multidimensional Model of Racial Identity (MMRI). The MMRI differs from Cross's Nigrescence Model in two important ways. First, it does not assume that racial identity is developmental. The second way that the MMRI differs from Cross's model is that it does not place any value or worth on the dimensions. In other words, no dimension or type of ideology is healthier or more developmentally sophisticated than any other.

The MMRI conceptualizes racial identity as consisting of multiple dimensions (i.e., centrality, salience, regard, and ideology). *Centrality* refers to whether race is a core part of an individual's self-concept. *Salience* refers to whether race is an important part of an individual's self-concept at a specific moment in time. Centrality is a stable dimension of identity, while salience is more situational. *Regard* refers to how individuals see themselves and feel about themselves. Regard consists of two components: private and public. Private regard refers to the degree to which an individual feels positively or negatively toward African Americans and about being a member in that group, while public regard refers to the degree to which an individual believes that non-African Americans feel positively or negatively about African Americans. According to Sellers et al. (1997), there are four types of ideologies: nationalist, oppressed minority, assimilationist, and humanist. A nationalist ideology emphasizes the importance and uniqueness of being African American. An oppressed minority ideology emphasizes the commonalities between other oppressed minorities and African Americans. An assimilationist ideology emphasizes the commonalities between African Americans and other Americans. A humanist ideology emphasizes the similarities of all human beings.

Empirical studies

Cross's (1991, 1995) model has enjoyed extensive research in the counseling psychology literature (Parham and Helms, 1981; Ponterotto and Wise, 1987; Pyant and Yanico, 1991). One likely reason is because of its developmental nature, where individuals are conceptualized as moving from a least healthy stage of identity (i.e., pre-encounter) to the healthiest stage of identity (i.e., internalization). This framework makes it easy for therapists to make treatment plans that incorporate a client's racial identity profile. To date, however, hardly anyone has tested Cross's theory in either educational or business settings.

That Cross's model and the others inspired by it can be empirically tested has, however, been demonstrated by work done on the model developed by Sellers. Schmerund et al. (2001) showed that Blacks for whom centrality is high, who have high private regard, and who have adopted an oppressed minority ideology, are more supportive than others of collective action solutions to the problem of discrimination. Especially strong are the links between centrality and private regard, on the one hand, and support for affirmative action, on the other. Blacks who embrace their ethnicity and like themselves also support affirmative action. Blacks who dislike affirmative action tend to shun their own Blackness and take little pride in being Black.

Applying Cross's model to organizational processes

Given that most American corporations are Eurocentric, and given the systemic processes that prolong White advantage even after blatant prejudice has subsided, life in corporate America poses challenges for Black employees. How Black employees meet the challenges depends in part, we think, on their racial identity. Blacks at different stages of racial identity are likely to attempt to cope with the anti-minority bias of America in different ways.

Most Eurocentric organizations surely reward African Americans who hold assimilationist attitudes. That is to say, African Americans who do not make race a salient part of their identity, who see themselves first and foremost as Americans, who think of themselves in individual rather than collective terms, who believe that hard work will usually result in positive and fair outcomes, and who believe in being a team player and not ever "rocking the boat," will typically be seen in a more positive light by their White supervisors and co-workers, and subsequently be rewarded in the form of social acceptance, informal social networking, and/or career advancement. The question of whether the organizational culture creates assimilationist attitudes or rewards preexisting assimilationist attitudes is difficult, if not impossible, to answer. It probably is the case that there is a reciprocal relationship, such that assimilationist African Americans are drawn to monocultural, Eurocentric organizations. Whatever the case may be, the climate of many organizations rewards non-threatening African Americans, and in this way shapes the identity of African Americans ultimately for the purpose of social control. Assimilationist African Americans are not naturally inclined to document discriminatory practices or behavior. However, if well-qualified assimilationist African Americans are passed over for promotions or other forms of career advancement, this may serve as a defining encounter that propels them into a psychological state of anti-Whiteness and pro-Blackness, where documentation of discrimination becomes more salient.

For those African Americans who are immersed in their Blackness and harbor anti-White attitudes, negotiating the terrain of Eurocentric monocultural organizations becomes an extremely difficult, if not impossible, task. These African Americans generally harbor a profound mistrust and, indeed, dislike of White people that is evidenced by their limited interactions with them. These limited interactions tend to be perfunctory and superficial, and in effect serve to isolate Blacks socially from their White co-workers and supervisors. Such African Americans, while wanting to advance in their careers, are naive because they have failed to understand that they are in an environment that is punitive of nonconformers. Although their generally aloof demeanor may appear threatening to some Whites, they are more often seen as having a chip on their shoulder. When qualified Immersion African Americans are passed over for promotion or other forms of career advancement, it reinforces their disdain of the system in general, and of Whites in particular. The end result is a perpetually unhappy and disgruntled employee whose motivation to excel is greatly diminished. This individual may possibly plant the seeds of discontentment in other like-minded African-American employees in order to build a racial alliance. Any discriminatory behaviors or the appearance of discriminatory behaviors will be documented for the purposes of exacting revenge on a racist organization. As mentioned previously, there is most likely a reciprocal relationship between the organizational culture and Immersion African Americans. However, it is probably the case that organizational culture has more influence in facilitating immersion attitudes among African Americans than that Immersion African Americans have an influence on organizational culture.

Unlike Immersion African Americans, Multiculturalist African Americans are able to negotiate the cultural demands of Eurocentric monocultural organizations and, unlike Assimilationist African Americans, they are able to maintain a positive racial/ethnic identity. Unlike Assimilationist and Immersion African Americans, Multiculturalists value forging coalitions across race, ethnicity, gender, and sexual orientation, and recognize their importance in maintaining positive interpersonal relations in the workplace. Multiculturalist African Americans are comfortable socially interacting with their White co-workers and supervisors, and indeed value these interactions as a means of tearing down racial barriers.

The culture of Eurocentric monocultural organizations superficially promotes multiculturalist attitudes to the extent that these organizations value a workforce of team players who respect and value each other. In this regard, Eurocentric monocultural organizations will encourage cooperation and teamwork amongst its diverse workforce. However, it is superficial because fundamentally the Eurocentric monocultural organization will not change its cultural moorings. That is to say, Eurocentric monocultural organizations will continue to be bastions of White, Eurocentric, male-centered, and individualistic mores. For the Multiculturalist African American, this is a frustrating reality, but one that she is willing and able to endure. Multiculturalist African Americans can work within this system while simultaneously trying to change it. Meyerson and Scully (1995) coined the term "tempered radicalism" to describe people who identify both with their organization and with ideals that are different from the dominant culture. Such individuals can help challenge the status quo to work toward effective organizational change. Similarly, Multiculturalist African Americans in monocultural organizations recognize the importance of forming coalitions across different social groups, which serves them well as they attempt to effect change within the organization. When qualified Multiculturalist African Americans are turned down for a promotion or other forms of career advancement, it may arouse a righteous anger that requires a plan of action. Because Multiculturalist African Americans have internalized a positive, non-reactionary Black identity, they are more motivated by obtaining justice for all people rather than exacting revenge for only African Americans. Like Immersion African Americans, they will document discriminatory behaviors and policies. However, Multiculturalist African Americans are more likely to enlist the help of non-African Americans, including White co-workers or supervisors, in documenting discriminatory behaviors and policies.

Multiculturalist African Americans will probably have a greater impact on organizational culture than Immersion African Americans because of their willingness to form coalitions. We believe that Eurocentric monocultural organizations will exert a greater negative influence on the attitudes of Immersion African Americans than Multiculturalist African Americans because the latter are more willing and perhaps better able to negotiate the cultural demands of the environment.

Summary

In summary, racial identity theory challenges the monolithic image of African Americans. The propositions regarding racial identity theory and organizational experiences for African-American employees discussed above are speculative and need to be supported by research. Nonetheless, there are several attitudes African Americans may hold regarding their racial identity, and the predominance of any one of these attitudes has implications for how African-American employees negotiate the demands of the workplace, for the career advancement of African-American employees, and ultimately for their productivity, well-being, and happiness. Panel 8.2 provides a critical thinking exercise that applies the concepts of institutional racism and racial identity theory to a hypothetical, but realistic organizational challenge.

SUMMARY AND CONCLUSIONS

Many factors impact the ability of African Americans to become fully integrated into the upper echelon of management in corporate America. In spite of relatively successful attempts to diversify the workforce, senior management positions in corporate America have remained virtually a bastion of White male privilege. The most obvious impediment to career advancement for African Americans and other racial/ethnic minorities is some form of racial bias.

Even when the people in control have managed to shed some of their racial prejudice, biased systems persist. Access to informal networks, social relationships, and mentoring plays an important role in the differential career advancement of African Americans and Whites. When one considers that it is human nature to establish social and mentoring relationships and extend opportunities to individuals who are most like oneself, it becomes easy to understand why White men continue to maintain a monopoly on senior management positions. It might even be argued that White men are not behaving any differently than any other social group would behave in the same circumstances.

8.2 *Critical thinking exercise*

Tryon Incorporated, an organization which manufactures textiles, has a performance appraisal process which determines who receives promotions. The performance appraisal process relies on both objective and subjective criteria. The objective criteria include scores on a general aptitude test, as well as an individual's productivity in a specific unit. The subjective criteria include subordinate and supervisor evaluations of an individual's performance, as well as ability to interact with people. An African-American employee, upon being denied a promotion, discovers that over the past five years, 75 percent of White employees who were eligible for promotion were promoted, while only 25 percent of African-American employees who were eligible for promotion were promoted. When confronted with the data, the CEO of Tryon maintained that there was no discrimination because each employee was evaluated by the same performance appraisal process using the same objective and subjective criteria.

Discussion questions

1 Is this an example of institutional racism? What is the evidence for and against this charge?
2 Using racial identity development theory, give examples of how African Americans might deal with this situation.

Strategies to reduce the influence of prejudicial attitudes and biased behaviors, such as affirmative action, have been criticized because they supposedly go against the notion of meritocracy. Individuals in corporate America, just like admissions officers in selective universities, often rely on standardized test scores to determine who has high managerial potential. As is the case in education, heavy reliance on standardized test scores reduces the numbers of qualified African Americans and Latinos considered for career advancement and promotion. Given the numerous debates over what constitutes meritocracy, multiple indicators of ability, motivation, and potential should be used so that all segments of the workforce are given equal consideration for advancement (Crosby, in press).

Finally, if corporate America is serious about managing its diversity, more attention should be paid to how the corporate culture challenges and negatively impacts the racial identity of African Americans in ways about which Whites may never have to be concerned. To work in an environment where African Americans and other ethnic minorities feel as if they have to compromise their identity and not be who they really are can have long-term negative psychological implications for ethnic minority employees in the form of unhappiness, depression, resentment, and anger. Thus far the psychological well-being of ethnic minority employees has not been given much attention. Preventive measures such as focus groups and surveys that address ethnic minority concerns would demonstrate that the workplace is invested in the satisfaction and well-being of its ethnic minority employees.

9

AGE, DISABILITY, AND OBESITY: SIMILARITIES, DIFFERENCES, AND COMMON THREADS

Myrtle P. Bell, Mary E. McLaughlin, and Jennifer M. Sequeira

Populations in the US and other developed nations are aging, the prevalence of obesity is considered "epidemic" in the US, and the incidence of disabling conditions is increasing, in part due to an older and heavier population. In this chapter we discuss why age, obesity, and disability are important aspects of workplace diversity, and how they are similar to and different from more commonly studied areas of diversity, such as race/ethnicity and gender. Importantly, growing older is something that everyone experiences, and people of all racial or ethnic backgrounds, religions, and sexualities may be obese or have a disability. We provide evidence that persons who are older, obese, or who have a disability are discriminated against in organizations, despite the lack of research showing their performance is inferior to that of others. We conclude with implications for diversity management and for researchers.[1]

Diversity issues are becoming more diverse. There was a time when sex and race were the only two characteristics that rose to conscious awareness in discussions of diversity. Now many other characteristics come to mind, including aspects of the body.

In this chapter we focus on three physical aspects of diversity: age, disability, and obesity. These body issues are understudied relative to other aspects of diversity, perhaps because federal laws prohibiting discrimination on the basis of age and disability are more recent and less well known than is the powerful Civil Rights legislation of 1964. Yet, body issues are of increasing importance to individuals, organizational decision-makers, policy-makers, and those interested in diversity research.

Populations in the US and in other developed nations are aging. The prevalence of obesity is considered "epidemic" in the US (CDC, 2001), and the incidence of disabling conditions is increasing. Men and women from all racial, ethnic, and national backgrounds, all religions, and all sexualities may be aged, obese, or have a disability. Although the characteristics of race, ethnicity, national origin, religion, and sex can allow people to be categorized into separate groups, *everyone* grows older. As people age, furthermore, they are more likely to become disabled and/or obese. People who are overweight are also more likely to develop health problems (e.g., hypertension, high cholesterol, diabetes, and coronary artery heart disease) that may lead to disabilities (Maranto and Stenoien, 2000; Martin, Leary, and Rejeshi, 2000). These concurrent relationships and multiple category memberships make these body issues particularly important for the study of workplace diversity.

The study of age, obesity, and disability as aspects of diversity is also interesting because these groups have permeable boundaries. Whereas sex and race are generally agreed as being genetic and immutable, as people age, gain weight, or become disabled, new members join the group. Members may also leave the group when defining features are lost (Gatz and Cotton, 1994); for example, by a person who maintains a significant loss of weight over a period of time or who no longer has a disability.

The boundaries for membership in the classes of the aged, obese, and disabled are also ill-defined. People differ in their judgments of who is overweight, obese, elderly, and sometimes even disabled. Just as beauty is in the eye of the beholder, so is being overweight and elderly. The age at which people become eligible for entitlement programs, such as Medicare in the US (65 years), may define "old" for some people. Others may consider "old" to be 40 or 50 years. Furthermore, as people grow older, their estimates of the age at which "old age" begins get higher and higher (Logan, Ward, and Spitze, 1992; Seccombe and Ishii-Kuntz, 1991). Women are judged to become old at a younger age than men and to decline more in physical attractiveness with age (Deutsch, Zalenski, and Clark, 1986; Seccombe and Ishii-Kuntz, 1991). Thus, gender differences, more commonly studied in diversity research, also exist regarding perceptions about age.

The boundaries for membership in the overweight category are also influenced by gender, in that there are differences in the amount of overweight considered acceptable for men and women. For example, the ideal weight standard for women is unrealistically low (thin), whereas the standard for men is much closer to natural body shape (Rodin, Silberstein, and Striegel-Moore, 1984). This gender difference is mirrored in the degree of obesity discrimination evident in wages, as the weight-based wage penalty starts earlier for women than for men (Maranto and Stenoien, 2000). Category membership may even be debatable for disability status: even though disability is defined in the Americans with Disabilities Act (ADA), whether a complainant possesses a disability or impairment is often argued in the courts.

This permeability of category membership not only has meaning for observers, but also has implications for the perspective of the individual who is elderly, overweight, or who has a disability. From the individual's perspective, there is an adjustment process to the consequences of growing older, becoming overweight, or acquiring a disability. If this adjustment happens during adulthood there may be strong implications for work behavior and treatment by others. As will be discussed later, persons with these body issues share the status of being regarded as less competent and experience discrimination and prejudice at work.

In this chapter we identify similarities, differences, and common threads in the experiences of people with these body issues, with the goal of promoting acceptance, reducing discrimination in organizations, and facilitating research in these areas. We first define briefly the categories of obese, aged, and disabled, presenting data on their prevalence. We then present legislation, federal guidelines, and judicial interpretations that are relevant to discrimination in employment based on body issues. We next use Dworkin and Dworkin's (1999) characterization of minority groups to demonstrate how persons who are older, obese, or have a disability are similar to people from other minority or non-dominant groups. As part of this discussion, we discuss the evidence for stereotyping and discrimination against people with these body issues. Finally, we offer practical suggestions to reduce employment discrimination against persons who are diverse with respect to age, disability, and obesity, and discuss the implications for researchers interested in these understudied aspects of diversity.

DEFINITIONS AND PREVALENCE

Age

Defining "older" workers is difficult; there is no particular age at which one is certain to move from being a younger worker who is free from older age discrimination, to an older worker who is subject to such discrimination. Federal law (discussed below) prohibits discrimination against workers who are at least 40 years old, implying that people who are 40 or older may be old enough to face age discrimination.

The bulging baby-boomer population (persons born between 1946 and 1964) and lower birth rates in the US mean the US population is aging. The median age in the US in 2000 was 35.3, up from 28 in 1970 and from 32.9 in 1990. By 2010, the median age is projected to be 37.4. Because of women's longer life spans, the age medians for women are higher, with a median age in 2000 of 37.4 and a projected median of 39 by 2010. In comparison, the median age for men in 2000 was 34.6 and is projected to be 36 by 2010.

Figures from the US Census Bureau indicate that the population is shifting toward older age ranges. Between 1990 and 2000, there were 9.1 percent and 6.2 percent fewer people in the age ranges of 25–29 and 30–34, respectively. On the other hand, people in the age ranges of 35–39 increased by nearly 14 percent, while those between 40 and 44 increased by 27.4 percent. More striking is the 45 percent increase in people aged 45–49 and the nearly 55 percent increase in those 50–54. People in the 55–59 age range increased by almost 28 percent. Overall, in the 2000 census, people aged 36–54 represented 28 percent of the total US population (Meyer, 2001).

Obesity

Conceptualizations of obesity vary. There is no set weight or body-fat proportion at which all people become obese and at which point obesity is clear and unequivocal. However, recognizing that one is "fat" is fairly simple and easily agreed upon – researchers find agreement, even with children as judges (see Staffieri, 1967). Formally, the Centers for Disease Control (CDC, 2001) define obesity as an excessively high amount of body fat in relation to lean body mass, still a vague description. Others have described obesity as occurring when a person is at least 20 percent above the weight recommended by actuarial tables (Roehling, 1999). As with age (and, to some extent, as a function of age), the US population is increasing in obesity. Weight tends to increase with age as metabolism slows and physical activity declines; thus, the concurrent age and weight increases in the US population are to be expected. About 40 million American adults are obese and these figures are growing. The percentage of obese Americans has nearly doubled in 20 years, up from 15 percent in 1980 to 27 percent in 1999 (CDC, 2001).

The prevalence of obesity varies by gender and race/ethnicity, compounding the effects of multiple aspects of diversity. Among African Americans, 28.6 percent are classified as obese. Twenty-one percent of Hispanics and 18 percent of Whites are obese. Women tend to be more overweight than men, and obesity more negatively affects women than men with respect to college attendance, employment, and earnings. We will discuss these negative consequences and their greater effect on women later in the chapter.

Disability

For some disabilities, such as complete inability to see or hear, there is clear and unequivocal recognition of and agreement about their existence. For other disabilities, such as slight impairments in vision or hearing, or the early stages of arthritis, recognition and agreement are less obvious. By law in the US, a disability is a real or perceived physical or mental impairment that substantially limits one or more major life activities (US Census Bureau, 1997). Both age and obesity increase one's likelihood of developing a disability (Maranto and Stenoien, 2000; Martin, Leary, and Rejeshi, 2000), and as we have mentioned, the US population is increasing in both age and obesity. More children living in poverty (resulting in more childhood onset disability) and medical advances associated with higher survival rates (Population Reference Bureau, 2002) are also related to increases in disability.

Today, over 20 percent of people in the US have a disability (Population Reference Bureau, 2002). Over 4.5 million adults with disabilities between ages 25 and 64 are in the workforce; about half are men and half are women. Although the percentage of people with disabilities who are *able to work* has remained relatively stable in the past decade, there has been an increase in the percentage of people with a disability who are actually working. In 1986, 46 percent of people with disabilities who were able to work were employed. By 2000, 56 percent of such persons were employed (NOD/Harris, 2000); a significant increase, but still leaving 44 percent of those who are able to work unemployed. This high unemployment reiterates the importance of including persons with disabilities in diversity research.

LEGAL PROHIBITIONS AGAINST WORKPLACE DISCRIMINATION

As with other diverse persons (e.g., people of color, women), increasing numbers of persons who are older, obese, or who have a disability occur concurrently with legislation prohibiting discrimination against them and fostering their acceptance in the workplace. We discuss the Age Discrimination in Employment Act (ADEA, 1967) and the Americans with Disabilities Act (ADA, 1990) in the following paragraphs.

The ADEA and subsequent amendments prohibit discrimination against persons aged 40 and older in employment-related matters. This law has been interpreted to protect older workers from being targeted in layoff actions and from discrimination in hiring, training and development, promotions, compensation, and benefits. Despite the prohibitions against discrimination, older workers frequently experience age-based discrimination in employment, as suggested by the proliferation of age discrimination lawsuits in the US (EEOC, 2001a).

Federal legislation protecting workers with disabilities began in 1973 with the Rehabilitation Act (RHA), which applies only to the federal government and federal contractors. Those protections were expanded to apply to private employers in 1990 with the ADA, which was not fully implemented until 1994. Employers are required to make reasonable accommodations to enable persons with disabilities (who are otherwise qualified) to work, as long as the accommodations do not cause the employer undue hardship.

At present, no federal legislation directly and unequivocally prohibits discrimination on the basis of weight. In rare instances, the RHA and ADA have covered instances of discrimination on the basis of obesity when it could be shown that the morbid obesity (being twice the normal weight for one's height) actually was, or was perceived as, a disability (see Maranto and Stenoien, 2000, for a discussion). In one of the earliest court cases to be decided in the obese plaintiff's favor (*Cook v. State of Rhode Island Department of Mental Health, Retardation, and Hospitals*), Bonnie Cook, who was 5 feet 3 inches tall and weighed 329 pounds, was determined to have an actual or perceived disability and thus be protected under the ADA. Though protections are limited to persons who are morbidly obese, employers who refuse to hire an obese applicant because of fear of health problems due to the obesity may be in violation of the ADA's prohibition of discrimination against those "perceived" to have a disability. Bonnie Cook's case was particularly disturbing because she had worked for the defendant before (when she was obese) and had an "excellent employment history during her previous tenure" (Martin, 1994: 141).

As few people (about 1 percent of the population) are morbidly obese, some cities and states, including Michigan, San Francisco, CA, Santa Cruz, CA, and Washington, DC, have passed specific legislation prohibiting any type of size discrimination (Anti-Weight Discrimination Laws, 2000). As is apparent in the recent decision under the San Francisco law (see panel 9.1), an overweight plaintiff need not be "morbidly obese" to experience illegal size discrimination. Despite this victory for overweight job applicants, the absence of widespread formal prohibitions against discrimination on the basis of weight, plus the ambiguity surrounding what constitutes overweight or obesity, make addressing such discrimination more difficult than for other diverse groups. In addition, because of the stigma associated with obesity, overweight people may be more reluctant than others to pursue discrimination claims (Byers, 1995).

In sum, the ADEA and the ADA have had some impact on employment of older workers, those who have a disability, and to a much lesser extent, those who are morbidly obese. However, these laws have been in effect for less time and there has been greater uncertainty regarding the relevant legislation as compared with protections afforded people who are diverse with respect to gender, race, and ethnicity. Thus, as we discuss in the next section, considerable employment-related discrimination against obese, older, or disabled workers remains.

Lawsuits and settlements: Evidence that the laws are working

The number of age-related discrimination claims filed with the Equal Employment Opportunity Commission (EEOC) is similar to the number of disability claims; about 14,000–20,000 claims of age and disability discrimination were filed per year in the period 1992–2000 (EEOC, 2001a). This compares with 22,000–26,000 sex-based claims and 26,000–32,000 race-based claims filed under Title VII of the Civil Rights Act during that same period. Though fewer in number, claims filed under the ADEA and the ADA are nonetheless quite substantial, and, importantly, represent large numbers of workers who are also diverse in other regards (e.g., race/ethnicity, gender). Further, average damage awards for claims filed under the ADEA are often higher than the average awards for claims filed under Title VII (EEOC, 2001b; Thompson and Kleiner, 1995). Thompson and Kleiner

9.1 *Fat people fight back, and win!*

America's obsession with size has led to "thin" people being admired and "fat" people being discriminated against. Societal attitudes and the stigmas associated with those who are overweight or obese have led to overweight people being ridiculed, ostracized, fired, denied promotions, and other negative consequences. This discrimination is especially harmful to children, whose developing self-esteem and success in school are placed in jeopardy. Even worse, this stigma tends to follow children through to adulthood.

In the workplace, some people who have been discriminated against have sought restitution under federal and state laws that prohibit discrimination on the basis of disability. Although these laws do not specifically prohibit weight discrimination, successful suits have been brought using the Rehabilitation Act of 1973. One such case occurred in 1993 when the court decided that obesity resulting from a metabolic dysfunction could be classified as a disability. The case of *Cook v. Rhode Island* involved an obese woman (Cook) who was denied re-employment at a state facility because the employer believed her obesity compromised her ability to do the job, even though she had been quite successful in the job previously. In addition, the employer claimed that because of Cook's greater risk for illness, she would have increased absenteeism and the state would face increased compensation claims. The court did not concur with the state facility and ruled in favor of Cook, finding that she had been discriminated against because of her obesity. However, although some individuals have been successful in seeking restitution, others have had difficulty proving discrimination. Given this difficulty, several organizations advocated the introduction of laws that would prevent this type of discrimination.

The National Association to Advance Fat Acceptance (NAAFA) and other advocacy groups are helping to change laws and thereby the lives of large people. The movement to stop continued discrimination against the overweight and obese has led to the introduction of statutory laws at local and state levels. These statutes and regulations open avenues to compensation for size discrimination. The most recent local ordinance was passed in May of 2000 when San Francisco joined Michigan, the District of Columbia, and the city of Santa Cruz, California in banning size discrimination. The city's board of supervisors added body size discrimination to its list of city laws that prohibit discrimination in other areas such as gender identity, sexual orientation, disability, place of birth, ancestry, age, and others as listed under Title VII. San Francisco's Human Rights Commission was thus enabled to investigate allegations of bias in some occupations (occupations that have fitness criteria are exempt).

San Francisco's Human Rights Commission began investigating one of its first cases under the new law in September 2001, when Jennifer Portnick, aged 38, filed a body size discrimination complaint against Jazzercise, Inc., the world's largest dance-fitness company. Though she weighed 240 pounds on a 5 feet 8 inch frame, Jennifer had been doing high-impact aerobics for 15 years and had incredible stamina. The trouble began when Jennifer's teacher, impressed by her stamina and ability, invited her to audition to be a certified Jazzercise instructor. The management at Jazzercise encouraged Jennifer to lose weight and avoid carbohydrates, noting that Jennifer needed to appear leaner than the public. Jennifer was told that "Jazzercise sells fitness" and that she should consider body sculpting (Fernandez, 2002). The case was settled in May of 2002, when Jazzercise, Inc. agreed to change its company policy, eliminating the requirement that aerobics instructors look fit. Applicants will now be evaluated based on their skill.

This case is an important victory for overweight people in San Francisco, and it is hoped that it will set a precedent for other decisions. NAAFA continues to work to educate people about the realities of obesity and discrimination. Changing attitudes and changing laws are processes that must go hand in hand.

Discussion questions

1 How are Bonnie Cook's case and Jennifer Portnick's case similar and dissimilar with regard to key points of their claims, legislation used, and employer defenses?
2 What can and should employers do to avoid discriminating against qualified overweight employees?
3 How is obesity discrimination similar to and different from other types of discrimination, such as race/ethnic or gender discrimination?
4 To what extent is obesity discrimination simply discrimination on the basis of appearance, as opposed to inferences about health or fitness? Is it fair to make judgments about employees and job applicants on the basis of appearance? Appearance-based judgments are commonplace and commonly accepted. When are they fair or unfair?

have argued that larger damage awards for age discrimination when compared with other types of discrimination may reflect the fact that aging is something everyone experiences. In other words, these damage awards may indicate that jurors see themselves as potentially suffering similar discrimination in the future. These awards also indicate that older and obese workers, and workers with disabilities, have discriminatory organizational experiences that are similar to those of other minority groups.

SHOULD THE OLD, OVERWEIGHT, OR DISABLED BE CONSIDERED MINORITY GROUPS?

Researchers have used visibility, differential power, differential and pejorative treatment (e.g., discrimination), and group awareness as determinants of whether a group may be characterized as a "minority" or non-dominant group. Visibility and differential power lead to differential treatment and discrimination, which help build group awareness and cohesion (Dworkin and Dworkin, 1999). By these standards, we believe the old, obese, and disabled should indeed be considered minority groups.

Visibility

If such defining characteristics as race/ethnicity or gender were not easily observable, categorization and development of in-groups and out-groups based on those characteristics would be more difficult (Tajfel, 1969, 1970; Tajfel and Turner, 1986). Group members must be able to recognize each other quickly and easily, as well as those who do not belong to the group. Age and obesity are easily identifiable characteristics. Despite plastic surgery, cosmetics, and hair coloring products, for most people, one's age range remains fairly obvious. Disability, however, may be easily identifiable (e.g., by use of a wheelchair), or not at all identifiable (e.g., HIV-positive).

Differential power

Dworkin and Dworkin (1999: 19) describe differential power as the relatively greater control of resources by one group compared to another. In the workplace, such things as decision-making power, and hiring, firing, and reward power, may be considered resources. It is well known that people of color and women, who occupy lower levels and fewer managerial and executive positions than others, control fewer organizational resources than Whites and males (Federal Glass Ceiling Commission, 1997). Similarly, in a study of obesity, occupational attainment, and earnings, Pagan and Davila (1997) found that most obese women worked in low-paid occupations and were largely excluded from higher levels and higher pay.

Wertlieb (1985) has described the dominant group in the workforce as White men without disabilities. We would further describe this group as including younger White men without disabilities who are not overweight. Despite this description, however, the relationship between age and power is not clear-cut. Overall, managers and other well-compensated persons in power tend to be older than non-managers (Barnum, Liden, and DiTomaso, 1995), yet research consistently shows that when hiring or promoting, decision-makers prefer younger people to older ones. Older workers are also provided with fewer opportunities for training and development and are perceived as being less promotable than younger workers (Cleveland and Shore, 1992; Lee and Clemmons, 1985).

Stigmas, stereotypes, and discrimination

The previous section discussed how persons who are older or obese, or who have a disability, generally have less power than persons without those body issues. This differential power, in some regards, reflects overt and covert stereotyping and discrimination against such persons, as evidenced by research, discrimination complaints, lawsuits, and damage awards.

Scholars have described stigma as a negative discrepancy between the actual or inferred attributes of an individual versus the expectations for typical (or "normal") individuals in that context, such that the individual is regarded as aberrant or atypical (Goffman, 1963; Stone, Stone, and Dipboye, 1992; see also Jones and Stone, 1995; Kleck and DeJong, 1983). In other words, stigmatization refers to the perception that someone is negatively different from most "normal" others. People who are obese, have disabilities, and who are older are often stigmatized when compared with those who are of normal weight or thin, who do not have disabilities, or who are young(er). We discuss stigmatization, stereotyping, and discrimination against people with these body issues in the following sections.

Ageism

"Ageism" is discrimination against persons because of their age (Kelchner, 1999). In the US, employers are prohibited from age discrimination against persons who are aged 40 and above. Further, it is illegal to prefer a person who is slightly older than 40 (for example, one who is 43) over a person who is considerably older than 40 (for example, one who is 59). Despite the legal prohibitions against age discrimination, such discrimination persists.

Various researchers have documented age bias in selection and promotion (e.g., Cleveland, Festa, and Montgomery, 1988; Morrow et al., 1990). Perry and Bourhis (1998) found that older applicants were preferred over younger applicants, particularly when jobs were more strongly "younger-typed," providing evidence of stereotyping and perceptions of job suitability based on age. In an early study involving business students and working realtors, Rosen and Jerdee (1974) found that both rated older workers lower on performance capacity and potential for development.

Ableism

"Ableism" is discrimination against persons because of their physical disabilities. The National Organization on Disability reports that people with disabilities work in jobs that are less challenging than persons without disabilities and experience other job-related discrimination. Specifically, of people working full- or part-time, 40 percent of people with disabilities and 48 percent of people without disabilities reported that their job requires them to use their full talent and abilities. Thirty-six percent of persons with disabilities reported having encountered some form of discrimination at work, varying from being denied an accommodation, interview, promotion, or job for which they were qualified, to being paid less for similar work than persons without disabilities (NOD/Harris, 2000). Johnson and Lambrinos (1985) concluded that 33–40 percent of wage differentials between persons with disabilities and those without disabilities were attributable to employment discrimination.

Researchers in various contexts (e.g., employment, education, public services, etc.) have documented considerable discrimination against people with disabilities (e.g., Borchert and Rickabaugh, 1995; Bordieri and Drehmer, 1988; Bordieri, Drehmer, and Taricone, 1990; Rush, 1998). Persons who are considered personally responsible for their disabling conditions receive little or no sympathy, and are more likely to be treated unfairly (e.g., DeJong, 1980; Stone and Colella, 1996). Bordieri and Drehmer (1988) and Bordieri, Drehmer, and Taricone (1990) reported bias against job applicants with disabilities, with persons who are believed to be responsible for their disability experiencing the most negative outcomes (cf., Borchert and Rickabaugh, 1995; Rush, 1998). In a field study of working managers, Florey and Harrison (2000) reported that persons with AIDS, partial deafness caused by playing in a rock band, or other disabilities believed by others to be self-caused, were viewed more negatively, and were less likely to receive accommodations on the job, than persons with congenital disabilities.

Obesity discrimination

Obesity discrimination is discrimination against people who are obese or overweight. As discussed earlier, there is no specific point at which people become obese or overweight, making its determination more difficult than age or physical ability. Despite this lack of specificity, being slightly overweight, extremely overweight, or obese are all generally viewed in various employment contexts as less desirable than being an average weight or thin (Allon, 1982). The former executive director of the National Association to Advance Fat Acceptance (NAAFA) has called weight discrimination "the last bastion of acceptable discrimination" (Fraser, 1994), further differentiating it from other, less readily accepted discrimination.

Persons who are overweight are generally construed as being responsible for their condition – that they lack self-control and self-discipline, and are incompetent and lazy (see Larkin and Pines, 1979; Maddox, Back, and Liederman, 1968), all negative traits in the employment context (as well as in most other contexts). These beliefs persist despite research which indicates that weight may be somewhat predefined or genetic, in some ways similar to race or gender (Angier, 1994; Rothblum et al., 1990).

In field and experimental studies, researchers have found that persons who are obese experience various types of employment discrimination (Pingitore et al., 1994; Rothblum et al., 1990). In an experiment, Bellizzi and Hasty (1998) found that sales managers were more likely to assign obese employees to telephone sales jobs than to jobs that involved face-to-face contact. Those managers were also more likely to discipline obese sales people for unethical behavior. In Jasper and Klassen's (1990) study, male participants rated obese targets more harshly and reported that they did so because of the target's weight; female participants did not rate overweight targets more harshly. Supporting findings from experimental studies, and using actual workers, Register and Williams (1990) found that young obese women (20 percent or more over their standard weight for height) earned 12 percent less than non-obese women. They found no weight effect for young men, however.

Obesity discrimination is particularly troubling in its ubiquity and the relative lack of sanctions against it. Crandall (1991: 606) noted that discrimination against the obese is "unusually pervasive across race, sex, age, and ethnic and occupational groups." In an article in *Working Woman* magazine, one woman reported that on her first day at work she was told she had "put on a lot of weight!" since her interviewed. As the director of public relations, she was constantly pressured to diet because of the "image" she presented. Despite on-the-job success, she was ultimately fired by the manager who had told her to wear dark colors and had continually scrutinized her appearance. Though she attributed the termination to her weight, she did not sue her employer (Fraser, 1994).

Group awareness

We have provided evidence that workplace discrimination against the aged, persons with disabilities, and the obese is common. Dworkin and Dworkin (1999) suggest that discrimination against non-dominant groups leads to group awareness. That is, being aware of belonging to a group that experiences differential, discriminatory treatment brings about group awareness, "we-ness," and subsequent resistance. For example, in the 1800s, women's awareness that they were unable to vote because of their sex brought about the women's suffrage movement (Lutz, 1940). For the aged, the obese, or people with disabilities, however, the differences among people within these categories limit the group awareness and solidarity that would be expected from other discernable groups that experience discrimination. Persons of all races and ethnic backgrounds, religions, and nationalities can and do have these body issues. Salience of other group memberships (e.g., being female) and other factors may make salience of membership in one of the categories of body issues less apparent or important. A recent survey of persons with disabilities shows that only 47 percent share a common identity with people with disabilities (NOD/Harris, 2000).

Another deterrent to the formation of group awareness concerns the numerous, accepted negative connotations associated with these body issues. Although most people would choose to grow old over dying young, the prevalence of hair color and cosmetic surgeons attest to people's aversion to looking their age. Similarly, "the disabled" and "the obese" are not generally viewed as categories to which most people would readily choose to belong or identify. Despite the negative connotations associated with obesity, NAAFA was formed in 1969 to help eliminate size discrimination, educate people, and empower the overweight and obese (www.naafa.org). Similarly, the American Association of Retired Persons in the US and the Gray Panthers have been successful in improving perceptions of older people (Cardinali and Gordon, 2002). The National Organization for Disability (www.nod.org) serves to unify and advocate for persons with disabilities.

WORKPLACE CONSEQUENCES AND IMPLICATIONS

We have argued that persons who are older, obese, or who have a disability experience stereotyping and discrimination similar to other minority group members. Research has indicated that some portion of the discrimination against people with these body issues can be attributed to perceived performance limitations. That is, people make assumptions that persons who are older, overweight, or disabled may not be able to perform their jobs as well as others. In previous disability research, we found that for persons with AIDS, recovering from stroke, or cerebral palsy (disabilities with very different features and causes), performance effects were the only aspect that consistently influenced acceptance (e.g., McLaughlin, Bell, and Stringer, in press). That is, regardless of the type or cause of a potential co-worker's disability, when the disability was viewed as limiting the co-worker's ability to perform the job, attitudes toward the co-worker were more negative than when the disability was believed to have no performance implications.

Whenever these beliefs about performance implications are unfounded, we recommend interventions to change and educate other workers about abilities, attendance, and performance of diverse workers (McLaughlin et al., in press). On the other hand, there are some jobs that should not or cannot be performed by some people who are aged, obese, or have certain disabilities. For example, although it is generally illegal to discriminate against people who are over age 40, mandatory retirement of pilots and certain vehicle drivers, and age limitations on new hires for certain public safety positions (e.g., police officers), are not illegal. Similarly, there are some jobs that cannot be performed by people who are legally blind or who are so overweight they are unable to move quickly (e.g., flight attendants). It is important to note that these exclusions are not due to simple discrimination against people who are older, overweight, or who have disabilities. On the contrary, they are because of real performance limitations due to these body issues. For employers and decision-makers, however, it is critical to ensure that performance limitations are real rather than imaginary or based on stereotypes, and to minimize misperceptions among co-workers.

Workers should be made aware that, for most jobs, the *lack* of a consistent relationship between age and job performance is well documented. In their meta-analysis of two decades of age–performance research, McEvoy and Cascio (1989) found no consistent relationships between age and performance across jobs (professional v. non-professional). Similarly, Crow (1993) has argued that persons with disabilities perform similarly to those without disabilities.

Suggestions for organizations

Results of research on social psychological processes underlying treatment of persons who are obese, older, or who have disabilities have broad implications for practice given the large (and growing) numbers of people who may be included in those categories. Simply having persons who are disabled, obese, or older working with other employees on cooperative tasks, in positions of equal status, may serve to reduce stigma (Greig and Bell, 2000). A straightforward way to promote fair treatment of persons in these groups is to provide information aimed at reducing stigmas and stereotypes. For example, as part of their regular training, employees could learn about research that establishes no relationship between age and performance. Information from medical research showing that obesity is often beyond an individual's control and that it does not necessarily correspond with functional impairments should also be presented. Candid presentation of information about disabilities (e.g., contagion, functional limitations imposed, and onset controllability) may help to reduce disability stigma (see Schneider and Anderson, 1980, for a summary of studies using this approach). Stigma reduction coupled with knowledge of legal protections may improve acceptance and treatment of persons with disabilities or those who are older or obese. These interventions could be modeled on successful interventions designed to improve employee attitudes toward ethnic, racial, and gender diversity (e.g., Gilbert and Stead, 1999; Wentling and Palma-Rivas, 1998).

In addition to education and training, as with other unacceptable discrimination (such as sexual harassment), it is important for organizations to have clear policies and swift punishment as deterrents. Although age and disability discrimination are clearly illegal, because obesity discrimination is not illegal in most cases, it is important for organizations to make clear that any form of non-job related discrimination will not be tolerated. We believe that the positive implications for valuing cultural diversity suggested by Cox and Blake (1991) – resource acquisition, marketing, creativity, and cost – are also relevant to persons who are aged, obese, or who have disabilities. The millions of people who fall into such categories will see inclusive organizations as ones to patronize and ones in which to work.

Suggestions for researchers

Because being an older employee can co-occur with obesity and disability, the impact of multiple category membership is a critical area for future research. Specifically, research is needed on self-perceptions and self-presentational concerns for persons who are in multiple groups, and on the joint influences of multiple group membership on acceptance and treatment in organizations. As persons who are obese, older, or who have a disability may also be members of an ethnic or racial minority group, and/or female, investigation of the work-related effects and consequences of multiple category membership is increasingly important. In addition, as the US workforce grows more diverse in various ways, it is important for researchers to broaden their conceptualization and study of diversity.

Note

1 Portions of this chapter were presented at the 2002 Academy of Management meetings in Denver, Colorado.

DIVERSITY AND SEXUAL ORIENTATION: INCLUDING AND VALUING SEXUAL MINORITIES IN THE WORKPLACE

Micah E. Lubensky, Sarah L. Holland,
Carolyn Wiethoff, and Faye J. Crosby

This chapter focuses on sexual orientation. It briefly articulates some basic concepts. It documents changes in attitudes toward and treatment of gays, lesbians, and bisexuals, both among the American public at large and at the workplace. It focuses on two corporations that are models for creation of gay-friendly workplaces – Eastman Kodak and IBM – and on one organization, the US Army, which serves as a contrast. The chapter concludes by considering some issues that require attention from practitioners and scholars alike.

It is difficult to estimate how many people in the United States are gay, lesbian, or bisexual (GLB). Although some people place the figure as low as 2 percent (Michael et al., 1994), most authorities agree that the percentage is higher. Calculations vary from 4 to 17 percent of the population (Gonsiorek and Weinrich, 1991), putting the number somewhere between 11 and 48 million Americans. At a minimum, 1 out of every 25 employed persons is gay, lesbian, or bisexual. At a maximum, the ratio is 1 in 6.

Although we can only hazard guesses about the number of Americans who are GLB, we do have more certainty that both attitudes and practices concerning sexual orientation are undergoing dramatic change. Throughout the business community, the stigma attached to minority sexual orientations is giving way to tolerance. In many organizations mere tolerance has evolved into genuine inclusiveness for GLB employees.

Sexual orientation is the focus of this chapter.[1] After briefly articulating some basic concepts, we document recent changes in attitudes toward and treatment of GLB individuals, both among the American public at large and in the workplace. We then take an in-depth look at how and why some companies implement change, while other organizations resist it. We focus on two corporations that are models for the creation of gay-friendly workplaces, and one organization – the US Army – that is not. We conclude by considering some issues that require attention for practitioners and scholars alike.

BASIC CONCEPTS

The scientific measurement of same-sex orientation began with the work of Kinsey and his associates in the late 1940s (Kinsey, Pomeroy, and Martin, 1948; Kinsey, Pomeroy, Martin, and Gebhard, 1953). At that time, homosexuality was classified as a mental disorder, and most social scientists who paid attention to the issue at all were engaged in the development of treatments to change into heterosexuals those who expressed gay or lesbian feelings (Silverstein, 1991). However, Kinsey and his colleagues took a broader view of sexual behavior. They created a 7-point continuum to describe sexual behavior, with 0 representing exclusively hetero-sexual behavior, 3 depicting more or less equally bisexual behavior, and 6 denoting exclusively homosexual behavior. This team of researchers challenged the dichotomous, either/or view of sexual orientation, paving the way for increased study of the nuances of same-sex behaviors.

Since the days of Kinsey, many social scientists have studied sexual orientation. Scholars now readily admit that sexual orientation comprises many elements, including self-image, fantasies, attractions, and behavior. The various elements may not always work in concert. For example, an individual who is equally attracted to men and women and has fantasies about both men and women may be exclusively heterosexual in behavior or exclusively homosexual. Behavioral choices may be constrained by many factors, including the availability of partners, adherence to a monogamous ideal, and fear of being stigmatized. The lack of absolute concordance between the different elements of sexuality is probably one of the reasons why precise estimates of the number of GLB persons are so hard to develop. The malleability of sexuality may be another reason. Some people, for example, come to the realization that they are GLB late in their lives (Gonsiorek and Rudolph, 1991). Other people form affectionate and/or erotic attachments to individuals of the other sex after years of same-sex orientation. For the majority of individuals who are not at either of the extreme ends of Kinsey's scale, it may make sense to think in terms of sexual orientation as something with multiple facets that is influenced by social context. Of course, some people are at the ends of the continuum. For them, sexual orientation is quite narrowly prescribed, and for them it makes little sense to speak in terms of "sexual preference."

Over time, most psychological experts have come to accept same-gender sexual orientations as a normal and healthy variant of sexual behavior. Their investigations have prompted some changes in other societal groups as well. In the next section, we explore current attitudes and behaviors toward the GLB community held by the population in general and corporate America in particular.

CHANGES IN ATTITUDES AND BEHAVIOR

Ours is an era of rapid but uneven change concerning issues of sexual orientation. As noted above, change has been visible in the positions of psychologists who are experts on human behavior. In this section we examine other arenas in which changes in attitudes toward the GLB community have been evident. Although change has occurred slowly and consistently among average Americans, discontinuous and dramatic change has taken place in some sectors of corporate America.

Attitudes and behavior in the general population

Only recently has the general population been surveyed for attitudes towards GLB individuals. The larger national polling organizations started to inquire about an increasing number of relevant GLB issues over the past 25 years. Within these two and a half decades, attitudes have noticeably changed for the better.

For example, the general population has steadily come to like GLB individuals more as a group, since the National Election Survey (NES) started to inquire in 1988 (Yang, 2001). The Gallup Poll finds that a GLB lifestyle has accordingly become more accepted over time. For the first time since Gallup started collecting the data in 1977, more than half of the general population feels that homosexual relations between consenting adults should be legal (Newport, 2001). With these improvements in attitudes about GLB people in general, attitudes about specific rights and protections have also seen marked changes. Gallup, NES, and the Harris Poll have researched attitudes about issues such as same-sex couples adopting children, GLB people serving openly in the military, and protection from job discrimination (Newport, 2001; Taylor, 2001; Yang, 2001). Their results indicate a trend for the general population's increased acceptance and inclusion of GLB members in society. Given that attitudes about homosexuality and GLB people are improving, anti-GLB attitudes and practices risk disapproval and increased pressure from sympathetic individuals and/or organizations (e.g., Human Rights Campaign, 2001a; see also Herek, 1990; Sweeney, 2001).

One behavioral indicator of the change in attitudes is the growth in the number of groups that advocate on behalf of GLB persons. One such organization is the Human Rights Campaign (HRC), founded in 1980 to give national voice to GLB issues. HRC lobbies Congress, mobilizes grassroots political activity, invests in election campaigns, and works to increase public understanding through education and communication. The increased strength of the HRC and other organizations that promote acceptance of GLB people has, of course, erased neither prejudicial feelings and thoughts nor the discriminatory behavior that results from prejudice. The Gallup Poll reports that 48 percent of Americans still disapprove of same-sex relations (Newport, 2001), although homosexual males elicit more disapprobation than do lesbians (Kite and Deaux, 1986).

Attitudes about homosexuality, heterosexuality, or indeed any form of sexuality, have increasingly interested social scientists. George Weinberg (1972: 4) coined the term "homophobia" to describe "the dread of being in close quarters with homosexuals." Some scholars have opined that homophobia springs from a fear of one's own homoerotic impulses or tendencies. It seems quite likely that – whether or not they worry about being gay – people who are uncomfortable with the issue of homosexuality are often uncomfortable with sexuality in general (Agnew et al., 1993).

Recently researchers have shifted away from an exclusive focus on homophobia to examine broader explanations for anti-GLB prejudice. Perhaps the most important theorist on the topic is Gregory Herek (1987, 1988, 1990, 1994, 2000). Herek (1987) notes that people often maintain prejudicial attitudes because of the psychological functions that those attitudes serve. For example, anti-GLB attitudes can serve an ego-defensive function, wherein people who are defensive about their own sexual orientation reject GLB people because they challenge the traditional heterosexual social structure. Homophobic attitudes are most likely to serve an ego-defensive function. Similarly, prejudicial attitudes toward GLB people can serve to affirm someone's personal or social values. This "value-expressive" function occurs when people reject GLBs in the name of their religious or social beliefs. Additionally, negative attitudes toward GLBs can simply be based on stereotypes, which help people make sense of the world by categorizing their past experiences. In this case, people are likely to change their prejudicial attitudes when they have contact with GLB people who challenge their previous beliefs (Bowen and Bourgeois, 2001). On the other hand, heterosexuals whose prejudicial attitudes serve value-expressive or ego-defensive functions are less likely to modify their anti-gay attitudes simply on the basis of favorable contacts with those in the GLB community (Nelson and Kreiger, 1997). As this analysis suggests, not all heterosexuals are prejudiced against GLB people. However, this functional analysis does help us identify some groups of people who are most likely to maintain negative attitudes toward the GLB community. For example, heterosexuals who strongly identify with traditional gender roles often see GLB people as a threat to traditional roles and develop negative attitudes as an ego-defensive move (Harry, 1995; Heaven and Oxman, 1999; Jome and Tokar, 1998; Kite and Whitley, 1998; Krulewitz and Nash, 1980; MacDonald et al., 1973; Newman, 1989; Weinberger and Millham, 1979; Whitley, 1987, 1999). Research also suggests that people with a strong conservative religious orientation are typically opposed to homosexuality on religious/biblical grounds (Hunter, 1991). People with fundamentalist Christian religious orientations, for example, report more prejudicial attitudes toward gays and lesbians than do less conservative or non-religious people (Kirkpatrick, 1993; McFarland, 1989). Numerous studies have demonstrated that membership in a traditionally conservative religion is associated with negative attitudes toward lesbians and gays (Agnew et al., 1993; Herek, 1994; Herek and Capitanio, 1995), as is frequent attendance at religious services affiliated with conservative religions (Fisher et al., 1994; Seltzer, 1992). Hunsberger (1996) found similar negative attitudes toward gays and lesbians in the Muslim and Hindu faiths. Rather than being related to specific religious tenets or beliefs, the tendency for conservative believers to reject homosexuality may be a reflection of the authoritarian tendencies of religious fundamentalists (Altemeyer, 1996; Hunsberger et al., 1996). In any event, because negative attitudes toward GLB people serve a value-expressive function for people with conservative religious orientations, these attitudes are not as likely to change.

Controlled laboratory studies have documented connections between prejudicial attitudes and discriminatory behavior. Haddock and Zanna (1998) found that individuals who are prejudiced against GLBs are likely to discriminate against them, largely because they believe that GLBs do not share their personal values (Pilkington and Lydon, 1997). In the same vein, laboratory studies found that heterosexuals sought to put more spatial distance between themselves and a gay man, than from a "straight" (non-homosexual) man, and that they treated gays more negatively than non-gays during the course of experiments (Kite and Deaux, 1986; Morin and Garfinkle, 1978). Participants in other studies have been seen to speak more rapidly to confederates believed to be gay (Cuenot and Fugita, 1982), to label gay men as less preferred partners in future experiments (Karr, 1978), and to offer less help to an individual wearing a pro-gay t-shirt than to one with a plain t-shirt (Gray, Russell, and Blockley, 1991).

Outside the controlled laboratory, too, research has shown the persistence of discrimination against sexual minorities. Nine out of ten gay men and lesbians report being victims of verbal abuse or threats, and more than one in five has been physically assaulted because of their sexual orientation (Elliott, 2000; Herek, 1989). In fact, gay men and lesbians are more likely to be victims of hate crimes in the United States than are members of any other social group (Nelson and Krieger, 1997). Where they exist, laws and company policies prohibiting discrimination against GLBs do improve the situation (Pratt, 1998). On May 28, 1998, President Clinton signed Executive Order 13087 prohibiting discrimination on the basis of sexual orientation in the federal government. By 2002 twelve states and a number of cities and counties had passed ordinances banning sexual orientation discrimination in housing, employment, and other forums. It is estimated that only 20 percent of GLB Americans live in areas that afford this protection (Button, Rienzo, and Wald, 1997). Discrimination against GLB people – or even those who are merely believed to be GLB – is still legal in many places (Badgett, 1996; Button, Rienzo, and Wald, 1997; Elliott, 2000; Kirby, 2000).

Attitudes and behavior in corporate America

Although relatively little research has examined the nature and effects of discrimination toward gay men and lesbians in the workplace (Croteau, 1996, 1999), the research that has been done shows that GLB individuals suffer discrimination at work. Various media sources indicate that discrimination still takes place with some regularity (e.g., Human Rights Campaign, 2001b; Lenihan, 1998; Taylor, 1997). Surveys of GLB employees reveal that more than two-thirds who disclosed their sexual orientations at work experienced discrimination on the job (Croteau, 1996; Croteau and Von Destinon, 1994; Crow, Fok, and Hartman, 1995; Welch, 1996), sometimes including termination of employment. Results from other studies suggest that discrimination has a harmful effect on the work attitudes and career trajectories of gay men and lesbians (Friskopp and Silverstein, 1996; Hall, 1986) and also that it negatively affects their productivity at work (Day and Schoenrade, 1997; Powers, 1996; Stangor, Carr, and Kiang, 1998). Other studies have documented the stress and resultant health hazards GLB people experience as a result of the discrimination they encounter both on and off the job (e.g., Bosanko, 1995; O'Hanlan et al., 1996). Moreover, many gay male workers earn significantly less than equally situated heterosexual male counterparts, although this is not necessarily the case for lesbian workers (Badgett, 1996; Ellis and Riggle, 1996). Other studies confirm that gay men have a high risk of discrimination during the hiring process (Crow, Fok, and Hartman, 1995).

Recognizing both the prevalence and the harms of discrimination toward GLB workers, a growing number of organizations provide resources for self-identified GLB employees and their employers. The HRC Foundation's WorkNet provides a national source of information on laws and policies surrounding sexual orientation and gender identity in the workplace. WorkNet collects, analyzes, and disseminates information to assist employees and employers in implementing policies and procedures aimed at treating GLB workers equally. It publishes an annual State of the Workplace report available to the public at http://www.hrc.org/worknet.

Another respected organization, the Visibility Project, argues that nothing demonstrates a company's commitment to diversity more convincingly than a workplace where that diversity is apparent. Diversity can be gauged by noticing the employees who join, stay in, and advance within the organization and by noticing who is visible, welcome, and valued. The Visibility Project helps corporations devise employment policies and procedures and develop marketing strategies that are gay-inclusive, and thereby add to the diversity of organizations. Their website (www.visibilityproject.org) can be accessed for further information about the Visibility Project.

In addition to organizations that work directly with companies to develop GLB-friendly cultures, other groups focus their efforts on GLB workers. For example, Out and Equal Workplace Advocates (O & E) provides support and advocacy to the GLB community through diversity training and networking. O & E's Workplace Summit has become the preeminent GLB-related conference for senior human resource professionals, and is held annually in major cities around the US. A highlight of the summit is the presentation of the Out and Equal workplace awards, dubbed the "Outies." Created both to recognize and encourage progress and to provide a platform for effective business practices, the Outies are offered to individuals and companies in a number of categories. The awards program has already become highly competitive. Such companies as Agilent, American Express, Bank One, Booz-Allen Hamilton, Coca-Cola, Disney, IBM, Kodak, Motorola, NCR, Raytheon, SBC, SC Johnson, Shell Oil, and Xerox vied for the 2001 awards. The winning initiatives become "best practices," and word of their success – a byproduct of the awards process – inspires competition and emulation, accelerating corporate change.

What do WorkNet, the Visibility Project, O & E, and similar organizations look for in a GLB-inclusive workplace? Essentially, they track three indicators of inclusiveness. The first is an explicit policy of non-discrimination on the basis of sexual orientation. Second is the existence of health and other benefits for same-sex domestic partners. Third is the presence of support and networking groups for GLB employees, often referred to as affinity groups.

Progress in all three of these areas has been substantial in the last two decades, although there is significantly more work to be done. At the time of writing, 59 percent of Fortune 500 companies include sexual orientation in their non-discrimination policies, a substantial increase from the two companies that articulated non-discrimination policies when the HRC was founded in 1980. Moreover, although none of the Fortune 500 companies offered domestic partner benefits 20 years ago, 30 percent have these programs now. Still, there is no widespread corporate support for GLB affinity groups. According to the Visibility Project, only about 10 percent of companies with written non-discrimination policies also have active affinity groups. On the more positive side is the fact that many large employers, like American Airlines and Microsoft, now list their GLB employee affinity groups on their corporate websites.

No matter how passionately gay rights advocates feel about the moral imperative for social change, businesses become more gay-friendly only when they embrace the business case for diversity in terms of sexual orientation. The business community recognizes several reasons why it should be gay-friendly. Some issues arise beyond the organization's walls, such as how the company is viewed by consumers in the GLB community. Other reasons crop up within the organization, such as how greater inclusiveness of GLB workers can benefit the company's productivity.

Some organizations may seek to avoid doing harm to gays, lesbians, and bisexuals out of concern for the adverse results of discrimination. Companies that are seen to routinely discriminate against GLB workers can run the risk of lawsuits (where they are allowed; e.g., Lenihan, 1998; Welch, 1996). In certain cases, they may even run the risk of a large-scale boycott by members of the GLB community and their sympathizers (e.g., Romano, 1993).

A more common and more compelling reason for GLB-friendly policies is that the GLB community is ripe for product marketing. Although the statistics used to make this argument are the subject of some debate (Badgett, 1998), many companies share a widespread belief in the relative affluence of GLB individuals and hence view GLB consumers as a virtually untapped gold mine (Fargo, 1999). Several corporations conclude that because lesbians and gay men have been neglected for so long (Levin, 1993), even modest attempts at marketing to the community in a positive light could generate sales and secure brand loyalty (Chow, 1998; Kiley, 1996; Seal, 1995; Snowdon, 1996).

Of course, there is a negative side to marketing to the community. The producers of any product, including dangerous ones, can try this approach and hope for added sales. For example, recent research on the internal marketing documents of the Philip Morris Company found that their marketers were taking large steps to increase the Marlboro Man's appeal to gay men. This ranged from making him more of a homoerotic image, to offering more ways of identifying with this stereotypically masculine icon (Engardio, 2000). Given that gays and lesbians have been found to smoke almost twice as much as their heterosexual counterparts (see Engardio, 2001a), Philip Morris's marketing could be just another way that the tobacco industry hopes to maintain and expand its appeal in the GLB community. Since tobacco is such a deadly and addictive drug (American Lung Association, 2002), attempts to increase market outreach to the GLB community should be greeted with caution.

Besides the more externally focused reasons, companies might also have intra-organizational reasons for appearing gay-friendly. These intra-organizational reasons focus on how the organization is best served, and perhaps even improved, with positive treatment of GLB workers. The bulk of this advice derives from two complementary rationales. The first centers on the current global economy and an expanded stage for business relations. Businesses face new challenges for success in today's larger market, and many believe that full inclusion of GLB employees adds to their overall diversity. They remind us that employee diversity benefits a company in several ways, such as increasing problem solving capacity and better enabling a company to confront the challenges of competitive markets (e.g., Taylor, 1997).

The complementary rationale considers GLB individuals who are already employed. To keep employees enthusiastic and hard-working, companies should strive to make everyone feel respected, accepted, and justly treated (Klara, 2000; Hernandez, 1996). Survey research implies that GLB employees are more comfortable at their jobs and less likely to leave when they feel accepted regardless of their sexual orientation (Day and Schoenrade, 1997, 2000). An accepting work environment simply preserves employee morale, which keeps employees productive. Gay-friendly policies may also have a beneficial effect on heterosexual employees. Knowing that the employer judges employees on the basis of their work, and not on the basis of factors irrelevant to work, is reassuring for many who see themselves as fitting only imperfectly the ideal prototype. A workplace that is tolerant on one dimension may be believed to be tolerant on many dimensions.

LOOKING IN DEPTH: THREE CASE STUDIES

To understand better how workplace policies are implemented in today's organizations, and the effects that these programs have, we will next turn our attention to three specific organizations that handle GLB-related challenges in different ways. The experiences of Eastman Kodak, IBM, and the United States military are enlightening examples of the treatment of GLB workers in America.

Eastman Kodak

A look at Eastman Kodak, a recent Outie winner, provides insight into how one company created a climate for GLB inclusiveness. The mid-1990s was a time of enormous market-driven change at Eastman Kodak. The board of directors introduced into a paternalistic and hierarchical corporate culture a dynamic CEO with a mandate to ready Kodak for the challenges of the digital age. The new CEO wasted no time in communicating his personal commitment to diversity. At Kodak, every aspect of business life would be conducted according to five core values: respect for the dignity of the individual, integrity, trust, credibility, and continuous improvement and personal renewal.

Although Kodak had always espoused institutional values, as with most American corporations they existed largely on paper. Kodak's new CEO insisted that these values achieve corporate prominence. They were stressed at every meeting and reinforced in every speech: Kodak employees were expected to live by them. Consequently, Kodak's longstanding non-discrimination policy, which included sexual orientation, began to mean more than a prohibition on firing employees for being GLB. Instead, these values provided a platform for Kodak's fledgling group of GLB employees.

Although Kodak was hardly the first major corporation to sanction a GLB affinity group – that honor goes to AT&T (1987) and then Microsoft (1991) – the history of its group is illustrative. In 1992, Kodak's Human Resource Diversity Initiative program was developing a workshop focusing on non-traditional families, when two gay employees asked to represent their non-traditional families in the discussion. As the initiative moved forward, officials sought other GLBs at Kodak who might also benefit from involvement in their activities. Formal discussions about forming a GLB affinity group gained further ground with the discovery of an informal support group focusing on the future of gay men and lesbians at Kodak. The two groups joined forces under the banner of the Lambda

Network at Kodak. By the end of 1992, Lambda was holding monthly meetings and had established mission and vision statements and by-laws.

By 1995 the Lambda Network had built its membership base, established working committees, developed support and education strategies, and had an official structured directorate. However, although the CEO's widely embraced core values supported the kind of diversity Lambda represented, membership was still small and the highest-ranking Lambda leaders were only middle managers.

In late 1995 Lambda held its first Education Event with Management, an occasion that would have lasting impact on Kodak's corporate climate for gay men and lesbians. Unknown to most of the workforce, the CEO's newly placed chief of staff was a lesbian. This senior executive, a fast-tracker at Kodak for a decade, was reasonably visible in the local gay community but had not made sexual orientation an issue at work. As she put it, "I didn't know there was another way to be. It was like being born in prison and never knowing what it's like on the outside." This executive's attendance at the Lambda Education Event galvanized her into action: she decided to come out.

Now there was a high-ranking executive, a recognized member of the senior management team, who was able to voice GLB issues at the highest level of Kodak. The impact on the Lambda Network was notable: the organization that began with only a handful of members grew in size and influence and began attracting non-GLB allies and sponsors at various levels of management. These allies provided critical visibility as well as monetary and moral support to the fledgling organization.

In subsequent years the Lambda Network developed tools for outreach to Kodak's employees. In addition to the Education Event with Management – an annual occurrence now attended by hundreds of Kodak employees – Lambda has partnered with other Kodak constituencies to create training methods and materials. None has been more successful than the "Can We Talk" workshop developed in 1996. Designed as an experiential learning opportunity, this workshop enables participants to listen to thoughts and concerns on the subject of sexual orientation and related issues affecting the workplace. Because Can We Talk is offered offsite and outside of regular working hours, it provides the opportunity to ask questions and have conversations about sexual orientation that are sometimes difficult to initiate in the work environment.

Can We Talk uses a format commonly known as a "fish bowl." At the beginning of the workshop, participants self-identify into gay or non-gay groups. The groups take turns listening to each other's intragroup dialogues about sexual-orientation related occurrences at work. The session begins with the gay group responding to a facilitator's questions. Sitting in an outer circle, the non-gay group listens to the gay group's discussion. A dinner break follows, during which all participants are encouraged to ask questions and share information or concerns with each other. After the dinner break, the groups switch roles and the non-gay group moves into the inner circle and responds to the facilitator's questions. At the conclusion of the workshop, the entire group discusses the experience together.

Can We Talk has dual objectives. The gay group experiences the importance of discussing GLB issues with non-gay people and can develop comfort and confidence while doing so. The non-gay group can examine personal feelings and perceptions toward GLB people and begin to learn how to talk about gay issues.

Today, the Lambda Network describes itself as a diverse group of Eastman Kodak employees and retirees who work to maintain a supportive work environment for all individuals. Their goals include increasing visibility of GLB employees to promote their inclusion in the organization, educating and sensitizing managers and employees about GLB issues, creating and expanding safe and open workplaces for GLB employees, and establishing helpful external contacts and internal networks that add value to both employees and the corporation as a whole.

In conjunction with other employee networks, Lambda contributes to Kodak's image as a high quality employer as well as to the company's overall business success. Over time, Lambda has helped Kodak meet the demands of a diverse marketplace by including people from all facets of that marketplace who understand its cultural and economic dimensions and know how to succeed there. Lambda's very existence prompts Kodak to think differently about how the company orients itself to a world of customers, which in turn makes Kodak a stronger and more valuable company.

IBM

The drive for business success and the image of a high quality employer have also motivated IBM to become an exemplary gay-friendly workplace. IBM's achievement on behalf of GLB workers is first and foremost a story about business. This company's decision was driven by business issues: market share, customer satisfaction, shareholder value, and winning the war for talent. Additionally, IBM's transformation into a GLB-friendly workplace demonstrates how an organizational commitment to inclusion, a mandate to maximize market potential, and a group of dedicated individuals can create a new corporate landscape. The IBM story also demonstrates the importance of top-down support for diversity initiatives.

IBM was justifiably proud of its longstanding commitment to corporate inclusion. The company that promoted its first female vice president in 1944 and hired its first African-American salesman in 1946 became, in 1984, the first major company to add sexual orientation to its US non-discrimination policy. In this open environment, some GLB employees began to risk being visible in the workplace; by the early 1990s, informal GLB networking was evident in IBM locations across North America.

However, it was not until 1994 that a new diversity initiative changed the way IBM did business. As in Kodak, the initiative was instigated by a powerful new

CEO. This CEO drew inspiration and direction from the dynamic Vice President of Global Workforce Diversity, whose long and illustrious tenure at IBM was itself a testimony to innovation and inclusion. The new CEO reasoned: "In order to serve markets, we have to understand them, reflect their diversity and build a workplace in which every individual knows their opportunity to contribute is gated only by the quality of their ideas and job performance, and the integrity of their work" (IBM, 2000). He also recognized that his employees – IBM's human resources – were a critical component in achieving that goal.

To fulfill his diversity mandate, the CEO commissioned eight executive task forces, including one for gay and lesbian workers. Their charge was to consider and respond to three key questions:

1 What will it take for your constituency to feel welcome and valued at IBM?
2 What needs to change at IBM to increase your productivity?
3 How can IBM gain market share with your identity group?

Although some task forces achieved quick and prominent success with their recommendations, it was a slow start for GLB workers at IBM. Service on the GLB task force required a level of visibility beyond the comfort level of many who would ultimately benefit from its efforts. There were simply insufficient numbers of executives who were openly GLB to perform the task force's roles. Consequently, the organizers decided to solicit members from the next lowest level of management. The move proved beneficial for the GLB constituency, since it tapped into employees who were already active in the unofficial network that would eventually become IBM's successful GLB affinity group. At the same time, the Vice President for Global Diversity persuaded a talented executive engineer to serve as co-chair of the task force, placing her as the first "out" lesbian in IBM's senior ranks.

What the vice president likely did not know when he convinced this executive to broaden her visibility at IBM is that the new co-chair agreed to serve, in part, due to enlightened self-interest. She had a same-sex partner without health insurance. As a couple, they would benefit greatly from domestic partner benefits –not yet offered at IBM. Indeed, within a year of the task force's start-up, IBM offered US employees same-sex domestic partner benefits. At the same time, cultural change was occurring from the bottom up. IBM's GLB employee group adopted the name "EAGLE" (Employee Alliance for Gay and Lesbian Equality) and secured IBM's support for the National Gay and Lesbian Business and Consumer Exposition, the first of myriad organizations, causes, and events that IBM sponsors on behalf of its GLB employees. By 1999, IBM's visible support of the GLB community had earned much acclaim. The company received the HRC Corporate Citizens and Corporate Courage Awards, the Parents and Friends of Lesbians and Gays (PFLAG) Flag Bearer Award, and was widely recognized as a "top company" for GLB employees. Today, the company offers additional benefits to domestic partners, including bereavement leave, domestic and international relocation benefits, and time off when entering a domestic partnership. IBM continues to provide active support to a variety of GLB community organizations and maintains a corporate intranet site with mentoring information, GLB executive biographies, marketplace recognition, and a calendar of GLB-related events. Perhaps more important, IBM has actively tracked and encouraged GLB executives. The number of high-ranking GLB managers at IBM has increased from 4 in 1998 to 12 in 2001.

This inclusion has translated into significant marketplace initiatives. IBM currently has an LGBT (Lesbian, Gay, Bisexual, Transgender) Sales and Talent Team, an industry first in business-to-business marketing. Their goal is to drive attributable revenue through a network of openly gay and lesbian decision-makers and influencers in global organizations and to recruit, retain, and motivate the world's best GLB talent. The team's director, herself an out lesbian, is within two reporting levels of the CEO and deals with top management on a regular basis.

10.1 *Ted Childs*

"Frankly, I don't know one company that dislikes diversity more than it loves money."[2]

This is the bottom line for Ted Childs. Leader, motivator, negotiator, and Vice President of Workforce Diversity at IBM Corporation, Ted Childs is passionate about employee diversity. With the savvy of a lifelong activist and the clout of his executive position, Childs brilliantly articulates the business case for inclusion and sets the standard for non-gay allies in corporate America.

In 1994, IBM's CEO Lou Gerstner instituted a corporate mandate to "build a workplace in which every individual knows their opportunity to contribute is gated only by the quality of their ideas and job performance, and [by] the integrity of their work."[3] Gerstner turned to Ted Childs to fulfill the mandate. Given IBM's economic woes at the time, the CEO believed that Childs understood how to make this accomplishment happen, and how it would be critical for IBM's global success.

If IBM wanted to prosper, Childs advised that the corporation should establish a work environment in which all employees felt welcome and valued. Gerstner therefore called for the creation of the Work Force Diversity Executive Task Forces, to represent IBM's key employee groups. Rounding up the "usual suspects" for IBM meant groups for women, African Americans, Latinos, and Asian Americans. Childs seized the opportunity to include people with disabilities, White men, and gays and lesbians.

His rationale was clear and principled: "We should not allow ourselves to be in a state of denial. We can't say that a group of people that legitimately exists really isn't there. You can't be a workforce of more than 300,000 people and feel that you've got some people who aren't IBM employees . . . And when you start down that road, you are endorsing unfair treatment . . . You cannot talk 'inclusive' and exclude any group of people."[4] As a result, gays and lesbians were an integral part of IBM's sweeping diversity initiative from the beginning.

In the mid-1990s, gays and lesbians were still largely invisible in the general workforce. They were not used to being included in the diversity conversation because they did not have the political influence of other, more visible minority groups. In addition, visibility was often risky because there was only limited legislation to protect them from potential anti-gay discrimination. So why was Ted Childs, a non-gay African-American man, willing to make a place for them at the corporate table? He traces the evolution of his gay-inclusive values to an IBM Social Service Leave in the early 1980s.

During his leave, Childs served as executive assistant to Benjamin Hooks, executive director of the NAACP. While in the position, he observed that the gay and lesbian community supported civil rights leaders of other groups, and marched side by side with Blacks and with women in their respective demonstrations. As far as Childs could tell, gay and lesbian activists identified with the justice content of the particular social struggles. Yet he also believed that these activists doubted their ability to win their own civil rights struggle and receive fair treatment in society. The asymmetry of these activists' situation thus inspired and influenced Ted Childs's attitudes and values.

However, it would take another ten years before gay and lesbian issues were talked about more openly. When the issue of sexual orientation began to gain importance as a business topic, it was discussed in the same manner as race, gender, religion, age, and disability. Ted Childs grasped the business implications and his gay-inclusive response has been emphatic: "The collective goal of business leaders today should be to ensure that our companies look like our customers, and that we leverage our differences to maximize America's competitive economic strength."[5]

Ted Childs has seen IBM's gay and lesbian employees, and the increasingly visible gay and lesbian consumer market, as valuable components of that competitive advantage. In the years since the CEO's diversity mandate, IBM has led the country, both in creating a gay-friendly workplace and in launching a successful campaign to attract the gay and lesbian market. The corporation consistently appears on the "Best" lists for gay and lesbian employees and received the 2001 Outie Award for Workplace Excellence from Out and Equal Workplace Advocates. In 2001, IBM also established a revenue-generating LGBT (Lesbian, Gay, Bisexual, Transgender) Sales and Talent Team, an industry first in business-to-business marketing.

Through his inspired diversity leadership, Ted Childs has enabled IBM to gain an edge in the global marketplace. By working tirelessly for an inclusive workplace, he has helped his employer become one of America's most gay-friendly companies. Childs champions diversity in all of its forms at IBM. As a result, he reminds IBM that "workforce diversity is the bridge between the workplace and the marketplace, and as such, victory with the customer begins with winning in the workplace."[6]

Discussion questions

1 Ted Childs values diversity, and his broad definition of diversity includes many demographic groups beyond the "usual suspects." Aside from making IBM's employees look even more like their broad customer base, in which other ways might the intentional inclusion of LGB employees be of benefit to a corporation?
2 Think of at least ten common human resources policies that might discriminate against LGB employees. In which ways could those policies be altered, in order to illustrate a corporation's commitment to the equal inclusion of LGB employees?
3 What are five additional, tangible ways in which a corporation can make its social atmosphere openly welcoming and inclusive to LGB employees?

The US military

In stark contrast to Eastman Kodak and IBM, the US military has long rejected GLB service members. The Army expelled a gay lieutenant as early as 1778 (Locke, 2001). Intolerance for homosexuality became an official policy for the armed forces during World War II, even though the policy was not always strictly enforced (University of California, Santa Barbara, Center for Study of Sexual Minorities in the Military, 2001). Nonetheless, annual statistics can be found for discharges due to "homosexual conduct" since the original policy was enacted (e.g., Garamone, 2000; Office of the Under Secretary of Defense, 1998).

The armed forces' rejection of GLB service members has been in the media spotlight since 1993, when President Clinton tried to create a way for GLB people to serve in the military with lower risk of expulsion. After a controversial and much contested series of exchanges with Congress and the Pentagon (see Kifner, 2000), Clinton signed Section 654 of the National Defense Authorization Act sanctioning the policy popularly known as "Don't Ask, Don't Tell." The "Don't Ask, Don't Tell" policy creates a large problem for GLB people in the military. According to the policy, service members are to be discharged for partnering people of the same gender, stating that they are gay or bisexual, or performing homosexual acts (a phrase that can mean anything from sexual encounters to holding hands; Department of Defense [DoD], December 21, 1993). The prohibitions apply even when individuals are in the privacy of their own homes or not on active duty (Kerr, 2000). However, no equivalent prohibitive standards exist for heterosexuals' behavior. Although "public displays of affection" are generally considered unprofessional in the military (Olivolo, 2000), the rules are applied and enforced unevenly for heterosexuals and homosexuals (Cullen, 2000).

The US military's devaluation of GLB individuals is also highlighted by its inconsistent treatment of anti-GLB harassment, behavior, and attitudes. After conducting an investigation that corroborated reports of harassment of individuals perceived to be gay (DoD, March 16, 2000), the US Department of Defense publicly condemned anti-gay harassment (DoD, March 24, 2000) and initiated attempts to ameliorate the general environment for GLB individuals (DoD, July 21, 2000). However, the DoD has applied the formal regulations unevenly and with little vigor (Servicemembers Legal Defense Network [SLDN], July 31, 2001; cf., Engardio, 2001b). Some high-ranking officers mock attempts to end harassment (SLDN, 2000), whereas others discount the severity of the military's anti-gay environment despite well-researched support of anti-gay sentiment and harassment (Aldinger, 2000; CBSNews.com, 2000; Myers, 2000). Others refuse to recognize the military's culpability in fostering anti-gay attitudes (Sanchez, 2000; Whitaker, 2000), or choose to reinterpret GLB service members' fear of harassment as an "easy way" out of the military (Suro, 2000, 2001).

SUMMARY

A summarized analysis of Kodak, IBM, and the US armed forces shows that the three organizations provide a stark contrast to how they treat GLB members. To start, Kodak provides explicit ethics for equal treatment of all employees, regardless of sexual orientation. The corporation supports GLB individuals in senior-level management who are public about their sexual orientation, and represent GLB issues when decisions are being made. Kodak institutionally creates dialogue between GLB and heterosexual employees in safe spaces, in order to maintain and build communication and bonds between employees of different sexual orientations. In addition, Kodak maintains a support group and an internal employee network whose focus is to increase visibility, education of GLB needs and issues, creation and maintenance of GLB-welcoming environments, and establishment of networks to support employees and the corporation as a whole.

IBM also has a demonstrated record of commitment to inclusion. This corporation established a task force to ascertain what GLB workers need to feel more welcomed and valued, to be most productive, and also to increase the market share for their community. IBM offers extensive domestic partner benefits that demonstrate respect for how GLB workers share their lives with their partners. Lastly, IBM recruits GLB workers, and tracks and encourages GLB executives.

In comparison, the US military has a demonstrated history of intolerance towards GLB service members. This organization expels people for acting on or expressing GLB identity or feelings. The military enforces regulations unfairly, in order to discriminate against GLB people. And even though the military has been proven to be a clear anti-GLB organization, highly visible representatives and ranking officers minimize the severity of this finding and the undesirable nature of its environment.

Issues for Practitioners and Scholars

The contrast between corporate America and the US armed forces is striking. What accounts for the differences? At one level, an adequate answer would reason that corporations have become relatively welcoming to sexual minorities because corporate leaders have seen the business necessity of inclusiveness and diversity while military leaders have not. Additionally, the contrast probably derives from the actual structure of the military. Recall that change at both Eastman Kodak and IBM was initiated by new CEOs. When highly placed individuals resist change, progress can be stymied, and the influence of resistant leaders may be exaggerated in a strict hierarchical structure such as the armed forces. However, should a set of high-ranking military officials decide that diversity is good for the armed forces, change is likely to come rapidly.

How solid and lasting would such change be? Indeed, how solid is the change in business culture? To answer this question, we believe it is useful to think in terms of the scheme put forward by Ely and Thomas (2001), referenced by many other authors in this volume. Ely and Thomas see organizations as exhibiting different levels of valuing diversity. Organizations that take the discrimination and fairness perspective seek to avoid prejudice and discrimination, but they do not envision any positive reasons to embrace diversity. Organizations that take the access and legitimacy perspective go one step further: they understand that "non-standard" workers may provide certain organizational assets, especially by helping the organization to mirror its client base. Yet underlying the access and legitimacy perspective is the assumption that minorities have more to gain from being in the organization than the organization has to gain from having them. In contrast, learning and effectiveness organizations prize diversity for the ways in which people who are different from each other need to learn from each other. Diversity is an integral part of strategic growth for organizations of the learning and effectiveness variety.

Our guess is that even the best employers have not yet reached the learning and effectiveness stage of embracing sexual diversity. Certainly, as long as GLB people feel a need to hide their sexual orientation, the changes we have witnessed are susceptible to reversal. And without a doubt, organizations that see that their own health and well-being is linked to being gay-friendly are the ones where changes are likely to be more permanent.

If a non-discrimination policy has substance, there should be few business reasons for remaining invisible on the job. Once GLB individuals feel as comfortable as heterosexuals when discussing their personal relationships, when displaying pictures of loved ones at the work station, and when bringing partners to company events, the workplace will become truly diverse. It is hard to maintain stereotypes when numerous individuals, all in one category, show their manifold differences. Just as some heterosexuals are politically conservative, some liberal, some are short, some tall, some are soft spoken, some brash, so too are some GLB individuals conservative while others are liberal, some are short while others are tall, some are soft spoken while others are brash.

By working side-by-side with non-apologetic and unafraid gay men and lesbians, most heterosexuals can learn to shed their prejudices. The fewer the prejudices, the safer and more wholesome the environment. The safer the environment, the more relaxed and visible will be all people, of all sexual orientations. As heterosexuals come to see GLB co-workers as "regular folk" with the same worries and joys as themselves, we will witness a desexualizing of issues of "sexual" orientation at work. In this way, everyone benefits when enough GLB people become visible, so that all can see that GLB people are as varied among themselves as are heterosexuals.

The desexualized American workplace, in which sexual diversity has no more importance than variety in hair color, may seem a distant ideal. Yet, given the strides of the last decades, and given strides in other aspects of human rights, the trip to the promised land may be shorter than we think.

Notes

1 We readily acknowledge that more work is needed to make the workplace equally inclusive for transgender individuals. Transgender people are typically welcomed and incorporated into the GLB community. However, although there are many overlaps between sexual orientations such as homosexuality and bisexuality and gender orientations such as transgenderism, the two concepts should not be conflated. Each subject merits a focused analysis of its relationship to workplace rights to most fully respect the host of accompanying issues. Because the parameters of this chapter could not allow an appropriate analysis of all the issues, our chapter focuses only on the GLB community. We encourage the further consideration of workplace issues facing the transgender community.

2 A promise held dear: An interview with Ted Childs. (2002, January/February). *Profiles in Diversity Journal, 4* (1), p. 9.

3 IBM (2000, April). *Valuing diversity: An ongoing commitment.* Armonk, NY: IBM, p. 1.

4 A promise held dear: An interview with Ted Childs. (2002, March/April). *Profiles in Diversity Journal, 4* (2), p. 46.

5 A promise held dear (2002, January/February), p. 8.

6 IBM (2000, April), p. 55.

CLASS DIVERSITY IN THE WORKPLACE

Heather E. Bullock

This chapter provides an overview of class-based power differences and stratification in the workplace. The role that organizational structures play in maintaining class privilege is discussed, as is the impact of differential treatment within organizational systems. Examples of institutional and interpersonal classism are provided and intersections with sexism and racism are explored. Stereotypes about low-wage workers and other barriers to class mobility are examined. Emphasis is placed on understanding the needs of low-income workers, especially welfare recipients, and the policies and supports needed to create greater economic justice in the workplace. Strategies for valuing class diversity in the workplace are offered.

In the film *Working Girl* (1988), the heroine moves from a cramped secretarial cubicle to a large windowed office when she is finally credited for her innovative ideas. A modern "rags to riches" story, the film tracks one woman's metaphorical ascent from the "mailroom to the boardroom." Through hard work and perseverance the central character makes it to the "top" despite her lack of formal training or broad-based support within the organization. Workplace "success" stories such as this one reflect dominant cultural beliefs about social mobility and the power of individuals to transcend class boundaries through personal achievement.

The belief that anyone can succeed in the workplace, regardless of how humble their origin, how recently they immigrated to the country, or how resource-poor they are, is a central component of American ideology (Hochschild, 1995). The United States is regarded as a "meritocracy" or a society in which rewards and training are distributed based on talent and ability, rather than unearned advantage (e.g., inheritance, family privilege), unfair practices (e.g., discriminatory hiring or advertising policies), or group membership (e.g., race, gender, class). These beliefs extend to the workplace, where occupation is thought to reflect individual skill or "merit," with the strongest, most capable candidate rising to the "top" of the organization regardless of ethnicity, gender, or class. Describing this process, Weakliem, McQuillan, and Schauer (1995: 271) explain: "If all people compete on an equal basis with no special preference given to any group, the most desirable positions will usually be won by the most talented people, and occupation will be closely tied to ability." Equal opportunity or a level playing field on which to compete is assumed, but equal outcomes are not. Instead, inequality in the workplace (and other spheres) is seen as the inevitable result of differences in ability and talent.

The danger of this perspective is that it obscures how factors such as gender, ethnicity (see chapters 7 and 8, this volume), and social class shape opportunities for entry and advancement in the workplace. It also assumes equal opportunity and access to the resources that make career advancement possible (e.g., high quality education, social networks). However, a large body of research documents pervasive and systemic stratification across social groups. Stratification refers to the hierarchical division of people into "distinct social groups, each having specific life chances" (Scott, 1996: 1). Challenging the fundamental assumptions of meritocracy, theories of stratification focus on how institutionalized inequality and power relations, rather than individual ability, influence the allocation of resources and rewards (Kerbo, 1996). Those who are positioned in more prestigious or socially valued strata (e.g., European Americans, men, the middle class) are afforded a greater number and wider variety of opportunities than those who occupy devalued strata (e.g., ethnic minorities, women, the poor). From this vantage point, whether someone is a janitor or an executive conveys more about access to resources and education than talent or drive.

Focusing on class-based stratification in the workplace and the risks associated with unquestioningly accepting the fundamental tenets of meritocracy, this chapter critically examines the ability of low-wage workers to break through class-based barriers. The analysis presented here tells a markedly different story about social class in the workplace than the success story of *Working Girl*. This chapter provides an overview of class hierarchies in the workplace, the ways in which power and class are communicated through organizational structure, how class status influences treatment within organizational systems, and classist discrimination. Interpersonal and institutional strategies for valuing and increasing class diversity in the workplace are offered. Emphasis is placed on understanding the needs of low-income workers, especially welfare recipients, and the policies and supports that are necessary to create an inclusive workplace.

CLASS HIERARCHY: STRATIFICATION AND STRUCTURE

Social class is arguably the most pervasive form of stratification in the United States, yet its impact on life chances has received far less attention in the social psychological and industrial/organizational literature than gender or race (Bullock and Lott, 2001; Saris and Johnston-Robledo, 2000). Social class refers to "a group of individuals or families who occupy a similar position in the economic system of production, distribution, and consumption of goods and services in industrial societies" (Rothman, 2002: 6). Although there is considerable debate within the field of sociology about how social class should be measured and the structure of contemporary class groupings, income, education, and occupation, or some combination of these indicators, are frequently used to define social class.

The United States is often characterized as a five-class system: the elite; the professional or "upper" middle class; the middle class; the working class; and the poor. The smallest group, the elite, located at the "top" of the class hierarchy, consists of two subgroups: the capitalist elite (i.e., individuals and families whose wealth and status are derived from ownership of land, property, businesses, and stock) and the institutional elite (i.e., those who hold powerful leadership positions in government and corporations) (Rothman, 2002). Estimated at no more than 1–2 percent of the US population, the elite owns the lion's share of financial resources and wealth (i.e., real estate, stocks). The wealthiest 1 percent of Americans own 38.5 percent of wealth; the richest 20 percent of the population own 83.9 percent of wealth (Keister and Moller, 2000). Perhaps most striking is the estimate that the financial assets of one man, Bill Gates, equals the assets of 40 million American households at the bottom of the wealth distribution (Wolff, 1998).

Unlike the elite, the middle class relies heavily on earned wages or salary for income rather than stocks and dividends. The professional middle class or "upper middle class" is comprised of a broad range of "white collar" workers, including those whose position is based on expert knowledge (e.g., professors, journalists, doctors, lawyers) and managers and administrators below the executive level. Entry into the professional middle class typically requires a baccalaureate degree and often a graduate or a doctoral degree. The middle class includes technicians such as data entry specialists, public school teachers, and lower-level personnel and managers. A baccalaureate, but not necessarily a graduate degree, is required to obtain these positions.

The high value placed on middle-class status is evident in the tendency to self-identify as middle class regardless of actual educational or occupational status. Survey research indicates that many Americans identify as middle class even if they do not meet objectively defined criteria (Kelley and Evans, 1995). This tendency reflects the widespread belief that the United States is a "classless" society (e.g., "this country is not divided by class," "the 'middle' is normative") and the greater social value placed on middle-class over poor and working-class groups.

"Working class" or "blue collar" is used to describe people who engage in physical labor in factories, mills, and construction sites. Although some working-class positions require considerable technical skills and apprenticeships (e.g., automobile mechanics, plumbers, bricklayers), these positions do not necessarily require the longer, formal education required for entry into the middle class. Other working-class positions, such as administrative assistant or assembly line worker, may require little formal training.

The poor are located at the "bottom" of the class hierarchy. Poverty is usually defined in terms of one's relationship to official poverty thresholds that are set annually by the federal government. In 2000 the official poverty threshold for a parent with one dependent child was $11,869 and $13,874 for a family of three (US Census Bureau, 2001b). This heterogeneous group includes children as well as women and men who are unemployed or work part- or full-time (typically in low-wage service jobs) but still live below official poverty thresholds. Female-headed households are overrepresented among the poor, especially families headed by women of color. Twenty percent of White female-headed households were poor in 2000, compared with 34.6 percent of Black and 34.2 percent of Hispanic female-headed households, respectively (US Census Bureau, 2001b).

Although a growing percentage of low-income families are employed part- or full-time, participation in the labor market does not guarantee an end to poverty. In 2000, 44.5 percent of poor families had one worker employed full-time outside the home, but their earnings were not enough to lift the family out of poverty (US Census Bureau, 2001b). Poor women and men typically work in low-status positions with little opportunity for professional advancement, such as the retail industry, and food and domestic service (i.e., housekeeping). Paying minimum wage or perhaps a bit above, these jobs are unlikely to offer benefits, paid vacations, or other "perks" associated with middle-class employment and some working-class positions.

OF MANAGERS AND JANITORS: SOCIAL CLASS IN THE WORKPLACE

Class-based differences permeate the workplace. In any organization, employees are likely to have different levels of educational attainment, work and earning histories, housing arrangements, and life experiences. These factors affect the type, range, and number of positions for which an individual is qualified. The organizational structure of the workplace, in turn, reinforces and reproduces the class-based differences that individuals bring to organizational settings. Examining the reciprocal nature of these relationships underscores how class privilege is maintained and the obstacles that outsiders confront when trying to break through class barriers.

Social class and workforce entrée

In the United States, middle-class cultural norms depict occupation as a freely chosen activity. Children are asked from a very young age what they would *like* to be when they grow up. Middle-class parents encourage their children to explore different career options during college and early adulthood, and then *select* what they would *like* to do for a living. From this vantage point, occupation is a matter of personal choice, unfettered by economic demands and class-based opportunities that open doors for some and close them to others. By depicting occupation as a "calling" rather than a necessity, situational demands that limit the career "choices" of poor and working-class youth – such as working at an early age to help support family members, or being unable to afford college tuition – are rendered invisible.

Although social class during childhood does not determine status across the lifespan, it does affect how different career options are perceived, the type of learning opportunities that are available, and access to resources that facilitate mobility. Even young children become aware of hierarchies in the workplace and class-based barriers. Weinger (1998) found that poor children perceived a smaller range of jobs as appropriate despite associating greater economic security with expanded career possibilities. Traditional "working-class" jobs were perceived as more suitable occupations, whereas more lucrative professions (e.g., business ownership, management) were regarded as unattainable. Yet these same children believed that middle-class youth could successfully pursue whatever careers they wished.

Social class not only shapes beliefs about the accessibility of various careers, it also influences schooling, a variable that is strongly correlated with income and occupational status. A large body of research indicates that growing up in a middle-class family is associated with higher educational attainment, whereas growing up in a poor family is associated with lower educational achievement (McLoyd, 1998). Recent statistics on the relationship between economic status and high school completion illustrate this point. Although most low-income youth finish high school, adolescents from the poorest 20 percent of families are six times more likely to leave high school than their peers in the wealthiest 20 percent of families. In 2000, only 1.6 percent of students from families with incomes in the top 20 percent of households dropped out of high school, compared with 10 percent of students from the poorest 20 percent of families (National Center for Educational Statistics [NCES], 2001).

For poor students who complete high school, significant barriers to higher education remain. Only 26 percent of all undergraduate students are from low-income families (NCES, 2000). Without a college degree, most low-income youth cannot compete for positions or incomes that will help them achieve middle-class status. Those who go to college may be unable to afford the more expensive, elite universities attended by their middle-class peers. Graduates of these privileged institutions benefit from the prestigious academic reputation of these schools as well as the strong networking opportunities they provide. These invaluable, and often intangible, social resources provide workforce entrée that less connected, low-income groups lack.

Individuals who enter the workforce with higher levels of education are able to compete for higher paying positions, further reinforcing their privileged status. Women and men across ethnic groups who have completed more years of school earn higher incomes than those with less formal education. Research that compares annual earnings by highest degree earned documents the financial rewards of education (US Census Bureau, 2001b). For example, in 2000 the median income for a White male college graduate was $58,777, compared with $36,378 for a White male high school graduate and $27,221 for a White male high school dropout.

Although education is positively correlated with higher earnings, ethnicity and gender moderate this relationship. Overall, European Americans continue to earn more than people of color even when they have similar educational backgrounds, and men on average still earn more than women even when they are less educated. In 2000, White and Black men who did not complete high school earned more on average at their full-time, year-round jobs ($33,105 and $27,415, respectively) than Black ($25,219) and Hispanic ($23,488) women who graduated from high school (US Census Bureau, 2001b). In fact, Black women with some college education and who work full-time earn the equivalent of White men who dropped out of school (Fine and Weis, 1998). Underscoring sexist and racist wage disparity, these figures document the differential impact education has on earning power.

Hierarchy in the workplace: Reifying class-based differences

The class-based differences that workers bring to the labor market are reified in the workplace, where position reinforces class status. Although in some contexts class may be a less visible marker than gender or ethnicity, class status is highly visible in the workplace, where one's job title or occupation conveys information about power, authority, and social status.

Since the 1920s, researchers have assessed the social value of different occupations by asking respondents to rate their relative status. Studies of occupational prestige reveal that judgments about various occupations have remained relatively stable over time (Rothman, 2002; Kerbo, 1996). Mirroring class relations in larger society, occupations associated with the professional middle class (e.g., surgeon, lawyer, department head in state government) are positioned at the top of the status hierarchy, whereas occupations associated with the working class (e.g., electrician, auto mechanic, post office clerk, hairdresser) and the poor (e.g., laundry worker, janitor, stock clerk, parking lot attendant) receive lower status rankings (Rothman, 2002). Judgments of occupational prestige not only reflect widely shared cultural beliefs about the relative value of different types of labor, but also justify differential rewards and treatment in the workplace by valuing some workers and skill sets over others.

Highly valued occupations, particularly those associated with the professional middle class, offer more rewards and benefits than lower-status jobs. These positions typically offer higher salaries, trajectories for advancement, medical benefits, comprehensive pension packages, stock options, and childcare assistance. Other "perks" such as autonomy (e.g., freedom to keep one's own hours, express individuality through personal appearance), opportunity to voice one's opinion, office space, paid vacation time and sick days, are also more common in middle-class positions. On the other hand, lower-status or working-class occupations tend to pay lower wages and provide fewer benefits or "perks" such as paid vacation or sick time, flexible working hours, employer paid health benefits, and pension plans. Because occupational entrée is largely dependent on education/training, class history shapes where and how one enters the workplace and, in turn, is reinforced by the income, status, and benefits associated with occupational position.

Income or salary disparity provides one of the most dramatic illustrations of how social class is reinforced by occupational structure. When cost of living expenses are controlled for, real hourly wages for high school graduates have fallen 11 percent since 1973, and those of school dropouts have fallen 18 percent, while college graduates have enjoyed a 17 percent increase in hourly wages (Gabel et al., 1999). In 2000, upper-middle-class professions paid an annual average salary of $107,780 to general practitioners, $91,320 to lawyers, and $70,220 to general and operations managers, while working-class employees such as word processors and typists were paid an average annual salary of $25,420, electrical and electronic equipment assemblers $22,950, childcare workers $16,350, and fast food workers $14,240 (US Department of Labor, 2001a). Yet even the salaries of upper-middle-class earners are dwarfed by CEOs at the 362 largest American businesses, who average approximately $12.4 million annually (Rothman, 2002).

Given these figures it comes as little surprise that the United States leads the industrial world in wage inequity between its top and bottom earners. In 1980 top executives earned 42 times the income of the average factory worker, but that ratio escalated to 209 times in 1996 and reached 475 times in 1999 (Rothman, 2002). Other industrialized countries such as Germany, Britain, and France only pay their executives 15 to 30 times more than manufacturing employees (Rothman, 2002).

Although income is one of the primary mechanisms through which class boundaries are maintained, other forms of workplace compensation and benefits also vary tremendously. Between 1996 and 1998, 76 percent of all employees had paid vacation and 67 percent had paid jury duty leave, but only 61 percent of employees had medical care, 51 percent paid sick leave, 39 percent dental care, and 27 percent long-term disability plans. Less educated, low-wage employees are significantly less likely to receive these benefits. Between 1992 and 1997 the percentage of families with a high school diploma or less that did not have health insurance rose from 26.2 percent to 28.6 percent (Gabel et al., 1999). During the same period, families without health insurance headed by college graduates increased slightly from 7.8 percent to 8.1 percent.

Class-based differences in employer-sponsored pensions programs are also pervasive. Fifty-three percent of the employed labor force, or 69 million persons, did not have a pension plan in 1998 (US General Accounting Office, 2000). Employees earning less than $20,000 a year (81 percent), working part-time or part of the year (79 percent), and employees who work at small businesses (82 percent) are particularly likely to lack pension plans (US General Accounting Office, 2000). People without a high school diploma are also less likely to have pension plans.

Class disparity exists even among middle- and upper-class employees who are fortunate enough to have defined benefit or defined contribution pension plans. Defined benefit plans provide a retirement income that is based on salary and years of service, whereas defined contribution programs are based on contributions that employers, employees, or both make to individual retirement accounts. Saving and profit sharing plans, 401(k) plans, and employee stock options are examples of defined contribution plans. Since the 1980s there has been a significant shift from defined benefit toward defined contribution plans, an option which tends to be less expensive for employers and riskier for employees (US General Accounting Office, 2002).

During the stock boom of the 1990s, millions of workers were encouraged to invest in stock plans for their retirement, particularly in their company's stock. Moreover, employers increasingly matched employee contributions to 401(k) plans with company stock rather than cash. Generally greeted with enthusiasm by workers, these investments were perceived as a way to access the same rising market that has traditionally benefited the wealthy (Uchitelle, 2002). However, recent market downturns and the high-profile Enron crisis have raised questions about this practice and increased awareness of corporate policies that protect top executives, but not middle-class employees, from losing their retirement savings.

Top executives are usually privy to the financial status of their company and, despite legal sanctions against insider trading, some may sell portions of their stock before it takes a public plunge. Other "perks" are institutionally supported. With assistance from financial advisers who are paid for by their corporation, top executives are able to develop more diversified portfolios and invest in safe capital, such as real estate. Most importantly, top executives receive company-funded cash pensions that are unavailable to most workers. Pensions range from 60 percent of an executive's pre-retirement pay after 30 years of service to 25 percent for an executive with 15 years. For example, Richard McGinn, former chief executive of Lucent, receives a pension of $870,000 a year, not far below his former salary. Meanwhile, employees earning $60,000 or less annually can expect $20,000 in 401(k) savings, hardly enough to support oneself (Uchitelle, 2002).

Poor and working-class occupations not only provide fewer benefits, they are also associated with higher risk of injury and death. In 2000, 5.7 million non-fatal injuries and illnesses were reported in private industry, resulting in a rate of 6.1 injuries per 100 full-time employees. That same year nearly 6,000 workplace fatalities were reported. The vast majority of accidents and deaths occurred in the working-class occupations, with manufacturing employees, drivers, construction workers, mechanics, miners, machine operators, equipment cleaners, and field laborers at greatest risk (US Department of Labor, 2001b, 2001c).

In sum, class influences entrance into the workforce which, in turn, influences status and privilege on the job, thereby perpetuating social class differences. The greater social value placed on middle-class positions is reflected in the elevated prestige, competitive salaries, generous benefits, and workplace safety associated with these occupations. On the other hand, positions associated with the poor and working classes tend to be devalued and consequently pay lower wages and offer few, if any, benefits. Because their work is essential to organizational effectiveness, appreciation days like "Administrative Professionals Day" is widely recognized, but these gestures do little to boost the status or pay associated with these positions.

CLASSISM IN THE WORKPLACE

In what ways do class-based institutional privileges legitimate workplace inequities? Classism refers to the oppression of low-income people through a network of everyday practices, attitudes, assumptions, behaviors, and institutional rules (Bullock, 1995; Lott, 2002). Classism is composed of three independent but related dimensions: classist prejudice refers to negative attitudes toward poor and working-class people; classist stereotypes describe widely shared and socially sanctioned beliefs about the poor and working classes; and classist discrimination refers to behaviors that distance, avoid, and/or exclude poor and working-class people (Bullock, 1995). As the previous discussion of salaries and pensions illustrates, classism is an institutional problem. Classism also occurs on the interpersonal level through covert forms of social distancing (e.g., ignoring, excluding, or ridiculing someone based on their class status) and overt behaviors (e.g., refusing to hire welfare recipients or people from working-class backgrounds).

Classist stereotypes undermine the perceived competency of poor and low-wage workers by depicting these groups as lazy, uninterested in self-improvement, and lacking initiative and intelligence (Bullock, 1995, 1999; Cozzarelli, Wilkinson, and Tagler, 2001; Furnham, 1982a; Lott, 2002). Consistent with meritocratic beliefs that emphasize personal achievement and upward mobility, classist stereotypes place the locus of responsibility on the individual by associating financial and/or class-based success with adherence to the Protestant work ethic. Emphasizing the importance of hard work, individual perseverance, and competition, the Protestant work ethic regards "success" (e.g., power, prestige, wealth) as a reflection of hard work and "failure" (e.g., low social and economic status) with lack of effort (Furnham, 1982b). As a result, classist stereotypes are particularly hurtful because unlike ethnicity and gender, which are regarded as beyond individual control, class standing tends to be perceived as a reflection of one's own effort and ability.

In the United States, individualistic explanations for poverty (e.g., lack of thrift, laziness) and wealth (e.g., hard work, ability) tend to be favored over structural or societal attributions for poverty (e.g., failure of society to provide strong schools, discrimination) and wealth (e.g., inheritance, political influence, and "pull"). However, attributional patterns vary as a function of ethnicity (Hunt, 1996), gender (Bullock, 1999), political affiliation (Zucker and Weiner, 1993), and income level (Bullock, 1999; Furnham, 1982a; Kluegel and Smith, 1986). European Americans, men, conservatives, and middle-income groups are particularly likely to endorse individualistic attributions for poverty and wealth, whereas African Americans, women, liberals, and low-income groups prefer structural attributions. Thus, it appears that the same groups (e.g., European Americans, members of the middle class, men) that hold significant institutional power in the workplace are more likely to endorse classist stereotypes and beliefs.

Very little research examines the prevalence of classist stereotypes among employers, but several studies suggest that this is a significant problem, affecting job recruitment and hiring decisions. Kennelly's (1999) study of White employers (e.g., company presidents, CEOs, human resource representatives, and supervisors) and their attitudes toward hiring Black women documents the extent to which discriminatory attitudes affect hiring decisions in the low-wage labor market. When asked about filling positions that required minimal skills and education (e.g., clerical worker, cashier, or sales associate), more than half of White employers identified lack of emphasis on education, reliance on public assistance, and poor role models as key problems with the Black labor force. Commenting on hiring "inner-city" employees, a thinly veiled code for poor, urban, African Americans, a White plant manager remarked:

> The people that I want, it would be hard to get those people to come downtown. And when we get into the inner-city, in my opinion, work values change because you're talking about people that are primarily raised in a single family. Very poor environment, don't have a role model that shows them that work is good, that you should do your very best and a good job no matter where it is or who it is for. (**Kennelly 1999: 184**)

Regardless of their actual parental status, Black women were assumed to be single mothers and as a consequence were regarded as unreliable workers (e.g., often tardy or having high rates of absenteeism). Although a small percentage of managers believed that Black single mothers were dependable employees because they desperately needed to support their families, employer perceptions were overwhelmingly negative.

Other studies reveal similar patterns of discrimination against poor, urban residents, suggesting that classism is commonly expressed as "locality" discrimination (Kasinitz and Rosenberg, 1996; Kirschenman and Neckerman, 1991). In their analysis of hiring practices for working-class jobs along the Brooklyn waterfront, Kasinitz and Rosenberg (1996) found that many employers regarded local residents as undesirable employees because of their minority status and their connection to low-income neighborhoods. The authors use their findings to argue that "empowerment zones" (i.e., economic development strategies based on geographically targeted tax incentives) will not lower unemployment rates among low-income urban residents unless local hiring requirements accompany tax incentives. Biased hiring practices, such as advertising for employees in largely White, working-class areas rather than in poor African-American neighborhoods, state agencies, and welfare offices, underscores this point (Neckerman and Kirschenman, 1991).

Experimental studies provide further confirmation of class and ethnic bias. In a study examining the effects of applicant ethnicity, job status, and racial attitudes on hiring decisions, Stewart and Perlow (2001) found that participants who held more racist attitudes expressed greater confidence in the decision to hire a Black applicant for a low-status job than a White applicant. These same respondents were more comfortable hiring a European-American applicant for a high-status job than a Black applicant. Reflecting "race–job" bias, African Americans were perceived as a better "fit" in low-status jobs (e.g., janitor), while European Americans were regarded as a closer "fit" with high-status jobs (e.g., architect). Such perceptions may make it difficult for ethnic minorities to break through classist barriers and expectations to obtain high-status positions even when they are qualified for middle-class positions.

With the exception of hiring decisions, which may involve face-to-face inter-class interactions, many workplaces are structured in ways that minimize inter-personal contact and reinforce class-based boundaries. For example, janitors clean middle-class offices in the evening after other employees have left for the day. In large corporations, parties and social gatherings may be organized by class status, with one event planned for middle-class professionals and another for working-class employees. In some cases, working-class employees are excluded completely from social events. In their study of perceived discrimination among low-income, elderly, part-time employees, Kaye and Alexander (1995) found that these workers were not invited to special workplace events because as part-timers they were not viewed as "regular" employees. This was especially true for employees who were paid through subsidized funds rather than by employers. Invisible to their employers, these workers were socially and professionally dis-advantaged in their organizations. Regarded as "second-class" workers, they were not asked to participate in training opportunities to advance their workplace skills.

Although many cross-class interactions are limited by physical arrangements (e.g., situating working-class and middle-class workers in different areas of a building) and social customs (e.g., informal class-based segregation in the lunch room), some workplace roles require interclass contact. For organizations to run smoothly, middle-class professionals and administrative assistants must be able to communicate effectively with one another. Likewise, in hospital and nursing facilities where effective treatment depends on cooperative teamwork, nurses and aides need to discuss effective procedures. Because these interactions are rooted in well-defined hierarchical roles that equate middle-class status with authority and the poor and working classes with subordinate status, they may reinforce rather than challenge classist stereotypes and beliefs.

Riemer's (1997) ethnographic study of former welfare recipients employed as nursing assistants provides just one illustration of how classism manifests itself in such relationships. Despite the low wages, enthusiasm among the new nursing assistants was strong, but class and race-based hierarchies soon led to resentment and conflict. Although the aides were largely responsible for their patients' daily care, their recommendations were dismissed and their behavior was monitored closely by supervisors who questioned their knowledge. Former recipients who responded with anger or frustration or left their jobs only confirmed supervisors' assumptions that they were unprofessional and unworthy. Classist stereotypes that degrade the importance of semiskilled labor and undercut the perceived reliability of low-wage workers are apt to underlie discriminatory behaviors.

Unfortunately, the procedures used by the Equal Employment Opportunity Commission (EEOC) to implement Title VII of the Civil Rights Act of 1964 may not adequately protect poor and working-class employees, particularly women of color, who file employment discrimination charges. In Wilhelm's (2001) analysis of nearly 180,000 complaints made by female employees, she found that EEOC's investigation procedures benefited White and Black middle-class women, but disadvantaged working-class Black women. Regardless of race, "withdrawal with benefit" (i.e., employer agrees to compensation and employee withdraws charge), one of the quickest, positive outcomes, was correlated with middle-class status. Cases brought by African-American women, particularly women with low levels of educational attainment, were significantly less likely to result in positive outcomes. Although the EEOC was designed to take the burden of Title VII disputes off the claimant, access to private legal representation emerged as one of the primary reasons for class disparity in successful outcomes. Wilhelm (2001) argues that without legal representation, working-class employees are not only less aware of what constitutes discrimination and how the EEOC should investigate the case, but also their claims may be taken less seriously by employers who regard the EEOC as ineffective. She concludes: "The EEOC, in poorly enforcing Title VII, has allowed employers to get away with paying those who cannot defend themselves lower wages. For every case that results in a resolution through the EEOC, black women with lower education levels lose ground" (p. 303).

MOVING FROM WELFARE TO WORK: BARRIERS TO ECONOMIC MOBILITY AND WORKPLACE INCLUSION

Recent changes to the welfare system make increasing class diversity in the workplace of the utmost importance. The passage of the Personal Responsibility and Work Opportunity Reconciliation of Act of 1996 (P.L. 104-193; PRWORA) dramatically changed the structure of the welfare system by ending the federal guarantee of cash assistance to poor families. PRWORA replaced Aid to Families with Dependent Children (AFDC), the program widely known as "welfare," with a new, more restrictive cash assistance program, Temporary Assistance for Needy Families (TANF).

Some of the most notable changes concern the implementation of time limits and work requirements. The new law adopts a "work first" philosophy that requires recipients to move quickly from welfare to work. The majority of recipients must engage in work activities within two years of receiving assistance.

Acceptable work activities include subsidized or unsubsidized employment, community service, on-the-job training, job search or job search readiness activities (limited to six weeks in a year and no more than four weeks consecutively per participant), or short-term vocational training. To avoid financial penalties, states must meet rising work participation rates. In fiscal year 1997, 25 percent of all single-parent families were required to participate in a minimum of 20 hours of work activities per week and as of fiscal year 2002, 50 percent of states' single-parent caseload needed to work 30 hours per week. A feminist critique of requiring poor women to work outside the home is presented in panel 11.1.

These regulations place heavy pressure on states to get recipients off welfare and into the paid workforce as quickly as possible. Despite the well-documented association between increased schooling and earning power (Rice, 2001), rules limit the percentage of recipients permitted to participate in education and training programs. Only 30 percent of a state's caseload can participate in training and educational programs as "work activities" at any given time. Vocational and/or post-secondary education is usually limited to a 12-month maximum and even in these cases recipients must work at least 20 hours per week (O'Connor, 2000). Time limits, which restrict the receipt of benefits to 24 consecutive months and impose a 60-months lifetime limit, serve to further push recipients into the workforce.

PRWORA's adoption has spurred a surge in psychological research on the barriers that prevent welfare recipients from moving into the workforce (Brooks and Buckner, 1996; Danziger et al., 2000; Corcoran et al., 2000; Olson and Pavetti, 1997; Danziger, Kalil, and Anderson, 2000; Jayakody and Stauffer, 2000). Collectively, these studies document the prevalence of multiple, interacting barriers to getting and keeping a job. For example, in a study involving more than 700 single mothers receiving welfare benefits, Danziger et al. (2000) found that almost two-thirds of respondents had two or more potential barriers to work, and over one-quarter experienced four or more. The more commonly reported barriers included the following: transportation problems (47.1 percent); not completing a high school education (31.4 percent); major depressive disorder (25.4 percent); children's health problems (22.1 percent); weak job skills (21.1 percent); personal health problems (19.4 percent); low work experience (15.4 percent); domestic violence (14.9 percent); and perceived discrimination (13.9 percent). In all cases in which comparisons were possible, the incidence of barriers was found to be greater among welfare recipients than women nationally, and not surprisingly, the more barriers women experienced, the less likely they were to be working.

Other barriers to work include lack of appropriate clothing (Turner-Bowker, 2001) and the shortage of affordable, high quality childcare. Although most mothers who work outside the home have a hard time securing reliable childcare, low-income women are particularly hard hit (Children's Defense Fund, 2000; Henly and Lyons, 2000). The average annual cost of childcare in a center-based facility is $4,000 to $6,000. An analysis of childcare costs by the Children's Defense Fund (2000) found that the average annual cost of childcare in urban centers was higher than public college tuition in all but one state.

11.1 *In defense of "motherwork"*

Requiring poor mothers to work outside the home is one of the most controversial aspects of "welfare reform." Feminist scholars such as Gwendolyn Mink (1999, 2002) and welfare rights advocacy groups argue that poor mothers have a right to raise their children and that they should not be compelled by law to work outside the home. Work requirements, they argue, are based on a societal "double standard" in which labor outside the home is regarded as "employment," but caring for one's own children is not. By mandating that welfare mothers work outside the home to receive their benefits, PRWORA reinforces "motherwork" status as invisible, unpaid labor. It also deepens the chasm between poor and middle-class mothers because unlike their middle-class counterparts, poor mothers cannot "choose" to stay home full-time with their children. The law mandates that they must enter the workforce to receive cash assistance.

Feminists believe that "motherwork" (e.g., caring for children, housework, meal preparation) is "labor" that deserves public recognition and compensation. Explaining this position, Mink (1999: 185) states, "We all know that care giving is work – household management and parenting – takes skill, energy, time and responsibility. We know this because people who can afford it *pay* other people to do it . . . If economists can measure the value of this work when it is performed for other people's families, why can't we impute value to it when it is performed for one's own?" If, in fact, family caregiving were considered in terms of its labor market value (i.e., dietician, laundress, chauffeur, cook, nurse), salaries above the poverty threshold would be paid.

Creating a guaranteed "caregivers income" for poor, single mothers is a top priority of campaigns for economic and gender justice. Survivors' insurance is often used to provide a conceptual framework for the creation of such a program and to illustrate the hypocrisy of work requirements (Gordon, 1995; Mink, 1999, 2002). Survivors' insurance entitles a widowed spouse and the children under her or his care to collect cash benefits. Similar to social security, survivors' insurance provides uniform benefits across the country and is paid automatically to eligible families. Moreover, beneficiaries are not subject to public scrutiny or perceived as welfare "dependent." Comparing welfare mothers to those receiving survivors' insurance, Mink (1999: 187) notes: "The only difference between a survivors' insurance parent and a welfare parent is that the former was married. Because she was once married to her children's father, a survivors' insurance mother is not required to work outside the home – though she may take a job and still receive benefits."

The discrepancy between these programs underscores the stigma associated with "unwed" mothers, raising questions about the legitimacy of providing government entitlements to certain types of families but not others. Feminists believe that limiting receipt of survivors' benefits to heterosexual, married couples reinforces patriarchal family structures that disadvantage single mothers. They suggest that similar income provisions, a so-called "caregiver's income," be allotted to all single parents, regardless of their marital history, so that full-time caregiving is economically feasible (Mink, 1999, 2002). A caregiver's wage would not only validate the social and economic value of "motherwork," but also give poor mothers the right to stay home with their children.

The idea of providing a caregiver's wage to poor mothers has been met with considerable resistance by political conservatives who believe that guaranteed assistance to single mothers would encourage "dependency" and discourage work incentive. They believe that any type of work outside the home, regardless of whether the wages lift a family out of poverty, is essential to building "self-sufficiency." It is also feared that any form of guaranteed support, particularly to single women, would increase "out-of-wedlock" births or divorce. These same claims, although unsubstantiated by empirical research, were also used to build support for the strict work requirements and time limits adopted under PRWORA (see Delgado and Gordon, 2002; Hardisty and Williams, 2002; Piven, 2002).

Gaining widespread support for a caregiver's income in the United States will be difficult. The general public has little sympathy for "stay-at-home" mothers who need assistance to do so (Hyde, 2000) and with more mothers of young children employed outside the home, at least part-time, women's labor force participation has become a normative expectation. Many Americans seem to believe that if a woman cannot afford to support children on her own, she shouldn't have them. Amidst policy discussions about what constitutes "work" and cultural debates about women's roles, feminists must now argue vigorously for access to and fair treatment in the labor market, as well as economic justice for "stay-home" mothers.

Discussion questions

1 Should "motherwork" receive economic compensation? Explain your position.
2 If the government provides economic support to low-income families (e.g., welfare), what, if anything, should the government ask of recipients in return? Is it legitimate for the government to make welfare benefits contingent on recipient behavior (e.g., work requirements) or are such stipulations intrusive and unethical?
3 Design a campaign in support of a caregiver's income. What would you emphasize to maximize your campaign's effectiveness?

Although states have adopted provisions to ease the impact of these barriers, significant problems remain. Although childcare subsidies are available for low-income families, the demand for these resources exceeds supply and funding. Families who receive subsidized childcare are given certificates that they can use to purchase care from the provider of their choice. No state serves all of the families who are eligible for assistance under federal guidelines (Children's Defense Fund, 2000) and nationally, only about 15 percent of children eligible for childcare subsidies receive them (US Department of Health and Human Services, 1999). As a result, low-income families spend a higher percentage of their income on childcare than middle-income families and rely more heavily on informal, and often unreliable, childcare arrangements (e.g., family members, neighbors) (Henly and Lyons, 2000). Parents who work afternoon or evening shifts face further hardship since most centers offer limited evening hours.

Other state strategies for easing the transition from welfare to work have focused on extending time limits or suspending work requirements for specific populations. Most states have adopted the Family Violence Option (FVO) which allows work requirements and time limits to be temporarily waived for domestic violence survivors (Tolman and Raphael, 2000), but few states offer similar exceptions for mental health difficulties (Jayakody and Stauffer, 2000). Systematic mental health screening is not conducted in most states, making the likelihood of treatment and successful integration into the workforce unlikely.

Studies of "welfare leavers" reveal slim prospects for workplace advancement or economic mobility. Although most women leaving welfare are able to find a job (Corcoran et al., 2000), they are concentrated in low-wage service and clerical positions. In a General Accounting Office (1999) study of former welfare recipients in seven states, average quarterly earnings ranged from $2,378 to $3,786 or from $9,512 to $15,144 annually, assuming ongoing employment. Consequently, many "welfare leavers" remain poor despite the fact that they are working. Based on national survey data, Loprest (2001) estimates that approximately 41 percent of those who left the welfare rolls lived below the federal poverty level even after taking into account the cash value of food stamps and the earned income tax credit. Few working recipients receive employer-sponsored health insurance (Loprest, 1999). Not surprisingly, job retention is a significant problem and many families return to welfare (Urban Institute, 2001). Of the 2.1 million adults who reported leaving welfare for at least a month between 1995 and 1997, almost a third returned to welfare and were receiving benefits in 1997 (Loprest, 1999). But the option of cycling in and out of the workforce is declining as families come up against time limits.

Employer response to hiring welfare recipients is mixed. Although research documents relatively strong employer interest in hiring welfare recipients, the demand for these workers is heavily contingent on larger economic and labor market trends (Holzer, 1999). Even under relatively favorable conditions, Holzer and Stoll (2002) found that the demand for African Americans and Latinas lagged behind their representation in the welfare population, suggesting that welfare-reliant ethnic minorities may have a harder time securing employment than European Americans.

The extent to which employers are willing and/or able to accommodate workers with multiple barriers raises further concerns about how well welfare-reliant families can fare in the workplace. Studies of employer attitudes reveal a strong preference for hiring "job-ready" employees (Holzer, 1999; Owen et al., 2000). When given a choice between receiving referrals for pre-screened, ready-to-work employees or receiving financial incentives (e.g., wage subsidies, tax credits) for hiring recipients who were not ready to work, Roberts and Padden (as cited in Owen et al., 2000) found that employers unanimously preferred the former. A study of 900 Michigan employers by Holzer (1999) revealed a similar emphasis on job preparation. The vast majority of employers surveyed wanted basic assurances about the job readiness of welfare-reliant workers. Absenteeism, tardiness, work attitudes, and substance abuse were cited as major worries. Concerns about criminal records and basic cognitive skills were also quite high, with 55–60 percent of employers rating assurances on these issues as "very important." Half of the employers surveyed said that they would run drug tests or criminal background checks before hiring welfare-to-work employees.

A great deal of employer concern seems to be rooted in the fear that they will have to provide "social services" to their staff. Some employers have expressed discomfort with the work-first model for this reason (Owens et al., 2000). Very few of the Michigan employers Holzer (1999) surveyed were willing to provide job retention services. Less than 10 percent wanted to provide childcare or transportation assistance, although a greater percentage said they would help with basic skills (34 percent) and job skills (80 percent). These findings suggest that employers may be willing to assist with basic skill development but not the other supports that are essential to sustained employment. As a result, workers with multiple obstacles are likely to face extended periods of unemployment and underemployment.

REDUCING WORKPLACE CLASSISM: STRATEGIES FOR CHANGE

Improving class relations in the workplace requires a multifaceted approach. On the interpersonal level, classist stereotypes about the work ethic of welfare recipients and competency of working-class employees must be challenged. In-service training sessions typically focus on gender and ethnic diversity, but rarely broach class diversity or stereotypes. Class must be fully integrated into such discussions, bringing to the forefront negative assumptions about the performance of African-American inner-city employees and poor, Black single mothers or what Kennelly (1999) refers to as "that single mother element." Organizations need to seriously consider how subtle forms of classism such as "talking down" to "subordinates" poisons the workplace climate and diminishes the potential of their employees. Changing these behaviors, so deeply rooted in cultural beliefs about meritocracy and deservingness, will not be easy.

A number of structural changes are also needed. Hiring and recruiting practices should be analyzed to assess whether prospective employees from poor, minority neighborhoods and schools are being systematically excluded. Organizations that are genuinely interested in developing inclusive practices must be willing to implement policies that benefit *all* employees. Even though it is unlikely that class privilege in the workplace will be eliminated, the inequities perpetuated by practices such as providing paid vacation time or medical benefits to one class of employees at the expense of others, warrants careful examination.

For many years, family advocates and feminists have called for the widespread adoption of "family friendly" policies, including paid and job-secure parental leave, flexible scheduling to work around family needs, and onsite childcare centers (Glass and Estes, 1997). Research on welfare reform and the obstacles facing the growing number of welfare-reliant women in the workforce underscores the necessity of these supports. These policies which are slowly reaching middle-class professionals are virtually non-existent among low-wage workers. A real commitment to helping parents locate and afford quality childcare is an essential part of developing inclusive workplaces, but it is unlikely that most organizations can afford to provide these resources without significant governmental support. Although PRWORA expanded childcare assistance to low-income families, increased funding is desperately needed. In New York alone, subsidized childcare, pre-kindergarten, or Head Start services were only provided to 24 percent of low-income children whose mothers were working in welfare-to-work activities in 1998 (Citizen's Committee for Children, cited by Meyers et al., 2001). Subsidies need to reach more families, quality care needs to be easily accessible regardless of shift, and the salaries paid to childcare workers need to be improved, or class hierarchies that privilege professional positions over service-oriented and caregiving occupations will be further reified.

There are many reasons why the middle class might resist changes in the workplace that make it less classist. Those who benefit from class-based inequities are likely to reject moving toward a more class-sensitive, economically just workplace, and, in the short run, working-class gains would be bought at the expense of the middle class. Creating entry and promotion opportunities for semiskilled workers, paying living rather than minimum wages, and providing medical benefits to *all* workers would undoubtedly cut into profit margins and, in the immediate future, erode the power of privileged social networks.

In addition to these material barriers, psychological obstacles also stand in the way of change. Creating a more just workplace requires middle-class managers and others in positions of authority to examine the implications of "business as usual" and take personal responsibility for the classist policies and practices within their own organization. For those who unquestioningly accept their class privilege as earned, this will likely be a difficult process. Reversing exploitative workplace practices (e.g., low wages, dangerous conditions), providing real opportunities for advancement (e.g., training, post-secondary education, continuing education classes), and appreciating the contributions made by all workers are changes that not only threaten the foundation of class stratification, but also interrupt the self-congratulations of the privileged who wish to see themselves a fair minded people participating in a true meritocracy.

Although class diversity receives far less attention in the psychological literature than ethnic/racial and gender diversity (Bullock and Lott, 2001; Lott, 2002), psychologists have much to offer in terms of improving interclass relations and promoting economic justice. The research discussed in this chapter underscores the need to incorporate class into analyses of workplace diversity. Moreover, the practices that exclude, exploit, and limit the potential of poor and working-class people disproportionately affect women and ethnic minorities. Studying class diversity along with other diversities provides us with a richer understanding of workplace problems and promises the greatest hope for achieving equity.

Part IV

FURTHER DEVELOPMENTS

Where do we go from here? The subject of workplace diversity has, for better or worse, evolved simultaneously in both scientific/intellectual domains and as a viable management development practice. It has also aroused worldwide interest. Certainly, fads have come and gone, and some initiatives have not fulfilled their promise. But even these failed attempts to implement and manage diversity in the workplace have led to greater understanding, greater sensitivity, and greater creativity, all of which sustain the hope that full multicultural inclusiveness will eventually be achieved.

The chapters in this section describe the state of the management of workplace diversity in the US and abroad. They also provide directions for future innovation, both in research and practice. Chapter 12 discusses the general processes of organizational change and how it can continue to undergird diversity management. Chapter 13 discusses efforts around the globe to address workplace discrimination and inclusiveness, and outlines unique challenges facing several different nations. Chapter 14 provides a thematic review of the entire volume with regard to the benefits, challenges, and strategies for future development of workplace diversity as a scholarly discipline and a business imperative.

CREATING AND SUSTAINING DIVERSITY AND INCLUSION IN ORGANIZATIONS: STRATEGIES AND APPROACHES

Evangelina Holvino, Bernardo M. Ferdman,
and Deborah Merrill-Sands

This chapter describes the key elements of diversity initiatives: defining a vision for the desired outcome, understanding the dynamics of change and designing an appropriate strategy, and selecting and combining the most effective interventions and best practices. We review approaches used in organizations to create change toward diversity and inclusion, articulate some of the challenges organizations face as they seek the benefits that diversity, inclusion, justice, and equity can bring, and outline some techniques for meeting those challenges. Visions of inclusion in organizations are described, as are three levels of organizational change (systemic, cultural, and behavioral) and two approaches to change (organization development and collaborative inquiry). The chapter concludes with a discussion of tactics and best practice for successful change.

Organizations in the United States and around the world are paying increased attention to diversity. Diversity is widely regarded as vital for organizations to reach their valued goals. More and more emphasis is placed on the need to leverage multiculturalism and to foster inclusion as a basis for organizational success. For most organizations, the road to multiculturalism is long and hard (Dass and Parker, 1999). Knowledge of how organizations change and evolve can help individuals and teams travel toward multiculturalism with greater assurance of success and the least risk of disappointment.

What can organizations do to obtain the full benefit of all the potential that their people bring to the workplace? How can the vast range of differences among people – all the things that make us both unique and similar to others – function as a source of strength to organizations? What can organizations do to make sure that they are the kinds of places to which people would like to belong and contribute, and where historical patterns of intergroup injustice and inequality are eliminated rather than continually reproduced?

The aim of this chapter is to help students and practitioners who are interested in fostering and sustaining diversity and inclusion in organizations understand the key elements of a diversity initiative, which we submit are the following:

1 Define a vision of the desired outcome: what is a successfully diverse organization?
2 Understand the dynamics of change and design an appropriate strategy: how will this organization move toward its desired future and what type of leadership will be required?
3 Select and combine the most effective interventions and best practices to achieve goals for change toward diversity and inclusion: what activities and steps will bring about change?

The chapter is divided into three sections. The first section articulates a model for increasing multiculturalism within organizations – the vision. The second section outlines three levels of organizational change and differentiates between two related but distinct approaches – the dynamics of change. The third section moves from the conceptual to the concrete in order to discuss tactics for successful change – the best practices.

MODEL OF ORGANIZATIONAL EVOLUTION

Holvino (1998) has developed a framework she terms the Model of Multicultural Organizational Development (MCOD).[1] The MCOD model (see table 12.1) proposes that organizations go through six phases as they move from being *monocultural* (exclusionary organizations in which the values of one group, culture, or style are dominant) to *multicultural* (inclusive organizations in which the perspectives and styles of diverse peoples are valued and contribute to organizational goals and excellence).

In the first *exclusionary* stage, organizations explicitly and actively base themselves on the norms and values of one cultural group and advocate openly for the privileges and dominance of that group. Today, not many public organizations are still at the exclusionary stage. In the *passive club* stage, organizations are based on one cultural group's informal rules, systems, and ways of doing things, and only admit those who are similar to or closely fit the dominant group. In this

Table 12.1 The multicultural organizational development model

Monocultural		Transitional		Multicultural	
Exclusionary	Passive club	Compliance	Positive action	Redefining	Multicultural
Actively excludes in its mission and practices those who are not members of the dominant group.	Actively or passively excludes those who are not members of the dominant group. Includes other members only if they "fit."	Passively committed to including others without making major changes. Includes only a few members of other groups.	Committed to making a special effort to include others, especially those in designated target groups. Tolerates the differences that those others bring.	Actively works to expand its definition of inclusion and diversity. Tries to examine and change practices that may act as barriers to members of non-dominant groups.	Actively includes a diversity of groups, styles and perspectives. Continuously learns and acts to make the systemic changes required to value and include all kinds of people.
Values the dominant perspective of one group, culture, or style.		Seeks to integrate others into systems created under dominant norms.		Values and integrates the perspectives of diverse identities, cultures, styles, and groups into the organization's work and systems.	

Source: Holvino (1998). © Chaos Management, Ltd., 1998, used by permission.

stage, organizations operate much like private social clubs, where the norms include passive exclusion and ignoring of differences.

Organizations in the third stage of development, *compliance*, are passively committed to including members of non-dominant groups, but do not make any substantive changes in their management approaches so as to include those who are different. At this stage, differences are more symbolic than real, such as in a predominantly Christian organization with one or two Muslim members where the cultural symbols and celebrations remain Christian.

Organizations become actively committed to including members of non-dominant groups, making special efforts to attract non-dominant group members and tolerating the differences they bring, in the *positive action* stage. However, the subtle ways in which the norms, structures, and methods of working still favor those in the dominant group make it hard for others who are different to feel that they can contribute and advance in the organization. Although there is tolerance and targeted use of differences, not enough cultural and structural change has occurred to provide equal opportunities for all. At this stage there may be a critical mass of non-dominant group members who help to question and change some existing practices. The imbalances that occur during the positive action stage often lead organizations to move toward more inclusion or retreat to an earlier stage.

In the *redefining* stage, organizations actively try to include all differences and to remove the subtle and not so subtle barriers to inclusion in norms, practices, relationships, structure, and systems. At this stage there may be acceptance of differences, but not full utilization, as members of dominant and non-dominant groups are still learning to deal with differences and diversity.

In the *multicultural* or inclusive and diverse stage – an ideal stage in the development process – organizations seek and value all differences and develop the systems and work practices that support members of every group to succeed and fully contribute. Inclusion in multicultural organizations means that there is equality, justice, and full participation at both the group and individual levels, so that members of different groups not only have equal access to opportunities, decision-making, and positions of power, but also are actively sought out *because* of their differences. In a multicultural, inclusive organization, differences of all types become integrated into the fabric of the business, such that they become a necessary part of doing its everyday work.

Visions of multicultural organizations

The vision of a diverse and fully multicultural organization embedded in Holvino's MCOD model is similar to other visions described in the literature. For example, Foster et al. (1988: 40) define a multicultural organization as

> [one] that (1) reflects the contributions and interests of the diverse cultural and social groups in the organization's mission, operations, products, or services; (2) commits to eradicate all forms of social discrimination in the organization; (3) shares power and influence so that no one group is put at an exploitative advantage; (4) follows through on its broader social responsibility to fight social discrimination and advocate social diversity.

Cox (1991) defines a multicultural organization as one characterized by pluralism, full structural and informal integration, absence of prejudice and discrimination, low levels of intergroup conflict, and similar levels of identifications with the organization among employees from both dominant and non-dominant groups. For Miller and Katz (1995), in multicultural, inclusive organizations, diversity is seen as "a fundamental enhancement" and a "wide range of values and norms are . . . connected to . . . [the organization's] values, mission and goals" (p. 278).

Most visions of multicultural organizations focus on inclusion as a key aspect of leveraging diversity (Davidson and Ferdman, 2001; Ferdman and Davidson, 2002). We see inclusion as a feature of good management in any organization; unfortunately, it has typically been less evident in the context of most diverse organizations, particularly for those who are also members of historically sub-ordinated groups. Inclusion is fundamental for incorporating equality and truly sharing power across a range of groups and their members.

Mor-Barak and Cherin (1998: 47) describe inclusion in diverse organizations as "the degree to which individuals feel part of critical organizational processes," which is indicated by how much access they have to information and resources, how involved they are in their work group, and how much they can influence decision-making. Gasorek (2000) describes inclusion at Dun and Bradstreet in the context of a diversity initiative and considers the degree to which (a) employees are valued and their ideas are taken into account and used, (b) people partner successfully within and across departments, (c) current employees feel that they belong and prospective employees are attracted to the organization, (d) people feel connected to each other and to the organization and its goals, and (e) the organization continuously fosters flexibility and choice and attends to diversity.

Wheeler (1999: 33–4) provides a succinct summary of the components of inclusion at the organizational level: "organizations that truly value inclusion are characterized by effective management of people who are different, ability to admit weakness and mistakes, heterogeneity at all levels, empowerment of people, recognition and utilization of people's skills and abilities, an environment that fosters learning and exchanging of ideas, and flexibility." Similarly, Thomas and Ely (1996) describe a learning and effectiveness paradigm that predominates in multicultural organizations that are able to connect members' contributions and perspectives to the principal work of the organization, allowing them to "enhance work by rethinking primary tasks and redefining markets, products, strategies, missions, business practices, and even cultures" (p. 85). In this type of organization there is equal opportunity for all, differences and their value are recognized, and most importantly, the organization is able to "internalize differences among employees so that it learns and grows because of them. Indeed . . . members of the organization can say, We are all on the same team, *with* our differences – not despite them" (p. 86).

In essence, we define a multicultural, inclusive organization as one in which the diversity of knowledge and perspectives that members of different groups bring to the organization has shaped its strategy, its work, its management and operating systems, and its core values and norms for success. Furthermore, in multicultural, inclusive organizations, members of all groups are treated fairly, feel included and actually are included, have equal opportunities, and are represented at all organizational levels and functions. The ultimate goal in working with diversity is to weave it into the fabric of the organization. Working with diversity connects directly to the work of the organization and the people within it. It implies that diversity is the work and responsibility of everyone, not just managers and leaders. It suggests that diversity is an asset to be used and developed, rather than a problem to be managed. Finally, it projects a sense of dynamism and continuity.

Thus, it is important to understand diversity as more than just a human resource strategy or an approach for managing the workforce. Instead, diversity permeates all the work of an organization and requires a comprehensive effort to change at the organizational level as well as internalization by members of the organization. As Miller and Katz (2002) point out, if such an effort is to be successful it ultimately requires making diversity a new way of doing business, as well as a way of life for the organization and its people. In our view this entails a commitment to addressing and redressing historical inequities and power imbalances (Foldy, 1999; Litvin, 2000) and discovering new ways of collaborating across difference that, in a sense, "work" for everyone (see, for example, Ely and Meyerson, 2000; Fletcher, 2002). This is what we call *working with* diversity.

LEVELS OF CHANGE

Authors and practitioners vary widely in their specific recommendations and approaches to diversity initiatives because, as Zane (1994) points out, they come from very different disciplinary backgrounds: organizational behavior, organization development, and sociological and feminist disciplines. Considerable differences exist in several areas, including the vision of a successful and diverse organization, the degree and type of change required to accomplish diversity, the levels of the system on which to focus (individual, group, organizational, societal), how to measure change and success, and the kind of change required – long or short term, radical or evolutionary. Yet, in spite of the many differences and the range of recommended strategies and activities, organizational theorists agree that changes can be conceptualized as occurring at three levels of analysis.

Diversity initiatives must address these three different levels of organizational change: structural change, cultural change, and behavioral change (Ragins, 1995). Structural, cultural, and behavioral changes are synergistic: they interact and build on each other. Each level of change becomes a key leverage point for intervening in a planned diversity initiative. For example, structural changes such as equitable performance and advancement systems may remove "glass ceiling barriers" to the participation of women, but if the culture of an organization does not support the advancement of women and individual managers behave in non-supportive ways, gender equity will not be achieved (Acker, 1990; Kolb et al., 1998; Merrill-Sands, 1998; Meyerson and Fletcher, 2000; Thomas and Ely, 1996). Although the levels of change are interrelated in a complex and mutually reinforcing manner, we identify below the scope and examples of specific interventions that are representative of each. One of the key challenges of a diversity initiative is to have the right mix of synergistic interventions that will maximize change.

Structural change

Structural interventions focus on the formal systems that guide and control the work of the organization. These interventions target policies, practices, and structures that support or hinder the goals of diversity, such as recruitment practices, equal pay and benefits, policies on work–family balance, and the achievement of proportional heterogeneity in positions across rank, departments, and specializations.

Cox (1994) states that structural integration – the integration of "minority" group members in key positions, vertically and horizontally across the organizational hierarchy – is an important component of working with diversity effectively. In addition to providing access to decision-making and organizational power, structural integration may help reduce stereotyping and prejudice, provide important role models for the incorporation of other groups, and diminish the dynamics of tokenism that often reduce the effectiveness of employees from non-dominant groups.[2]

Recruitment, advancement, and retention programs usually accompany structural integration goals. These can include advising and mentoring, recruiting from new pools of talent, and setting up career development programs and career paths. They can also include changes in current recruitment practices, such as requiring that all interview panels be diverse in their makeup, changing the weight of the interview in the selection process, and reviewing jobs and job descriptions to focus on requirements as opposed to style preferences. Nevertheless, structural integration is not a sufficient component for achieving equity and inclusion, and when mishandled through practices such as rigid quotas and non-standard procedures, it may harm more than benefit a diversity initiative.

Other formal procedures that act as barriers to the inclusion, advancement, and effectiveness of employees across lines of difference must also be changed. For example, flexible work schedules, part-time scheduling, compressed work weeks, job sharing and job rotation, and flexible vacation and sick-leave policies have been shown to bring about the inclusion of different groups by providing more flexibility and helping attract and retain a diversity of employees such as working mothers and fathers, employees with elder-care responsibilities, and employees from non-dominant religions (see Lobel, 1999). This is not an exhaustive list. Other examples of important policies that should be reviewed or implemented are pay equity, benefits for domestic partners of gay and lesbian workers, and employee support programs that address the special needs of employees and enhance the quality of life in the workplace, such as counseling services and health and exercise clinics. Miller and Katz (2002) urge organizations to truly create and sustain inclusion by developing "new baselines" in policies and practices that go much further than in the past to support people from a wide range of groups.

Cultural change

Cultural change concerns the basic assumptions, values, beliefs, and ideologies that define an organization's view of itself, its effectiveness, and its environment. Organizational cultures, in large part, consist of the informal norms, or *mental models*, that support or hinder diversity and that have differential impact on different groups in the organization. Senge et al. (1994) describe mental models as deeply ingrained "images [and] assumptions . . . which we carry in our minds of ourselves, other people, institutions . . . Like a pane of glass, framing and subtly distorting our vision, mental models determine what we see . . . [They] also shape how we act . . . Because mental models are usually tacit, existing below the level of awareness, they are often untested and unexamined" (pp. 235–6). This is what makes them particularly hard to transform.

Changing the culture of an organization in order to value diversity and difference and to redress power imbalances is thus one of the most difficult parts of a diversity initiative. Cox suggests that the change goal is to develop a pluralistic culture "characterized by tolerance for ambiguity, an acceptance of a wide range of work styles and behaviors, and the encouragement of diversity in thought, practice, and action" (Ragins, 1995: 92). As Reynolds (1987: 38) advises, the difficulty with changing organizational culture is that

> culture is not the official system of values promulgated by management but a whole range of shared models of social action containing both real and ideal elements. Each layer of the cultural onion is affected by the social context and the channel of communication: the observed behavior; the official document; the things said at meetings; the things said when alone with one's boss; the things said to one's boss when the boss's boss is present; the verbal expression of what the ideal situation should be; and humorous rendering of all of the above.

Many attempts have been made to study and characterize organizational cultures according to their major traits, such as a power culture, a role culture, a support culture, and an achievement culture (Harrison and Stokes, 1992). Changes are then prescribed accordingly, depending on the strengths and weaknesses of the organizational culture identified. Education and training interventions may also be made with the aim of *changing* the culture of an organization, but it is important to understand that training interventions do *not* change organizational culture. We believe the best way to change organizational culture is to identify the informal practices and beliefs that make up that culture, to analyze their consequences (especially in terms of their impact on different groups of employees), and then to introduce small experiments designed to change everyday practices (Kolb and Merrill-Sands, 1999; Merrill-Sands, Fletcher, and Acosta, 1999; Meyerson and Fletcher, 2000; Rao, Stuart, and Kelleher, 1999).

Cultural audits are a good way of understanding and changing the assumptions and norms that predominate in an organization. The purpose of a diversity cultural audit is to identify key elements or characteristics of the organizational culture and how these influence the treatment and opportunities of members of different groups. Cultural audits may include studying the socialization of new members, analyzing responses to critical incidents in the organization's history, analyzing artifacts, symbols, rites and rituals, beliefs, values, stories, and even physical layout, and jointly exploring their meaning and impact on organizational climate and effectiveness (Chung, 1997).[3]

Other interventions that support organizational culture change include sanctioned affinity, support, or interest groups and alliances, which meet to share problems and solutions, learn the organizational norms, and develop supportive relations and change strategies (see chapter 10 for a discussion of GLB affinity groups); and ideological negotiations and forms of multicultural conflict resolution that help resolve conflicts of interest by directly or indirectly addressing value and ideological differences and settling disputes in democratic and participatory ways (Chesler, 1994; Jackson and Holvino, 1988).

Behavioral change

Behavioral change interventions seek changes in behaviors, attitudes, and perceptions within and between individuals, and within and between work groups, that support or hinder the goals of diversity. Targeted behaviors can range from the hostile to the thoughtless. Even without intending to do so, majority group members can negatively affect minority group members. Language use and humor, for example, can denote stereotyping and negative intergroup attitudes. These behaviors have been called micro-inequities because they support exclusion and differential treatment towards some people in practices such as restricted information and feedback from supervisors and co-workers, inequitable delegation of tasks, and exclusion from informal social networks and peer support (Cole and Singer, 1991; Ragins, 1995).

A common intervention to address individual and interpersonal behavior is education and training (see panel 12.1). Although many organizations and consultants equate diversity with training programs, we wish to emphasize that training is just one of the interventions that focus on changing individual behavior and is limited to that level of change. For example, training by itself cannot change organizational culture, except indirectly when a critical mass of people go through intense and successful training programs and become internal change agents (see Ferdman and Brody, 1996).

Ellis and Sonnenfeld (1994) identify some of the advantages of diversity training, such as raising awareness about indirect discrimination and conferred privilege, providing voice to those who have been historically underrepresented, substituting knowledge and facts for myths and stereotypes about co-workers, and sending a message that diversity is an important initiative throughout the organization. On the other hand, ill-designed and inappropriately conducted

12.1   *Training: A rich and focused intervention*

There are many options for implementing training and education programs to support a diversity initiative (Ferdman and Brody, 1996). Some
authors and consultants define education as a general approach to developing knowledge, attitudes, and skills in diversity. They differentiate education
from training interventions. Others define competency-based training as
knowledge-based and behavioral in nature, especially targeted to develop
"proven" skills that support diversity. To help decide which type of education and training program to implement, elements such as the overall
purpose, the audience, the content, and delivery style desired should be
considered.

Purposes of training programs

- *Awareness training:* To increase knowledge, ability to empathize, and understanding of the differential impact of the corporate culture by sharing
  stories and hearing about others' experiences and challenges. Deals with
  emotional and rational content of human interactions, exploring how
  people feel and act in the face of differences.
- *Skill building:* To increase skills in behaving and acting in ways that
  promote diversity, such as cross-cultural communication and conflict
  resolution.
- *Orientation and information dissemination:* To increase knowledge by disseminating information about new policies that impact diversity –
  such as sexual harassment – or communicating the status of a diversity
  initiative.
- *Dialogue groups:* To increase the opportunity for candid conversations
  between individuals and groups in a relatively unstructured format on
  an ongoing basis.

Types of content

- Cross-cultural training, bias reduction, managing diversity, and general
  policy orientation programs are just a few of the types of content areas
  that differentiate training programs.

Target audience

- Programs may be developed for different target populations, such as
  mid-level managers, first-line supervisors, technical staff, working teams,
  general population and internal change agents.

- Other choices must be made between training that is off-the-shelf or customized, internally delivered or delivered by external consultants, offsite or on-the-job, short or long duration, stretched over a period of time or one-time, phased into a sequence of programs, and voluntary or mandatory.

Discussion questions

1 In what kinds of training have you participated? What made these training experiences successful (or unsuccessful)? What lessons can you draw for diversity training?
2 In what ways might diversity training be similar to other types of training in organizations? How is it different? What implications do these similarities and differences have for the design and delivery of diversity training?
3 Discuss the pros and cons of participating in diversity training with the same people as are in your workgroup (as opposed to participating with people with whom you do not work every day).
4 What are some of the topics and issues that you believe could or should be addressed in diversity training? Why?

training may do considerable harm to diversity efforts. For example, it can create additional stereotypes if the content is too simplistic, or it can alienate dominant groups if the process of training is believed to favor some groups at the expense of others. Training interventions can also backfire if they are delivered as one-shot events without appropriate follow-up or reinforcement (Grace, 1994).

Other important interventions to change behaviors for increased diversity and inclusion are coaching and multicultural team-building. Coaching provides one-on-one support to managers, especially at senior levels, to help them identify areas that need development and to encourage them to take action. Multicultural team-building enhances the effectiveness of working teams by developing skills in managing cultural and other social differences that may impact tasks, the roles members play, their relationships, and the methods and procedures used to accomplish their work. One important note of caution is that behavioral change interventions can rely too much on "fixing the people" or "equipping the minorities" while ignoring the systemic structural and cultural factors that influence individual and group behavior (Kolb et al., 1998; Smith, Simmons, and Thames, 1989).

Effective diversity efforts require a multi-level approach that includes structural, cultural, and behavioral change and a variety of specific interventions that reinforce and augment each other. Morrison (1996) summarized the ten most important diversity interventions identified in her benchmarking research with corporations in the United States. We list them here in the order of importance assigned by her team, based on their survey and interview information:

- personal involvement of the top management and organizational leaders;
- recruitment of diverse staff in managerial and non-managerial positions;
- internal advocacy and change agent groups;
- emphasis on collection and utilization of statistics and diversity organizational profiles;
- inclusion of diversity in performance appraisal and advancement decisions;
- inclusion of diversity in leadership development and succession planning;
- diversity training programs;
- support networks and internal affiliation groups;
- work–family policies;
- career development and advancement.

APPROACHES TO CHANGE

This section describes two major approaches to organizational change: the organization development approach and the collaborative inquiry approach. Although similar, the two approaches differ in certain particulars.

Organization development approach

The organization development (OD) approach to diversity is an integrated, planned, system-wide, and long-term process of change. Holvino's MCOD model (see above) is an example of an OD approach to diversity (Chesler, 1994; Jackson and Holvino, 1988; Katz and Miller, 1988; Miller and Katz, 1995). OD approaches are characteristically managed from the top, cascade down the organization to other organizational levels, and make use of external consultants as experts who support the organization throughout the process of change.

The OD approach requires an initial assessment of where the organization is in relation to diversity and its vision of where it wants to be in the future. From an analysis of the gap between where the organization is and where it wants to be, specific interventions are then designed to accomplish the identified change goals. Holvino's MCOD model (see table 12.1) provides a useful way for an organization to frame an initial diagnosis and vision of diversity.

Processes and sequence of change

Although many organizations come up with their own blueprints for developing and implementing a diversity initiative, the following five-step process is representative of common practices in the OD approach (Arredondo, 1996; Cox, 2001; Cross, 2000; Jackson and Hardiman, 1994; Katz and Miller, 1988; Loden, 1996; Miller, 1998; Miller and Katz, 2002; Thomas, 1992):

1 Preparing for the initiative.
2 Assessing needs related to diversity.
3 Developing a vision, goals, and a strategic plan.
4 Implementing the interventions selected.
5 Monitoring and evaluating progress and results.

It is important to note that even though these steps appear to be linear, this is actually a cyclical process in which the last step informs prior work. Because diversity is so complex it is recommended – especially in its initial stages – that the plan remain open and flexible until data gathering, learning, and needs assessment have taken place to better inform the initial decisions. For example, the concept of diversity is usually unclear in the beginning. During data collection a great deal of learning takes place about the barriers to diversity and inclusion, the specific meaning of these concepts in the context of the organization, and the vision of inclusion and diversity that will galvanize members to work towards and embrace the change effort.

Preparing for an initiative (step 1) involves creating the foundation for the change process, including securing leadership support and involvement and developing an initial plan of action. The most important elements at this stage are to communicate the intent of the initiative, allocate resources, assign responsibilities, and frame the initial tasks, as well as to ensure that the initiative responds to strategic organizational imperatives for diversity (see, for example, Robinson and Dechant, 1997; Wheeler, 1995). Miller and Katz (2002) highlight the importance of beginning to create a belief in the organization that new ways of working together inclusively are actually possible, and of identifying points of leverage so that actions taken have maximal payoff.

Once the intent of a diversity initiative has been identified, data need to be gathered in order to assess needs related to diversity (step 2). Cultural audits (e.g., Cox, 2001; Potts, 1996), employee surveys, and focus groups are typical ways in which consultants help organizations gather information about which aspects of diversity should be explored, given the strategic imperative. The consultant analyzes the data and makes recommendations, which are then fed back to key members of the organization for action (see, for example, Cox, 2001; Potts, 2000). The purpose of the analysis and feedback process is to connect interrelated themes into a meaningful picture that suggests important areas of need and goals for change. Strengths as well as limitations should be identified and categorized under some broad areas of change.

The MCOD model helps define the diversity change goal by providing a framework to interpret the data into a picture of the current level of multicultural development. Usually the change goal becomes the means to move the organization to the next stage of development. In doing an assessment, one needs to look at all of the important dimensions of an organization and all the social groups that may need to be included to determine the level of current multiculturalism. For example, it is important to consider how the mission, culture, language, informal systems, policies, structures, leadership, and reward systems support (or do not support) an inclusive and diverse organization for women; for members of racial, ethnic, language, or religious minorities; for gays, lesbians, bisexuals, and transgendered people; for people with disabilities; for members of poor and working socioeconomic classes; and for members of other subordinated social groups (Davidson and Ferdman, 2002). Because it is not usually possible to identify all issues or all identity groups at the early stages of an initiative, it is vitally important to design the change effort so as to be able to respond to new demands and to expand the agenda for change. As the critical mass of internal and external change agents increases, gradually incorporating the needs and perspectives of new stakeholders may help to reduce the resistance of those who feel that they may not benefit from the change effort. In any case, attending to this resistance and finding ways to be inclusive of members of dominant groups who are willing to participate as champions of the initiative are often key aspects of successful change efforts (see, for example, Cross, 2000; Nash, 2000).

Developing a strategic plan is the third step. An organizational change strategy is a comprehensive plan based on a thorough analysis of organizational needs and goals. It is designed to bring about specific changes and ensure that appropriate steps are taken to maintain those changes. It includes definitions of end objectives, outlines of specific actions designed to produce the desired outcomes, time frames, and a monitoring and evaluation system. A strategy must specify the priority goals, primary interventions, and sequence of activities, resources, and responsibilities. It also needs to take into consideration the power dynamics and the culture of the organization, as well as the processes involved in implementing organizational innovations (Loden, 1996).

A well-developed strategic plan guides a diversity initiative by (a) informing the organization about the importance and flow of the change effort; (b) defining goals for management and targets of change; (c) providing a structure, clarity, and accountability for the initiative; and (d) linking the change effort to the competitive advantage and gains that will be derived from the initiative. Arredondo (1996: 96) states that the strategic plan is "the document that can reflect the goals and actions that will respond to concerns and recommendations that emerge from needs assessments and other relevant sources."

Part of the strategic plan (though this may also be an additional phase in the process) must include a vision and a definition of diversity and inclusion that are specific to the organization. The important task at this point is to explore, come to terms with, and provide a definition of diversity for the organization that is inclusive and that guides and connects to the core vision and mission of the organization. Many times, the vision and definition of diversity and inclusion are generated too early in the process and are vague or incomplete, and can then become easy targets of criticism. We recommend that organizations do not attempt to develop a final diversity vision before assessing needs and collecting information and examples through educational and benchmarking activities. Paradoxically, some type of vision is also necessary at the earliest stages, to begin and help pull the process of change in the first place. The problem comes when that vision is not modified or enhanced on the basis of the needs assessment and the strategic planning process. A good example of an aspirations statement that incorporates diversity is the one developed by Levi Strauss, a retail company, for its leadership:

> [The leadership of Levi Strauss] values a diverse workforce (age, sex, ethnic group, etc.) at all levels of the organization, diversity in experience, and diversity in perspectives. We have committed to taking full advantage of the rich backgrounds and abilities of all our people and to promoting a greater diversity in positions of influence. Differing points of view will be sought; diversity will be valued and honestly rewarded, not suppressed. (**Howard, 1990: 135, quoted in Kossek and Lobel, 1996: 10**)

Roosevelt Thomas (Thomas and Woodruff, 1999) suggests that strategic plans in diversity-mature organizations have the following characteristics: (a) they derive from compelling and strategic motives; (b) they identify the diversity-related issues that must be addressed in response to an organizational assessment; and (c) they delineate a clear sequence in which the tasks must be implemented. Dass and Parker (1999) distinguish among episodic, freestanding, and systemic approaches to diversity initiatives, with the latter being more likely when the pressures for diversity are high and the priority for working with diversity is seen as having strategic importance. Organizations adopting systemic approaches integrate the various components of their diversity initiatives with each other and into a larger strategic framework.

As with any other organizational action plan, the key questions in the implementation step (step 4) are: Who? What? When? For whom and with whom? and Where? A variety of options are available to address these questions. For example, in answer to the "Who?" question, leadership and accountability for the intervention can be provided by a task force, committee, or council; departments, business units, or occupational groups; the office of the designated diversity leader and staff, such as a Gender Unit; the most senior levels in the organization, such as the chief executive; or other key stakeholders, such as the board of directors and unions.

The types of interventions, activities, and programs to be selected, the timelines and sequence of events, who will participate, what their roles will be, in which locations, and at what hierarchical levels and functional units these various components will take place, are the essence of the implementation plan. Many decisions must be made and a multicultural development model such as Holvino's can help guide these decisions.

Regardless of the specifics, the key enablers of a strategic plan are communication, credibility, and accountability (Arredondo, 1996). Without appropriate communication throughout the organization to all employees and at all levels, without a plan of action that makes sense and sets clear priorities, and without clarity about responsibilities, accountability, and measures of success, the best intervention plan will fail. Thus, a key aspect of implementing a strategic plan is defining communication and rollout strategies, assigning responsibilities to credible members of the organization, and identifying clear targets of change and measures of success for different organizational members and divisions. Clearly, the involvement of those affected in the planning process will be crucial to the success of the plan. In addition, we want to emphasize the importance of visible leadership from the top, engagement of middle managers responsible for operations, and involvement of "everyday" leaders – "seed carriers" – who will lead the effort through everyday activities and work practices (Meyerson and Scully, 1999; Senge, 1990).

Monitoring and evaluating the diversity plan (step 5) is an important component of a diversity initiative. By monitoring, we mean making sure that what was planned is being accomplished. By evaluating, we mean determining the impact and results of the planned interventions. Evaluation is one of the most neglected aspects in diversity initiatives and also requires careful planning regarding the scope of the evaluation, the information that will be sought from the evaluation process, how and for whom information will be gathered, the use of the data, and to whom and how it will be fed back (Comer and Soliman, 1996; Digh, 1998; Martineau and Preskill, 2002; McEnrue, 1993; Stephenson and Krebs, 1993). When goals and expected outcomes have been made clear during the initial planning process and data have been collected that can serve as a baseline to assess change over time, the evaluation process is easier to implement, because it provides its own measurements of comparison for before and after the interventions.

Monitoring the representation, advancement, and retention of members of previously underrepresented groups is the most common method of assessing diversity efforts, but this approach to monitoring is more appropriate for organizations in the positive action stage of the MCOD model. In comprehensive long-term initiatives, other areas to evaluate – addressing outcomes of the intervention as well as effective implementation of the interventions – should include (a) changes in individual attitudes and behavior; (b) the impact of specific interventions to promote change in organizational culture; (c) the integration of particular diversity strategies in the daily business systems and structures; (d) changes in costs and in profitability; and (e) the level of satisfaction of members of different groups in the organization (see panel 12.2). Specific evaluation methods that can be used include program evaluations, such as evaluation of training or career development programs; organizational surveys to assess workplace climate; benchmarking with other organizations for comparison purposes; surveys of

12.2 *Evaluating diversity through employee surveys, not numbers of employees*

Comer and Soliman (1996) state that very few organizations that have invested in diversity efforts monitor and assess whether they are actually achieving their objectives and promoting multiculturalism. They suggest several indicators that move beyond monitoring numerical representation and promotions of diverse groups. These indicators can be grouped into two areas: (1) employee assessment of a positive working climate and (2) assessment of increased organizational performance. New questions to be explored are:

- Do all employees consider systems of performance appraisals, rewards, and promotions to be fair and unbiased?
- Do all employees have access to important information that enables them to do their jobs and contribute?
- Do all employees have the ability to influence decision-making?
- Do all employees perceive that they have opportunities to acquire and develop new skills and advance their careers?
- Do all employees perceive that they have opportunities for formal and informal mentoring and coaching?
- Have absenteeism and turnover costs declined among all employees?
- Has patronage of diverse customers or clients flourished?
- Has creativity and innovation blossomed?
- Has organizational responsiveness and flexibility increased?

Often, appropriate items can be incorporated into an organization's regular employee survey. It is important to collect data for different groups of employees so as to determine the impact of changes on a range of employees, especially those who are different from the majority. In this way, well-constructed surveys that take diversity into account can play an important role in monitoring and evaluating an ongoing diversity initiative. Falletta and Combs (2002) point out that when surveys are used as part of an organization development effort, they should be grounded in systems theory, model driven, action research oriented, and viewed as a tool for change planning.

Discussion questions

1 What impact do you think including questions about diversity and inclusion on regular employee surveys might have on an organization and its members? Why?
2 What criteria or indicators could be used in your school or work environment to assess diversity and inclusion? How are these tied to particular goals or objectives with regard to changes in the organization?

external recognition and reputation awards such as "best employer" or "community service"; and analysis of indicators of overall performance such as profits, market share, and new markets, and of executive performance such as leadership and business unit or departmental performance.

It is important to note that evaluation is crucial if organizational learning on diversity is to occur. Moreover, not paying attention to this step in the process of developing a diversity initiative can undo important progress made and sends a message that diversity is not as serious as other organizational goals.

Strengths and limitations of the organization development approach

The OD approach to diversity has some key strengths. It provides a clear focus to the change effort. It is similar to other planning processes commonly used in organizations and thus more familiar. It is management driven, and it involves a logical and deliberate pace of change that promotes a certain amount of organizational security amidst a process that can be experienced as potentially threatening.

However, success in implementing OD approaches to diversity also requires considering how their application differs from more traditional OD change efforts (Chesler, 1994; Chesler and Delgado, 1987; Jackson and Hardiman, 1994; Prasad et al., 1997). For example, Chesler points out that MCOD, because of its equity goal, needs to pay more attention to the role of conflict, intergroup dynamics, coalition and alliance building, and power and resistance issues within the context of change than do other OD interventions.

Some of the limitations to the OD approach to diversity are that unforeseen organizational changes such as top leadership shifts, restructuring, or a bad economic year, can derail the initiative. If the organization is not able to adapt, learn from the implementation process, and revise the initial plans, the effort will be difficult to sustain. It is also important not to rely too heavily on educational programs, policy changes, and accountability measures – all of which are common interventions in the OD approach – as a way of changing the organizational culture. Moreover, the effort should not be viewed as simply a human resource initiative, because this removes the managers and other staff from their responsibility to provide leadership. Indeed, Dass and Parker (1999) point out that a distinguishing feature of systemic diversity initiatives is that responsibility for them typically lies with line managers.

Panel 12.3 provides an example of an OD approach to diversity (see also White, 1996). OD approaches to diversity are particularly suitable for organizations operating in stable environments, in hierarchical organizations where there is strong leadership championing the diversity change agenda, and when there is a critical mass of people who desire change. Collaborative approaches to change, to which we turn in the next section, offer an alternative that may work best under a different set of organizational conditions (Bunker and Alban, 1997; Chesler, 1994; Holvino, 1993).

12.3 *An example of an organization development approach to diversity: MOBA manufacturing*

The initiative started with a request from the CEO of MOBA manufacturing, a multinational corporation, via his human resource manager, to engage in "diversity management." After initial conversations with members of the top management team, the plan of action summarized here was implemented during the first three years.

Activities for the first year focused on developing an initial strategy with the top management team that included: (1) defining the overall global business context and determining the organizational imperative for diversity; (2) informing the workforce of the initiative and the intention to begin to collect information; (3) forming and developing a diversity advisory group composed of representatives of diverse groups in the organization across levels and functions; and (4) identifying and educating the internal liaison for the initiative in the office of a Manager for Inclusion and Organizational Change.

The set of activities implemented at the end of the first year and during the second year were: (5) refining, developing, and disseminating the "business imperative" for diversity, which identified workforce skills needed for the future, requirements for a successful organizational culture, and leadership competencies required for the future; (6) implementing education and awareness sessions with the top management team and the advisory group; (7) selecting three country sites, plus headquarters, for initial data collection through employee surveys and focus groups; and (8) reviewing recruitment, placement, advancement policies, and other human resource practices.

The third set of activities implemented during the second and third year were: (9) analysis of the survey and focus group results and preparation of a report with recommendations by an external diversity consulting firm; (10) discussion of key data and recommendations from the report in joint session with the top management team, the advisory group, and selected interviewees from representative groups in the organization; and (11) agreement on a plan of action to respond to the recommendations. These included: (a) in-depth diversity education sessions for managers and advocates; (b) changes in recruitment practices, development of new career development paths, and implementation of a 360-degree feedback system; and (c) an intervention involving large numbers of staff in-country to address issues of workplace culture and climate.

Responsibility for implementation of the selected diversity initiatives was assigned to the department heads and other working unit heads. The diversity advisory group, the Office of Inclusion and Organization Change, and the consultants acted as resources. The top management team continued to receive reports and monitor the implementation and results during the first three years.

Discussion questions

1 What suggestions do you have for how MOBA manufacturing might go about assessing the effectiveness of its diversity initiatives?
2 What components would you recommend including in a diversity initiative in your organization? Why?

Collaborative inquiry approaches to diversity

Collaborative inquiry approaches are usually more fluid than traditional OD approaches to diversity. We explore three examples of collaborative inquiry approaches: action research, appreciative inquiry, and future search conferences. Although some authors (e.g., Waclawski and Church, 2002) see these as also falling under the rubric of OD, we distinguish them to emphasize the somewhat different orientation adopted by those using these methods with regard to the degree and type of collaboration with the organization and its members, the flexibility of the change process and the roles of internal v. external change agents, and the orientation to change. Specifically, external consultants who practice collaborative inquiry approaches emphasize a high degree of partnership with the client organization and its members, with concomitant involvement of the latter in all phases of planning and implementation of the diversity initiative. In so doing, practitioners of collaborative inquiry seek to approach new situations without many preconceived models, and are prepared to generate new frameworks and new strategies as needed. Finally, those adopting collaborative inquiry approaches, in contrast to those focusing on the more traditional OD methods described earlier, are more likely to see change as constant. (For more details on collaborative inquiry, see Rapoport et al., 2002.)

Action research is a collaborative inquiry approach to organizational change that focuses on joint learning between internal and external change agents (Greenwood and Levin, 1998; Rapoport, 1970; Whyte, Greenwood, and Lazes, 1991). Rapoport (1970: 499) provides the following definition: "Action research aims to contribute to the practical concerns of people in an immediate problematic situation and to the goals of social science by joint collaboration within a mutually acceptable ethical framework."

Action research usually proceeds with the following seven phases (Greenwood and Levin, 1998; Merrill-Sands, Fletcher, and Acosta, 1999; Merrill-Sands, Fletcher, Acosta, Andrews, and Harvey, 1999; Whyte, Greenwood, and Lazes, 1991):

1 *Entry and set-up*: the inquiry and change goals are agreed upon and internal and external research collaborators develop an initial design and "contract" to collect information.
2 *Data collection and inquiry:* information is collected through interviews, focus groups, surveys, and other mechanisms.
3 *Analysis:* the data are assembled, summarized, and organized according to identifiable patterns.
4 *Feedback and action planning:* the analysis of the data is shared with members of the organization to develop a joint interpretation, identify change goals, and develop action plans.
5 *Implementation and experimentation:* actions agreed upon are implemented and organizational experiments to support the change goals are conducted.
6 *Monitoring and evaluation:* data are collected to assess the impact of the change initiatives and experiments.
7 *Learning, adaptation, and further experimentation:* the process is repeated, as needed. Eventually, it becomes a normal part of the organization's processes.

This process of data collection, analysis, and experimentation initiates another cycle of action research, engaging the organization in a continuous and iterative process of inquiry and change. Central to the process of action research is the idea that learning derives from introducing changes or experiments into the system and observing their effects. This may then lead to further adaptations or new interventions. Although less is published on action research and collaborative inquiry approaches to diversity initiatives than on the OD methods described earlier, Cumming and Holvino (1997) provide a concrete example from the practice of collaborative action research with a multicultural board development intervention (see panel 12.4).

Because collaborative approaches to change are more fluid and are planned in distinct cycles of inquiry, analysis, and implementation, Holvino (2000) suggests that an action research approach to diversity may be more appropriate than long-term and more traditional OD approaches. This may be especially so for social change organizations where more stakeholders expect to participate in key organizational decisions, where human and financial resources are scarce, and where changes in the external environment – such as donors' priorities or national politics – are unpredictable or frequent.

Large group collaborative interventions for organizational change, such as future search conferences (Weisbord, 1992; Weisbord and Janoff, 2000) and appreciative inquiry methodology (Bunker, 1990; Cooperrider, 1990; Cooperrider and Srivasta, 1987; Elliott, 1999; Fitzgerald, Murrell, and Newman, 2002; Hammond, 1996), could also prove to be very powerful in diversity efforts. A unique characteristic of large group interventions is that they simultaneously involve internal and external stakeholders in the change effort and bring the whole system into the room to work together, energizing and involving many organizational members in the process of change.[4]

12.4 *BEC: An example of collaborative inquiry
with a social change organization*

BEC is a small organization whose mission is to advocate on a variety of
social issues that affect a very diverse community with a high population of
immigrants in the heart of a major US city. A multicultural board made up
of representatives of the key groups in the community and an executive
director, a White bilingual man, manage the affairs of the organization with
a skeleton staff of part-timers and community volunteers.

The consultants were enlisted to assist the board of directors in becoming
more sensitive and effective at managing the cultural, language, and class
differences among its members. The monthly board meetings were conducted
in English and simultaneously translated into three other languages: Portu-
guese, Spanish, and Khmer. The board was having trouble working effectively, yet recognized the importance of learning from, and finding better
ways of working with, their very rich and representative social differences.

A collaborative inquiry approach was agreed upon. A videotape was made
at a regular board meeting. After the meeting, board members attending
the meeting were asked to identify at least one problematic moment they
had observed in the meeting and to assess the effectiveness of the meeting
using a short evaluation form. A problematic moment is a moment when
the group has the opportunity to creatively struggle with its differences and
solve a particular problem.

An edited 15-minute version of the videotape was produced containing
four problematic moments, which were identified in the course of the two-
hour meeting. The tape was shown to the board during a one-day retreat.
Analysis of each moment helped the members assess strengths and areas
for improvement in the way the board managed itself and its differences.
Based on the assessment and discussions, the group drew up action plans
designed to improve the board's work and multicultural relations. As a
result of the analysis of the problematic moments, the following sustainable
improvements were brought to the operation of BEC's board:

- Responsibilities and roles were clarified and an internal board structure
  was set up consisting of a community outreach committee, a program/
  staff committee, and a financial/fundraising committee.
- A glossary of multicultural terms used frequently by board members
  was produced. Interpreters now sit behind, not next to, people receiving
  interpretation. A way for non-English speaking members to have more
  input into the agenda was formalized.
- The board members worked on improving their meeting skills and developed multicultural norms for their meetings. The board now meets

every month to discuss 5–6 issues instead of every two months with 10–12 issues.
• Experienced board members began mentoring new board members on key issues affecting the community.

Discussion questions

1 What similarities and differences do you see in the approaches taken at BEC and that taken at MOBA manufacturing (panel 12.3)? How might one reasonably combine the two approaches?
2 What can your organization and its members do to work more effectively with and learn from your differences?
3 Based on your reading so far, what aspects of the work groups that you belong to might benefit from a collaborative inquiry such as that described here? Why?

By James Cumming and Evangelina Holvino, © Copyright 1997, Chaos Management, Ltd. Used with permission.

A future search conference is a three-day large group event that helps the various stakeholders of an organization create a shared vision of the future and generate action steps for accomplishing it. Typically, 60–70 participants – representative of the whole system – gather in one room and engage in a highly structured set of activities to explore their past and common history, identify the conditions that are impacting them in the present, and develop scenarios for the desired future. The meeting enables all stakeholders to discover shared intentions and common ground on such issues as how multicultural they want their organization to be. It encourages participants to take responsibility for their own action plans and to make their visions happen.

Appreciative inquiry (AI) has also led to some notable successes in organizations seeking to better capitalize on staff diversity (see panel 12.5). The appreciative inquiry process consists of a four-part cycle: discovery, dreaming, design, and delivery (Elliott, 1999; Hammond 1996; Hammond and Royal, 1998). What distinguishes this from other approaches is its assumption that in every organization, and for every member thereof, something is going right, and that there have been at least occasional high points of performance and achievement. Rather than diagnose problems and shortcomings in the discovery phase, appreciative inquiry sets out to document the organization's best moments and the conditions and individual contributions that made them possible. Here the process resembles an internal benchmarking of best practices, identified and narrated by the people who experienced them. As the organization amasses stories, it can

12.5   *From sexual harassment to best cross-gender relations:*
An appreciative inquiry case

A large manufacturing organization located in Mexico wanted to make a dramatic cut in the incidence of sexual harassment. In conversations with the appreciative inquiry consultants, the purpose of the intervention was redefined as "develop a model of high-quality cross-gender relationships in the workplace for the new-century organization."

A small pilot project started with pairs of women and men who worked together nominating themselves to share their stories of creating and sustaining high-quality cross-gender workplace relationships. Hundreds of pairs nominated themselves and a hundred people were trained in appreciative inquiry interviewing. During the next several weeks, 300 interviews were completed, using volunteer interviewees to interview new pairs. The stories collected and documented provided examples of achievement, building trust, joint leadership, practices for effective conflict management, ways of dealing with sex stereotypes, stages of development in cross-gender relations, and methods of career advancement.

A large group forum was held after the stories had been collected and disseminated, with the interview stories providing the fuel to develop proposals for the future. Some thirty practical proposals were created, such as "Every task or committee, whenever possible, is co-chaired by a cross-gender pair." Changes in systems and structures were made to implement the propositions. One of the most dramatic examples of the impact of the appreciative inquiry intervention was the change made in the composition of the senior leadership group to include more women. In 1997 the organization was chosen as the best company in the country for women to work.

Discussion questions

1 Think of a situation in which you have participated in a high-quality and productive cross-gender work relationship. What were its key features? What allowed the partnership to succeed? What lessons can you draw from that experience for future cross-gender collaborations?
2 Why do you think that this intervention had the results that it did?
3 Based on your reading, experience, and observation, what do you think can be done to improve the experience and results of cross-gender work partnerships? What can/should organizations do in this regard? What can/should you do?

This intervention was designed and facilitated by Marge Schiller and Marcia Worthing; from Holman and Devane (1999: 250–1).

create a new image of itself based on the qualities it has manifested in its moments of excellence.

Some of the resulting action steps to put the "dream" – as it is referred to in AI – into operation may involve extending the conditions that enabled successful practices, so that these become the norm rather than the exception. But the very process of AI frequently leads to breakthroughs in an organization's own sense of what it is capable of achieving and in its members' awareness of the richness of resources that were previously latent. Several AI scholar-practitioners attribute this to the deep dialogue of the interview process, which enables the members of an organization to talk about their successes in their own terms (Bushe, in press; Elliott, 1999). AI proponents argue that this approach does not generate the defensiveness that typically comes with traditional organization development diversity change interventions because, rather than asking people to change what they have been doing wrong, it encourages them to do more of what they have already been doing right.

Strengths and limitations of collaborative inquiry approaches to diversity

The action research and other collaborative inquiry approaches to diversity have some key strengths. These approaches involve many stakeholders in the stages of the change effort, thus generating energy and commitment throughout the whole system. They develop internal capacity by increasing the knowledge and skills of internal change agents. They promote organizational dialogues, which help to identify and illuminate deep norms affecting equity and effectiveness and the practices that reinforce them. Furthermore, collaborative inquiry approaches generate less resistance than top-down approaches because they tend to involve those likely to be affected by the changes as integral participants in the process, and they provide access to important information rapidly. Finally, such approaches integrate the expertise of internal and external change agents.

The collaborative inquiry approaches also have some limitations. First, it may be difficult to get leadership commitment and resources because specific outcomes are not predictable or set at the beginning of the initiative. Second, the participatory process may generate too many agenda items and create unrealistic expectations about change throughout the organization. Third, the unbounded nature of the process requires ongoing negotiation. Fourth, the external researchers' lack of grounding in the culture of the organization and their lack of an established long-term relationship with the organization and its leaders may hinder the continuing viability of the initiative.

TACTICAL CONSIDERATIONS IN DIVERSITY INITIATIVES

For each of the levels of change and for either approach to change, there exists a wide range of specific interventions or activities that can be applied. Many interventions, such as mentoring, impact more than one level of change. In a diversity initiative, the purpose of mentoring programs is to support the career development of "targeted" groups by helping identify and develop specific individuals in the organization. The assumption is that members of non-dominant groups do not have the same access to informal mentoring opportunities that may accrue more easily to members of dominant groups. Catalyst (1999b), a non-profit research organization focusing on gender issues in corporations, found that the single greatest barrier to advancement as reported by women of color in the United States was the lack of mentors. The importance of mentoring for individual advancement, effectiveness, and well-being is well established (see, for example, Murrell, Crosby, and Ely, 1999; Ragins, 1999).

In addition, different interventions are more appropriate for different stages of multicultural OD. For example, in the exclusive stage, organizations benefit most from legal interventions and having to respond to external pressures for change. In the passive club stage, organizations will benefit from revising and opening up the recruitment process to increase the numbers of underrepresented groups, making a special effort to recruit "pioneers" who are willing to lead organizational change, and adopting policies to prevent socially based harassment.

In the compliance stage, mentoring, networks, and education programs help create a climate for change and a critical mass of employees to support change. In the positive action stage, an expanded vision of diversity, identifying and developing internal change agents, working with pockets of readiness to initiate culture change experiments, and instituting diversity accountability measures in performance evaluations, have proven to be successful interventions.

In the redefining and multicultural stages, inclusive policies and structures such as self-managed teams, win-win conflict skills training, organizational learning, reviewing and renegotiating norms, and involvement of external stakeholders, are interventions that support a continuous change process for inclusion and diversity.

Although organization-wide interventions such as training programs and support networks are an important part of a diversity change initiative, diversity initiatives must also include interventions that address the needs and opportunities of work within specific work units; for example, conducting a multicultural team-building intervention with a virtual project team. It is often in the smaller work units that experiments can be designed and tested. Innovations can then be dispersed throughout the organization (Merrill-Sands, Fletcher, and Acosta, 1999; Meyerson and Fletcher, 2000).

Maximizing impact

To maximize the impact of a diversity change effort, it is important to involve and deploy both external and internal change agents in the selection and implementation of specific interventions, because their different perspectives, roles, and skills can complement each other. Usually, the role of an external consultant is to provide expertise and support to the designated persons accountable for the initiative. This person (or team of people) will recommend particular approaches and help develop a strategy for the effort, including how to organize internal resources, involve different constituencies, and design and implement specific interventions. But an organization may also choose to implement a diversity initiative only with internal resources. In this case, a good way to organize human resources is to have a director of diversity, a diversity council, and an executive group sharing responsibility and accountability for the initiative.

Unfortunately, it is often difficult for internal change agents to have the organizational credibility, enough power and influence, and the overall support required to create and manage a diversity initiative on their own. The strength of internal change agents lies in their knowledge of the organizational culture and systems and their ability to access resources and organize targeted interventions such as recruitment, mentoring, statistical analysis of the workforce, and training. However, large organizational change efforts require the support of external change agents who bring an outsider's perspective and external credibility and experience. In our opinion, the combination of internal change agents, external consultants, executive leadership, and other key stakeholders produces the best results for developing and implementing a successful diversity initiative.

Common diversity "traps"

Various authors (e.g., Katz and Miller, 1988; Kirkham, 1992; Thomas and Woodruff, 1999) have identified – from experience and from practice – common mistakes to avoid in trying to bring about diversity change, especially in the context of US-based organizations and their international affiliates. Based on their work and our own, some of these "traps" are:

- assuming that short-term training will be enough;
- failing to relate diversity to the organizational mission and key products;
- waiting to collect all possible data and ignoring employee perceptions as data for taking action;
- waiting for everyone important to be thoroughly behind the effort;
- not paying attention to the impact of resistant people in important positions;
- isolating the effort in one department (such as human resources) or under one person;
- not differentiating between good intentions, usually contained in verbal expressions of support of diversity, and the impact of specific institutional actions that go against diversity;
- not building coalitions and support with different stakeholders who may fear that the diversity effort will not include them;
- assuming that managing diversity is just "good common sense and people skills";

- measuring success by the quantity and magnitude of diversity activities and events, rather than the impact on work and people.

Helpful conditions

For diversity initiatives to accomplish the goals of maximizing both inclusion and performance, it is important to have a number of conditions in place. On the basis of the literature (e.g., Arredondo, 1996; Cox, 2001; Ferdman and Brody, 1996; Hayles and Russell, 1997; Kotter, 1995b; Loden, 1996; Merrill-Sands, 1998; Miller and Katz, 2002) and our own experience we have identified 13 tactics that promote successful diversity initiatives:

1. Work from an inclusive definition of diversity that goes beyond race and gender issues to include other dimensions of difference.
2. Develop a strategic vision and plan with clear objectives, focus, and appropriate financial and human resources to support it. Communicate the plan widely.
3. Align the initiative to the core work of the organization and its strategic goals; connect it to a clear statement of needs that conveys the urgency and benefits the organization will derive from embracing change.
4. Engage many forces and people to create a broad sense of ownership, for example by supporting the development of a cadre of internal change agents and building alliances and coalitions among diverse internal constituencies and networks to support change. Engage respected and credible people to help guide and champion the change.
5. Have clear leadership and involvement of senior management in the change process beyond verbal and symbolic support. Identify internal champions with defined responsibilities for implementing the initiative.
6. Pay attention to internal and external factors that may support or hinder the initiative, such as budget constraints, changes in the internal and external political climate, and potential alliances with external pressure groups, such as clients, donors, or partners.
7. Build the change strategy from a solid analysis of diversity issues in the organization. Develop the analysis from multiple perspectives throughout the organization.
8. Provide freedom to pilot and experiment. Encourage an environment of learning from experience where flawless implementation is not expected.
9. Convey the importance of engaging in a dynamic and systemic process, not a static program or a single "quick-fix" solution.
10. Encourage an open climate that allows for the expression of passion, compassion, and forgiveness throughout the change and learning process.
11. Assign accountability across all levels and types of employees, including senior management.

12 Ensure the competence of consultants and other resources in designing and facilitating relevant initiatives aligned to the organizational culture and strategic imperatives.

13 Recognize, celebrate, and connect "small wins" so as to aggregate small changes into a larger change process with more impact (Meyerson and Fletcher, 2000; Weick, 1984).

Tips for international organizations

Based on our experience of initiating, designing, and implementing diversity change efforts in international contexts, we add the following tips for working with diversity across national boundaries and outside the United States:

1 Make special efforts to identify and utilize in-country resources to provide demographic data, cultural and social science research, and other relevant diversity information on an ongoing basis. National universities, local research organizations and think-tanks, social action groups, and other profit and non-profit organizations working on diversity are often overlooked, but are important local resources to be integrated into a diversity initiative, especially at the beginning of the change effort.

2 Partner local resources with external resources in order to develop the capacity of country nationals to work on organizational diversity and to ensure that external consultants understand and respond to the local context. Nurture and provide the opportunity for these partnerships to become role models of successful cross-mentoring and multicultural teamwork.

3 Pay attention and respond to the national social context and constraints, but also accept responsibility for providing leadership in changing accepted patterns of social behavior that are no longer suitable in a multicultural and global environment. For example, low accountability to government agencies with regard to anti-discrimination laws should not be taken as a reason for "not taking action" by international organizations initiating diversity efforts.

Indicators of progress

To guide and instill momentum into the change effort, it is important to identify success indicators and develop realistic, but not complacent, measures of progress. This is essential for working with diversity in a way that responds to the organizational vision and to the social and cultural realities of the specific organizational context. Panel 12.6 provides an example of indicators of diversity progress that can be adapted to specific organizational and national realities.

12.6 *Indicators of progress in effectively managing diversity*

An organization is working creatively with diversity when the following apply:

- Diversity strategies are integral to organizational strategies and objectives.
- Diversity is viewed as contributing to organizational effectiveness.
- Diversity is recognized as a long-term organizational investment that naturally involves complexity and constructive conflict.
- Managers take ownership for the strategy by setting visible goals and by serving as positive role models.
- People of diverse backgrounds work at all levels and departments of the organization.
- Diversity is an explicit goal in recruitment strategies.
- There is equity in employment actions and systems.
- Diversity is integral to the organization's operating principles and values and these are recognized as driving organizational behavior.
- Diversity objectives are set and met, from the top to the bottom of the organization.
- Organizational issues and personnel grievances are resolved effectively, with active and appropriate input/participation from all levels.
- Employee issues are raised and heard with respect and honesty, and are resolved in an effective, timely manner.
- Information flows unencumbered to those who need it to work effectively.
- Expertise is tapped in strategic decision-making no matter where it resides in the organization.
- Individuals hold themselves accountable for their actions.
- Managers are trained, assessed, held accountable, and rewarded for managing people of diverse backgrounds effectively.
- Managers are rewarded for integrating diversity objectives and practices within their work initiatives and programs.
- The organization is viewed by its employees, clients, and other stakeholders as an ethical player in its professional area and in the community where it is located.
- The organization is viewed as a benchmark for best practices in diversity, by employees and by the public.
- The organization's products and outputs reflect a broad and diverse client base and partner network.
- The organization continually assesses and learns about the dynamics of diversity and their impact on the people and the work of organizations.

Discussion questions

1 What do you think about the list of indicators of progress listed here? Why? How applicable might these be to your organization? Why?
2 What additional (or alternative) indicators of effective diversity management can you list?
3 How do the indicators in the panel and the ones you listed connect to particular goals and objectives regarding diversity and inclusion?
4 What benefits do you believe would accrue to organizations that display these characteristics?

Revised and adapted from Laura Moorhead, Joppa Consulting, 1999.

CONCLUSION

As we hope this chapter has shown, the steps that organizations and their leaders must take to create and sustain diversity and inclusion are demanding and challenging; to be effective, they require a substantial degree of planning, resources, and commitment. The path to multiculturalism is not one on which organizations should embark simply because other organizations are doing it or because it seems trendy. Yet, for many if not most of today's organizations, future success and in many cases even survival, will depend on what they begin to do now to make sure that they use their diversity as a source of strength, and that they seek inclusion and justice in their everyday ways of working. We believe that, ultimately, this is a rewarding and highly worthwhile path that most organizations will find ample reason to take.

Notes

1 This model is similar to those developed by Adler (2002), Cox (1991), Jackson and Holvino (1988), Katz and Miller, (1988), and Kolb et al. (1998). Also, work by such authors as Ferdman (1997), Palmer (1994), R. Thomas (1990), and Thomas and Ely (1996) on paradigms of diversity such as affirmative action, fairness, valuing differences, and managing diversity, imply that different perspectives and visions of diversity guide the process of organizational change.
2 Kanter (1977) explored four key dynamics of tokenism that occur when minority members are a small proportion of a group or organization: increased visibility, pressures to assimilate, emphasis on differences from the dominant group, and stereotyping. See also Ely (1994).

3 For example, Kossek and Zonia (1993) define diversity climate as the individual's perceptions and attitudes regarding the importance of diversity in the organization and the perceived qualifications of women and racioethnic minorities.

4 Stakeholders refer to actors or parties who have some involvement or interest in the outcomes or business of an organization. Weisbord and Janoff (2000) identify stakeholders important to consider in an organizational intervention as people with information, people with authority and resources to act, and people affected by what happens.

13

INTERNATIONAL PERSPECTIVES ON WORKPLACE DIVERSITY

Rana Haq

Workplace diversity is a fact, not only in North America but also in most countries around the globe, as the world's working population has become more diverse than ever before. The challenge for organizations is to understand the similarities and differences of the new workforce, make systemic changes in policies and procedures designed for the traditional employee base, empower all employees to contribute to their full potential, and create synergies for operating effectively as truly multicultural entities. The general concept and complexities of workplace diversity have been discussed in previous chapters. The purpose of this chapter is to explore the international perspectives on workplace diversity, focusing on gender, age, ethnicity, and religion. An overview of the historical, legal, social, and cultural influences is presented to better understand the diversity issues faced by organizations in ten countries: the USA, Canada, Sweden, the United Kingdom, Northern Ireland, South Africa, India, Japan, Australia, and New Zealand.

Diversity is a global issue. As technology shrinks our world, the number of international and multinational organizations increases. These organizations, exposed to foreign cultures in working closely with clients and employees in other countries, use international cross-cultural diversity training and research for developing successful business partnerships. Generally, the diversity focus is specific to the host country involved and is used primarily for facilitating inter-action and designing expatriate and repatriation programs. However, workplace diversity is not limited to international business. Global demographic trends are diversifying the domestic labor force in most countries of the world. Therefore, an understanding of different heritages *between* as well as *within* national boundaries is important for successfully managing diversity.

Loden and Rosener (1991: 20) have classified diversity into six primary dimensions and several secondary dimensions. The primary dimensions are those that human beings cannot change: gender, age, ethnicity, physical abilities, race, and sexual orientation. The secondary dimensions are those which can be changed, such as education, geographic location, social status, income, marital status, parental status, religious beliefs, work experience, and so on (see also Harrison, Price, and Bell's (1998) discussion of surface- and deep-level dimensions of diversity, discussed in chapters 2 and 3 of this volume). This chapter addresses three primary diversity dimensions – gender, age, and ethnicity – and one secondary dimension, religion.

The aim of this chapter is to provide a survey of diversity issues around the globe. The chapter starts with some basic information on global demographic developments that have implications for workforces around the world. Thumbnail sketches are then presented of the diversity issues in ten nations on five continents. These sketches clearly indicate that North America is not alone in coping with the trials of workforce diversity. "The prevalence of common responses suggests a commonality of structural problems that liberal democratic societies encounter in coping with rapid change, increased diversity, and growing minority assertiveness" (Fleras and Elliott, 1995: 268).

THE WORLD

United Nations statistics reveal that the world population reached 6 billion in 1999 and is growing at a rate of 1.3 percent annually. Over the last 12 years the world added 1 billion people, making it the shortest time period in history during which such large numbers were added to the human population. The world's population is projected to reach 7 billion by 2013, 8 billion by 2038, 9 billion by 2054, and 10 billion by 2183 (United Nations, 1999).

Populations are growing faster in the under-developed regions of the world. Of the 78 million or more people added to the world population each year, 95 percent live in the less developed regions. In fact, due to current patterns in childbearing, 80 percent of the world currently resides in the less developed regions, compared to 70 percent at the beginning of the twentieth century (United Nations, 1999).

In terms of continents too, population shifts are occurring. In 1750, Asia accounted for 64 percent of the world population; Europe, 21 percent; and Africa, 13 percent. By 1900, Europe increased to 25 percent, North America to 5 percent, and Latin America to 5 percent, while Asia decreased to 57 percent, and Africa decreased to 8 percent. However, this trend has now reversed. It is projected that by 2050, Asia will be 60 percent, Africa will have more than doubled to 20 percent, and Latin America will also have nearly doubled to 9 percent. Meanwhile, Europe will decline by two-thirds to only 7 percent. Interestingly, in 1900 the population of Europe was three times that of Africa, but by 2050 the population of Africa is projected to be nearly three times that of Europe (United Nations, 1999).

Within each continent, people are moving from rural to urban areas. Currently, 46 percent of the world population is living in cities; urban dwellers are expected to surpass 50 percent by 2006 (United Nations, 1999). Higher urbanization rates exist in developed countries than in under-developed countries; for example, Census 2001 reported Canada as 80 percent urban (*Globe and Mail*, 2002).

Across national boundaries, too, the world population is becoming increasingly mobile. In particular, there is record net migration from Africa, Asia, Latin America, and the Caribbean into Europe and North America. These migration patterns will have major implications for the workforce composition of the traditionally White populations in the host countries. Canada, for example, had about 95 percent of its immigrants from Europe before 1961, down to 75 percent between 1961–70, and only 22 percent between 1991–6, when over 78 percent of immigrants came from Africa, Asia, and South America (Statistics Canada, 1998). Foot (1996) explains how Canada has used an immigration system of numerical targets and points allocation in its selection criteria as a tool to screen for qualifications and control the profile of the incoming labor force in attempts to match it with the country's changing labor requirements.

The world's population is aging. The United Nations Population Division (United Nations, 2001) reports that people over the age of 60 are the fastest growing segment of the world population. In 2000, Japan had the oldest population, with a median of 41 years, followed by Italy, Switzerland, Germany, and Sweden at 40 years each. Africa reported the youngest population at a median of 18.4 years. China at 11.5 million, the USA at 6.1 million, Japan at 4.8 million, Germany at 3 million, and the Russian Federation at 3 million together accounted for 54 percent of the world's people of 80+ years.

The ratio of working-age persons to older persons is declining rapidly, placing a larger dependency burden on the working population. The *potential support ratio*, that is, the number of working persons (aged 15–64 years) per older person (aged 65 years or older), is projected to decline from 5 to 2 working persons per senior in developed countries and from 12 to only 4 working-aged persons per senior in developing countries (United Nations, 1999). Weeks (1994) has documented the replacement-level fertility rate as about 2.1 for industrialized countries to successfully replace each generation and maintain a healthy workforce. However, *below*-replacement fertility rates are now the norm in many industrialized countries. This trend raises serious implications for labor force availability, as well as for supporting healthcare and social security systems.

The aging population is increasingly female. Among people aged 60 years or older, 55 percent are women and among those 80 years or older, 65 percent are women (United Nations, 1999). Adler and Izraeli (1994) have documented in detail how women's career patterns and experiences in employment are significantly different than that of men throughout the world. Using workforce data from the Organization for Economic Co-operation and Development (OECD), Marshall (2001) documents the increasing international trends in part-time workers, less than 30 hours per week, among industrialized countries over the last three decades,

especially for older workers and women trying to balance work and family responsibilities. The International Labor Organization (2002) reports that although
women around the world have achieved higher levels of education than ever
before and now represent more than 40 percent of the global workforce, they still
continue to face serious equity challenges in the workplace. Senior management
positions seem to be particularly elusive for women worldwide and they are
overcoming this barrier by opting out of large corporations and starting their
own companies.

Global demographic trends clearly indicate that workplace diversity will continue to increase as more women, older people, and visible minorities participate
in the paid labor force. In addition, economic trends indicate the emergence of
highly competitive global marketplaces as trade barriers between countries are
reduced. Further, technological trends indicate that organizations can operate
successfully using sophisticated information network systems. The opportunities
are boundless, but there are also significant challenges. Organizations, whether
national or international in scope and public or private in mandate, will need to
understand and manage workplace diversity in the present and well into the
future. Diversity, however, must be understood within the historical, legal, social, and cultural context in which it exists and the unique ways in which it is
manifested in the workplace, since diversity issues within individual nations
differ as a result of the underlying latent causes specific to that environment. Let
us now take a closer look at ten individual countries on five continents.

North America

Originally inhabited by diverse tribes of the North American Indians or Aboriginal Peoples followed by over 200 years of mass immigration, both the USA
and Canada have similarities in their diversities. Two widely used metaphors –
"the melting pot," where minority groups are encouraged to homogenize into
the dominant group, and "the mosaic," where minority groups are encouraged to
maintain their distinctiveness as colorful pieces in a kaleidoscope – are reflective
of the national approaches adopted by the USA and Canada in living, working,
and socializing with people of different heritages. As nations of immigrants, both
these countries have experienced a shift from the traditionally White European
immigrants to more visible minority immigrants from around the world. Both
countries are internationally recognized as pioneers in their diversity efforts.
Using North America, therefore, as the baseline benchmark will help us to better
understand, compare, and contrast the challenges faced by other countries in
their diversity experiences and approaches.

United States of America

Although the US comprises only 5 percent of the world population, it is the third
most populous country, after China and India, with a total population of over

281 million in the 2000 census. Unique in their long history of slavery, African Americans or Blacks traditionally formed the most significant minority group in the US, but Hispanics or Latinos, defined as "persons of Cuban, Mexican, Puerto Rican, South or Central American, or other Spanish culture or origin regardless of race," have now become the fastest growing minority group at 12.5 percent. With the introduction of multiple responses to the question of race in the 2000 census, 6.8 million people identified themselves as multi-racial and three in ten people reported themselves as belonging to minorities. Asked to self-identify their race, Americans reported 75 percent White, 13 percent Black or African American, 4 percent Asian American and Pacific Islanders, 1 percent American Indian and Alaska Native, and 6 percent other (US Census Bureau, 2002). The 2000 census was printed in five languages to accommodate non-English speaking residents and the Census Bureau projects that by the year 2050, only 53 percent of the US population will be Anglo (see panel 13.1 for further discussion on international measures of ethnicity).

E Pluribus Unum is the motto of the United States and it appears on the nation's coins, bank notes, and many public monuments. It means, "From many, one." Yet, undoubtedly, the richest workplace diversity research has emerged from the United States. As described in other chapters in this book, a number of forces have combined to make American scholars and practitioners very concerned with issues of workplace diversity. They maintain that the time has come to move beyond legislated measures for affirmative action toward voluntary programs in valuing and managing diversity.

Canada

The first White settlers in Canada were the French, followed by the English. They are considered as the two founding nations. Canada is officially bilingual and all services provided by the federal government are available in both English and French. For years, diversity issues in Canada revolved around the Francophone–Anglophone divisions. The majority of French Canadians live in the province of Quebec, where they make up about 80 percent of the population and are assertive in their efforts to preserve their language and culture, to the extent of fiercely supporting an independent Quebec.

More recently, multiculturalism has overtaken biculturalism as other minority groups have begun to assert themselves. Canada's indigenous peoples, referred to as Native Peoples, First Nations Peoples, or Aboriginal Peoples, made up about 3 percent of the 28.5 million Canadian population in 1996. The 1996 census was the first Canadian census to ask a direct question to collect data on visible minorities for purposes of the Employment Equity Act (EEA). It reported that visible minorities, defined as "persons other than Aboriginal peoples, who are non-Caucasian in race and non-White in color," represented about 11.2 percent of the Canadian population (up from 6.3 percent in 1986) and projected further increases in the future. Of the visible minorities, the largest groups are Chinese,

13.1 *International measures of ethnicity*

There is a multitude of ways in which individual countries collect data on ethnicity. There are no internationally recognized standards for classification of ethnic groups, as these vary from country to country and have different connotations (for example, "race," "origin," "tribe") which make it difficult to establish one single uniform measure across countries. There are also differences in how a group is defined, how the question is asked, and how the answer options are presented in the survey. Some respondents may not understand the meaning of ethnic group and respond on the basis of nationality (country by birth or citizenship), ancestry (by family descent), or race (by physical characteristics). These measures are not the same as ethnicity (by self-identification of affiliation) but can play an important role in determining to which ethnic group(s) people feel that they belong. Many countries have traditionally not collected data on ethnicity and are only beginning to do so, while others still consider it irrelevant or unnecessary.

Within individual countries there are frequent reviews and changes in how to measure ethnic group affiliation. This makes the continuity of comparisons from census to census very difficult, since they are based on varying definitions and measure a different subgroup. There are also variations in views among producers, users, and respondents about the measures of ethnicity and the use to which the statistics should be put. These differences in data have an impact on the overall information about groups, the resulting analysis, the conclusions reached, and the projections made. Consequently, public policy issues and resource decisions can be influenced, impacting areas such as education, employment, housing, healthcare, justice, social security programs, etc. New standards and classifications are being developed by many countries to reflect their multiethnic population (Allan, 2001). The following table highlights some of the census variables in the countries covered in this chapter.

Country	Ethnicity-determining variables in census information
USA	(Race, Ethnicity for Hispanics, Place of birth, Citizenship, Ancestry, Language) The first census took place in 1790 and occurs every ten years in the year ending in zero. The 2000 census, printed in five languages, was the first time respondents could indicate more than one race.
Canada	(Race, Language, Ancestry, Aboriginal or First Nations: Inuit, or Metis peoples) The 1996 census was the first to collect data on visible minorities for the purposes of the Employment Equity Act.
UK	(Country of birth, Ethnic group) Decennial censuses have been held since 1801. In 1991, ethnic identification was introduced, requiring the respondent to give an answer based on color.

Country	Ethnicity-determining variables in census information
Ireland	(Place of birth, Nationality)
	Decennial censuses have been held since 1841. A question on religion has been asked in each census, but there is no question on ethnicity.
Sweden	In contrast to other countries, population statistics in Sweden are based on church register information, a unique record system used since 1686, that records all individual demographic changes at the parish level. With no formal census process in place, census data is extracted from these administrative collections.
South Africa	(Population group, Citizenship, Country of birth, Languages spoken)
	In the 1996 census, defining color and degree of color of a person for political rights was replaced by racial self-affiliation.
India	(Caste, Tribe)
	The 2001 census was the sixth since independence from Britain in 1947. No question asked on ethnicity, ancestry, or race.
Japan	(Nationality)
	The 2001 census was the seventeenth since 1920, on a five-year cycle. No question on ethnicity, ancestry, or race.
Australia	(Citizenship, Indigenous identity, Ancestry, Country of birth, Parents born overseas, Language(s) spoken)
	The 2001 census was the fourteenth, held every five years since 1961. While ancestry was asked in 1986, ethnicity questions were introduced in 2001.
New Zealand	(Ethnic group, Maori descent, Country of birth, Language(s) spoken)
	The first census in 1851 counted only the European population. Maori were enumerated separately from 1867 and Chinese from 1874 until 1951. The 2001 census asked a question on ethnicity and one on Maori descent. Ethnicity is defined as the ethnic group or groups that a person identifies with or feels they belong to. Ethnicity is self-perceived and people can belong to more than one ethnic group.

Discussion questions

1 From your personal experience or perceptions, what are the five main diversity dimensions that you have encountered in your workplace, university, or college? What have you learned about diversity and about yourself from these experiences?

2 Compare and contrast the advantages and disadvantages of using census data for estimating workplace diversity and designing diversity initiatives in an organization.

3 Do you think it is important to develop global consistency in diversity measures? Explain why, or why not.

at 27 percent, and South Asian, at 21 percent, all mostly concentrated in British Columbia and Ontario (Statistics Canada, 1998).

Canada's constitution guarantees equality under the law to all of its citizens. The Canadian Human Rights Act of 1977 prohibits discrimination on the basis of "race, national or ethnic origin, color, religion, age, sex, sexual orientation, marital status, family status, disability or conviction for an offence for which a pardon has been granted." The federal Multiculturalism Act of 1988 was the first of its kind in the world, reaffirming Canada's fundamental mosaic characteristic through an official policy to preserve, enhance, and share the cultural heritage of its people and encouraging institutions to be respectful and inclusive of other cultures (Berry and LaPonce, 1994: 8). The Charter of Rights and Freedoms (1982) protects every individual's right to equality without discrimination, in Section (15), and permits laws, programs, or activities designed to eliminate barriers. It also protects language rights, aboriginal rights, diversity of cultural heritage, and gender equality, and promotes equal opportunities and the reduction of economic disparity (Abella, 1984: 13). *Equality in Employment: A Royal Commission Report* by Judge Abella (1984: 9, 10) affirmed that "systemic discrimination requires systemic remedies . . . Equality demands enforcement. It is not enough to be able to claim equal rights unless those rights are somehow enforceable. Unenforceable rights are no more satisfactory than unavailable ones." It became instrumental in the creation of the Employment Equity Act of 1986. The term "employment equity" (Abella, 1984: 7) was adopted in Canada "to describe programs of positive remedy for discrimination in the Canadian workplace." It identified four specific designated groups: women, aboriginal peoples, persons with disabilities, and visible minorities. The Act, revised in 1995, applies to about 1,400 federally regulated private and public sector organizations, with 100 or more employees. It covers almost 2 million people or 12 percent of the Canadian labor force. It requires them to (a) identify employment barriers against the four designated groups; (b) determine the degree of underrepresentation as compared with their availability in the Canadian labor force; (c) prepare, implement, review, and revise plans to promote employment equity; and (d) submit annual reports to the Human Resource Development Canada. The Act gives the Canadian Human Rights Commission the authority to conduct audits and gain compliance. In addition, it sets out the Federal Contractors Program for Employment Equity requiring service providers to the government to comply with employment equity requirements.

Europe

Europe is the second smallest continent, after Australia. The European Union (EU), which currently comprises 15 member states (Austria, Belgium, Denmark, Finland, France, Germany, Greece, Ireland, Italy, Luxembourg, the Netherlands, Portugal, Spain, Sweden, and the United Kingdom), is an unprecedented partnership of nations to create an economy where labor, capital services, and goods can circulate freely for greater economic prosperity. On January 1, 2002, the Euro became the official currency in 12 of the 15 EU countries, eliminating conversion problems and encouraging cross-border movement. Undoubtedly, financial harmonization – despite its complications – will prove to be much easier than cultural harmonization, as distinct national customs, and social, cultural, and language differences, remain. Organizations operating across the EU will need to comply with the complex legislative and regulatory environment, and be sensitive to each country's specific diversity issues.

A report published by Eurostat (2001) details recent patterns and future projections for the labor force in the EU for the period 1995–2025. In 1995 the EU labor force was 169 million, with an increased participation of women in the workforce in every member nation, a growing number of older workers (55–64 age group), and more part-time workers. The population within the EU is growing as a result of net migration, accounting for 70 percent of the increase, yet there is a lack of constitutional protection for people of different races as compared to the relatively specific provisions for gender equality. Documenting research findings that half of the Dutch personnel officers interviewed admitted to using negative stereotypes when making employment decisions, Forbes and Mead (1992) confirm that racial discrimination, especially in recruitment and selection procedures, plays a significant role in the underemployment of racial/ethnic minorities. Even in terms of gender equality, considerable differences still remain between the progressive Scandinavian countries, which have a better standard than that mandated by EU legislation, and other nations such as Portugal and Greece, which remain the most backward (Rossilli 1999). The EU's 1998 Employment Guidelines include "strengthening equal opportunities" as one of the four guidelines for member states' employment policies and the three Action Programs on Equal Opportunities require member states to develop fairly comprehensive measures to promote affirmative action in both private and public sectors. While EU legislation has helped national laws to move closer toward a common standard across the member states, EU-wide enforcement of legislation is required in order to prevent sporadic and differential attention to diversity issues across the member countries. Sweden, the United Kingdom (UK), and Northern Ireland (part of the UK) provide a glimpse of the variety of diversity issues salient in the different member nations of the EU.

Sweden

Sweden has a population of 8.8 million, and almost half its labor force of 4.3 million are women. As a result of strong political consensus and support for the principles of gender equality, Sweden has achieved impressive success in women's employment (see panel 13.2 for a discussion on Sweden's gender equality index). A separate Division for Gender Equality and an Office of Equal Opportunity Ombudsman were established in central government when the first Equal

Opportunity Act came into force in 1980, later reinforced in 1992. The most prominent results were achieved in Sweden's political system. The number of women in parliament has tripled since 1971, to 43.6 percent of the 349 members in 1998. In 1999, Sweden became the first country in the world to have a female majority in government, with 11 women ministers to 9 men. Twelve women, of a total of 27, were at the state secretary's rank immediately below that of the cabinet minister. Municipalities, at 41 percent, and counties, at 48 percent, also reflected strong representation of women at almost all levels of the public sector decision-making hierarchy (Swedish Institute, 2000). Senior management leadership in the private sector, however, remains dominated by men. A Business Leadership Academy was formed in 1995 by the government to develop women in business.

Although Sweden has served as the exemplar in dealing with gender issues, it has stumbled along unsuccessfully on the question of immigrants. In Sweden, the concept of workforce "diversity (*mangfald*) is first and foremost related to ethnicity and heterogeneity in terms of citizenship or national origin" (Reyes, 2000: 255). Immigration to Sweden was insignificant until World War II. Over the last few decades, however, Sweden has changed from being mainly monolingual and ethnically homogeneous to a multilingual society with a number of ethnic minorities. Today, about one-fifth of Sweden's population is composed of immigrants or individuals who have at least one foreign-born parent. About 50 percent of all foreign nationals in Sweden are from other Nordic countries, such as

---

13.2   *Gender equality index*

In the early 1990s Sweden developed a gender equality index for tracking and measuring actual figures on gender equality, for the purpose of relating policies with practice (Thermaenius, 2001). The index compares outcomes for women and men in several areas, such as paid work, education, childcare, income, and representation in municipal councils, based on statistics gathered on ten key factors. The weighted average of these variables forms a score. The results of each factor are added up to produce the index, which is then used to rank the municipalities and counties by their index score. The higher the score, the greater the equality between women and men within that region. Since the variables are results-based numerical measures, they are useful in measuring the gender equality position achieved, by each factor, for municipalities and counties and comparing with the national average. Results are presented in maps and tables for Sweden's 289 municipalities and counties and are disseminated via the Internet. Clicking on a county or municipality on the map reveals the values of all the variables: red for women, blue for men, and green for rank or score.

The gender equality index has three principal components:

1 An index comparing women and men on the ten variables at the municipal level in different parts of the country, which can then be rolled up to a national level.
2 A section that enables the user to construct a personalized gender equality index by allowing a change in the weight assigned to each variable.
3 A database of statistics, taken from various sources, which can be personalized by changing the key variables used in the measures.

The standard variables currently used in the index (all measured by gender) are as follows:

- Proportion of people with post-secondary education
- Proportion of people in gainful employment
- Proportion employed in full-time work
- Proportion of job-seekers
- Total income from gainful employment
- Days of parental leave benefit
- Days of temporary parental leave benefit
- Proportion of children in municipal day care
- Sickness rates
- Municipal Council
- Municipal Executive Board
- Entrepreneurs with at least nine employees
- Mean age of people 20–64 years of age

Many European countries have shown an interest in using the gender equality index, and Statistics Sweden would like to cooperate with other countries to make this an international product. The index is accessible at Statistics Sweden's website address: http://www.scb.se/scb/bor/scbboju/jam_htm_en/index.html

Discussion questions

1 Using your knowledge of culture and gender issues in the workplace, evaluate why some countries are further ahead than others in promoting gender equality in the workplace. What strategies, in your opinion, have the best (or worst) results in achieving the intended goals and outcomes?
2 Assess the usefulness of the gender equality index. Do you think it is important to develop an international gender equality index? Why? What key measures would you suggest for inclusion in such an index?
3 What are your thoughts on the development of national and international indices for other diversity dimensions?

Denmark, Finland, Iceland, and Norway, who can become Swedish citizens after two years in Sweden. Citizens of non-Nordic countries become eligible for Swedish citizenship after five years in Sweden (Swedish Institute, 1999). These immigrants, seen as the "other" and even stigmatized as a "problem," face an enormous imbalance of power resulting from ethnic segregation in Swedish workplaces. Integration problems are particularly serious for the refugees from non-European countries who form the majority of the newcomers since the 1970s, because second and third generation individuals of immigrant background are still considered as foreigners (Reyes, 2000). In 1998 the government set up the National Integration Office to prevent xenophobia, racism, and discrimination in the Swedish workplace.

United Kingdom

The UK is roughly the size of Oregon or Colorado. Its population was about 57 million in 2000, estimated at 90 percent urban with a high population density of 244 persons per square kilometer. More than 93 percent of the British population is White, despite an influx of immigrants during the 1940s and 1950s from its many colonies. The remaining 7 percent comprise Africans, Indians, Pakistanis/ Bangladeshis, and others (UK Office for National Statistics, 2000). Racial tensions in the UK have never been as great as they are at present, with hostility, violence, and destruction witnessed over the last few years in frequent outbreaks of ethnic rioting across the country. Despite this, the UK's focus for diversity remains primarily on gender equality.

Storey (1999) documents the progress of the Equal Opportunities Commission (EOC) of Great Britain, in existence for more than 20 years, with a focus solely on gender equality. The key legislation to date has been the Equal Pay Act of 1970, the Sex Discrimination Act of 1975, and the Race Relations Act of 1976. These and other related Acts are currently under review, as the EOC plans a single, strengthened, and consolidated Sex Equity Act incorporating EU laws requiring employers to monitor their workforce in terms of gender, job title or grade, and rates of pay, making this information available upon request. Although the Equal Pay Act has been in existence for over 30 years, women working full-time earn only 72 percent of the average male weekly earnings and 80 percent of hourly wages. Women also tend to be employed in occupations different from men and are generally poorly paid even though the concept of "equal pay for work of equal value" was incorporated into the equal pay legislation in 1984. Hammond (1992) explains that the UK's business-led initiative, Opportunity 2000, arose as a result of frustration over the slow progress of women at all levels in organizations and the competitive need to acquire and retain talented employees. Envisioned by 17 chairmen, chief Executives, and directors of major UK companies, this initiative was primarily aimed at increasing the numbers of women in senior management.

Liff (1999) examines some examples of best practice, as defined by Opportunity 2000, to see whether institutional discrimination has been better addressed through different types of initiatives and practices focusing on culture change and managing diversity. She doubts that a procedural approach embedded in codes of practice "can be effective in addressing inequality created by organizational structures and cultures which favor members of some social groups over others" (p. 65). Noting the limits of the procedural interventions in managing diversity initiatives within deep-seated cultural and structural constraints, she proposes that the organization itself must change rather than simply allowing women and other minorities to fit into it. Although there seems to be widespread adoption of equality policies in the UK, there continues to be evidence of differential labor market experience by members of disadvantaged groups.

Northern Ireland

The diversity situation in Northern Ireland revolves around religious differences. The 1971 census was the first to provide data on employment conditions and religion, indicating Catholic disadvantage in the labor and housing markets. A series of reports and legislation followed, but they appear to have made little difference to the prevailing division between the two major religious communities, namely the Catholics and Protestants. In 1972 the Van Straubenzee Committee was set up "to consider what steps, whether in regard to law or practice, should be taken to counter religious discrimination where it may exist in the private sector of employment in Northern Ireland" (Van Straubenzee, cited in McCormack and McCormack, 1994: 38). Its report, delivered in 1973, recognized the need for specific action and for measuring the capacity to produce change. The Northern Ireland Constitution Act 1973, which replaced the Government of Ireland Act 1920, provided for a legislative Assembly for Northern Ireland and also established the Standing Advisory Committee on Human Rights, outlawing discrimination on the grounds of religious belief or political opinion.

The Fair Employment (Northern Ireland) Act of 1976 (FEA) made direct discrimination in employment on the basis of religion or political belief illegal in Northern Ireland. Although the FEA was enacted to remove the economic inequities between Catholics and Protestants in Northern Ireland, it appears to have had little effect. Over a decade later, the Standing Advisory Commission on Human Rights (SACHR) commissioned research on the FEA. Its 1987 report confirmed that not much had changed over the ten years of the legislation. Two-fifths of all workplaces continued to be composed almost exclusively of one religious group, the Protestants, and this was unlikely to be the result of existing geographic and residential segregation of the Catholics. These discouraging findings led to the development of the 1989 Fair Employment Act, which required employers to carry out a review of their employment composition and practices within three years and thereafter submit annual reports. A review of equal employment in Northern Ireland by the Central Community Relations Unit (CCRU) reports that there continues to be major inequalities between Catholics and Protestants in employment. According to the Labour Force Survey in

1991, the economically active population of Northern Ireland was 59 percent Protestant and 41 percent Catholic, of which 62 percent of Protestants and only 38 percent of Catholics were employed. Catholics were underrepresented in professional and managerial positions (71 percent Protestants and 29 percent Catholics) and overrepresented in unskilled manual labor (54 percent Protestants and 46 percent Catholics) (Melaugh, 1995).

Africa

South Africa

Black Africans comprise three quarters of South Africa's population yet, until recently, Whites dominated the non-White majority population under a political system of racial segregation known as apartheid (Afrikaans for separateness, a doctrine of White supremacy). Although racial segregation and inequality had traditionally existed as a matter of custom and practice, in 1948 they were enshrined in the law. Race influenced education, occupation, place of residence, choice of partner, freedom of movement, and use of facilities and amenities.

International pressure against apartheid, beginning in 1952 at the General Assembly of the United Nations, eventually resulted in resolutions in the 1980s that described apartheid as a crime against humanity. On April 27, 1994, the South African population voted in the country's first democratic election, ending 45 years of official apartheid and over 300 years of segregated rule of minority Whites over majority Blacks. All apartheid legislation was immediately repealed. The South African parliament approved a new constitution in 1996, designating 11 official languages, reflective of the South African population. South Africa is both multiracial and multiethnic, with Blacks constituting 78 percent of the population; Whites, 11 percent; Colored (of mixed race) people, 9 percent; and Asians (mainly Indians) 2 percent.

South African organizations are multicultural in their workforce. The Human Rights Commission Act (1994), the Labor Relations Act (1995), and the 1996 constitution all support affirmative action and employment equity programs. The Employment Equity Act of 1998 is applicable to employers with 50 or more employees. It prohibits unfair discrimination in the workplace on the following grounds: "race, gender, sex, pregnancy, marital status, family responsibility, ethnic or social origin, color, sexual orientation, age, disability, religion, HIV status, conscience, belief, political opinion, culture, language, and birth" (ch. 2, 6.1). In addition, it requires "affirmative action measures, to redress the disadvantages in employment experienced by designated groups in order to ensure their equitable representation in all occupational categories and levels in the workforce." The designated groups under this Act are Black people (including Africans, Coloreds, and Indians), women, and people with disabilities. The Act also requires annual Employment Equity Plans to be submitted by designated employers.

Gender is another key diversity issue in South Africa, with women comprising 38 percent of the estimated 16.7 million workers in 1999. Although women are thought to be more disadvantaged in South African society than in Europe or North America, gender issues take a back seat to racial issues in South Africa. Whites earn an estimated 104 percent more than Africans, and men receive 43 percent higher wages than similarly qualified women in similar sectors and occupations. Of course, a person can be both a woman and a Black. Erwee (1994) documents the experiences and career patterns of Black working women in South Africa as they face the "double challenge." Cox and Nkomo (1990) call this the "double-whammy" effect, which is also known in Canada as the "double-disadvantage" (Abella, 1984). Louw (1995) presents "ubuntu" as a concept central to understanding diversity in South Africa. Ubuntu means that "a person is a person not alone but through other people," reflecting the South African cultural values of community and belonging. Noting the differences in culture, many scholars recommend an Afrocentric rather than a Eurocentric view of understanding organizational cultures and for managing workplace diversity issues in South Africa (Bowmaker-Falconer et al., 1997).

Asia

India

India is the second country in the world, after China, with a population that has surpassed 1 billion (Census India, 2001). The people of India are diverse in language, culture, and religion. The country has 28 states, each with its own distinct culture, customs, and official language (imagine the diversity challenge if this was the case in the USA). English and Hindi are the two national languages. India is constitutionally a secular nation, but religion is the primary source of workplace diversity. About 82 percent of Indians are Hindu. It is important to note, however, that the Hindus cannot collectively be considered as one homogeneous group, since significant differences exist among them, not only in terms of caste but also in terms of religious beliefs and devotion to different deities. A further 12 percent of Indians are Muslims, divided into two major conflicting communities: the more progressive Sunni and the traditionally conservative Shia. In many cities in northern India, Muslims are close to one-third or more of the population (and up to two-thirds in Jammu and Kashmir). The remaining 6 percent of Indians comprise Christians (2.3 percent), Sikhs (2 percent), Buddhists (0.7 percent), Jains (0.4 percent), Zoroastrians, Jews, and others.

India's indigenous tribal peoples are known as adivasis ("original inhabitants" in Hindi). Officially designated for affirmative action purposes as "Scheduled Tribes," they make up about 8 percent of India's population, or over 65 million people (more than twice the population of Canada). Eighty-seven percent of these identify themselves as Hindus, about 7 percent as Christians, and about

5 percent exclusively practice traditional tribal religions. Living in areas preserved by government policies that restrict the sale of these lands to tribe members only, much like the First Nations reserves in Canada, they are mostly engaged in agriculture or traditional methods of hunting and gathering.

Workplace diversity issues in India are primarily based upon intraracial and not interracial differences, as in most countries with high immigration patterns. Although there are provincial differences in physical characteristics, diversity issues are based more on religion and caste than on appearance, and Indian affirmative action policies address discrimination based on class and status arising from the traditional Hindu culture and religious teachings. *The Times of India* (2001a) reported on a seminar in New Delhi, organized by the National Human Rights Commission, on whether "caste" should be included at the 2001 UN Conference on Race in Durban, South Africa. The global members' agreement at this conference to consider caste discrimination as serious as racism was a victory for non-governmental organizations that had been lobbying for years to bring about this recognition.

The caste system remains pervasive in India. It is not limited solely to workplace issues, but pervades every aspect of life, from birth, to marriage, to death. Caste (*Jati*, in Sanskrit) is determined by profession and based on perceptions of purity and pollution. It is identified upon birth into a family and remains unaltered over the generations, through the family name. Even though a child may follow a different profession than that of its forebears, upward mobility remains virtually impossible. Nesiah (1997: 37) compares the stark simplicity of the American Black–White divide with the complexity of the Indian caste system, which is grouped into four varnas and a fifth outcaste. According to Hindu mythology, the four varnas emerged from different parts of Brahma, the creator. From his head came the Brahmins (priests, philosophers, and scholars); from his arms, the Kshatriyas (rulers and warriors); from his thighs, the Vaisyas (merchants); and from his feet, the Sudras (artisans and peasants). A fifth catchall category was commonly referred to as the Untouchables. This included all other "non-persons" outside the caste system, mostly the people involved in janitorial and sanitation occupations and so forth, generally regarded as unclean and polluting.

The Untouchables were required to maintain a physical distance from "Caste Hindus," as even their shadow was believed to be polluting. They were segregated from the mainstream in every aspect of life, from separate water wells, to separate temples, to separate crematoriums. Most of these discriminatory practices were made unlawful decades ago, but are so deeply entrenched that they have not been totally eradicated. Even today, individual and collective acts of violence against the Untouchables are prevalent in rural India, a very disturbing fact given that the country is 75 percent rural. It was Mahatama Gandhi who renamed the Untouchables as "Harijans" ("People of God" in the Hindi language) and regularly interacted with them, including eating and drinking with them at their homes, to bring down the walls of discrimination. Although the practice of labeling people as Untouchables was outlawed by the 1950 Indian constitution, Harijans continue to face discrimination in many aspects of life, including employment and housing. Today, many of them prefer to be called Dalits ("the oppressed" in the Indian Marathi language) and are included in the list of designated groups for affirmative action programs as the Scheduled Castes. Interestingly, at least 50 percent of Christians in India are Dalits, through mass conversions to Christianity in attempts to gain equality through the church. However, this strategy proved to be unsuccessful because they continue to be treated as Dalits, even after their conversion. Moreover, under the constitution, they are no longer protected, since they are now officially Christians and not Scheduled Caste. Since the Dalit Sikhs and the Dalit Buddhists were granted this benefit by the central government, Dalit Christians and Muslims are demanding the removal of religion from affirmative action reservation policies (*Times of India*, 2001a).

The Indian constitution specifically endorses affirmative action in Article 15 (4), permitting "special provision for the advancement of any socially and educationally backward classes of citizens or for the Scheduled Castes and Scheduled Tribes" (Nesiah, 1997: 57). Sivaramayya (1984: 51) outlines the following four principles as the basic rationale for India's preferential policies: compensation (for past injustices), protection (of the weak), proportional equality, and social justice. For the purposes of affirmative action, the Indian government publishes lists of the Scheduled Tribes, Scheduled Castes, and Other Backward Classes as the only designated groups. The 2001 census documented 1,221 Scheduled Castes and 664 Scheduled Tribes in India (Census India, 2001). India has the world's oldest system of affirmative action, but more than 3,000 years of bias against the lower castes still persists (Cooper, 1997). Interestingly, gender and religions other than Hinduism, Sikhism, and Buddhism do not qualify under India's affirmative action policies. Also, the private sector is not bound by reservation policies and has taken no voluntary measures to support affirmative action.

Japan

Japan's population is approaching 126 million, making it the ninth most populous country in the world (Japan, Census 2000). The Japanese workforce, like Japanese society, is very homogeneous and does not exhibit any ethnic, religious, and class divisions typical of many countries.

Diversity issues in Japan center on gender and age. Japan's labor force of 68 million is increasingly female, constituting 41 percent of the workforce in 1999, up from 34 percent in 1980. Lu (1987) has noted the gendered aspect of the concept of lifetime employment for men in most Japanese organizations. Women, on the other hand, appear to have a transitory career path, with more tenuous employment, few benefits, and more part-time work. Ogasawara (1991) describes this two-track system, split along gender lines, as one of the most important aspects of the career patterns of Japan, where men are recruited for managerial positions and women are streamed into clerical occupations. Tasker (1987), referring to the clerical-track office ladies as "decorative" and hired primarily to make the workplace comfortable, notes that the majority of these women are stuck in repetitious clerical jobs that offer no prospects of advancement. Ogasawara (1991) discusses female employment patterns and notes that Japanese women's presence in the labor force resembles the traditional M-shaped or double-peak pattern coinciding with different types of jobs. First, women in their twenties enter the workforce after finishing school, representing the first peak, becoming full-time employees recruited by large firms directly from universities. Then a significant percentage leave the workforce in their thirties to raise a family. The second and lower peak occurs with women returning to the workplace, mostly in their forties after their children are grown, gaining employment in small firms or as part-time workers, often working as many hours as regular employees but with lower pay and few benefits. Compared with other industrialized nations, Japan exhibits a large gender gap in pay. Differential treatment based on gender seems to be well accepted in Japanese society, which is still very male dominated. Saso (1990) compares the treatment and experiences of working women in Japan, Britain, and Ireland. Based on statistical data and interviews with women on the shop floor, she compares wages, working conditions, training, union involvement, and attitudes to work and childcare, highlighting an ironic example of the inverse relationship between gender and jobs in Japan. For a male employee, a family is an advantage in furthering his career, as salaried men in Japan can be penalized if they do not have a family. In Japan, if a man is not a father in a stable marriage he is thought to be irresponsible, whereas a family is a severe impediment for Japanese women, who are penalized for attempting to combine family with a career.

In terms of the regulatory environment, some progress against sexism has been made. Under the Equal Employment Opportunity Law of 1986, neither companies nor individual executives could be fined or held accountable for violations, as there were no provisions for enforcement. Under the Revised Equal Employment Opportunity Law of 1999, non-compliant companies can now have their transgressions publicized (Ursaki, 2001). Other barriers to women's employment opportunities were revised by the Act Amending Several Acts to Guarantee Equal Opportunity and Treatment between Men and Women in Employment. No. 92, 1997. This Act changed several associated legislations, such as the Labor Standards Act No. 49 of 1947, removing limits on women's overtime, holidays, and night-time work and improving measures to protect maternity and family responsibilities; and the Guarantee of Equal Opportunity and Treatment between Men and Women in Employment Act No. 113 of 1972, prohibiting discrimination in recruitment, assignment and promotion, and promoting positive measures (Kampo Gogai, 1997). Japan's Fundamental Law Designed to Promote a Gender-Equal Society of 1999 sets out five areas of policy development: (1) respect for the rights of men and women, (2) taking into account systems or customs of society, (3) participation of men and women in decision-making processes, (4) harmonization of activities at home with other activities, and (5) international cooperation

(Kampo Gogai, 1999). It mandates the government with legislative action and financial measures to implement policies for creating a gender-equal society and requires central and local governments to submit annual reports. Implementation, however, has not been as forceful as one might hope, and attitudes toward working women in Japan are not changing rapidly. Attitudes toward working Japanese men, on the other hand, have undergone more rapid change. The 1990s recession in Japan resulted in the disappearance of lifetime job security for men, once a hallmark of Japan's economy, as companies struggled to survive the economic downturn by laying-off older workers.

Age is the other major diversity issue facing the Japanese workforce. Japan is aging at a faster rate than North America because it did not experience a postwar baby-boom, has negligible immigration rates, and has the lowest mortality rate and the highest life expectancy rate in the world. Martin (1989) documented Japan's rapidly aging population and projects that, by the year 2025, Japan will have the most elderly population, with 23 percent over the age of 65. Meanwhile, the younger age group between 20 and 29 is projected to decline by one-third. This combined effect of an aging population, a decreasing youth group, and no immigration has resulted in an annual population increase of only 0.2 percent (Seike, 1997). The Japanese have considered several solutions to the problem of a workforce that is too small to support the retired population. One solution is to increase the birth rate, and despite the overcrowding in Japan, the government has looked with favor on some pronatalist policies (Keidanren, 1999). Another potential solution is immigration, but few expect immigration to work well in Japan because it is an insular nation where foreigners (*gaijin* or outsiders) are very small in number relative to the population. Japan appears to have difficulties integrating outsiders into its labor force and its society. Indeed, Thurow (1992: 251) refers to Japan as the country "least willing or able to absorb immigrants." Perhaps the most popular solution is a proposal to maintain the size of the labor pool by extending the retirement age to 65 (Seike, 1997), since Japan's present retirement age, at 55–60 years, is early relative to a long life expectancy. Currently, the law allows organizations to re-hire their retired workers at lower wages for part-time work, resulting in 65+ labor force participation rates at more than three times those of Canada and other industrialized countries (Venne, 2002).

Australasia

Australia

Australia is the world's sixth largest country and the smallest continent. It is similar to North America, in that its indigenous population was displaced by White European settlers who later opened up the country to high levels of immigration. In 1967 a national referendum granted full citizenship to Aboriginal

Australians, giving them the right to vote. In 1993 the Australian government passed legislation allowing Aborigines and Torres Strait Islanders to file land claims. However, as in Canada, Aborigines continue to struggle for social, political, cultural, and economic prosperity, and serious efforts are required to address widespread disparities.

A spacious country, with a sparse population of 3 persons per square kilometer, Australia has experienced growing diversity in its workforce over the past two decades after opening up to aggressive immigration from Asia. The many advantages traditionally enjoyed by British immigrants ended as recently as 1983. The first major intake of Asian immigrants began in the first year of the Fraser Liberal/ National government. The White Australia policy finally ended during the Whitlam Labor government (Jupp, 1995). The 1991 census reported the Australian population approaching 17 million, with 95 percent of European descent, 1 percent indigenous Aborigines and Torres Strait Islanders, and about 4 percent Asians. English is the only official language, although aboriginal and other minority languages are spoken in ethnic communities.

Australia has recently become very active in its diversity policies, embracing multiculturalism as an official government policy at the federal and provincial levels and recognizing the importance of managing diversity for social and economic prosperity. Australia is moving quickly towards a culturally and ethnically diverse workforce and has implemented an extensive national and provincial Affirmative Action (Equal Opportunity for Women) and Human Rights Legislation covering both the public and private sectors (*Australia: Equality of opportunity and treatment, 1984–2000*). The Affirmative Action (Equal Opportunity for Women) Act of 1986 requires all private sector employers in Australia with more than 100 employees to report annually on programs developed to improve women's employment opportunities. Although most of this protective legislation is built around equality in the workplace for women, Sheridan's (1995) research, based on a comparative profile of Australian organizations, suggests that simple quantitative measures of the effect of affirmative action are clearly inadequate to capture women's employment experiences. Sinclair's (2000) research in forwarding the understanding of gender relations in organizations recommends ceasing to focus solely on women and concentrating instead on men and the construction of masculinities in management, describing the challenges of this approach through her experiences in management development and education activities. Recent research reported by the Australian Center for International Business reveals that despite increasing diversity in the Australian workplace, including ethnicity, gender, age, religion, sexual orientation, socioeconomic status, education, family status, and physical and mental ability, few companies are capturing the diversity dividend. "Although in some firms diversity management has evolved from equal opportunity compliance into a proactive approach to the management of valuable human resources . . . few Australian firms have prioritized diversity management and even fewer have developed diversity capabilities" (O'Flynn et al., 2001: 34–5).

New Zealand

New Zealand, situated southeast of Australia, comprises a heavily populated Northern Island, a Southern Island, and numerous smaller islands in the South Pacific. It is an independent state within the Commonwealth. Its constitutional history as a British colony began in 1840 when the indigenous Maori and the English settlers signed the Treaty of Waitangi. New Zealand gained its independence from Britain and moved to Dominion status in 1907. Queen Elizabeth II is represented by the governor-general, and the prime minister is the political head of state, as in Canada. Since the 1950s the Polynesians and other Pacific Islanders have contributed primarily to New Zealand's ethnic diversity, but over the last two decades there has been significant immigration from Asian countries. The 1996 census reported over 3.4 million people in New Zealand, approximately 80 percent of European descent (mainly British); 14 percent Maori; and 6 percent of other ethnic peoples, including Chinese, Indians, and those of Polynesian descent (New Zealand, Statistics 2001).

New Zealand was the first country to grant women's suffrage, doing so in 1893. Jenny Shipley became New Zealand's first female prime minister in 1997, followed by Helen Clark in 1999. Other high-profile positions such as the governor general, attorney general, and chief justice are also occupied by women. In fact, women comprise 31 percent of the New Zealand parliament, compared to 22 percent in Australia and only 18 percent in the United Kingdom. However, the private sector does not appear to be as progressive. The Equal Employment Opportunity Trust (2000) reports that women are seriously underrepresented among the business leadership and continue to earn less than men.

New Zealand is unique in its workplace diversity issues in that the Maori asserted and succeeded in their right, as a founding nation of New Zealand, for a bicultural rather than a multicultural national policy. With English and Maori as the two official languages, other minority languages were not recognized. The Maori favored biculturalism over multiculturalism as they still far outnumbered the immigrants and other ethnic minorities in New Zealand. They referred to the 1840 Treaty of Waitangi, which recognized the unique status and special rights of the Maori as the original occupants of the land. Due to a reduction in immigration restrictions, however, increasing numbers of Polynesian islanders and other Pacific Rim immigrants began entering the country. This led to Maori discord and distrust of the pakeha (White) people.

> The [Treaty of Waitangi] was an acknowledgment of Maori existence, of their prior occupation of the land and of an intent that the Maori presence would remain and be respected. It made us one country, but acknowledged that we were two peoples. It established the regime not for uni-culturalism but for bi-culturalism. (**"Waitangi Tribunal," cited in Fleras and Elliott, 1995: 262**)

Although recognition for the tangata whenua (indigenous people) resulted from native activists' demands in a policy known as tu tangata (stand tall) designed to revitalize the Maori through self-directed initiatives, the Maori occupy only a peripheral status in New Zealand as compared with the Whites. Similar to the Canadian Aboriginal peoples, the Maori remain overrepresented in unemployment and underrepresented in education, economic power, and participation (Fleras and Elliott, 1995: 259). The trend seems to be moving from biculturalism towards multiculturalism in New Zealand, as public institutions attempt to reflect the new cultural and racial diversity within the country.

Parting Observation

These brief snapshots of a few countries are only the tip of the diversity iceberg. Culture is deep and slow moving. The bulk of information lies below the surface and more comparative diversity research is required to document the evolution of diversity strategies used and the outcomes achieved in countries around the world. There is growing worldwide awareness of the importance of managing diversity in organizations, as countries adapt to their rapidly changing demographic, legislative, economic, and social environments. In reality the results have been slow, especially in the upper echelons, indicating that change at the macro or institutional and systemic level must be accompanied with change at the micro or individual level, and vice versa, in order to ensure enduring positive results of diversity.

Acknowledgment

The author would like to acknowledge the Social Sciences and Humanities Research Council of Canada (SSHRC) for partial funding support for this research.

14

LOOKING BACK AND HEADING FORWARD: MAJOR THEMES OF *THE PSYCHOLOGY AND MANAGEMENT OF WORKPLACE DIVERSITY*

Margaret S. Stockdale and Feng Cao

The preceding 13 chapters provide a wealth of information. This chapter integrates that information and considers three themes: (1) the benefits of diversity management; (2) the barriers and challenges to full multicultural inclusiveness; (3) strategies for future directions for workplace diversity research and practice.

In the late 1980s and early 1990s, a number of publications documented the advent of demographic and social changes in the workplace (e.g., Johnston and Packer, 1987; Morrison and Von Glinow, 1990). Scholars such as Taylor Cox, Stacey Blake, and R. Roosevelt Thomas provided a vision and an agenda for the Workplace Diversity Movement that emphasized the competitive advantage for organizations that managed diversity well. In particular, Cox and Blake (1991) outlined six strategic reasons why diversity management is not only good for people, but also good for business. According to Cox and Blake, organizations that manage diversity well reduce turnover, increase productivity, gain an edge in attracting talented White women and minorities, increase successful marketing to under-exploited subpopulations, increase the potential for creative problem solving and innovation, and improve their ability to adapt to other inevitable forces for change. Such theories, coupled with demographic changes, helped spark a revolution in the nature and direction of research and practice relating to equal employment opportunity.

Now, more than a decade later, scholarship and practice in the field of workplace diversity has grown immensely. For example, at the 2002 meeting of the Society for Industrial and Organizational Psychology there ·were more sessions on workplace diversity and work–family balance than on any other topic except personnel selection. Currently, diversity management is not only a sub-discipline of industrial and organizational psychology, but also of human resource management, organizational development, organizational sociology, political science, and other esteemed disciplines.

The chapters in this book approach diversity from a variety of perspectives, yet it is possible to discern several themes common to them all. First, one can see the benefits to individuals, groups, and organizations of diversity management. Second, emphasis is also placed on the barriers and challenges to full multicultural inclusiveness. Third, implicit in the recognition of barriers is the understanding that some methods for becoming multicultural are more effective than others. One of the special contributions of many of our authors is their attention to strategies for change.

The purpose of this chapter is to summarize and integrate the wealth of information already provided in this book. We alert the reader to new research directions and we indicate ways of applying our new learning to help improve human relations in the new multicultural workplace.

IMPETUS AND BENEFITS OF DIVERSITY MANAGEMENT

Anyone who has not yet jumped on the diversity bandwagon will soon learn that there are forces that push and pull organizations to make such an effort. Demographic, economic, and legal developments make it compulsory for most organizations to deal with diversity. Clearly, the demographic changes predicted by Johnston and Packer (1987) and further articulated by early diversity scholars have come to pass. Hays-Thomas (chapter 1, this volume) noted that the 2000 US census not only bore out earlier projections about changes in the demographic configuration of population growth, but also anticipated the popularity of the new "multiracial" category for ethnic identity – a sign that diversity is becoming more diverse and perhaps more complicated. Hays-Thomas also reviewed the variety of economic forces that are changing the very nature of the workplace and work itself. These include a tremendous growth in multinational strategic alliances and growth in the service sector, requiring both technical and human-relations competence. Because the marketplace has become multicultural, the skills necessary to survive and thrive are fundamentally grounded in multicultural competence.

Also important is the changing legal climate. Within the United States, the US Civil Rights Act of 1964, combined with Executive Order 11246 which promulgated affirmative action, were arguably the most important influences in spurring diversity-related concerns and practices in US organizations. Subsequent legal interpretations and updates to the Civil Rights Act and affirmative action orders, as well as new laws such as the Age Discrimination in Employment Act of 1967 and the Americans with Disabilities Act of 1991, have created a sophisticated legal structure that undergirds and sometimes complicates diversity practices. Internationally, as Haq (chapter 13) outlines, legal structures shape diversity practices in nations around the world. An important motivation for many organizations to engage in pro-diversity practices, both at home and abroad, is to avoid breaking the law and having to submit to costly penalties.

The impetus to manage diversity may have originated in external forces, but for many, the thrust toward multiculturalism is now less a matter of reaction and more a matter of motivation. To be sure, as Thomas et al. (chapter 2) show, many of the old myths about the costs of multicultural inclusiveness still persist. Yet, increasingly, scholars and practitioners are coming to see diversity as an asset, not simply an exigency.

The benefits of good diversity management to individuals

Many individuals reap advantages when their employers become more inclusive. Clearly, those who have been discriminated against or stigmatized – including women (Stroh et al., chapter 7), people of color (Cokley et al., chapter 8), lower-class and poor people (Bullock, chapter 11), gay people (Lubensky et al., chapter 10), and the physically challenged or non-conforming (Bell et al., chapter 9) – benefit in both the short and long term from working in a genuinely inclusive environment. Improved salaries and opportunities are obvious gains. Less obvious perhaps, but no less real, are the gains in both mental and physical health that accrue to minority workers in inclusiveness workplaces (Sagrestano, chapter 6).

It is not just the erstwhile underdogs who benefit from well-managed organizational diversity. Potential benefits extend to the entire workforce. The work environment for heterosexual workers, for example, improves when sexual orientation is no longer a frightening issue; the sexually inclusive workplace is a desexualized workplace (Lubensky et al., chapter 10). Furthermore, as Bell et al. (chapter 9) point out in relation to aging, obesity, and disability, everyone has the potential to be a member of an "underrepresented" social identity group. The young will someday be old, so it is reassuring for them to see the old being well treated.

The benefits of good diversity management to organizations

It is easy to focus on individuals, but the gains to organizations of good diversity management are just as important – perhaps more so. As is clear from many of the chapters in this book, especially those by Chrobot-Mason and Ruderman (chapter 5), Stroh et al. (chapter 7), and Cokley et al. (chapter 8), serious benefits accrue to organizations when they develop the leadership potential of organizational members from minority groups. The processes that allow an organization to utilize talent, no matter what the external packaging of that talent, also serve as a blueprint for the types of competencies needed in the new millennium. Everyone in an organization benefits from increased awareness of the operation of bias, especially from enhanced insights into their own biases, prejudices, and attitudes toward dissimilar others. Everyone benefits from awareness of their own cultural heritage. Everyone wins with the development of conflict management skills, interpersonal communication skills, feedback-seeking and role-modeling skills. Thus, as all our authors noted – especially those in parts two and four of the book – organizations that endeavor to become fully inclusive and to maximize multicultural understanding and sensitivity tend to realize benefits to their entire operations.

Contemporary organizations that do not develop multicultural competency face a number of challenges. White-dominated environments expose an organization to legal difficulties, whereas good diversity management is an effective prophylactic against costly discrimination suits (Hays-Thomas, chapter 1). Non-inclusive work environments, furthermore, create health problems for their workers (Sagrestano, chapter 6). In contrast, good diversity management should help reduce organizational costs related to high turnover, low productivity, and other forms of withdrawal, and help reduce health insurance costs resulting from stress-related illness brought on by unfair treatment.

The benefits of good diversity management to societies

Bullock (chapter 11) notes that workplaces reproduce and reinforce social inequities that exist in broader society. In her analysis, societal class structures are compounded in organizations because of prejudice and structural barriers. For example, low-level employees such as clerks and janitors have little or no opportunity to advance on career tracks that offer upward mobility. Cokley et al. (chapter 8) also noted that African Americans and other racial–ethnic minorities tend to be segregated into jobs and occupations that offer little opportunity for upward mobility and career advancement. Therefore, the extent to which these inequities and disparities are addressed within organizations may very well lead to reforms in broader society. Certainly, if marginalized groups of people gain access to powerful and influential positions in organizations, and if pay inequities are eliminated, they will bring greater wealth and resources to their families and communities and thus break the chains of poverty.

The benefits of increasing knowledge of diversity and of moving organizations toward full multiculturalism also have the potential to impact worldwide diversity practices. Haq (chapter 13) noted that there is probably no nation that does not have its own workplace diversity concerns. Knowledge of diversity management issues developed and applied in the US can be extended to diversity efforts abroad. Similarly, the US can and should learn from the successes and failures of diversity practices in other countries. In the modern world – forever changed by the events of September 11, 2001 – greater knowledge of cultural issues around the world should help shrink our globe in salutary ways and halt the advance of destruction.

Benefits of understanding diversity to scholarship on organizations

Theories provide a framework for understanding observations around a particular phenomenon and permit us to make meaningful predictions about the behavior of related phenomena in the future. Thus, theories are very useful in helping us understand and solve socially important problems. In the words of Kurt Lewin: *there's nothing more practical than a good theory.*

Yet theories are only as good as those observations used to develop and test them. For decades, American theories of organizational behavior were based on the understanding that the typical, if not only, person of concern was a White, male, able bodied, heterosexual manager. The diversity Zeitgeist has contributed to broadening our understanding of human behavior in organizational settings (if not beyond) and thus has improved our theories of human behavior. Several authors have documented such theoretical developments.

Stone and Stone-Romero (chapter 4) take a very central theory in organizational behavior, Katz and Kahn's (1978) role-taking model, and expand it to consider cultural factors that may influence many of the linkages in the role-taking process. For example, individuals who come from high power distance cultures are likely to interpret supervisory cues about role expectations much differently than individuals who come from low power distance cultures. Similarly, Cokley et al. (chapter 8) expand Campbell et al.'s (1970) well-established theory of career attainment to show that race, through its effects on differential access to social and educational capital, impacts the association between opportunity and career success. Furthermore, because of race-based dynamics in the ability and opportunity to form important social connections in organizations (such as mentoring), race further modifies the extent to which background credentials, motivational forces, and other forces translate into career success. In other words, the career success model for African Americans may not be quite the same as the career success model for Whites. These basic tenets are echoed by Stroh et al. (chapter 7) and Thomas et al. (chapter 2), who remind us that human capital and merit never fully accounted for career success, despite many early and contemporary theories to the contrary. Finally, Chrobot-Mason and Ruderman (chapter 5) suggest that most of our well-established theories of leadership have rarely considered cultural and other related differences among followers or between followers and leaders. Incorporating these dynamics into leadership theories not only helps us to develop mutliculturally competent leaders; it also enriches our understanding of leadership generally.

Barriers and Challenges to Full Multicultural Inclusiveness

We have a long way to go before individuals, organizations, and society fully reap the benefits of multiculturalism. Every chapter in this volume has identified problems and challenges that must be overcome before true multiculturalism can be attained in our organizations. We think the factors they identify can be roughly organized into three levels of analysis: individual, interpersonal, and organizational. Table 14.1 sets out these factors.

Table 14.1 Themes related to barriers and obstacles to full multicultural inclusiveness

Level of analysis	*Theme*	*Example*	*Chapter*
Individual	Stereotypes	Social identity perceptions	3
		Stereotypes	3, 7, 8, 9
		Stigma associated with perceptions of onset controllability	10
	Prejudice	Classism (classist prejudice, classist stereotypes, and classist discrimination)	11
		Forms of homosexual prejudice (ego-defensive, value expressive, and anti-gay attitudes)	10
		Legacy of legalized segregation both within US and abroad (e.g., apartheid)	8, 13
	Behavioral effects	Threat rigidity	3
		Race discrimination in cross-race jobs	8
		Sex discrimination in cross-gender jobs	7
		Sexual harassment creating stress	6
		Sexual harassment inhibiting mobility	7
	Unsupportive attitudes	Misunderstanding of affirmative action	1, 2
		Backlash sentiments toward diversity	2
		Justice perceptions (special help programs believed to violate social justice)	3
		Other myths of meritocracy, colorblind ideal, melting pot	2
	Individual deficiencies	Gender differences in negotiating skills	7
		Biases in attaining educational and social capital	8
Interpersonal and group	Group conflict	Lack of group cohesiveness and greater emotional conflict	5

Table 14.1   *(cont'd)*

Level of analysis	Theme	Example	Chapter
	Homophily processes and networking barriers	Attraction–Selection–Attrition process affects team and organizational diversification	5
		Homophily tendencies interfere with ability to create cohesive teams and develop high exchange leader–member relationships	5
		Homophily tendencies interfere with ability to develop important influential mentoring relationships	8
	Communication barriers	Cultural miscommunication at various stages in the role-taking process	4, 11
Organizational/ occupational	*Stratification and compositional barrier*	Class stratification and factors within organizations that reproduce and reinforce this stratification	11
		Structural barriers and facilitators, e.g., number of women in top executive ranks affects stereotypes of women as leaders and salaries of women	11, 7
		Tokenism	
	Lack of top management support	Lack of top management support for diversity initiatives	6 10
	Occupational stress	Disparities in emotional labor burdens	6
		Occupational and job segregation affects occupational health risks	6
	Access to power and resources	Differential power and access to resources	9
		Occupational and job segregation affects pipeline mobility	8
Societal/extra- organizational	*Work–family balance*	Gender imbalance in handling domestic chores v. working extreme hours	8
		Work schedule inflexibility and lack of supervisor support for work–family balance	6
	Legal barriers	Barriers created by legislation, e.g., new welfare to work legislation and TANF	11
		Difficulties in enforcing anti-discrimination/pro-diversity laws	9, 10, 13 4
	Cultural barriers	Cultural differences in preferences and ability to work in different types of organizational structures	

Individual level

Stereotyping and prejudice are perhaps the most fundamental psychological processes that create discrimination and stand in our way of enjoying a multicultural workforce. Racism, sexism, classism, heterosexism, ageism, and sizeism are problems that persist in contemporary America. They affect many individuals.

Often, prejudice goes underground (see Thomas et al., chapter 2), so that the prejudiced individual can stymie attempts at full integration and equality without ever having to recognize his or her own prejudiced attitudes or the role that those attitudes play in perpetuating unfair systems. Reactions to affirmative action illustrate the process by which prejudice is masked by concerns with justice. To many Americans, any form of preferential or special treatment based on non-job relevant characteristics, such as social group identity, smacks of unfairness. Crosby (in press) has meticulously examined the structure of such sentiments. In American society, it is felt that fairness occurs when the ratio of one person's inputs and outcomes in an important arena, such as a job or in school, matches the ratio of another person's inputs and outputs (Adams, 1965). So, for example, if we see that Jack, with his Harvard degree and 45 hours of work per week, gets a handsome management promotion, whereas Jerry, with a high school diploma and 35 hours of work per week, maintains a steady but career-limited shipping clerk position, we feel all is fair. Jack and Jerry don't have the same outcomes, but their outcomes are comparable to their level of inputs (e.g., skills, ability, and level of effort). What seems unfair, however, is when Harvard-educated Jack is passed by for a promotion in favor of State University-educated (and African-American) John. Because of Jack's superior educational credentials, it seems that he should have the edge over a less credentialed person in promotion or job selection decisions, all else being equal. The problems with such seemingly fair-minded objections to affirmative action reveal the role of closed mindedness. As Crosby (in press) points out, any equity judgment subjectively weighs the relevant inputs and outcomes. Insensitive Whites may overlook the existence of racial barriers and thus underestimate all the effort and skill needed for African-American John to obtain his State University degree. After all, Harvard gives more places to legacees than to racial minority candidates; and not all the legacees are brilliant. Reliance on the apparently neutral input–outcome ratio for deciding fairness also allows aversive racists to give undue weight to certain criteria. Research shows that the majority of selection criteria, such as college credentials, are mediocre predictors of job performance (see Salgado, Viswesvaran, and Ones, 2001, for a review). The most robust type of predictor of job performance – measures of general mental ability – only accounts for between 14 and 20 percent of the variability in job performance. If Americans were to become more educated about how affirmative action really works, they might come to embrace the policy with vigor, but many of them appear to have resisted education (Crosby, in press), which is probably why scholars have found a strong association between prejudice and resistance to affirmative action among the privileged (Crosby, Ferdman, and Wingate, 2001).

Interpersonal and group level

Increasingly, work is conducted in teams (West, 2001) where members interact regularly to produce a product, perform a service, manage, plan, and problem solve. Teams with members who trust each other, share common perspectives, and feel comfortable with each other are inevitably more cohesive and effective than teams that don't. Team member diversity poses many challenges for team effectiveness. There are powerful psychological forces that work both to limit the extent to which teams become diverse and exaggerate any differences that remain. As described by Chrobot-Mason and Ruderman (chapter 5) and Cokley et al. (chapter 8), people tend to group with others whom they believe to be similar. This "similarity/attraction" or "homophily" bias is well documented in the literature of social psychology (e.g., Bryne, 1971) and organizational demography (e.g., Pfeffer, 1983). Social categorization processes make any differences among team members stand out (see Tajfel, 1981). In perceiving others, we categorize people by salient characteristics. Although the situation can make some categories more salient (e.g., being the only philosopher in a group of mechanics), some demographic characteristics, such as age, race, and gender, are chronically salient. When team members are grouped in such fashion, there is a tendency for conflict and tension to arise (see Williams and O'Reilly, 1998, for a review of research demonstrating negative effects of team diversity).

Team member diversity does not inevitably lead to bad outcomes. There is evidence that diverse teams outperform homogeneous teams (McLeod, Lobel, and Cox, 1996; Watson, Kumar, and Michaelsen, 1993), and there have been several theoretical and empirical efforts to understand the factors that affect the extent to which team member diversity burdens (e.g., increases conflict) or benefits (e.g., increases creativity and problem solving) team performance (see Jehn, 1999; Jehn, Northcraft, and Neale, 1999; Lawrence, 1997; Lau and Murnighan, 1998; Milliken and Martins, 1996; Pelled, 1996; Pelled, Eisenhardt, and Xin, 1999). Leaders must develop skills to manage the inevitable interpersonal conflict that arises when diversity in teams and groups increases and channel it into productive, task-based conflict that results in improved problem solving, creativity, and innovation (see Chrobot-Mason and Ruderman, chapter 5). Otherwise, a negative cycle can persist in which members of the dominant group avoid having members of minority groups on their teams unless they are forced, which almost invariably leads to more tension and conflict.

Organizational and occupational level

Additional barriers to multiculturalism are created by organizations that stratify the workforce by class, race, and gender (among other characteristics) and that maintain structural barriers that limit opportunities for women and members of other non-hegemonic groups. Job and occupational segregation (a) hinders the ability for members of diverse groups to gain access to influential networks and mentoring relationships (Cokley et al., chapter 8), (b) facilitates the debilitating effects of tokenism (Sagrestano, chapter 6; Stroh et al., chapter 7), and (c) perpetuates stereotypes about identity groups (e.g., Bullock et al., chapter 11). For example, the stereotype that poor people are lazy may be based on the observation that people in low-paying, low-prestige jobs have higher absenteeism than people in high-paying, high-prestige jobs. The stereotype overlooks the fact that jobs that poor people occupy provide little motivational incentive and turns a blind eye to impediments such as poor transportation systems, lack of day care, and inadequate healthcare systems that poor people face.

Job and occupational segregation is a strong organizational barrier to multiculturalism. When people of different identity groups disproportionately occupy various classes of jobs, inclusiveness is hard to achieve. As noted by Sagrestano (chapter 6), the jobs that tend to be reserved for women and minorities have low pay and low opportunity for advancement, and they tend also to lack autonomy and control, be physically demanding and unsafe, and in other ways are more stressful than the jobs occupied by the dominant majority.

Hierarchical segregation tends also to be self-perpetuating. People feel comfortable with others like themselves. When all the executives are White and male, there may be no one in the executive suite who spontaneously reaches out to mentor or sponsor women or people of color. As Stroh et al. (chapter 7) note, research shows that the more executive women there are in an organization, the less are women stereotyped throughout the organization and the less the pay gap for women and men at all levels. Generally, the more top management, no matter what its demographic composition, actively supports a comprehensive approach to diversity management, the greater the chances for constructive change (Holvino et al., chapter 12; Lubinsky et al., chapter 10).

Societal/extra-organizational level

Organizations do not exist in a vacuum. They are embedded in larger social, cultural, and political contexts. Cultures help shape the behavior, attitudes, and values of people who work in organizations. Societies help dictate the policies and practices by which organizations operate.

One of the most important social systems that shapes and is shaped by organizational practices is the family. Most working adults have family responsibilities as well as work responsibilities. Furthermore, these responsibilities can encompass many roles, such as being a spouse/partner, parent, and adult. In collectivistic/ interdependent cultures, meaningful and time-consuming family responsibilities and roles can be even broader, such as being a grandparent, sibling, aunt/uncle, or cousin. Sagrestano (chapter 6) reviews the family-related issues that impact the health and well-being of workers, such as access to flextime, telecommuting, quality day care, the magnitude of time and resource demands from multiple roles, and the amount and quality of support that other family members provide to help fulfill these responsibilities (see also Stroh et al., chapter 7). Although women – especially those who have limited resources – may experience more work–family stress than others, Sagrestano notes that balancing multiple family roles can also lead to mental health benefits, especially when role demands are not excessive and individuals find their various roles to be satisfying. Increased attention and dedication to developing a fully functioning multicultural workforce will compel organizations to adopt family-inclusive and multiple-role inclusive perspectives in managing the workforce. Although laws in many nations, including the United States, have generally moved in the direction of assuring rights to more and more people, the laws have been uneven both in their form and in their enforcement. In the US, one cannot discriminate against women, for instance, but in many states it is still perfectly legal to discriminate against homosexuals. In some cases, laws may actually hinder effective diversity practices. For example, the Personal Responsibility and Work Reconciliation Act of 1996 dramatically restructured the US welfare system by requiring recipients to be employed or to engage in work-related activities and by restricting their TANF (Temporary Aid for Needy Families) benefits to two years. Not only are limits placed on the number of people who can participate in job-readiness related programs, but also the law does not adequately deal with the many barriers that TANF participants experience in getting and keeping high-quality jobs (see Bullock, chapter 11).

Finally, culture is perhaps the broadest extra-organizational dimension that shapes diversity philosophies, values, and practices. Understanding and appreciating cultural dimensions and differences are an important part of diversity training programs and other sorts of diversity practices. These very dimensions can also present challenges to effective implementation and maintenance of pro-diversity and general management practices. By its very nature, multiculturalism means that life in organizations is likely to be more complicated than it is in monolithic organizations. Depending on their orientation toward power and power distance, individuals and groups will vary in their preferences for tight versus loose supervision, for example. Stone and Stone-Romero (chapter 4) note that based on cultural differences, groups vary in their preference for working in different types of organizational structures. Individuals from high power distance cultures prefer top-down management styles and impute credibility to elders and those with greater structural power, whereas those from low power distance and high achievement striving cultures prefer participative management structures and impute credibility to those with greater expertise, intelligence, and track records of accomplishments. Differences in orientation toward time present particular challenges for multicultural groups that need to develop common norms for task engagement, meetings, and interpersonal interactions. These kinds of cultural differences not only need to be understood and valued, but also need to be negotiated in finding effective ways to work together harmoniously and with mutual respect.

STRATEGIES FOR MULTICULTURAL ORGANIZATIONAL DEVELOPMENT: NOW AND IN THE FUTURE

What are managers and leaders to do? Efforts to effectively manage the complex web of multicultural challenges and opportunities require attention to processes at many levels. Most chapters in this book provide suggestions for strategies that organizational members can consider for managing the multitude of issues discussed. Table 14.2 summarizes these strategies, discussed in further detail below. We also highlight some exemplary multicultural organizational practices gleaned from the research, popular, and trade literature.

Individual development among the targets of discrimination

Many scholars have pointed out the dangers of stressing self-improvement as a means of social change. Such an approach runs the risk of implying that differences are deficiencies. Worse, the focus on the individual can detract from a more appropriate focus on important systemic barriers that need to be removed (see Riger and Galligan, 1980).

Kept in the proper perspective, however, attention to individual change among members of previously excluded or under-rewarded groups forms an important part of many diversity initiatives. Most individuals could benefit from some personal development to equip themselves for managing their own careers and for working effectively with others. Furthermore, because of past and current inequities, some individuals, by virtue of their social identity, have had less access than others to formal and informal sources of career socialization and other forms of education and training. Such individuals may benefit from receiving a "jump start" at critical points in their working lives.

In addressing the problems of the glass ceiling, Stroh et al. (chapter 7) relay advice from women who have succeeded in attaining top-level leadership positions in corporations. As reported in a study by Catalyst (1996), female executives endorse personal strategies of working hard and working smart consistently to exceed expectations and to prove to others that they can handle any assignment. The highly placed women also recommend developing a style that is comfortable for male managers (see also Adler, Brody, and Osland, 2001). Research shows that managerial women are viewed less favorably if they act too feminine or too masculine (see Cleveland, Stockdale, and Murphy, 2000, for a review), so

Table 14.2 Themes related to strategies for effective multicultural development in organizations

Theme	Example	Chapter
Individual development	Career tracking	7
	Individual strategies for women to shatter the glass ceiling	7
	Training; counter-stereotype training	9
Group and interpersonal development	Expanding discussion of forms of prejudice and oppression in diversity training, e.g., classism	11
	Developing multicultural competence	5
	Improving social networks through mentoring relationships, esp. with White males	7, 8
	Developing women's networks/affinity groups	7, 10
Organizational development	OD v. Action Research and Collaborative Inquiry	12
	Structural, cultural, and behavioral processes	12
	Kottke and Agars' model of organizational change: issue identification, implementation maintenance; and Holvino's Multicultural Organizational Development (MCOD) model of change	2, 12
	Organizational initiatives to shatter glass ceiling	7
	Top management support	10 and others
	Developing and maintaining work–family balance programs	7

developing a favorable style may be like trying to walk a tightrope. The same applies to African-American individuals. Cokley et al. (chapter 8) explain that Whites have different levels of comfort when they interact with African Americans, depending not only on White racism but also on the African American's stage of racial identity. Although educating Whites about racial identity is fundamentally important, it is also sometimes helpful to have African Americans analyze their interpersonal effectiveness.

Individual development among the privileged

Of course, most of the responsibility for change must be borne not by those least favored but rather by those in positions of responsibility. Managers need to be aware of the importance of developing others and to pay particular attention to factors that may bias their efforts in developing others who have not been part of the traditional dominant group, as well as to factors that are of particular relevance to members of non-dominant groups. Chrobot-Mason and Ruderman (chapter 5) discuss four key areas for leaders to consider in developing others: challenge, assessment, feedback, and support.

An example of a good mechanism that can be used by managers to help develop talent is the technique of making a career plan (Gilbert and Ivancevich, 1999; Iverson, 2000; Wentling and Palma-Rivas, 1998). In addition to noting strengths, weaknesses, goals, and potential mobility, a career plan should also consider the fit between personal attributes and job demands. Like all other diversity practices, career plans need management commitment and accountability in order for their benefits to be realized. One strategy is to link the development and implementation of employees' career plans to managers' performance and pay (Gilbert and Ivancevich, 1999).

Diversity training

Given the historically high levels of cultural insensitivity, prejudice, and discrimination in the USA, it would be unrealistic to expect managers and leaders to become instantly multiculturally competent. Nor would it be fair or effective to expect the change to be primarily self-engineered. Education and training are needed.

Many of our authors advocate the use of training in organizational transformations. Chrobot-Mason and Ruderman (chapter 5) endorse the use of training. Bell et al. (chapter 9) suggest that counter-stereotype training would be helpful for developing sensitivities toward misunderstood diverse groups such as the obese, the disabled, and the aged. Similarly, Bullock (chapter 11) calls for diversity trainers to expand sessions on prejudice to include the issues of classism and oppression. Holvino et al. (chapter 12) argue that training is important for providing opportunities for underrepresented groups to be heard, so that myths and stereotypes can be replaced with facts and knowledge.

Not all programs make for good diversity training. As Chrobot-Mason and Ruderman (chapter 5) point out, a one-day session can be worse than inconsequential. Research corroborates their claim. For example, Ellis and Sonnenfeld (1994) surveyed 92 employees of United Communications Corporation who attended a Valuing Diversity seminar. They found that only 59 percent of employees who participated in the diversity training thought it worthwhile, only 60 percent thought it enhanced awareness of the benefits of diversity, and only 44 percent thought it improved their ability to work with diverse employees. Poorly conceived or poorly executed training programs have been known to provoke disdain among White males (Ellis and Sonnenfeld). Even among those who liked the training, behaviors may not change as much as people would like (Kirkpatrick, 1987). In fact, few organizations have seriously evaluated the behavioral effects of training (cf., Linnehan, Chrobot-Mason, and Konrad, 2002; Linnehan et al., in press).

What makes training succeed? Some processes have been identified as effective. McKee and Schor (1999), for example, suggest a framework to teach diversity content: (1) inform participants what prejudices and stereotypes are; (2) ask them to think about when they are victims; (3) encourage them to expose their pre-judice against others; (4) help them develop empathy.

Whether one uses the McKee and Schor model or another, support from the top is absolutely essential. It is also critical to select qualified trainers. One poll reported in the newsletter *Cultural Diversity at Work* (see "The Diversity Indus-try," 1993) suggested that as many as 50 percent of trainees thought that trainers did not have sufficient knowledge of diversity management issues. Trainers can be selected on the basis of their teaching skills, educational background, prior work experiences, and cultural self-awareness (Arredondo, 1996).

A common issue is whether to use internal managers or external consultants to facilitate the training. Organizations must be careful when using internal man-agers. Although they may establish trust with participants easily, they may also create confusion, resentment, or misinformation if they themselves have not yet resolved biases and prejudice, or if they lack the skill and sensitivity in handling group dynamics (Ellis and Sonnenfeld, 1994). Training programs that honestly deal with prejudice and stereotypes may be so sensitive and volatile that many but the best trainers fear to discuss them.

Another issue of concern to many organizations is whether participation should be voluntary or mandatory. Allowing voluntary participation sends the mess-age that employees themselves can decide the importance of the issue and that leaders do not support the training (Arredondo, 1996). Conversely, mandatory participation can generate resentment among employees in an organization which has a culture of being progressive and informal. Organizations need to design and implement training programs that best fit their cultures.

Despite the potential pitfalls, training programs that are well designed and carefully implemented may help many individuals who are not themselves in the targeted minority groups understand the processes of change. Training may help the privileged become good allies to the disadvantaged. Training many also empower individuals to work constructively for organizational change.

Group and interpersonal development

A great deal of work and career development is achieved by working with others. Thus, skills in building effective groups and interpersonal relationships are critical to the success of any diversity management program. The Catalyst (1996) study reviewed by Stroh et al. (chapter 7) mentions the importance of devel-oping effective mentoring relationships for helping to catapult the careers of minority and female employees. The importance of mentoring and sponsorship is echoed in other research studies (Gilbert and Ivancevich, 1999; Murrell, Crosby, and Ely, 1999; Friedman, 1999; Wentling and Palma-Rivas, 1998). According to Ragins (1995), a mentor will serve three purposes. First, in the "counselor" role, mentors assist minority employees to become aware of and to understand the organization's standards, norms, and politics. Second, in the "protector" role, mentors shield protégés from negative influences and situations. Third, in the "guardian" role, mentors keep protégés informed of good opportunities, offer feedback on performance, suggest strategies for career advancement, and encourage meeting high performance standards. Moreover, the mentoring relationship also influences organizational culture, structure, and behaviors. Cokley et al. (chapter 8) discuss research showing that developing mentoring relationships with senior White managers, as well as with other senior-level individuals whose social identity is similar to that of protégés, has differential advantages for diverse protégés.

In addition to fostering mentoring relationships, managers and leaders should also support formal and informal networking efforts among members of diverse groups. Stroh et al. (chapter 7) and Lubensky et al. (chapter 10) conclude that members of diverse groups gain support, guidance, recognition, and powerful allies by networking with similar others and participating in affinity groups. Network groups are informal groups without organizational sponsorship, established by minority or female employees voluntarily, but often open to any interested organizational (or extra-organizational) members. Friedman (1999) found that Black managers in companies that have network groups are more optimistic about their careers than those in companies without network groups. But he also pointed out possible problems with network groups. Managers may fear that network groups might engender employee resistance, akin to unionization. Network members may worry that they are regarded as too radical, which may negatively influence their career-growth opportunities. Friedman (1999) believes these concerns can become a self-fulfilling prophecy: "if one side expects the other to be angry and confrontational, they are likely to act in ways that generate angry and confrontational behaviors in the other side. If one side expects the other to be sincere and helpful, they are likely to act in ways that generate sincere and helpful responses in the other side" (p. 159). Managers and leaders who seek to excel in diversity management should support network groups to guide this tendency in a positive direction.

Leaders and managers play an important role in helping individuals work well in teams and groups. Chrobot-Mason and Ruderman (chapter 5) discuss the skills leaders need to learn and impart to help foster team development in a diverse context. Many of these skills are fundamental to any group task: fostering good communication skills and managing conflict. Yet, as Chrobot-Mason and Ruderman point out, these skills are particularly critical in teams composed of diverse members. Minority group members tend to be marginalized and left out of important communication loops. Diverse groups tend to engage in destructive emotional conflict. Chrobot-Mason and Ruderman call on leaders to channel such conflict into more productive task conflict (see Pelled, Eisenhardt, and Xin, 1999) or informational conflict (Jehn, Northcraft, and Neale, 1999), where the conflict centers on ideas, strategies, and approaches to task engagement as opposed to values, personalities, and attitudes. Similarly, Bell et al. (chapter 9) encourage managers to have diverse employees work together on cooperative tasks in which members share common goals and where task interdependence is essential to group success.

Multicultural organizational development

Organizational change efforts are comprehensive, multi-level, planned, but typically flexible, addressing the policies, practices, norms, attitudes, values, and behaviors of entire organizations or sizable units within organizations. Interventions may focus on structural, cultural, or behavioral processes, or all three together (Holvino et al., chapter 12). Davidson (1999: 174) claims that "if diversity change initiatives address ways of building structural and psychological inclusiveness for organizational members, they are more likely to be successful." Diversity scholars and practitioners have developed models of what multicultural organizations may look like with regard to structural, cultural, and behavioral dimensions and have discussed various ways that organizations can or should change to reach these desired states.

Agars and Kottke (chapter 3) and Holvino et al. (chapter 12) identify several theorists' definitions of desired goals or end-states for multicultural organizational development. Cox's (1991) multicultural organization is one that contains diversity (pluralism), has eliminated barriers to structural and informal integration, has eliminated prejudice and discrimination, has low levels of intergroup and interpersonal conflict, and allows all employees, regardless of social identity, to feel valued and attached to the organization (see also R. R. Thomas, 1991, 1996; Golembiewski, 1995). Foster et al. (1988) go further, suggesting that in addition to the outcomes stated by Cox, multicultural organizations commit to a broader social responsibility to fight discrimination and advocate social diversity.

How organizations achieve the desired goals has been contemplated by many theorists and put in to practice by diversity practitioners. Agars and Kottke (chapter 3) suggest that organizations progress through three stages: (1) issue identification, in which awareness of existing perceptions and attitudes occurs and members become of the aware of the need to change; (2) implementation, in which formal and informal organizational policies and practices that support diversity are implemented; and (3) maintenance, in which the organizational culture is modified and aligned with multicultural perspectives. Holvino et al. (chapter 12) discuss a six-stage model of organizational change showing how organizations evolve from being monocultural to multicultural. They further identify several organizational change strategies that can be used to help organizations move through these stages. Organizational development (OD) involves planned, top-down, integrated, system-wide and long-term change efforts. Needs assessment and evaluation are critical components of OD efforts and change targets include behaviors, values, and structural policies and practices. Action research and its cousin, collaborative inquiry, are more dynamic organizational change approaches that involve joint learning by internal and external agents, experimentation and evaluation, and in-depth dialogue to uncover the deep beliefs and norms that may both hinder and facilitate the adoption of multicultural processes, as well as serve as valuable information to assess the success of change efforts.

Many of the tactical activities that have been used in multicultural change efforts include ideas and strategies already discussed, such as gaining top management support, developing mentoring opportunities, changing recruiting and selection practices, attending to career development, and providing ongoing training to address multicultural competence. Furthermore, equitable pay and promotion based only on reliable and valid performance appraisal, as well as flattening and decentralizing organizational structures to reduce feelings of separation among hierarchical levels, have been forwarded as critical objectives for organizational change. Gilbert and Ivancevich (1999) provide concrete examples of successful organizational change strategies geared toward improving multicultural effectiveness. Programs to unify employees include financially rewarding employees for experiences that provide contact with a variety of individuals; encouraging majority managers to belong to volunteer groups where they are minority members; giving credit to non-managers for volunteering in schools or serving as big brother or sister; and organizing employee forums. These efforts are designed to develop empathy and understanding between majority and minority members. Some organizations have also tied bonuses and salary increases to attainment of diversity objectives.

Parting Thoughts

Managing diversity will continue to be a major task for organizations that seek productivity and financial profits from a diverse workforce. One of the most important strategies at the organizational level is to eliminate discrimination and foster conditions that promote structural and informal inclusiveness at all levels. To help organizations achieve these goals, we have highlighted some strategies and exemplary practices that have proven to be effective at different levels. These include strong leadership and good management skills, training, mentoring programs, network groups, career planning, and tying multicultural competence and achievement of multicultural objectives to managers' performance-contingent rewards.

We believe that efforts to manage diversity in intelligent and thoughtful ways will bring benefits to individuals, groups, organizations, and society as a whole. Will frustrations occur? Of course. Will mistakes be made? Plenty. Will there be times when all the new endeavors seem like silly fads? Probably. But in the end, those organizations that have made efforts to practice good strategies will reap a rich harvest, and thoughtful individuals in those organizations will know the rewards of true multiculturalism.

REFERENCES

Abella, R. S. (1984). *Equality in employment: A Royal Commission report*. Minister of Supply and Services Canada. Catalogue No. MP42–157/1–1984E. Ottawa: Canadian Government Publishing Centre.

Acker, J. (1990). Hierarchies, jobs, bodies: A theory of gendered organizations. *Gender & Society, 4* (2), 139–58.

Adams, J. S. (1965). Inequity in social exchange. In L. Berkowitz (ed.), *Advances in experimental social psychology*, vol. 2 (pp. 267–96). New York: Academic Press.

Adamson, J. B. (1998). The Denny's discrimination story – and ways to avoid it in your operation. *Restaurant News*, 40, October 5.

Adamson, J. B., with McNatt, R. and McNatt, R. F. (2000). *The Denny's story: How a company in crisis resurrected its good name and reputation*. New York: John Wiley.

Adelman, P. K. (1995). Emotional labor as a potential source of job stress. In S. L. Sauter and L. R. Murphy (eds.), *Organizational risk factors for job stress* (pp. 371–82). Washington, DC: American Psychological Association.

Adler, N. J. (2002). *International dimensions of organizational behavior*, 4th edn. Cincinnati, OH: South-Western Press.

Adler, N. J., Brody, L. W., and Osland, J. C. (2001). Advances in global leadership: The women's global leadership forum. *Advances in Global Leadership, 2*, 351–83.

Adler, N. J. and Izraeli, D. N. (eds.) (1994). *Competitive frontiers: Women managers in a global Economy*. Cambridge, MA: Blackwell.

Adler, N. J. and Matthews, K. (1994). Health psychology: Why do some people get sick and some stay well? *Annual Review of Psychology, 45*, 229–59.

Adler, P. S. and Kwon, S. (2002). Social capital: Prospects for a new concept. *Academy of Management Review, 27*, 17–40.

"After years of planning, euro arrives" (2002). *Pensacola News Journal*, January 1, 10C.

Agars, M. D. and Kottke, J. L. (2002). An integrative model of diversity. Paper presented as part of M. D. Agars and J. Kottke (Chairs), *Integrating theory and practice in gender diversity initiatives*. Symposium presented at the 17th Annual Conference of the Society for Industrial and Organizational Psychology, April. Toronto, Canada.

Agnew, C. R., Thompson, V. D., Smith, V. A., Gramzow, R. H., and Currey, D. P. (1993). Proximal and distal predictors of homophobia: Framing the multivariate roots of outgroup rejection. *Journal of Applied Social Psychology, 23*, 2013–42.

Alderfer, C. P. (1992). Changing race relations embedded in organizations: Report on a long-term project with the XYZ Corporation. In S. E. Jackson and Associates (eds.), *Diversity in the workplace* (pp. 138–66). New York: Guilford Press.

Aldinger, C. (2000). Pentagon moves to curb harassment of gays. July 21. Retrieved September 9, 2001, from http://www.gaymilitary.ucsb.edu/ResearchResources/NewsMagArticlesHome.htm

Allan, J. (2001). *Review of the measurement of ethnicity: International concepts and classifications.* Statistics New Zealand. Retrieved July 10, 2002, from http://stats.govt.nz

Allen, R. S. and Montgomery, K. A. (2001). Applying an organizational development approach to creating diversity. *Organizational Dynamics, 30,* 149–61.

Allon, N. (1982). The stigma of overweight in everyday life. In B. Wolman (ed.), *Psychological aspects of obesity: A handbook* (pp. 130–74). New York: Van Nostrand Reinhold.

Allport, G. W. (1954). *The nature of prejudice.* Reading, MA: Addison-Wesley.

Altemeyer, B. (1996). *The authoritarian specter.* Cambridge, MA: Harvard University Press.

American Lung Association (2002). Facts about tobacco. Retrieved July 29, 2002 from http://www.lungusa.org

Angier, N. (1994). Researchers link obesity in humans to flaw in genes. *New York Times,* December 1, pp. A1, A8.

Anti-Weight Discrimination Laws (2000). Council on Size and Weight Discrimination, Inc. Accessed 28 January, 2003. http://www.cswd.org/disclaws.html

Arredondo, P. (1996). *Successful diversity management initiatives: A blueprint for planning and implementation.* Thousand Oaks, CA: Sage.

Arvey, R. D. and Cavanaugh, M. A. (1995). Using surveys to assess the prevalence of sexual harassment: Some methodological problems. *Journal of Social Issues, 51* (1), 39–52.

Ashford, S. J., Rothbard, N. P., Piderit, S. K., and Dutton, J. E. (1998). Out on a limb: The role of context and impression management in selling gender-equity issues. *Administrative Science Quarterly, 43* (1), 23–57.

Austin, J. R. (1997). A cognitive framework for understanding demographic influences in groups. *International Journal for Organizational Analysis, 5,* 342–59.

Australia: Equality of opportunity and treatment, 1984–2000. Retrieved October 29, 2001, from http://natlex.ilo.org/Scripts/natlexcgi.exe?lang=E&doc=query&ctry=AUS&llx=02.03

Ayman, R. (1993). Leadership perception: The role of gender and culture. In M. M. Chemers and R. Ayman (eds.), *Leadership theory and research: Perspectives and directions* (pp. 137–67). New York: Academic Press.

Badgett, M. V. L. (1996). Employment and sexual orientation: Disclosure and discrimination in the workplace. In A. L. Ellis and E. D. B. Riggle (eds.), *Sexual identity on the job: Issues and services* (pp. 29–52). New York: Haworth Press.

Badgett, M. V. L. (1998). Income inflation: The myth of affluence among gay, lesbian, and bisexual Americans. Retrieved November 29, 2001, from the National Gay and Lesbian Task Force website: http://www.ngltf.org/downloads/income.pdf

Baltes, B. B., Briggs, T. E., Huff, J. W., Wright, J. A., and Neuman, G. A. (1999). Flexible and compressed workweek schedules: A meta-analysis of their effects on work-related criteria. *Journal of Applied Psychology, 84* (4), 496–513.

Barker, V. E., Abrams, J. R., Tyiaamornwong, V., Seibold, D. R., Duggan, A., Park, H. S., and Sebastian, M. (2000). New contexts for relational communication in groups. *Small Group Research, 31* (4), 470–503.

Barnett, R. C. and Baruch, G. K. (1985). Women's involvement in multiple roles and psychological distress. *Journal of Personality and Social Psychology, 49,* 135–45.

Barnett, R. C. and Hyde, J. S. (2001). Women, men, work, and family. *American Psychologist*, *56* (10), 781–96.

Barnett, R. C. and Marshall, N. L. (1991). The relationship between women's work and family roles and their subjective well-being and psychological distress. In M. Frankenhaeuser, U. Lundberg, and M. Chesney (eds.), *Women, work, and health: Stress and opportunities* (pp. 111–36). New York: Plenum.

Barnett, R. C., Marshall, N. L., and Pleck, J. H. (1992). Men's multiple roles and their relationship to men's psychological distress. *Journal of Marriage and the Family*, *54*, 358–67.

Barnett, R. C., Marshall, N. L., and Sayer, A. (1992). Positive-spillover effects from job to home: A closer look. *Women and Health*, *19* (2), 13–41.

Barnum, P., Liden, R. C., and DiTomaso, N. (1995). Double jeopardy for women and minorities: Pay differences with age. *Academy of Management Journal*, *38*, 863–80.

Barrier, M. (2001). Mixed signals. *HR Magazine*, *46* (12), 64–8.

Baruch, G. K., Biener, L., and Barnett, R. C. (1987). Women and gender in research on work and family stress. *American Psychologist*, *42* (2), 130–6.

Battaglia, A. (1999). Cracker Barrel workers allege discrimination, file lawsuit. *Nation's Restaurant News*, *33*, 1, 138.

Baugh, S. G., Lankau, M. J., and Scandura, T. A. (1996). An investigation of the effects of protégé gender on responses to mentoring. *Journal of Vocational Behavior*, *49*, 309–23.

Baum, A. (1994). Behavioral, biological, and environmental interactions in disease process. In S. Blumenthal, K. Matthews, and S. Weiss (eds.), *New research frontiers in behavioral medicine: Proceedings of the national conference* (pp. 61–70). Washington, DC: NIH Publications.

Baum, A. and Posluszny, D. M. (1999). Health psychology: Mapping biobehavioral contributions to health and illness. *Annual Review of Psychology*, *50*, 137–63.

Becker, G. (1964). *Human capital*. New York: National Bureau of Economic Research.

Begany, J. J. and Milburn, M. A. (2002). Psychological predictors of sexual harassment: Authoritarianism, hostile sexism, and rape myths. *Psychology of Men and Masculinity*, *3*, 119–26.

Bell, C. A. (1991). Female homicides in United States workplaces, 1980–1985. *American Journal of Public Health*, *81* (6), 729–32.

Bell, E. L. (1990). The bicultural life experiences of career-oriented Black women. *Journal of Organizational Behavior*, *11*, 459–77.

Bell, E. L. J. E. and Nkomo, S. M. (2001). *Our separate ways: Black and White women and the struggle for professional identity*. Boston, MA: Harvard Business School Press.

Bellinger, L. and Hillman, A. J. (2000). Does tolerance lead to better partnering? The relationship between diversity management and M and A success. *Business and Society*, *39*, 323–37.

Bellizzi, J. A. and Hasty, R. W. (1998). Territory assignment decisions and supervising unethical selling behavior: The effects of obesity and gender as moderated by job-related factors. *Journal of Personal Selling and Sales Management*, *18*, 35–49.

Bennett, C. E. (1993). *We the Americans: Blacks* (WE–1). Washington, DC: US Department of Commerce.

Bergmann, Barbara R. (1986). *The economic emergence of women*. New York: Basic Books.

Berry, J. W. (1984). Cultural relations in plural society: Alternatives to segregation and their sociopsychological implications. In N. Miller and M. Brewer (eds.), *Groups in contact*. New York: Academic Press.

Berry, J. W. (1990). Psychology of acculturation. In J. Berman (ed.), *Cross-cultural perspectives: Nebraska symposium on motivation* (pp. 201–34). Lincoln: University of Nebraska Press.

Berry, J. W. and Laponce, A. (1994). Evaluating research on Canada's multiethnic and multicultural society: An introduction. In J. W. Berry and A. LaPonce (eds.), *Ethnicity and culture in Canada: The research landscape* (pp. 3–16). Toronto: University of Toronto Press.

Betancourt, H. and Lopez, S. R. (1993). The study of culture, ethnicity, and race in American psychology. *American Psychologist, 48*, 629–37.

Bhawuk, D. P. S. and Brislin, R. W. (2000). Cross-cultural training: A review. *Applied Psychology: An International Review, 49*, 162–91.

Bierman, L. (2001). OFCCP affirmative action awards and stock market reaction. *Labor Law Journal, 52*, 147–56.

Biles, G. E. and Pryatel, H. A. (1978). Myths, management and women. *Personnel Journal, 57*, 572–7.

Black, J. S. and Mendenhall, M. (1990). Cross-cultural training effectiveness: A review and a theoretical framework for future research. *Academy of Management Review, 15*, 113–36.

Blanchard, F. A. and Crosby, F. J. (eds.) (1989). *Affirmative action in perspective.* New York: Springer-Verlag.

Blau, F. D. and Ferber, M. A. (1992). *The economics of women, men and work.* Englewood Cliffs, NJ: Prentice-Hall.

Board of Trustees (University of Alabama) v. Garrett, 531 US 356 (2001).

Bobko, P., Roth, P. L., and Potosky, D. (1999). Derivation and implications of a meta-analytic matrix incorporating cognitive ability, alternative predictors, and job performance. *Personnel Psychology, 52*, 561–89.

Boise, L. and Neal, M. B. (1996). Family responsibilities and absenteeism: Employees caring for parents versus employees caring for children. *Journal of Mangerial Issues, 8* (2), 218–38.

Boitano, M. (2000). Buying the firm. *Fortune, 142* (5), 345–6.

Bolles, R. N. (1992). *What color is your parachute?* Berkeley, CA: Ten Speed Press.

Bond, M. H. (1988). Finding universal dimensions of individual variation in multicultural studies of values: The Rokeach and Chinese value surveys. *Journal of Personality and Social Psychology, 55*, 1009–15.

Borchert, J. and Rickabaugh, C. A. (1995). When illness is perceived as controllable: The effects of gender and mode of transmission on AIDS-related stigma. *Sex Roles, 33*, 657–68.

Bordieri, J. E. and Drehmer, D. E. (1988). Causal attribution and hiring recommendations for disabled job applications. *Rehabilitation Psychology, 33*, 239–47.

Bordieri, J. E., Drehmer, D. E., and Taricone, P. F. (1990). Personnel selection bias for job applicants with cancer. *Journal of Applied Social Psychology, 20*, 244–53.

Bosanko, D. (1995). Stress and the gay life. *American Demographics, 17*, 23–36.

Boudreau, J. W. (1991). Utility analysis for decisions in human resource management. In M. D. Dunnette and L. M. Hough (eds.), *Handbook of industrial and organizational psychology*, 2nd edn., vol. 2 (pp. 621–745). Palo Alto, CA: Consulting Psychologist Press.

Bowen, A. M. and Bourgeois, M. J. (2001). Attitudes toward lesbian, gay, and bisexual college students: The contribution of pluralistic ignorance, dynamic social impact and contact theories. *Journal of American College Health, 50* (2), 91–6.

Bowes-Sperry, L. and Tata, J. (1999). A multiperspective framework of sexual harassment: Reviewing two decades of research. In G. N. Powell (ed.), *Handbook of gender and work.* Thousand Oaks, CA: Sage.

Bowl, K. (2001). Diversity means good business, survey says. *HRNews*, 46, 12.

Bowler, M. (1999). Women's earnings: An overview. *Monthly Labor Review*, December, 13–21.

Bowmaker-Falconer, A., Horwitz, F. M., Jain, H., and Tagger, S. (1997). Employment Equality programmes in South Africa: Current trends. *Industrial Relations Journal*, 29 (3), 222–33.

Brass, D. J. (1985). Men's and women's networks: A study of interaction patterns and influence in an organization. *Academy of Management Journal*, 28, 327–43.

Brenner, O. C., Tomkiewicz, J., and Schein, V. E. (1989). The relationship between sex role stereotypes and requisite management characteristics revisited. *Academy of Management Journal*, 32, 662–9.

Brett, J. M. and Stroh, L. K. (1998). Jumping ship: Who benefits from an external labor market career strategy. *Journal of Applied Psychology*, 82, 331–41.

Brett, J. M. and Stroh, L. K. (under review). Why do managers work over 61 hours?

Brewer, M. B. and Brown, R. J. (1998). Intergroup relations. In D. T. Gilbert, S. T. Fiske, and G. Lindzey (eds.), *The handbook of social psychology*, vol. 2, 4th edn. (pp. 554–95). New York: McGraw-Hill.

Brief, A. P., Buttram, R. T., Reizenstein, R. M., Pugh, S. D., Callahan, J. D., McCline, R. L., and Vaslow, J. B. (1997). Beyond good intentions: The next steps toward racial equality in the American workplace. *Academy of Management Executive*, 11 (4), 59–72.

Brief, A. P., Dietz, J., Cohen, R. R., Pugh, S. D., and Vaslow, J. B. (2000). Just doing business: Modern racism and obedience to authority as explanations for employment discrimination. *Organizational Behavior and Human Decision Processes*, 81, 72–97.

Brody, E. M., Kleban, M. H., Johnsen, P. T., Hoffman, C., and Schoonover, C. B. (1987). Work status and parental care: A comparison of four groups of women. *Gerontological Society of America*, 27, 201–8.

Brooks, M. G. and Buckner, J. C. (1996). Work and welfare: Job histories, barriers to employment, and predictors of work among low-income single mothers. *American Journal of Orthopsychiatry*, 66, 526–37.

Brush, C. G., Wong-MingJi, D. J., and Sullivan, S. E. (1999). Women entrepreneurs: Moving beyond the glass ceiling. *Academy of Management Review*, 24 (3), 585–6.

Bryne, D. (1971). *The attraction paradigm*. New York: Academic Press.

Bullock, H. E. (1995). Class acts: Middle-class responses to the poor. In B. Lott and D. Maluso (eds.), *The social psychology of interpersonal discrimination* (pp. 118–59). New York: Guilford Press.

Bullock, H. E. (1999). Attributions for poverty: A comparison of middle-class and welfare recipient attitudes. *Journal of Applied Social Psychology*, 29, 2059–82.

Bullock, H. E. and Lott, B. (2001). Building a research and advocacy agenda around issues of economic justice. *Analyses of Social Issues and Public Policy*, 1, 147–62.

Bunker, B. B. (1990). Appreciating diversity and modifying organizational cultures: Men and women at work. In S. Srivasta, D. Cooperrider, and Associates (eds.), *Appreciative management and leadership: The power of positive thought and action in organizations* (pp. 126–49). San Francisco, CA: Jossey-Bass.

Bunker, B. B. and Alban, B. T. (1997). *Large group interventions*. San Francisco, CA: Jossey-Bass.

Burke, R. J. and McKeen, C. A. (1997). Benefits of mentoring relationships among managerial and professional women: A cautionary tale. *Journal of Vocational Behavior*, 51, 43–57.

Burlington v. Ellerth, 118 S.Ct. 2257 (1998).

Burt, R. S. (1992). *Structural holes: The social structure of competition.* Cambridge, MA: Harvard University Press.

Bushe, G. (in press). *The new basics: Interpersonal competence and organizational learning.* Unpublished manuscript. Chapters can be accessed via http://www.bus.sfu.ca/homes/gervase/gervase.html

Button, J. W., Rienzo, B. A., and Wald, K. D. (1997). *Private lives, public conflicts: Battles over gay rights in American communities.* Washington, DC: CQ Press.

Button, S. B. (2001). Organizational efforts to affirm sexual diversity: A cross-level examination. *Journal of Applied Psychology, 86,* 17–28.

Byers, J. B. (1995). Comment: Cook v. Rhode Island: It is not over until the morbidly obese woman works. *Iowa Journal of Corporation Law, 20,* 389–412.

Byrne, D. E. (1971). *The attraction paradigm.* New York: Academic Press.

Callanan, J. A. (1984). *Communicating: How to organize meetings and presentations.* New York: Franklin Watts.

Campbell, J. P., Dunnette, M. D., Lawler, E. E., and Weick, K. E. (1970). *Managerial behavior, performance, and effectiveness.* New York: McGraw-Hill.

Caplan, R. D. and Jones, K. W. (1975). Effects of work load, role ambiguity, and Type A personality on anxiety, depression, and heart rate. *Journal of Applied Psychology, 60* (6), 713–19.

Cardinali, R. and Gordon, Z. (2002). Ageism: No longer the equal opportunity stepchild. *Equal Opportunities International, 21* (2), 58–68.

Carr-Ruffino, N. (2002). *Managing diversity: People skills for a multicultural workplace,* 4th edn. Boston, MA: Pearson Custom Publishing.

Cascio, W. F. (1995). Whither industrial and organizational psychology in a changing world of work? *American Psychologist, 50* (11), 928–39.

Catalyst (1996). *Women in corporate leadership: Progress and prospects.* New York: Catalyst Institute.

Catalyst (1998). *Advancing women in business – the Catalyst guide: Best practices from the corporate leaders.* San Francisco, CA: Jossey-Bass.

Catalyst (1999a). *Women entrepreneurs: Why companies lose female talent and what they can do about it.* New York: Catalyst Institute.

Catalyst (1999b). *Women of color in corporate management: Opportunities and barriers.* New York: Catalyst Institute.

Catalyst (2000). *Census of women corporate officers and top earners of the Fortune 500.* New York: Catalyst Institute.

Catalyst gives Bayer, Fannie Mae, and Marriott prestigious Catalyst Award for redefining diversity in the 21st century workplace. Retrieved March 15, 2002, from www.catalystwomen.org

CBSNews.com (2000). Army gets no blame for gay murder. July 17. Retrieved September 9, 2001, from http://cbsnews.cbs.com/now/story/0,1597,216083-412,00.html

Census India (2001). Provisional population totals: http://www.censusindia.net/results/resultsmain.html

"Census:12 million immigrants arrived in '90s" (2001). *Pensacola News-Journal.* March 23, 3A.

Centers for Disease Control (CDC) (2001). Basics about overweight and obesity. United States Department of Health and Human Services: Centers for Disease Control and Prevention.

Cervinka, R. (1993). Night shift dose and stress at work. *Ergonomics, 36,* 155–60.

Chapman, N. J., Ingersoll-Dayton, B., and Neal, M. B. (1994). Balancing the multiple roles of work and caregiving for children, adults, and elders. In G. P. Keita and J. J. Hurrell (eds.), *Job stress in a changing workforce*. Washington, DC: APA.

Chavez, L. (2000). Key dates in the battle over Affirmative Action policy. In F. J. Crosby and C. VanDeVeer (eds.), *Sex, race, and merit: Debating Affirmative Action in education and employment* (pp. 21–5). Ann Arbor: University of Michigan Press.

Chemers, M. M. and Murphy, S. E. (1995). Leadership and diversity in groups and organizations. In M. M. Chemers, S. Oskamp, and M. A. Costanzo (eds.), *Diversity in organizations: New perspectives for a changing workplace* (pp. 157–88). Thousand Oaks, CA: Sage.

Chen, C. C. and Eastman, W. (1997). Toward a civic culture for multicultural organizations. *Journal of Applied Behavioral Science*, 33, 454–70.

Chen, C. C. and Van Velsor, E. (1996). New directions for research and practice in diversity leadership. *Leadership Quarterly*, 7 (2), 285–302.

Chesler, M. (1994). Organization development is not the same as multicultural organizational development. In E. Y. Cross, J. H. Katz, F. A. Miller, and E. W. Seashore (eds.), *The promise of diversity: Over 40 voices discuss strategies for eliminating discrimination in organizations* (pp. 240–51). Burr Ridge, IL: Irwin.

Chesler, M. and Delgado, H. (1987). Race relations training and organizational change. In J. W. Shaw, P. G. Nordlie, and R. M. Shapiro (eds.), *Strategies for improving race relations: The Anglo American experience* (pp. 182–204). Manchester, UK: Manchester University Press.

Children's Defense Fund (2000). The high cost of child care puts quality care out of reach for many families. Washington, DC: Author.

Chow, L. (1998). G'ay day, mate. *Far Eastern Economic Review*, 161 (2), 80.

Chrobot-Mason, D. and Quiñones, M. A. (2001). Training for a diverse workplace. In K. Kraiger (ed.), *Creating, implementing, and managing effective training and development* (pp. 117–59). San Francisco, CA: Jossey-Bass.

Chrobot-Mason, D. L. and Thomas, K. M. (2002). Minority employees in majority organizations: The intersection of individual and organizational racial identity in the workplace. *Human resource management review*, 1, 323–44.

Chung, B. G. and Lankau, M. J. (2001). *Do minority managers fit Caucasians' successful manager prototype?* Paper presented at the annual meeting of the Society for Industrial Organizational Psychology, San Diego, CA.

Chung, W. (1997). Auditing the organizational culture for diversity: A conceptual framework. In C. D. Brown, C. C. Snedeker, and B. Sykes (eds.), *Conflict and diversity* (pp. 63–83). Cresshill: Hampton Press.

Clark, M. M. (2001). ADA outlaws disability-based harassment, two courts say. *HRNews*, June, pp. 1, 7.

Cleveland, J. N., Festa, R. M., and Montgomery, L. (1988). Applicant pool composition and job perceptions: Impact on decisions regarding an older applicant. *Journal of Vocational Behavior*, 32, 112–25.

Cleveland, J. N. and Shore, L. M. (1992). Self- and supervisory perspectives on age and work attitudes and performance. *Journal of Applied Psychology*, 77, 469–84.

Cleveland, J. N., Stockdale, M., and Murphy, K. R. (2000). *Women and men in organizations: Sex and gender issues at work*. Mahweh, NJ: Lawrence Erlbaum Associates.

Cobb-Clark, D. A. and Dunlop, Y. (1999). The role of gender in job promotions. *Monthly Labor Review*, December, 32–8.

Cohen, P. N. and Bianchi, S. M. (1999). Marriage, children, and women's employment: What do we know? *Monthly Labor Review*, December, 22–31.

Cole, J. R. and Singer, B. (1991). A theoretical explanation. In H. Zuckerman, J. Cole, and J. Bruer (eds.), *The outer circle: Women in the scientific community* (pp. 277–310). New York: W. W. Norton.

Coltrane, S. and Adams, M. (1997). Work–family imagery and gender stereotypes: Television and the reproduction of difference. *Journal of Vocational Behavior, 50* (2), 323–47.

Comer, D. and Soliman, C. (1996). Organizational efforts to manage diversity: Do they really work? *Journal of Management Issues, 8,* 470–83.

Cook v. State of Rhode Island Department of Mental Health, Retardation, and Hospitals, 2 A.D. Cases 1476 (1st Cir. 1993).

Cooper, K. J. (1997). Classes clash over quotas in India. *Washington Post,* July 18. Employment Equity Act, 1995. http://www.justice.gc.ca/en/E–5.401/43300.html

Cooperrider, D. L. (1990). Positive image, positive action: The affirmative basis of organizing. In S. Srivasta, D. L. Cooperrider, and Associates (eds.), *Appreciative management and leadership: The power of positive thought and action in organizations* (pp. 91–125). San Francisco, CA: Jossey-Bass.

Cooperrider, D. L. and Srivasta, S. (1987). Appreciative inquiry in organizational life. In W. A. Pasmore and R. W. Woodman (eds.), *Research in organizational change and development,* vol. 1 (pp. 129–69). Greenwich, CT: JAI Press.

Corcoran, M., Danziger, S. K., Kalil, A., and Seefeldt, K. S. (2000). How welfare reform is affecting women's work. *Annual Review of Sociology, 26,* 241–69.

Cox, T. H., Jr. (1991). The multicultural organization. *Academy of Management Executive, 5,* 34–47.

Cox, T. H., Jr. (1994). *Cultural diversity in organizations: Theory, research, and practice.* San Francisco, CA: Berrett-Koehler.

Cox, T. H., Jr. (1997). Linkages between managing diversity and organizational performance. In T. Cox, Jr., and R. L. Beale (eds.), *Developing competency to manage diversity* (pp. 35–42). San Francisco, CA: Berrett-Koehler.

Cox, T. H., Jr. (2001). *Creating the multicultural organization: A strategy for capturing the power of diversity.* San Francisco, CA: Jossey-Bass.

Cox, T. H., Jr., and Beale, R. L. (1997). *Developing competency to manage diversity.* San Francisco, CA: Berrett-Koehler.

Cox, T. H., and Blake, S. (1991). Managing cultural diversity: Implications for organizational competitiveness. *Academy of Management Executive, 5(3),* 45–57.

Cox, T. H., Jr., and Finley-Nickelson, J. (1991). Models of acculturation for intra-organizational cultural diversity. *RCSA/CJAS, 8,* 90–100.

Cox, T. H., Jr., and Nkomo, S. M. (1990). Invisible men and women: A status report as a variable in organizational behavior and research. *Journal of Organizational Behavior, 11,* 419–31.

Cox, T. H., Jr., and Nkomo, S. M. (1991). A race and gender-group analysis of the early career experience of MBAs. *Work and Occupations, 18* (4), 431–46.

Cox, T. H., Jr., and Nkomo, S. M. (1992). Candidate age as a factor in promotability ratings. *Public Personnel Management, 21,* 197–210.

Cox, T. H., Jr., Welch, J., and Nkomo, S. M. (2001). Research on race and ethnicity: An update and analysis. In R. T. Golembiewski (ed.), *Handbook of organizational behavior* (pp. 255–86). New York: Marcel Dekker.

Cozzarelli, C., Wilkinson, A. V., and Tagler, M. J. (2001). Attitudes toward the poor and attributions for poverty. *Journal of Social Issues, 57,* 207–27.

"Cracker Barrel customers sue the restaurant chain for racial discrimination" (2001). Retrieved September 27, 2002, from http://www.bet.com/articles/1,,c1gb1144–1797,00.html

Crandall, C. S. (1991). Do heavyweight students have more difficulty paying for college? *Personality and Social Psychology Bulletin, 17,* 606–11.

Crosby, F. J. (1991). *Juggling: The unexpected advantages of balancing career and home for women and their families.* New York: Free Press.

Crosby, F. J. (in press). *Affirmative action is dead; long live affirmative action.* New Haven, CT: Yale University Press.

Crosby, F. J., Bromley, S., and Saxe, L. (1980). Recent unobtrusive studies of black and white discrimination and prejudice: A literature review. *Psychological Bulletin, 87,* 546–63.

Crosby, F. J. and Clayton, S. (2001). Affirmative action: Psychological contributions to policy. *Analysis of Social Issues and Public Policy, 1,* 71–87.

Crosby, F. J., Ferdman, B. M., and Wingate, B. R. (2001). Addressing and redressing discrimination: Affirmative action in social psychological perspective. In R. Brown and S. Gaertner (eds.), *Blackwell handbook of social psychology: Intergroup processes* (pp. 495–513). Boston, MA: Blackwell.

Crosby, F. J. and VanDeVeer, C. (eds.) (2000). *Sex, race, and merit: Debating Affirmative Action in education and employment.* Ann Arbor: University of Michigan Press.

Cross, E. Y. (2000). *Managing diversity: The courage to lead.* Westport, CT: Quorum Books.

Cross, W. E., Jr. (1971). The Negro-to-Black conversion experience. *Black World, 20,* 13–27.

Cross, W. E., Jr. (1991). *Shades of Black: Diversity in African-American identity.* Philadelphia, PA: Temple University Press.

Cross, W. E., Jr. (1995). The psychology of nigrescence: Revising the Cross model. In J. G. Ponterotto, J. M. Casas, L. A. Suzuki, and C. M. Alexander (eds.), *Handbook of multicultural counseling* (pp. 93–122). Thousand Oaks, CA: Sage.

Croteau, J. M. (1996). Research on the work experiences of lesbian, gay, and bisexual people: An integrative review of methodology and findings. *Journal of Vocational Behavior, 48,* 195–209.

Croteau, J. M. and Von Destinon, M. (1994). A national survey of job search experiences of lesbian, gay, and bisexual student affairs professionals. *Journal of College Student Development, 35,* 40–5.

Crouter, A. C., Bumpus, M. F., Maguire, M. C., and McHale, S. M. (1999). Linking parents' work pressure and adolescents' well-being: Insights into dynamics in dual-earner families. *Developmental Psychology, 35,* 1453–61.

Crow, S. M. (1993). Excessive absenteeism and the Disabilities Act. *Arbitration Journal, 48,* 65–70.

Crow, S. M., Fok, L. Y., and Hartman, S. J. (1995). Priorities of hiring discrimination: Who is at greatest risk – women, blacks, or homosexuals? *Academy of Management Journal Special Issue, Best Papers Proceedings,* 443–5.

Cuenot, R. G. and Fugita, S. S. (1982). Perceived homosexuality: Measuring heterosexual attitudinal and nonverbal reactions. *Personality and Social Psychology Bulletin, 8,* 100–6.

Cullen, D. (2000). A heartbreaking decision. Salon.com. Retrieved September 9, 2001, from http://www.salon.com/news/feature/2000/06/07/relationships/index.html

Cumming, J. and Holvino, E. (1997). *BEC: An example of collaborative inquiry with a social change organization.* Unpublished handout. Brattleboro, VT: Chaos Management.

"Current labor statistics" (1999). *Monthly Labor Review, 122,* 99–100. *Customer/provider interactions.* San Francisco, CA: Jossey-Bass.

D'Souza, D. (1995). *The end of racism*. New York: Simon and Schuster.

Dalton, D. R. and Daily, C. M. (1998). Not there yet. *Across the Board, 35* (10), 16–20.

Daniels, C. (2001). Too diverse for our own good? *Fortune, 144,* 116.

Danto, E. (2000). Conflict vs. cohesion: EAP-based diversity training in small groups. *Employee Assistance Quarterly, 15,* 1–14.

Danziger, S. K., Corcoran, M., Danziger, S., Heflin, C., Kalil, A., Levine, J., et al. (2000). Barriers to the employment of welfare recipients. In R. Cherry and W. M. Rodgers, III (eds.), *Prosperity for all? The economic boom and African Americans.* (pp. 245–78). New York: Russell Sage.

Danziger, S. K., Kalil, A., and Anderson, N. J. (2000). Human capital, physical health, and mental health of welfare recipients: Co-occurrence and correlates. *Journal of Social Issues, 56,* 635–54.

Dass, P. and Parker, B. (1999). Strategies for managing human resource diversity: From resistance to learning. *Academy of Management Executive, 13* (2), 68–80.

Davidson, M. J. (1997). *The Black and ethnic minority woman manager: Cracking the concrete ceiling.* London: Paul Chapman.

Davidson, M. N. (1999). The value of being included: An examination of diversity change initiatives in organizations. *Performance Improvement Quarterly, 12* (1), 164–80.

Davidson, M. N. and Ferdman, B. M. (2001). A matter of difference – diversity and inclusion: What difference does it make? *The Industrial-Organizational Psychologist, 39* (2), 36–8.

Davidson, M. N. and Ferdman, B. M. (2002). A matter of difference – inclusion and power: Reflections on dominance and subordination in organizations. *The Industrial-Organizational Psychologist, 40* (1), 62–7.

Davison, H. K. and Burke, M. J. (2000). Sex discrimination in simulated employment contexts: A meta-analytic investigation. *Journal of Vocational Behavior, 56,* 225–48.

Day, N. E. and Schoenrade, P. (1997). Staying in the closet versus coming out: Relationships between communication about sexual orientation and work attitudes. *Personnel Psychology, 50,* 147–63.

Day, N. E. and Schoenrade, P. (2000). The relationship among reported disclosure of sexual orientation, anti-discrimination policies, top management support and work attitudes of gay and lesbian employees. *Personnel Review, 29,* 346–63.

Deaux, K. and Kite, M. E. (1985). Gender stereotypes: Some thoughts on the cognitive organization of gender-related information. *Academic Psychology Bulletin, 7,* 123–44.

DeJong, W. (1980). The stigma of obesity: The consequences of naive assumptions concerning the causes of physical deviance. *Journal of Health and Social Behavior, 21,* 75–87.

del Pinal, J. (1993). *We the Americans: Hispanics* (WE–2R). Washington, DC: US Department of Commerce.

Delgado, G. and Gordon, R. (2002). From social contract to social control: Welfare policy and race. In *From poverty to punishment: How welfare reform punishes the poor* (pp. 25–52). Oakland, CA: Applied Research Center.

Deloria, V. (1994). *God is red: A native view of religion.* Golden, CO: Fulcrum Publishing.

Denison, D. R., Hart, S. L., and Kahn, J. A. (1996). From chimneys to cross-functional teams: Developing and validating a diagnostic model. *Academy of Management Journal, 39,* 1005–23.

Department of Defense (DoD) (1993). December 21. Directive No. 1332.14. Retrieved November 18, 2001, from http://www.dtic.mil/whs/directives/corres/pdf/d133214wch1_122193/d133214p.pdf

Department of Defense (DoD) (2000). March 16. Audit report on the military environment with respect to the homosexual conduct policy (DoD Audit Report No. D–2000–101). Retrieved September 9, 2001, from http://www.dodig.osd.mil/audit/reports/00report.htm

Department of Defense (DoD) (2000). March 24. Secretary Cohen calls for action plan to reduce harassment. Retrieved September 9, 2001, from http://www.defenselink.mil/news/Mar2000/b03242000_bt146–00.html

Department of Defense (DoD) (2000). July 21. Department of Defense issues anti-harassment guidelines. Retrieved September 9, 2001, from http://www.defenselink.mil/news/Jul2000/b07212000_bt432–00.html

Deutsch, F. M., Zalenski, C. M., and Clark, M. E. (1986). Is there a double standard of aging? *Journal of Applied Social Psychology, 16,* 771–85.

Devine, P. G. and Monteith, M. J. (1993). The role of discrepancy-associated affect in prejudice reduction. In D. M. Mackie and D. L. Hamilton (eds.), *Affect, cognition and stereotyping: Interactive processes in group perception* (pp. 317–44). San Diego, CA: Academic Press.

Devine, P. G. and Vasquez, K. A. (1998). The rocky road to positive intergroup relations. In J. L. Eberhardt and S. T. Fiske (eds.), *Confronting racism: The problem and the response* (pp. 234–62). Thousand Oaks, CA: Sage.

DHHS (2000). *Healthy People 2010.* Washington, DC: US Department of Health and Human Services.

Dickens, F., Jr., and Dickens, J. B. (1991). *The Black manager: Making it in the corporate world,* revd. edn. New York: AMACOM.

Digh, P. (1998). The next challenge: Holding people accountable. *HR Magazine, 43* (11), 63–9.

Dipboye, R. L. (1987). Problems and progress of women in management. In K. S. Koziara, N. H. Moskow, and L. D. Turner (eds.), *Working women: Past, present, future* (pp. 118–53). Washington, DC: Bureau of National Affairs.

DiTomaso, N. and Friedman, J. J. (1995). A sociological commentary on Workforce 2000. In D. B. Bills (ed.), *The new modern times: Factors reshaping the world of work* (pp. 207–33). Albany: State University of New York Press.

DiTomaso, N. and Hooijberg, R. (1996). Diversity and the demands of leadership. *Leadership Quarterly, 7* (2), 163–87.

"Diversity in US on upswing as America grows." (2001). *Pensacola News-Journal,* March 13, 8A.

Dobbs, M. (1998). Managing diversity: The Department of Energy initiative. *Public Personnel Management, 27,* 161–73.

Dovidio, J. F. and Gaertner, S. L. (1991). Changes in the nature and assessment of racial prejudice. In H. Knopke, J. Norrell, and R. Rodgers (eds.), *Opening doors: An appraisal of race relations in contemporary America* (pp. 201–41). Tuscaloosa: University of Alabama Press.

Dovidio, J. F. and Gaertner, S. L. (1998). On the nature of contemporary prejudice: The causes, consequences, and challenges of aversive racism. In J. Eberhardt and S. T. Fiske (eds.), *Confronting racism: The problem and the response* (pp. 3–32). Newbury Park, CA: Sage.

Dovidio, J. F. and Gaertner, S. L. (2000). Aversive racism and selection decisions: 1989 and 1999. *Psychological Science, 11* (4), 315–19.

Doyle-Anderson, A. (2002). Wanted: Minority candidates with excellent credentials for academic jobs. Letter to the editor, August 16. *Chronicle of Higher Education,* pp. B4, B16.

Dreher, G. F. and Ash, R. A. (1990). A comparative study of mentoring among men and women in managerial, professional, and technical positions. *Journal of Applied Psychology, 75,* 539–46.

Dreher, G. F. and Cox, T. H. (1996). Race, gender, and opportunity: A study of compensation attainment and the establishment of mentoring relationships. *Journal of Applied Psychology, 81* (3), 297–308.

Dreher, G. F. and Cox, T. H. (2000). Labor market mobility and cash compensation: The moderating effects of race and gender. *Academy of Management Journal, 43,* 890–900.

Dreher, G. F. and Dougherty, T. W. (2002). *Human resource strategy: A behavioral perspective for the general manager.* New York: McGraw-Hill/Irwin.

Dreher, G. F. and Ryan, K. C. (2000). Prior work experience and academic performance among first-year MBA students. *Research in Higher Education, 41,* 505–25.

Drew, R. (1999). Who takes bigger risks. *Management Review, 88* (9), 9.

Durr, M. and Logan, J. R. (1997). Racial submarkets in government employment: African-American managers in New York State. *Sociological Forum, 12,* 353–70.

Dworkin, A. G. and Dworkin, R. J. (1999). *The Minority Report: An introduction to racial, ethnic, and gender relations,* 3rd edn. Orlando, FL: Harcourt Brace. e_archive/gov_reports/ GlassCeiling/documents/GlassCeilingNewsRelease.pdf

Eagle, B. W., Icenogle, M. L., Maes, J. D., and Miles, E. W. (1998). The importance of employee demographic profiles for understanding experiences of work–family interrole conflicts. *Journal of Social Psychology, 138* (6), 690–709.

Eagly, A. H. and Johannesen-Schmidt, M. C. (2001). The leadership styles of women and men. *Journal of Social Issues, 57* (4), 781–97.

Earley, P. C. and Erez, M. (eds.) (1997). *New perspectives on international Industrial/Organizational Psychology.* San Francisco, CA: New Lexington Press.

Elliott, C. (1999). *Locating the energy for change: An introduction to appreciative inquiry.* Winnipeg, Canada: International Institute for Sustainable Development.

Elliott, D. (2000). Nondiscrimination laws now cover 60 million Americans, new report finds. Press release, January 3. National Gay and Lesbian Task Force. Retrieved January 4, 2000, from http://www.ngltf.org

Ellis, A. L. and Riggle, E. D. B. (1996). The relation of job satisfaction and degree of openness about one's sexual orientation for lesbians and gay men. *Journal of Homosexuality, 30,* 75–85.

Ellis, C. and Sonnenfeld, J. A. (1994). Diverse approaches to managing diversity. *Human Resource Management, 33* (1), 79–109.

Ellison v. Brady (CA9 1991) 924 F.2d 872.

Ellison, N. B. (1999). Social impacts: New perspectives on telework. *Social Science Computer Review, 17* (3), 338–56.

Ely, R. J. (1994). The effects of organizational demographics and social identity on relationships among professional women. *Administrative Science Quarterly, 39,* 203–38.

Ely, R. J. (1995). The power of demography: Women's social constructions of gender identity at work. *Academy of Management Journal,* June, 589.

Ely, R. J. and Meyerson, D. E. (2000). Theories of gender in organizations: A new approach to organizational analysis and change. *Research in Organizational Behavior, 22,* 105–53.

Ely, R. J. and Thomas, D. A. (2001). Cultural diversity at work: The effect of diversity perspectives on work group processes and outcomes. *Administrative Science Quarterly, 46* (2), 229–73.

Employee tenure summary (2000). US Bureau of Labor Statistics, August 29. Retrieved October 10, 2000, from http://stats.bls.gov/news.release/tenure.nr0.htm

"Employers win more ADA court cases" (2000). *Pensacola News-Journal*, December 18, 6D.

Employment Equity Act of 1998 of the Republic of South Africa (No. 55 of 1998) *Government Gazette*, 400 (19370): 55.

Engardio, J. P. (2000). Outing the Marlboro Man. *SF Weekly*, February 16. Retrieved July 28, 2002, from http://www.sfweekly.com/issues/2000–026/bayview.html/1/index.html

Engardio, J. P. (2001a). The adventures of Capt. GayMan: The Bush administration has released the first-ever Army training manual on homosexual policy – as a comic book. *SF Weekly*, August 22. Retrieved September 9, 2001, from http://www.sfweekly.com/issues/2001–08–22/bayview.html/1/index.html

Engardio, J. P. (2001b). Smoking gun. *SF Weekly*, May 2. Retrieved July 29, 2002, from http://www.sfweekly.com/issues/2001–05–02/bayview.html/1/index.html

Equal Employment Opportunity Commission (EEOC) (1980a). Guidelines on discrimination because of sex. *Federal Register*, 45, 74676–7.

Equal Employment Opportunity Commission (1980b). Discrimination because of sex under Title VII of the 1964 Civil Rights Act as amended: Adoption of interim guidelines – Sexual harassment. *Federal Register*, 45, 25024–5.

Equal Employment Opportunity Commission (2000). Occupational employment in private industry by race/ethnic group/sex, and by industry, United States, 2000. Retrieved July 2, 2002 from http://www.eeoc.gov/stats/jobpat/2000/national.html

Equal Employment Opportunity Commission (2001a). Age Discrimination in Employment Act (ADEA) charges FY 1992–FY 2000. http://www.eeoc.gov/stats/adea.html

Equal Employment Opportunity Commission (2001b). EEOC litigation statistics, 1992–FY 2000. http://www.eeoc.gov/stats/litigation.html

Equal Employment Opportunity Commission (2002a). Sex-based charges: FY 1992 to FY 2001. Retrieved October 10, 2002, from http://www.eeoc.gov/stats/sex.html

Equal Employment Opportunity Commission (2002b). Sexual harassment charges EEOC and FEPAs combined: FY 1992–FY 2001. Retrieved October 10, 2002, from http://www.eeoc.gov/stats/harass.html

Equal Employment Opportunity Trust (2000). *Making the most of a diverse workforce*. Retrieved October 29, 2001, from http://www.eeotrust.org.nz

Erez, M. and Earley, P. C. (1993). *Culture, self-identity, and work*. New York: Oxford University Press.

Erwee, R. (1994). South African Women: Changing career patterns. In N. J. Adler and D. N. Izraeli (eds.), *Competitive frontiers: Women managers in a global economy* (pp. 325–42). Oxford: Blackwell.

Eurostat (2001). Report: Regional labour force in the EU: Patterns and future perspectives. *Statistics in focus, general statistics 02/2001*. Retrieved October 29, 2001, from http://europa.eu.int/comm/eurostat/Public

Eyring, A. and Stead, B. A. (1998). Shattering the glass ceiling: Some successful corporate practices. *Journal of Business Ethics*, 17, 245–51.

Faircloth, A. (1998). Guess who's coming to Denny's. *Fortune*, 138, pp. 108–10.

Falletta, S. V. and Combs, W. (2002). Surveys as a tool for organization development and change. In J. Waclawski and A. H. Church (eds.), *Organization development: A data-driven approach to organizational change* (pp. 78–102). San Francisco, CA: Jossey-Bass.

Faragher v. City of Boca Raton, 524 US 775 (1998).

Fargo, J. (1999). Gay marketing: A profitable niche? *Credit Card Management, 11* (12), 48–54.

Fassinger, R. E. (2002). Hitting the ceiling: Gendered barriers to occupational entry, advancement, and achievement. In L. Diamant and J. A. Lee (eds.), *The psychology of sex, gender, and jobs.* Westport, CT: Praeger.

Federal Glass Ceiling Commission (1997). The glass ceiling. In D. Dunn (ed.), *Workplace/ women's place: An anthology* (pp. 226–33). Los Angeles, CA: Roxbury Publishing.

Feingold, A. (1995). The additive effects of differences in central tendency and variability are important in comparisons between groups. *American Psychologist, 50,* 5–13.

Fenwick, R. and Taussig, M. (2001). Scheduling stress: Family and health outcomes of shift work and schedule control. *American Behavioral Scientist, 44* (7), 1179–98.

Ferdman, B. M. (1997). Values about fairness in the ethnically diverse workplace. Special Issue: Managing in a global context: Diversity and cross-cultural challenges. *Business and the Contemporary World: An International Journal of Business, Economics, and Social Policy, 9,* 191–208.

Ferdman, B. M. and Brody, S. E. (1996). Models of diversity training. In D. Landis and R. Bhagat (eds.), *Handbook of intercultural training,* 2nd edn. (pp. 282–303). Thousand Oaks, CA: Sage.

Ferdman, B. M. and Davidson, M. N. (2002). A matter of difference – Inclusion: What can I and my organization do about it? *The Industrial-Organizational Psychologist, 39* (4), 80–5.

Fernandez, E. (2002). Exercising her right to work: Fitness instructor wins weight-bias fight. *San Francisco Chronicle,* May 7.

Fernandez, J. P. (1981). *Racism and sexism in corporate life: Changing values in American business.* Lexington, MA: Lexington.

Fernandez, J. P. (1999). *Race, gender, and rhetoric.* New York: McGraw-Hill.

Ferrie, J. E., Shipley, M. J., Marmot, M. G., Stansfeld, S. A., and Smith, G. D. (1998). An uncertain future: The health effects of threats to employment security in white collar men and women. *American Journal of Public Health, 88* (7), 1030–6.

Fine, M. and Weis, L. (1998). *The unknown city: Lives of poor and working-class young adults.* Boston, MA: Beacon Press.

Finn, A. V. (1997). What race am I? *Mademoiselle, 103–4,* 74.

Fisher, R. D., Derison, D., Polley, C. F., III, Cadman, J., and Johnston, D. (1994). Religiousness, religious orientation, and attitudes toward gays and lesbians. *Journal of Applied Social Psychology, 24,* 614–30.

Fitzgerald, L. F., Drasgow, F., Hulin, C. L., Gelfand, M. J., and Magley, V. J. (1997). Antecedants and consequences of sexual harassment in organizations: A test of an integrated model. *Journal of Applied Psychology, 82* (4), 578–89.

Fitzgerald, L. F. and Hesson-McInnis, M. (1989). The dimensions of sexual harassment: A structural analysis. *Journal of Vocational Behavior, 35,* 309–26.

Fitzgerald, L. F., Hulin, C. L., and Drasgow, F. (1994). The antecedents and consequences of sexual harassment in organizations: An integrated model. In G. P. Keita and J. Hurrell (eds.), *Job stress in a changing workforce: Investigating gender, diversity, and family issues* (pp. 55–73). Washington, DC: American Psychological Association.

Fitzgerald, S. P., Murrell, K. L., and Newman, H. L. (2002). Appreciative inquiry: The new frontier. In J. Waclawski and A. H. Church (eds.), *Organization development: A data-driven approach to organizational change* (pp. 203–21). San Francisco, CA: Jossey-Bass.

Fleras, A. and Elliott, J. L. (1995). *The challenge of diversity: Multiculturalism in Canada.* Scarborough, Ontario: Nelson.

Fletcher, J. K. (2002). *The greatly exaggerated demise of heroic leadership: Gender, power, and the myth of the female advantage.* CGO Insights Briefing Note No. 13. Boston: Simmons School of Management Center for Gender in Organizations. Downloaded from http://www.simmons.edu/gsm/cgo/insights_13.pdf

Florey, A. T. and Harrison, D. A. (2000). Responses to informal accommodation requests from employees with disabilities: Multistudy evidence on willingness to comply. *Academy of Management Journal, 43*, 224–33.

Foldy, E. (1999). *Managing diversity: Identity and power in organizations.* Paper presented at the First International Critical Management Studies Conference, July, Manchester, UK.

Folkard, S., Totterdell, P., Minors, D., and Waterhouse, J. (1993). Dissecting circadiean performance rhythms: Implications for shiftwork. *Ergonomics, 36*, 283–8.

Foot, D. K. (1996). *Boom, bust and echo: How to profit from the coming demographic shift.* Toronto: Mcfarlane, Walter, and Ross.

Forbes, I. and Mead, G. (1992). *Measure for measure: A comparative analysis of measures to combat racial discrimination in the member countries of the European community.* London: Equal Opportunities Study Group, University of Southampton.

Forthofer, M. S., Markman, H. J., Cox, M., Stanley, S., and Kessler, R. C. (1996). Associations between marital distress and work loss in a national sample. *Journal of Marriage and the Family, 58*, 597–605.

Foster, B. G., Jackson, G., Jackson, B, and Hardiman, R. (1988). Workforce diversity and business. *Training and Development Journal, 42* (4), 38–42.

Fowers, B. J. and Richardson, F. C. (1996). Why is multiculturalism good? *American Psychologist, 51*, 609–21.

Fox, M. L., Dwyer, D. J., and Ganster, D. C. (1993). Effects of stressful job demands and control on physiological and attitudinal outcomes in a hospital setting. *Academy of Management Journal, 36* (2), 289–318.

Fraser, L. (1994). The office F word (Job discrimination against fat people). *Working Woman, 6* (53–4), 88–91.

Freeman, L. (2000). The top 500 women-owned businesses. *Working Woman, 25* (6), 51–94.

French, J. R., Jr., and Caplan, R. D. (1970). Psychosocial factors in coronary heart disease. *Industrial Medicine, 39*, 383–8.

Friedman, R. A. (1999) Employee network groups: Self-help strategy for women and minorities. *Performance Improvement Quarterly, 12* (1), 148–63.

Friskopp, A. and Silverstein, S. (1996). *Straight jobs, gay lives: Gay and lesbian professionals, the Harvard Business School, and the American workplace.* New York: Simon and Schuster.

Frone, M. R., Russell, M., and Cooper, M. L. (1995). Job stressors, job involvement and employee health: A test of identity theory. *Journal of Occupational and Organizational Psychology, 68*, 1–11.

Frone, M. R., Russell, M., and Cooper, M. L. (1997). Relation of work–family conflict to health outcomes: A four-year longitudinal study of employed parents. *Journal of Occupational and Organizational Psychology, 70*, 325–35.

Frone, M. R., Yardley, J. K., and Markel, K. S. (1997). Developing and testing an integrative model of the work–family interface. *Journal of Vocational Behavior, 50*, 145–67.

Fulkerson, J. R. and Schuler, R. S. (1992). Managing worldwide diversity at Pepsi-Cola International. In S. E. Jackson and Associates (eds.), *Diversity in the workplace* (pp. 248–78). New York: Guilford Press.

Furchtgott-Roth, D. and Stolba, C. (1999). *Women's figures. An illustrated guide to the economic progress of women in America.* Washington, DC: AEI Press.

Furnham, A. (1982a). Why are the poor always with us? Explanations for poverty in Britain. *British Journal of Social Psychology, 21*, 311–22.

Furnham, A. (1982b). The Protestant work ethic and attitudes towards unemployment. *Journal of Occupational Psychology, 55*, 277–86.

Gabel, J., Hurst, K., Whitmore, H., and Hoffman, C. (1999). Class and benefits at the workplace. *Health Affairs, 18*, 144–50.

Gaertner, S. L. and Dovidio, J. F. (1986). The aversive form of prejudice. In J. F. Dovidio and S. L. Gaertner (eds.), *Prejudice, discrimination, and racism* (pp. 61–89). Orlando, FL: Academic Press.

Galinsky, E., Bond, J. T., and Friedman, D. E. (1993). *The changing workforce: Highlights of the national study.* New York: Families and Work Institute.

Gallup Organization (2002) Black/White relations in the United States – 1997. Retrieved August 18, 2002, from http://www.gallup.com/poll/specialreports/socialaudits/sa970610.asp

Ganster, D. C., Fox, M. L., and Dwyer, D. J. (2001). Explaining employees' health care costs: A prospective examination of stressful job demands, personal control, and physiological reactivity. *Journal of Applied Psychology, 86* (5), 954–64.

Garamone, J. (2000). DoD approves "Don't Ask, Don't Tell, Don't Harass" plans. *American Forces Press Service.* Retrieved November 19, 2001, from www.defenselink.mil/news/Feb2000/n02022000_20002021.html

Gardiner, M. and Tiggemann, M. (1999). Gender differences in leadership style, job stress, and mental health in male- and female-dominated industries. *Journal of Occupational and Organizational Psychology, 72*, 301–15.

Gasorek, D. (2000). Inclusion at Dun and Bradstreet: Building a high-performing company. *The Diversity Factor*, summer, 25–9.

Gatz, M. and Cotton, B. (1994). Age as a dimension of diversity: The experience of being old. In E. J. Trickett, R. J. Watts, and D. Birman (eds.), *Human diversity* (pp. 334–55). San Francisco, CA: Jossey-Bass.

Gelfand, M. J., Fitzgerald, L. F., and Drasgow, F. (1995). The structure of sexual harassment: A confirmatory factor analysis across cultures and settings. *Journal of Vocational Behavior, 47*, 164–77.

Gerstner, C. R. and Day, D. V. (1997). Meta-analytic review of leader–member exchange theory: Correlates and construct issues. *Journal of Applied Psychology, 82*, 827–44.

Gilbert, J. A. and Ivancevich, J. M. (1999). Organizational diplomacy: The bridge for managing diversity. *Human Resource Planning, 22* (3), 29–39.

Gilbert, J. A. and Stead, B. A. (1999). Stigmatization revisited: Does diversity management make a difference in applicant success? *Group and Organization Management, 24*, 239–56.

Glass, J. L. and Estes, S. B. (1997). The family responsive workplace. *Annual Review of Sociology, 23*, 289–313.

Glick, P. and Fiske, S. T. (2001). An ambivalent alliance: Hostile and benevolent sexism as complementary justifications for gender inequality. *American Psychologist, 56*, 109–18.

Globe and Mail (2002). Canada is 30 million, but will it last? Wednesday, March 13, pp. A1, A7.

Glomb, T. M., Munson, L. J., Hulin, C. L., Bergman, M. E., and Drasgow, F. (1999). Structural equation models of sexual harassment: Longitudinal explorations and cross-sectional generalizations. *Journal of Applied Psychology, 84* (1), 14–28.

Goff, S. J., Mount, M. K., and Jamison, R. L. (1990). Employer supported child care, work/family conflict, and absenteeism: A field study. *Personnel Psychology, 43*, 793–809.

Goffman, E. (1963). Stigma: Notes on the management of spoiled identity. Englewood Cliffs, NJ: Prentice-Hall.

Golden, L. (2001). Flexible work schedules: Which workers get them? *American Behavioral Scientist, 44* (7), 1157–78.

Goleman, D. (1998). *Working with emotional intelligence.* New York: Bantam Books.

Golembiewski, R. (1995). *Managing diversity in organizations.* Tuscaloosa: University of Alabama Press.

Gonsiorek, J. C. and Rudolph, J. R. (1991). Homosexual identity: Coming out and other developmental events. In J. C. Gonsiorek and J. D. Weinrich (eds.), *Homosexuality: Research implications for public policy* (pp. 161–76). Newbury Park, CA: Sage.

Gonsiorek, J. C. and Weinrich, J. D. (1991). The definition and scope of sexual orientation. In J. C. Gonsiorek and J. D. Weinrich (eds.), *Homosexuality: Research implications for public policy* (pp. 1–12). Newbury Park, CA: Sage.

Gordon, L. (1995). Pitied but not entitled: Single mothers and the history of welfare. New York: Free Press.

Gore, S. and Mangione, T. W. (1983). Social roles, sex roles, and psychological distress: Additive and interactive models of sex differences. *Journal of Health and Social Behavior, 24,* 300–12.

Gottfredson, L. S. (1992). Dilemmas in developing diversity programs. In S. E. Jackson and Associates (eds.), *Diversity in the workplace: Human resources initiatives* (pp. 279–305), New York: Guilford Press.

Gowing, M. K. and Payne, S. S. (1992). Assessing the quality of the federal workforce: A program to meet diverse needs. In S. E. Jackson and Associates (eds.), *Diversity in the workplace* (pp. 89–118). New York: Guilford Press.

Grace, P. (1994). Danger – diversity training ahead: Addressing the myths of diversity training and offering alternatives. In J. W. Pfeiffer (ed.), *The 1994 annual: Developing human resources* (pp. 189–200). San Diego, CA: Pfeiffer.

Graen, G. B. and Uhl-Bien, M. (1995). Development of leader–member exchange (LMX) theory of leadership over 25 years: Applying a multi-level–multi-domain perspective. *Leadership Quarterly, 6,* 219–47.

Graham, H. (1993). *Health and hardship in women's lives.* London: Harvester/Wheatsheaf.

Graham, M. E. and Welbourne, T. M. (1999). Gainsharing and women's and men's relative pay satisfaction. *Journal of Organizational Behavior,* December, 1027–42.

Granovetter, M. S. (1973). The strength of weak ties. *American Journal of Sociology, 6,* 1360–80.

Gratias, M. B. and Hills, D. A. (1997). Social loafing in individuals versus groups: Assessing quantity, quality, and creativity. Poster presented at the annual conference of the Society for Industrial and Organizational Psychology, St. Louis, MO.

Gray, C., Russell, P., and Blockley, S. (1991). The effects upon helping behavior of wearing pro-gay identification. *British Journal of Social Psychology, 30,* 171–8.

Gray, J. D. (2001). *City of Atlanta ordinance broadens job shield on office romances.* Retrieved on February 22, 1002, from http://www.law.com/cgi–bin/gx.cgi/AppLo . . . mmary =0anduseoverridetemplate=ZZZHCC0Q95C

Greenberg, J. (1987). A taxonomy of organizational justice theories. *Academy of Management Review, 12,* 9–22.

Greenberger, E. and O'Neil, R. (1993). Spouse, parent, worker: Role commitments and role-related experiences in the construction of adults' well-being. *Developmental Psychology, 29* (2), 181–97.

Greenhaus, J. H., Parasuraman, S., and Wormley, W. M. (1990). Effects of race on organizational experiences, job performance evaluations, and career outcomes. *Academy of Management Journal, 33,* 64–86.

Greenwood, D. J. and Levin, M. (1998). *Introduction to action research: Social research for social change.* Thousand Oaks, CA: Sage.

Greig, T. C. and Bell, M. D. (2000). Work to reduce stigma. *American Psychologist, 55,* 1068–9.

Greller, M. M. (1997). Extending workers' careers: US implications from the European experience. *Human Resource Planning, 20,* 13–14.

Griggs v. Duke Power, 401 US 424 (1971).

Grover, S. L. and Crooker, K. J. (1995). Who appreciates family-responsive human resources policies? *Personnel Psychology, 48,* 271–88.

Gruber, J. E. (1990). Methodological problems and policy implications in sexual harassment research. *Population Research and Policy Review, 9,* 235–54.

Gutek, B. A. (1985). *Sex and the workplace: Impact of sexual behavior and harassment of women, men and organizations.* San Francisco, CA: Jossey-Bass.

Gutek, B. A. (1993). Asymmetric changes in men's and women's roles. In B. C. Long and S. E. Kahn (eds.), *Women, work, and coping: A multidisciplinary approach to workplace stress* (pp. 11–31). Montreal: McGill–Queen's University Press.

Gutek, B. A. (1995). *The dynamics of service: Reflections on the changing nature of customer/ provider interactions.* San Francisco, CA: Jossey-Bass.

Gutek, B. A. and Koss, M. P. (1993). Changed women and changed organizations: Consequences of and coping with sexual harassment. *Journal of Vocational Behavior, 42,* 28–48.

Gutek, B. A. and O'Connor, M. (1995). The empirical basis for the reasonable woman standard. *Journal of Social Issues, 51,* 151–66.

Gutek, B. A., O'Connor, M., Melancon, R., Stockdale, M. S., Geer, T. M., and Done, R. (1999). The utility of the reasonable woman legal standard in hostile environment sexual harassment cases: A multimethod, multistudy examination. *Psychology, Public Policy and the Law, 5* (3), 596–629.

Gutierres, S. E., Saenz, D. S., and Green, B. L. (1994). Job stress and health outcomes among white and Hispanic employees: A test of the person–environment fit model. In G. P. Keita and J. J. Hurrell (eds.), *Job stress in a changing workforce: Investigating gender, diversity, and family issues* (pp. 107–25). Washington, DC: American Psychological Association.

Gutman, A. (1993). *EEO law and personnel practices.* Newbury Park, CA: Sage.

Gutman, A. (2000). *EEO law and personnel practice,* 2nd edn. Thousand Oaks, CA: Sage.

Hacker, A. (1995). *Two nations: Black and White, separate, hostile, unequal.* New York: Ballantine Books.

Haddock, G. and Zanna, M. P. (1998). Authoritarianism, values, and the favorability and structure of antigay attitudes. In G. M. Herek (ed.), *Stigma and sexual orientation: Understanding prejudice against lesbians, gay men, and bisexuals* (pp. 82–107). Thousand Oaks, CA: Sage.

Hall, E. (1989). Gender, work control and stress: A theoretical discussion and an empirical test. *International Journal of Health Services, 19,* 725–45.

Hall, M. (1986). The lesbian corporate experience. *Journal of Homosexuality, 12,* 59–75.

Hammond, S. (1996). *The thin book of appreciative inquiry.* Plano, TX: Thin Book Publishing.

Hammond, S. and Royal, C. (eds.) (1998). *Lessons from the field: Applying appreciative inquiry.* Plano, TX: Practical Press.

Hammond, V. (1992). Opportunity 2000: A culture change approach to equal opportunity. *Women in Management Review, 7* (7), 3–10.

Hanover, J. and Cellar, D. (1998). Environmental factors and the effectiveness of workforce diversity training. *Human Resource Development Quarterly, 9*, 105–24.

Hardisty, J. and Williams, L. A. (2002). The right's campaign against welfare. In *From poverty to punishment: How welfare reform punishes the poor* (pp. 53–72). Oakland, CA: Applied Research Center.

Hare-Mustin, R. T. and Maracek, J. (1988). The meaning of difference: Gender theory, postmodernism, and psychology. *American Psychologist, 43*, 455–64.

Hare-Mustin, R. T. and Marecek, J. (eds.) (1990). *Making a difference: Psychology and the construction of gender.* New Haven, CT: Yale University Press.

Harris v. Forklift Sys., 114 S.Ct. 367 (1993).

Harrison, D., Price, K., and Bell, M. P. (1998). Beyond relational demography: Time and the effects of surface- and deep-level diversity on work group cohesion. *Academy of Management Journal, 41*, 96–107.

Harrison, J. (2000). M and A Timeline. *Mergers and Acquisitions, 35* (8), 24–30.

Harrison, R. and Stokes, H. (1992). *Diagnosing organizational culture.* San Francisco, CA: Jossey-Bass.

Harry, J. (1995). Sports ideology, attitudes toward women, and anti-homosexual attitudes. *Sex Roles, 32*, 109–17.

Hartigan, J. A. and Wigdor, A. K. (eds.) (1989). *Fairness in employment testing: Validity generalization, minority issues, and the General Aptitude Test Battery.* Washington, DC: National Academy Press.

Haslam, S. A. (2000). *Psychology in organizations: The social identity approach.* Thousand Oaks, CA: Sage.

Hayles, V. R. and Russell, A. M. (1997). *The diversity directive: Why some initiatives fail and what to do about it.* Chicago, IL: Irwin/ASTD.

Haynes, S. G. (1991). The effect of job demands, job control, and new technologies on the health of employed women. In M. Frankenhaeuser, U. Lundberg, and M. Chesney (eds.), *Women, work, and health: Stress and opportunities* (pp. 157–69). New York: Plenum.

Haynes, S. G. and Feinleib, M. (1980). Women, work, and coronary artery disease: Prospective findings of the Framingham Heart Study. *American Journal of Public Health, 70*, 133–41.

Hazen Paper Co. v. Biggins, 507 US 604 (1993).

Healy, D., Minors, D. S., and Waterhouse, J. M. (1993). Shift work, helplessness and depression. *Journal of Affective Disorders, 29*, 17–25.

Heaney, C. A. (1993). Perceived control and employed women and men. In B. C. Long and S. E. Kahn (eds.), *Women, work, and coping: A multidisciplinary approach to workplace stress* (pp. 193–215). Montreal: McGill–Queen's University Press.

Heaven, P. C. L. and Oxman, L. N. (1999). Human values, conservatism, and stereotypes of homosexuals. *Personality and Individual Differences, 27*, 109–18.

Hecker, D. (1998). How hours of work affect occupational earnings. *Monthly Labor Review,* October, 8–18.

Heilman, M. E. (1996). Affirmative action's contradictory consequences. *Journal of Social Issues, 52* (4), 105–9.

Heilman, M. E., Block, C. J., Martell, R. F., and Simon, M. C. (1989). Has anything changed? Current characterizations of men, women, and managers. *Journal of Applied Psychology, 74* (6), 935–42.

Hemphill, H. and Haines, R. (1997). *Discrimination, harassment, and the failure of diversity training: What to do now.* Westport, CT: Quorum Books; Hillsdale, NJ: Lawrence Erlbaum Associates.

Henly, J. R. and Lyons, S. (2000). The negotiation of child care and employment demands among low income parents. *Journal of Social Issues, 56,* 683–706.

Herek, G. M. (1987). Can functions be measured? A new perspective on the functional approach to attitudes. *Social Psychology Quarterly, 50,* 285–303.

Herek, G. M. (1988). Heterosexuals' attitudes toward lesbians and gay men: Correlates and gender differences. *Journal of Sex Research, 25,* 451–77.

Herek, G. M. (1989). Hate crimes against lesbians and gay men: Issues for research and policy. *American Psychologist, 4,* 948–55.

Herek, G. M. (1990). The context of anti-gay violence: Notes on cultural and psychological heterosexism. *Journal of Interpersonal Violence, 5,* 316–33.

Herek, G. M. (1994). Assessing heterosexuals' attitudes toward lesbians and gay men: A review of empirical research with the ATLG scale. In B. Greene and G. M. Herek (eds.), *Lesbian and gay psychology: Theory, research, and clinical applications* (pp. 206–28). Thousand Oaks, CA: Sage.

Herek, G. M. (2000). The psychology of sexual prejudice. *Current Directions in Psychological Science, 9,* 19–22.

Herek, G. M. and Capitanio, J. P. (1995). Black heterosexuals' attitudes toward lesbians and gay men in the United States. *Journal of Sex Research, 32,* 95–105.

Hernandez, D. G. (1996). Do ask – do tell. *Editor and Publisher, 129* (25), 13, 56.

Herrnstein, R. J. and Murray, C. (1994). *The bell curve: Intelligence and class structure in American life.* New York: Free Press.

Heydebrand, W. (1978). Critical issues in organizations. *Administrative Science Quarterly, 23,* 640–5.

Hill, E. J., Hawkins, A. J., and Miller, B. C. (1996). Work and family in the virtual office: Perceived influences of mobile telework. *Family Relations, 45,* 293–301.

Hillier, J. (1990). *An integrated framework for examining CEO background, board memberships and corporate performance: Test of a model.* Unpublished doctoral dissertation, Indiana University, Bloomington.

Hillman, A. J., Harris I. C., Cannella, A. A., and Bellinger, L. (1998). *Diversity on the board: An examination of the relationship between director diversity and firm performance.* Paper presented at the annual meeting of the Academy of Management, San Diego, CA.

Hochschild, A. R. (1983). *The managed heart.* Berkeley: University of California Press.

Hochschild, A. R. (1989). *The second shift: Working parents and the revolution at home.* New York: Viking.

Hochschild, J. L. (1995). *Race, class, and the soul of the nation: Facing up to the American Dream.* Princeton, NJ: Princeton University Press.

Hofstede, G. (1980). *Culture's consequences: International differences in work-related values.* Beverly Hills: Sage.

Hofstede, G. (1991). *Cultures and organizations: Software of the mind.* London: McGraw-Hill.

Holder, J. C. and Vaux, A. (1998). African-American professionals: Coping with occupational stress in predominantly white work environments. *Journal of Vocational Behavior, 53,* 315–33.

Holman, P. and Devane, T. (1999). *The change handbook: Group methods for changing the future.* San Francisco, CA: Berrertt-Koehler.

Holvino, E. (1993). *Organization development from the margins: Reading class, race and gender in OD.* Unpublished doctoral dissertation, University of Massachusetts, Amherst.

Holvino, E. (1998). *The multicultural organizational development model.* Unpublished training materials. Brattleboro, VT: Chaos Management.

Holvino, E. (2000). Social diversity in social change organizations: Standpoint learnings for organizational consulting. In R. T. Carter (ed.), *Addressing cultural issues in organizations: Beyond the corporate context* (pp. 211–28). Thousand Oaks, CA: Sage.

Holzer, H. J. (1999). Will employers hire welfare recipients? Recent survey evidence from Michigan. *Journal of Policy Analysis and Management, 18,* 449–72.

Holzer, H. J. and Stoll, M. A. (2002). *Employer demand for welfare recipients by race.* Washington, DC: Urban Institute.

Hooijberg, R. and DiTomaso, N. (1996). Leadership in and of demographically diverse organizations. *Leadership Quarterly, 7* (1), 1–15.

Hopkins, W., Hopkins, S., and Mallette, P. (2001). Diversity and managerial value commitment: A test of some proposed relationships. *Journal of Managerial Issues, 13,* 288–306.

Horne, G. (1992). *Reversing discrimination: The case for affirmative action.* New York: International Publishers.

Hosoda, M., Chen, D., and Stone, D. L. (2001). *Race, gender, and job satisfaction.* Paper presented at the April meeting of the Society for Industrial and Organizational Psychology. San Diego, CA.

Hossain, J. L. and Shapiro, C. M. (1999). Considerations and possible consequences of shift work. *Journal of Psychosomatic Research, 47* (4), 293–6.

House, R. J. (1995). Leadership in the twenty-first century: A speculative inquiry. In A. Howard (ed.), *The changing nature of work* (pp. 411–50). San Francisco, CA: Jossey-Bass.

House, R. J. and Mitchell, T. R. (1997). Path–goal theory of leadership. In R. P. Vecchio (ed.), *Leadership: Understanding the dynamics of power and influence in organizations* (pp. 259–73). Notre Dame, IN: University of Notre Dame Press.

Hudson, J. and Hines-Hudson, B. (1996). Improving race relations in a public service agency: A model workshop series. *Public Personnel Management, 25,* 1–11.

Huffcutt, A. I. and Roth, P. L. (1998). Racial group differences in employment interview evaluations. *Journal of Applied Psychology, 83* (2), 179–89.

Hughes, D. L. and Galinsky, E. (1994a). Gender, job, family conditions, and psychological symptoms. *Psychology of Women Quarterly, 18,* 251–70.

Hughes, D. L. and Galinsky, E. (1994b). Work experiences and marital interactions: Elaborating the complexity of work. *Journal of Organizational Behavior, 15,* 423–38.

Hughes, G. and Kleiner, B. H. (1995). New developments in disability discrimination. *Equal Opportunities International, 14,* 17–23.

Hultin, M. and Szulkin, R. (1999). Wages and unequal access to organizational power: An empirical test of gender discrimination. *Administrative Science Quarterly,* September, 453.

Human Rights Campaign (2001a). 12 states (and the District of Columbia) that prohibit work discrimination based on sexual orientation. Retrieved November 29, 2001, from http://www.hrc.org/issues/federal_leg/enda/background/map.asp

Human Rights Campaign (2001b). ENDA quickfacts: The right solution for a real need. Retrieved November 29, 2001, from http://www.hrc.org/issues/federal_leg/enda/enda_quickfacts.asp

Hunsberger, B. (1996). Religious fundamentalism, right-wing authoritarianism, and hostility toward homosexuals in non-Christian religious groups. *International Journal for the Psychology of Religion, 6,* 39–49.

Hunsberger, B., Alisat, S., Pancer, S. M., and Pratt, M. (1996). Religious fundamentalism and religious doubts: Content, connections, and complexity of thinking. *International Journal for the Psychology of Religion, 6,* 201–20.

Hunt, M. O. (1996). The individual, society, or both? A comparison of Black, Latino, and White beliefs about the causes of poverty. *Social Forces, 75,* 293–322.

Hunter, J. D. (1991). *Culture wars: The struggle to define America.* New York: Basic Books/ Harper Collins.

Hurley, A. E., Fagenson-Eland, E. A., Sonnefeld, J. A. (1997). Does cream always rise to the top? An investigation of career attainment determinants. *Organizational Dynamics,* autumn, 65–71.

Hyde, C. (2000). Feminist approaches to social policy. In J. Midgley, M. B. Tracy, M. Livermore (eds.), *The handbook of social policy* (pp. 421–34). Thousand Oaks, CA: Sage.

Hyde, J. S., Klein, M. H., Essex, M. J., and Clark, R. (1995). Maternity leave and women's mental health. *Psychology of Women Quarterly, 19,* 257–85.

Iannuzzi, J. (1997). Reaping diversity's competitive rewards. *Business Forum, 22,* 4–5.

Ibarra, H. (1993). Personal networks of women and minorities in management: A conceptual framework. *Academy of Management Review, 18* (1), 56–87.

Ibarra, H. (1995). Race, opportunity, and diversity of social circles in managerial networks. *Academy of Management Journal, 38* (3), 673–703.

IBM (2000). *Valuing diversity: An ongoing commitment.* Armonk, NY: IBM.

Ilgen, D. (1999). Teams embedded in organizations: Some implications. *American Psychologist, 54,* 129–39.

Imai, M. (1986). *Kaizen: The key to Japan's competitive success.* New York: Random House.

International Labor Organization (ILO) (2002). *Breaking through the glass ceiling: Women in management.* Department of Communication. http://www.ilo.org/communication

India: Census (1991). http://censusindia.net/stateprofile.html

Ireland. Central Statistical Office. http://www.cso.ie/principlestats/cenrel1.html

Ivancevich, J. M. and Gilbert, J. A. (2000). Diversity management: Time for a new approach. *Public Personnel Management, 29,* 75–92.

Iverson, K. (2000). Managing for effective workforce diversity: Identifying issues that are of concern to employees. *Cornell Hotel and Restaurant Administration Quarterly, 41* (2), 31–8.

Jackson, B. and Hardiman, R. (1994). Multicultural organization development. In E. Cross, J. H. Katz, F. A. Miller, and E. W. Seashore (eds.), *The promise of diversity: Over 40 voices discuss strategies for eliminating discrimination in organizations* (pp. 221–39). Burr Ridge, IL: Irwin.

Jackson, B. and Holvino, E. (1988). Developing multicultural organizations. *Journal of Religion and the Applied Behavioral Sciences, 9* (2), 14–19.

Jackson, P. B., Thoits, P. A., and Taylor, H. F. (1995). Composition of the workplace on psychological well-being: The effects of tokenism on America's black elite. *Social Forces, 74* (2), 543–57.

Jackson, S. E. (1992). Team composition in organizational settings: Issues in managing an increasingly diverse workforce. In S. Worchel, W. Wood, and J. A. Simpson (eds.), *Group process and productivity* (pp. 138–73). Newbury Park, CA: Sage.

Jackson, S. E. and Alvarez, E. B. (1992). Working through diversity as a strategic imperative. In S. E. Jackson and Associates (eds.), *Diversity in the workplace: Human resource initiatives* (pp. 13–29). New York: Guilford Press.

Jackson, S. E. and Associates (eds.) (1992). *Diversity in the workplace: Human resource initiatives.* New York: Guilford Press.

Jackson, S. E., May, K. E., and Whitney, K. (1995). Understanding the dynamics of diversity in decision-making teams. In R. A. Guzzo, E. Salas, and Associates (eds.), *Team effectiveness and decision making in organizations* (pp. 204–61). San Francisco, CA: Jossey-Bass.

Jackson, S. E. and Schuler, R. S. (1985). A meta-analysis and conceptual critique of research on role ambiguity and role conflict in work settings. *Organizational Behavior and Human Decision Proccesses, 36* (1), 16–78.

Jacques, E. (1989). *Requisite organization: The CEO's guide to creative structure and leadership.* Arlington, VA: Cason Hall.

James, K. (1994). Social identity, work stress, and minority worker's health. In G. P. Keita and J. J. Hurrell (eds.), *Job stress in a changing workforce: Investigating gender, diversity, and family issues* (pp. 127–45). Washington, DC: American Psychological Association.

Japan, Census (2000). www.stat.go.jp/english/15ld1.htm

Jasper, C. R. and Klassen, M. L. (1990). Perceptions of salespersons' appearance and evaluation of job performance. *Perceptual and Motor Skills, 71,* 563–6.

Javidan, M. and House, R. J. (2001). Cultural acumen for the global manager: Lessons from project GLOBE. *Organizational Dynamics, 29* (4), 289–308.

Jayakody, R. and Stauffer, D. (2000). Mental health problems among single mothers: Implications for work and welfare reform. *Journal of Social Issues, 56,* 617–31.

Jehn, K. A. (1999). Diversity, conflict and team performance: Summary of program of research. *Performance Improvement Quarterly, 12,* 6–19.

Jehn, K. A., Northcraft, G. B., and Neale, M. A. (1999). Why differences make a difference: A field study of diversity, conflict, and performance in workgroups. *Administrative Science Quarterly, 44,* 741–63.

Jencks, C. (1979). *Who gets ahead? Determinants of success in America.* New York: Basic Books.

Jex, S. M. (1998). *Stress and job performance: Theory, research, and implications for managerial practice.* Thousand Oaks, CA: Sage.

Johnson, L. A. (1991). Effectiveness of an employer sponsored child care center. *Applied Human Resource Management Research, 2* (1), 38–67.

Johnson, W. G. and Lambrinos, J. (1985). Wage discrimination against handicapped men and women. *Journal of Human Resources, 20,* 264–77.

Johnston, W. B. and Packer, A. H. (1987). *Workforce 2000.* Indianapolis, IN: Hudson Institute.

Jome, L. M. and Tokar, D. M. (1998). Dimensions of masculinity and major choice traditionality. *Journal of Vocational Behavior, 52,* 120–34.

Jones, G. E. and Stone, D. (1995). Perceived discomfort associated with working with persons with varying disabilities. *Perceptual and Motor Skills, 81,* 911–19.

Joplin, J. R. W. and Daus, S. (1997). Challenges of leading a diverse workforce. *Academy of Management Executive, 11* (3), 32–47.

Jordan, A. T. (1995). Managing diversity: Translating anthropological insight for organization studies. *Journal of Applied Behavioral Science, 31,* 124–40.

Judge, T. A., Cable, D. M., Boudreau, J. W., and Bretz, R. D. (1995). An empirical investigation of the prediction of executive career success. *Personnel Psychology, 48,* 485–519.

Judiesch, M. K. and Lyness, K. S. (1999). Left behind? The impact of leaves of absence on managers' career success. *Academy of Management Journal,* December, 641–51.

Judy, R. W. and D'Amico, C. (1997). *Workforce 2020: Work and workers in the 21st century.* Indianapolis, IN: Hudson Institute.

Jupp, J. (1995). Public policy and diversity – migration patterns and policy selection and rejection – twenty years of Australian Immigration. In 1995 Global Cultural Diversity Conference Proceedings, Sydney, Australia. http://www.immi.gov.au/multicultural/confer/speech7a.htm

Kahn, R. L., Wolfe, D. M., Quinn, R. P., Snoek, J. D., and Rosenthal, R. A. (1964). *Occupational stress: Studies in role conflict and ambiguity.* New York: Wiley.

Kampo Gogai (1997). *Act amending several Acts to guarantee equal opportunity and treatment between men and women in employment.* No. 92, vol. 1/2. No. 121: 30–3. http://natlex.ilo.org/Scripts/natlexcgi.exe?lang=Eanddoc=queryandctry=JPNand11x=02.03

Kampo Gogai (1999). *Fundamental law designed to promote a gender-equal society.* Vol. 1/3. No. 118: 7–8. http://natlex.ilo.org/Scripts/natlexcgi.exe?lang=Eanddoc=queryandctry=JPNand11x=02.03

Kandel, D. B., Davies, M., and Raveis, V. H. (1985). The stressfulness of daily social roles for women: Marital, occupational and household. *Journal of Health and Social Behavior, 26,* 64–78.

Kandola, R. (1995). Managing diversity: New broom or old hat? In C. L. Cooper and I. T. Robertson (eds.), *International Review of Industrial and Organizational Psychology,* vol. 10 (pp. 131–67). London: Wiley.

Kandolin, I. (1993). Burnout of female and male nurses in shift work. *Ergonomics, 36,* 141–7.

Kanter, R. M. (1977). *Men and women of the corporation.* New York: Basic Books.

Karasek, R. (1979). Job demands, job decision latitude and mental strain: Implications for job redesign. *Administrative Science Quarterly, 24,* 285–308.

Karasek, R., Russell, R. S., and Theorell, T. (1982). Physiology of stress and regeneration in job-related cardiovascular illness. *Journal of Human Stress,* March, 29–42.

Karasek, R. and Theorell, T. (1990). *Healthy work: A comparison of men's and women's jobs.* New York: Basic Books.

Karasek, R., Theorell, T., Schwartz, J. E., Schnall, P. L., Pieper, C., and Michela, J. L. (1988). Job characteristics in relation to the prevalence of myocardial infarction in the US HES and the US HANES. *American Journal of Public Health, 78,* 910–18.

Karr, R. G. (1978). Homosexual labeling and the male role. *Journal of Social Issues, 34,* 73–83.

Kasinitz, P. and Rosenberg, J. (1996). Missing the connection: Social isolation and employment on the Brooklyn waterfront. *Social Problems, 43,* 180–96.

Kasl, S. V. and Cobb, S. (1982). Variability of stress effects among men experiencing job loss. In L. Goldberg and S. Breznitz (eds.), *Handbook of stress: Theoretical and clinical aspects* (pp. 445–65). New York: Wiley.

Katz, D. and Kahn, R. (1978). *The social psychology of organizations,* 2nd edn. New York: Wiley.

Katz, J. H. and Miller, F. A. (1988). Between monoculturalism and multiculturalism: Traps awaiting the organization. *OD Practitioner, 20* (3), 1–5.

Kauffman, N. (1987). Motivating the older worker. *S.A.M. Advanced Management Journal, 52,* 43–8.

Kaye, L. W. and Alexander, L. B. (1995). Perceptions of job discrimination among lower-income, elderly part-timers. *Journal of Gerontological Social Work, 23,* 99–120.

Keaveny, T. J. and Inderrieden, E. J. (1999). Gender differences in employer-supported training and education. *Journal of Vocational Behavior, 54,* 71–81.

Keidanren (1999). Finding specific answers to the problem of declining birth rate. www.keidanren.or.jp/english/policy/polo98.htm

Keister, L. A. and Moller, S. (2000). Wealth inequality in the United States. *Annual Review of Sociology, 26,* 63–81.

Keita, G. P. and Jones, J. M. (1990). Reducing adverse reaction to stress in the workplace: Psychology's expanding role. *American Psychologist, 45* (10), 1137–41.

Kelchner, E. S. (1999). Ageism's impact and effect on society: Not just a concern for the old. *Journal of Gerontological Social Work, 32* (4), 85–100.

Kelley, J. and Evans, M. D. R. (1995). Class and class conflict in six western nations. *American Sociological Review, 60,* 157–78.

Kelley, K. and Streeter, D. (1992). The roles of gender in organizations. In K. Kelley (ed.), *Issues, theory, and research in industrial/organizational psychology* (pp. 285–337). Amsterdam, NY: Elsevier Science Publishing.

Kennelly, I. (1999). "That single-mother element:" How White employers typify Black women. *Gender and Society, 13,* 168–92.

Kerbo, H. R. (1996). *Social stratification and inequality: Class conflict in historical and comparative perspective,* 3rd edn. New York: McGraw-Hill.

Kerr, M. R. (2000). Army "tells" gay politician "no." *Tucson Weekly Observer/PlanetOut.com.* Retrieved September 9, 2001, from http://www.planetout.com/news/article.html?2000/09/18/1

Kifner, J. (2000). Clinton says he felt pushed into gay policy. *New York Times.* Retrieved September 9, 2001, from http://www.nytimes.com

Kiley, K. (1996). The gay market gains industry acceptance. *Catalog Age, 13* (10), 10.

Kimel v. Florida Bd. of Regents. 528 US 62 (2000).

King, L. A. and King, D. W. (1990). Role conflict and role ambiguity: A critical assessment of construct validity. *Psychological Bulletin, 107* (1), 48–64.

Kinsey, A. C., Pomeroy, W. B., and Martin, C. E. (1948). *Sexual behavior in the human male.* Philadelphia, PA: W. B. Saunders.

Kinsey, A. C., Pomeroy, W. B., Martin, C. E., and Gebhard, P. H. (1953). *Sexual behavior in the human female.* Philadelphia, PA: W. B. Saunders.

Kirby, M. (2000). Psychiatry, psychology, law and homosexuality – Uncomfortable bedfellows. *Psychiatry, Psychology, and Law, 7,* 139–49.

Kirby, S. and Richard, O. (2000). Impact of marketing work-place diversity on employee job involvement and organizational commitment. *Journal of Social Psychology, 140,* 367–77.

Kirkham, K. (1992). Destination 2000: Six traps in managing diversity. *Diversity Factor, 1* (1), 6–8.

Kirkpatrick, D. L. (1987). Evaluation of training. In R. L. Craig (ed.), *Training and development handbook,* 3rd edn. (pp. 301–19). New York: McGraw-Hill.

Kirkpatrick, L. A. (1993). Fundamentalism, Christian orthodoxy, and intrinsic religious orientation as predictors of discriminatory attitudes. *Journal for the Scientific Study of Religion, 32,* 256–68.

Kirschenman, J. and Neckerman, K. M. (1991). "We'd love to hire them, but . . ." The meaning of race for employers. In C. Jencks and P. E. Peterson (eds.), *The urban underclass* (pp. 203–32). Washington, DC: Brookings Institution.

Kiselica, M. and Maben, P. (1999). Do multicultural education and diversity appreciation training reduce prejudice among counseling trainees? *Journal of Mental Health Counseling, 21,* 240–54.

Kite, M. E. and Deaux, K. (1986). Attitudes toward homosexuality: Assessment and behavioral consequences. *Basic and Applied Social Psychology, 7,* 137–62.

Kite, M. E. and Whitley, B. E., Jr. (1998). Do heterosexual women and men differ in their attitudes toward homosexuality? A conceptual and methodological analysis. In G. M. Herek (ed.), *Stigma and sexual orientation: Understanding prejudice against lesbians, gay men, and bisexuals* (pp. 39–61). Thousand Oaks, CA: Sage.

Klara, R. (2000). Don't ask don't tell. *Restaurant Business, 99* (2), 30–6.

Kleck, R. and DeJong, W. (1983). Physical disability, physical attractiveness, and social outcomes in children's small groups. *Rehabilitation Psychology, 28,* 79–103.

Kleiman, L. S. and Faley, R. H. (1988). Voluntary affirmative action and preferential treatment: Legal and research implications. *Personnel Psychology, 41,* 481–96.

Klein, M. H., Hyde, J. S., Essex, M. J., and Clark, R. (1998). Maternity leave, role quality, work involvement, and mental health one year after delivery. *Psychology of Women Quarterly, 22,* 239–66.

Kluegel, J. R. and Smith, E. R. (1986). *Beliefs about inequality: Americans' views of what is and what ought to be.* New York: Aldine De Gruyter.

Knapp, D. E., Faley, R. H., Ekeberg, W. C., and Dubois, C. L. Z. (1997). Determinants of target responses to sexual harassment: A conceptual framework. *Academy of Management Review, 22* (3), 687–729.

Knight, D., Pearce, C., Smith, K., Olian, J., Sims, H., Smith, K. A., and Flood, P. (1999). Top management team diversity, group process, and strategic consensus. *Strategic Management Journal, 20,* 445–65.

Kochman, T. (1974). Orality and literacy as factors of "Black" and "White" communicative behavior. *International Journal of the Sociology of Language, 3,* 91–115.

Kochman, T. (1981). *Black and White styles in conflict.* Chicago, IL: University of Chicago Press.

Kolb, D., Fletcher, J., Meyerson, D., Merrill-Sands, D., and Ely, R. (1998). *Making change: A framework for promoting gender equity in organizations* (CGO Insights, No. 1). Boston, MA: Simmons Graduate School of Management, Center for Gender in Organizations.

Kolb, D. and Merrill-Sands, D. (1999). Waiting for outcomes: Anchoring a dual agenda for change to cultural assumptions. *Women in Management Review, 14* (5), 194–202.

Konrad, A. M. and Linnehan, F. (1995a). Formalized HRM structures: Coordinating equal employment opportunity or concealing organizational practices? *Academy of Management Journal, 38,* 787–820.

Konrad, A. M. and Linnehan, F. (1995b). Race and sex differences in line managers' reactions to equal employment opportunity and affirmative action interventions. *Group and Organization Management, 20,* 408–38.

Konrad, A. M. and Linnehan, F. (1999). Affirmative action: History, effects, and attitudes. In G. N. Powell (ed.), *Handbook of gender and work* (pp. 429–74). Thousand Oaks, CA: Sage.

Korabik, K. and Rosin, H. M. (1995). The impact of children on women managers' career behavior and organizational commitment. *Human Resource Management, 34,* 513–28.

Korunka, C., Weiss, A., and Karetta, B. (1993). Effects of new technologies with special regard for the implementation process per se. *Journal of Organizational Behavior, 14* (4), 331–48.

Koss, M. P., Goodman, L. A., Browne, A., Fitzgerald, L. F., Keita, G. P., and Russo, N. F. (1994). *No safe haven: Violence against women at home, at work, and in the community.* Washington, DC: American Psychological Association.

Kossek, E. E. and Lobel, S. A. (1996). Introduction: Transforming human resource systems to manage diversity – An introduction and orienting framework. In E. E. Kossek and S. A. Lobel (eds.), *Managing diversity: Human resource strategies for transforming the workplace* (pp. 1–19). Cambridge, MA: Blackwell.

Kossek, E. E. and Nichol, V. (1992). The effects of on-site child care on employee attitudes and performance. *Personnel Psychology, 45,* 485–509.

Kossek, E. E. and Ozeki, C. (1998). Work–family conflict, policies, and the job–life satisfaction relationship: A review and directions for organizational behavior–human resources research. *Journal of Applied Psychology, 83* (2), 139–49.

Kossek, E. E. and Zonia, S. C. (1993). Assessing diversity climate: A field study of reactions to employer efforts to promote diversity. *Journal of Organizational Behavior, 14,* 61–81.

Kossek, E. E., Zonia, S. C., and Young, W. (1995). The limitations of organizational demography. Paper presented at the conference "Work team dynamics and productivity in the context of diversity," Center for Creative Leadership and American Psychological Association, Greensboro, NC.

Kotter, J. P. (1995a). *The new rules: How to succeed in today's post-corporate world.* New York: Free Press.

Kotter, J. P. (1995b). Leading change: Why transformation efforts fail. *Harvard Business Review,* March–April, 59–67.

Kovach, K. A. and Millspaugh, P. E. (1996). Employment Nondiscrimination Act: On the cutting edge of public policy. *Business Horizons, 39,* 65–73.

Kraiger, K. and Ford, J. K. (1985). A meta-analysis of ratee race effects in performance ratings. *Journal of Applied Psychology, 70,* 56–65.

Kram, K. E. (1985). *Mentoring at work: Developmental relationships in organizational life.* Glenview, IL: Scott, Foresman.

Kram, K. E. and Hall, D. T. (1996). Mentoring in a context of diversity and turbulence. In E. E. Kossek and S. A. Lobel (eds.), *Managing diversity: Human resource strategies for transforming the workplace* (pp. 108–36). Cambridge, MA: Blackwell.

Kravitz, D. A. and Platania, J. (1993). Attitudes and beliefs about affirmative action: Effects of target and respondent sex and ethnicity. *Journal of Applied Psychology, 78,* 928–38.

Krulewitz, J. E. and Nash, J. E. (1980). Effects of sex role attitudes and similarity on men's rejection of male homosexuals. *Journal of Personality and Social Psychology, 38,* 67–74.

Kuczynski, S. (1999). If diversity, then higher profits? *HR Magazine, 44* (13), 66–74.

LaCroix, A. Z. and Haynes, S. G. (1987). Gender differences in the health effects of workplace roles. In R. C. Barnett, L. Biener, and G. K. Baruch (eds.), *Gender and stress* (pp. 96–121). New York: Free Press.

LaFromboise, T., Coleman, H., and Gerton, J. (1993). Psychological impact of biculturalism: Evidence and theory. *Psychological Bulletin, 114,* 395–412.

Lambert, S. (2000). Added benefits: The link between work–life benefits and organizational citizenship behavior. *Academy of Management Journal, 43* (5), 801–15.

Landau, J. (1995). The relationship of race and gender to managers' ratings of promotion potential. *Journal of Organizational Behavior, 16,* 391–400.

Larkin, J. C. and Pines, H. A. (1979). No fat persons need apply. *Sociology of Work and Occupations, 6,* 312–27.

Larson, R. W. and Almeida, D. M. (1999). Emotional transmission in the daily lives of families: A new paradigm for studying family process. *Journal of Marriage and the Family, 61*, 5–20.

Lau, D. C. and Murnighan, J. K. (1998). Demographic diversity and faultlines: The compositional dynamics of organizational groups. *Academy of Management Review, 23*, 325–40.

Lawler, E. E., III, and Finegold, D. (2000). Individualizing the organization: Past, present, and future. *Organizational Dynamics, 29*, 1–15.

Lawlor, J. (1994). Executive exodus. *Working Woman*, November, 39–87.

Lawrence, B. S. (1997). The black box of organizational demography. *Organizational Science, 8*, 1–22.

Lazarus, R. S. and Folkman, S. (1984). *Stress, appraisal, and coping.* New York: Springer.

Lee, J. A. and Clemmons, T. (1985). Factors affecting employment decisions about older workers. *Journal of Applied Psychology, 70*, 785–8.

Lefkowitz, J. (1994). Race as a factor in job placement: Serendipitous findings of ethnic drift. *Personnel Psychology, 47*, 497–513.

Leland, J. and Beals, G. (1997). In living colors. *Newsweek, 129* (18), 58–60.

Lenihan, R. (1998). McCann-Erikson, Peter Kim named in anti-gay bias lawsuit; at least $1 Mil. in damages sought. *Adweek (Eastern Edn.), 39* (10), 3.

Levin, G. (1993). Mainstream's domino effect. *Advertising Age, 64* (3), 30, 32.

Lewan, L. S. (1990). Diversity in the workplace. *HR Magazine, 35* (6), 42–5.

Lewin, K. (1951). *Field theory in social science.* New York: Harper Row.

Lichtenstein, R., Alexander, J., Jinnett, K., and Ullman, E. (1997). Embedded intergroup relations in interdisciplinary teams: Effects on perceptions of level of team integration. *Journal of Applied Behavioral Science, 33*, 413–34.

Liff, S. (1999). Diversity and equal opportunities: Room for a constructive compromise? *Human Resource Management Journal, 9* (1), 65–75.

Lin, N. (1990). Social resources and social mobility: A structural theory of status attainment. In R. L. Breiger (ed.), *Social mobility and social structure* (pp. 247–71). New York: Cambridge University Press.

Linnehan, F., Chrobot-Mason, D., and Konrad, A. M. (2002). The importance of ethnic identity to attitudes, subjective norms and behavioral intentions toward diversity. Paper presented at the annual meeting of the Academy of Management, Denver, CO.

Linnehan, F. and Konrad, A. M. (1999). Diluting diversity. Implications for intergroup inequality in organizations. *Journal of Management Inquiry, 8* (4), 399–414.

Linnehan, F., Konrad, A. M., Reitman, F., Greenhalgh, A., and London, M. (in press). Behavioral goals for a diverse organization: The effects of attitudes, social norms, and racial identity for Asian Americans and Whites. *Journal of Applied Social Psychology.*

Litvin, D. R. (2000). *Defamiliarizing diversity.* Unpublished doctoral dissertation, University of Massachusetts, Amherst.

Lobel, S. A. (1999). Impacts of diversity and work–life initiatives in organizations. In G. N. Powell (ed.), *Handbook of gender and work* (pp. 453–74). Thousand Oaks, CA: Sage.

Locke, M. (2001). Prospect of war brings military policy on gays "into sharper focus." Retrieved October 20, 2001, from http://www.gaymilitary.ucsb.edu/ResearchResources/NewsMagArticlesHome.htm

Loden, M. (1996). *Implementing diversity: Best practices for making diversity work in your organization.* Chicago, IL: McGraw-Hill.

Loden, M. and Rosener, J. (1991). *Workforce America: Managing employee diversity as vital resource.* Homewood, IL: Business One Irwin.

Logan, J. R., Ward, R., and Spitze, G. (1992). As old as you feel: Age identity in middle and later life. *Social Forces, 71* (2), 451–67.

Loprest, P. (1999). *Families who left welfare? Who are they and how are they doing?* Washington, DC: Urban Institute.

Loprest, P. (2001). *How are families that left welfare doing? A comparison of early and recent welfare leavers.* Series B, no. B–36. Washington, DC: Urban Institute.

Lott, B. (2002). Cognitive and behavioral distancing from the poor. *American Psychologist, 57,* 100–10.

Lott, B. and Maluso, D. (eds.) (1995). *The social psychology of interpersonal discrimination.* New York: Guilford Press.

Louw, L. (1995). Chapter in L. B. Griggs and L. Louw (eds.), *Valuing diversity: New tools for a new reality.* New York: McGraw-Hill.

Loy, P. H. and Stewart, L. P. (1984). The extent and effects of the sexual harassment of working women. *Sociological Focus, 17* (1), 31–43.

Lu, D. (1987). *Inside corporate Japan.* Cambridge, MA: Productivity Press.

Lutz, A. (1940). *Created equal.* New York: John Day.

Lyness, K. S. and Judiesch, M. (1999). Are women more likely to be hired or promoted into management positions? *Journal of Vocational Behavior, 54* (1), 158–73.

Lyness, K. S. and Thompson, D. E. (1997). Above the glass ceiling? A comparison of matched samples of female and male executives. *Journal of Applied Psychology, 82* (3), 359–75.

Lyness, K. S. and Thompson, D. E. (2000). Climbing the corporate ladder: Do female and male executives follow the same route? *Journal of Applied Psychology, 85* (1), 86–101.

McCall, M. W., Jr., Lombardo, M. M., and Morrison, A. M. (1988). *The lessons of experience: How successful executives develop on the job.* Lexington, MA: Lexington Books.

McCambley, E. (1999). Testing theory by practice. In A. J. Murrell, F. J. Crosby, and R. J. Ely (eds.), *Mentoring dilemmas* (pp. 173–88). Mahwah, NJ: Lawrence Erlbaum Associates.

McCammon, H. J. and Griffin, L. J. (2000). Workers and their customers and clients: An editorial introduction. *Work and Occupations, 27,* 278–93.

McCauley, C. D., Ruderman, M. N., Ohlott, P. J., and Morrow, J. E. (1994). Assessing the developmental components of managerial jobs. *Journal of Applied Psychology, 79* (4), 544–60.

McClelland, D. C. (1961). *The achieving society.* New York: Free Press.

McConahay, J. B. (1983). Modern racism and modern discrimination: The effects of race, racial attitudes, and context on simulated hiring decisions. *Personality and Social Psychology Bulletin, 9,* 551–8.

McConahay, J. B. (1986). Modern racism, ambivalence, and the modern racism scale. In J. F. Dovidio and S. L. Gaertner (eds.), *Prejudice, discrimination, and racism.* Orlando, FL: Academic Press.

McCormack, V. and McCormack, I. (1994). Equalizing advantages, lessening discrimination: Reviewing Northern Ireland's fair employment laws. *Review of Employment Topics. Labour Relations Agency, 2* (1), 36–55.

McDaniel, R. R. and Walls, M. E. (1997). Diversity as a management strategy for organizations: A view through the lenses of chaos and quantum theories. *Journal of Management Inquiry, 6,* 363–75.

MacDermid, S. M. and Williams, M. L. (1997). A within-industry comparison of employed mothers' experiences in small and large workplaces. *Journal of Family Issues, 18*, 545–66.

MacDonald, A. P., Jr., Huggins, J., Young, S., and Swanson, R. A. (1973). Attitudes toward homosexuality: Preservation of sex morality or the double standard? *Journal of Consulting and Clinical Psychology, 40*, 161–70.

McEnrue, M. P. (1993). Managing diversity: Los Angeles before and after the riots. *Organizational Dynamics, 21* (3), 18–29.

McEvoy, G. M. and Cascio, W. F. (1989). Cumulative evidence of the relationship between employee age and job performance. *Journal of Applied Psychology, 74*, 11–17.

MacEwen, K. E. and Barling, J. (1994). Daily consequences of work interference with family and family interference with work. *Work and Stress, 8*, 244–54.

McFarland, S. G. (1989). Religious orientation and targets of discrimination. *Journal for the Scientific Study of Religion, 28*, 324–36.

McGrath, J. E. (1998). A view of group composition through a group-theoretic lens. In M. A. Neale, E. A. Mannix, and D. H. Gruenfeld (eds.), *Research on managing groups and teams*, vol. 1 (pp. 255–72). Greenwich, CT: JAI Press.

McGuire, G. M. (1999). Do race and sex affect employees' access to and help from mentors? Insights from the study of a large corporation. In A. J. Murrell, F. J. Crosby, and R. J. Ely (eds.), *Mentoring dilemmas: Developmental relationships within multicultural organizations* (pp. 105–20). Mahwah, NJ: Lawrence Erlbaum Associates.

McGuire, G. M. (2000). Gender, race, ethnicity, and networks: The factors affecting the status of employees' network members. *Work and Occupations*, November, 500–23.

McIntosh, P. (1993). White privilege and male privilege: A personal account of coming to see correspondences through work in women's studies. In A. Minas (ed.), *Gender Basics*. Belmont, CA: Wadsworth.

McKee, A. and Schor, S. (1999). Confronting prejudice and stereotypes: A teaching model. *Performance Improvement Quarterly, 12* (1), 181–99.

McKinnon, J. and Humes, K. (1999). The Black population in the United States. *Current Population Reports*. Washington, DC: US Census Bureau.

McLaughlin, M. E., Bell, M. P., and Stringer, D. Y. (in press). Stigma and acceptance of coworkers with disabilities: Understudied aspects of workforce diversity. *Group and Organization Management*.

McLeod, P. L., Lobel, S. A., and Cox, T., Jr. (1996). Ethnic diversity and creativity in small groups. *Small Group Research, 27*, 248–64.

McLoyd, V. C. (1998). Socioeconomic disadvantage and child development. *American Psychologist, 53*, 185–204.

McWhirter, E. H. (1997). Perceived barriers to education and career: Ethnic and gender differences. *Journal of Vocational Behavior, 50*, 124–40.

Maddox, G. L., Back, K., and Liederman, V. (1968). Overweight as social deviance and disability. *Journal of Health and Social Behavior, 9*, 287–98.

Magley, V. J., Hulin, C. L., Fitzgerald, L. F., and DeNardo, M. (1999). Outcomes of self-labeling sexual harassment. *Journal of Applied Psychology, 84*, 390–402.

Maranto, C. L. and Stenoien, A. F. (2000). Weight discrimination: A multidisciplinary analysis. *Employee Responsibilities and Rights Journal, 12*, 9–24.

Marin, G. and Marin, B. V. (1991). *Research with Hispanic populations*. Newbury Park, CA: Sage.

Marks, S. R. and MacDermid, S. M. (1996). Multiple roles and the self: A theory of role balance. *Journal of Marriage and the Family, 58*, 417–32.

Markus, H. R. and Kitayama, S. (1991a). Culture and the self: Implications for cognition, emotion, and motivation. *Psychological Review, 98*, 224–53.

Markus, H. R. and Kitayama, S. (1991b). Cultural variation and self-concept. In G. R. Goethals and J. Strauss (eds.), *Multidisciplinary perspectives on the self* (pp. 18–48). New York: Springer-Verlag.

Marshall, K. (2001). Part-time by choice. *Perspective on labour and income. Statistics Canada, 13* (1), 20–7.

Martens, M. F. J., Nijhuis, F. J. N., Van Boxtel, M. P. J., and Knottnerus, J. A. (1999). Flexible work schedules amd mental and physical health: A study of a working population with non-traditional working hours. *Journal of Organizational Behavior, 20* (1), 35–46.

Martin, C. J. (1994). Protecting overweight workers against discrimination: Is disability or appearance the real issue? *Employee Relations Law Journal, 20* (1), 133–42.

Martin, K., Leary, M., and Rejeshi, W. (2000). Self-presentational concerns in older adults: Implications for health and well-being. *Basic and Applied Social Psychology, 22* (3), 169–80.

Martin, L. (1989). The greying of Japan. *Population Bulletin, 44* (2), 2–42.

Martin, L. (1991). *A report on the glass ceiling initiative.* Washington, DC: US Department of Labor.

Martin, P. Y. (1992). Gender, interaction, and inequality in organizations. In C. L. Ridgeway (ed.), *Gender, interaction, and inequality* (pp. 208–31). New York: Springer-Verlag.

Martineau, J. W. and Preskill, H. (2002). Evaluating the impact of organization development interventions. In J. Waclawski and A. H. Church (eds.), *Organization development: A data-driven approach to organizational change* (pp. 286–301). San Francisco, CA: Jossey-Bass.

Mateyaschuk, J. (1999). Gender gap is smaller in technology. *Information Week*, April 26: 54.

Mattis, M. (2001). Advancing women in business organizations. *Journal of Management Development, 20*, 371–88.

Matuszek, P. A. C., Nelson, D. L., and Quick, J. C. (1995). Gender differences in distress: Are we asking all the right questions? *Gender in the Workplace, 10* (6), 99–120.

Mays, V. M. (1995). Black women, work stress, and perceived discrimination: The focused support group model as an intervention for stress reduction. *Cultural Diversity and Mental Health, 1* (1), 53–65.

Mays, V. M., Coleman, L. M., and Jackson, J. S. (1996). Perceived race-based discrimination, employment status, and job stress in a national sample of black women: Implications for health outcomes. *Journal of Occupational Health Psychology, 1* (3), 319–29.

Melamed, S., Ben-Avi, I., Luz, J., and Green, M. S. (1995a). Objective and subjective work monotony: Effects of job satisfaction, psychological distress, and absenteeism in blue-collar workers. *Journal of Applied Psychology, 80* (1), 29–42.

Melamed, S., Ben-Avi, I., Luz, J., and Green, M. S. (1995b). Repetitive work, work underload and coronary heart disease risk factors among blue-collar workers: The Cordis study. *Journal of Psychosomatic Research, 39* (1), 19–29.

Melamed, S., Fried, Y., and Froom, P. (2001). The interactive effect of chronic exposure to noise and job complexity on changes in blood pressure and job satisfaction: A longitudinal study of industrial employees. *Journal of Occupational Health Psychology, 6* (3), 182–95.

Melamed, S., Kristal-Boneh, E., Harari, G., Froom, P., and Ribak, J. (1998). Variation in the ambulatory blood pressure response to daily work load: The moderating role of job control. *Scandinavian Journal of Work, Environment, and Health, 24* (3), 190–6.

Melamed, T. (1995). Career success: The moderating effect of gender. *Journal of Vocational Behavior, 47*, 35–60.

Melaugh, M. (1995). Majority–minority differentials: Unemployment, housing, and health. In S. Dunn (ed.), *Facets of the conflict in Northern Ireland*. Basingstoke, UK: Macmillan. http://cain.ulst.ac.uk/issues/discrimination/melaugh.htm

Mergenhagen, P. (1997). Enabling disabled workers. *American Demographics, 19*, 36–42.

Meritor Sav. Bank, FSB v. Vinson, 477 US 57 (1986).

Merrill-Sands, D. (1998). Moving towards gender equity: Strategies for change. Paper presented at the Inter-Center Consultation on Gender Staffing: Lessons Learned and Future Directions (ISNAR), April 28–30, The Hague.

Merrill-Sands, D., Fletcher, J., and Acosta, A. (1999). Engendering organizational change: A case study of strengthening gender-equity and organizational effectiveness in an international agricultural research institute. In A. Rao, R. Stuart, and D. Kelleher (eds.), *Gender at work: Organizational change for equality* (pp. 77–128). West Hartford, CT: Kumarian Press.

Merrill-Sands, D., Fletcher, J., Acosta, A., Andrews, N., and Harvey, M. (1999). *Engendering organizational change: A case study of strengthening gender equity and organizational effectiveness at CIMMYT* (CGIAR Gender Staffing Program, Working Paper no. 20). Washington, DC: World Bank, CGIAR Secretariat.

Messick, D. M. and Brewer, M. B. (1983). Solving social dilemmas: A review. In L. Wheeler and P. Shaver (eds.), *Review of personality and social psychology*, vol. 4. Beverly Hills, CA: Sage.

Meyer, J. (2001). *Age 2000: Census 2000 brief*. Washington, DC: US Census Bureau.

Meyers, M. K., Han, W. J., Waldfogel, J., and Garnfinkel, I. (2001). Child care in the wake of welfare reform: The impact of government subsidies on the economic well-being of single-mother families. *Social Service Review*, 29–59.

Meyerson, D. E. and Fletcher, J. K. (2000). A modest manifesto for shattering the glass ceiling. *Harvard Business Review, 78* (1), 127–36.

Meyerson, D. E. and Scully, M. A. (1995). Tempered radicalism and the politics of ambivalence and change. *Organization Science, 6*, 585–600.

Meyerson, D. E. and Scully, M. A. (1999). *Tempered radicalism: Changing the workplace from within* (CGO Insights no. 6). Boston, MA: Simmons Graduate School of Management Center for Gender in Organizations.

Michael, R. T., Gagnon, J. H., Laumann, E. O., and Kolata, G. (1994). *Sex in America: A definitive survey*. New York: Warner Books.

Milkovich, G. and Gomez, L. R. (1976). Child care and selected work behaviors. *Academy of Management Journal, 19*, 111–15.

Miller, F. A. (1998). Strategic culture change: The door to achieving high performance and inclusion. *Public Personnel Management, 27*, 151–61.

Miller, F. A. and Katz, J. H. (1995). Cultural diversity as a developmental process: The path from monocultural club to inclusive organization. In J. Pfeiffer (ed.), *The 1995 Annual: Volume 2, Consulting* (pp. 267–81). San Diego, CA: Pfeiffer.

Miller, F. A. and Katz, J. H. (2002). *The inclusion breakthrough: Unleashing the real power of diversity*. San Francisco, CA: Berrett-Koehler.

Milliken, F. J. and Martins, L. L. (1996). Searching for common threads: Understanding the multiple effects of diversity in organizational groups. *Academy of Management Review, 21* (2), 402–33.

Minehan, M. (1997). The aging baby boomers. *HR Magazine, 42* (4), 208.

Mink, G. (1999). Aren't poor single mothers women? Feminists, welfare reform, and welfare justice. In G. Mink (ed.), *Whose welfare?* (pp. 171–88). Ithaca, NY: Cornell University Press.

Mink, G. (2002). Valuing women's work. In *From poverty to punishment: How welfare reform punishes the poor* (pp. 139–47). Oakland, CA: Applied Research Center.

Mirchandani, K. (1999). Legitimizing work: Telework and the gendered reification of the work–nonwork dichotomy. *CRSA/RCSA, 36* (1), 87–107.

Moe, J. L., Nacoste, R. W., and Insko, C. A. (1981). Belief versus race as determinants of discrimination: A study of Southern adolescents in 1966 and 1979. *Journal of Personality and Social Psychology, 41,* 1031–50.

Moore, D. P. and Buttner, E. H. (1997). *Women entrepreneurs: Moving beyond the glass ceiling.* Thousand Oaks, CA: Sage.

Mor-Barak, M. E. (2000). The inclusive workplace: An ecosystem approach to diversity management. *Social Work, 45,* 339–52.

Mor-Barak, M. E. and Cherin, D. A. (1998). A tool to expand organizational understanding of workforce diversity: Exploring a measure of inclusion–exclusion. *Administration in Social Work, 22,* 47–64.

Mor-Barak, M. E., Cherin, D., and Berkman, S. (1998). Organizational and personal dimensions in diversity climate: Ethnic and gender differences in employee perceptions. *Journal of Applied Behavioral Science, 34,* 82–104.

Morgan, R. (2002). Fire guts home of professor at U. of Montana days after she sues for domestic-partner benefits. *Chronicle of Higher Education.* Retrieved February 11, 2002, from http://chronicle.com/daily/2002/02/2002021104n.htm

Morin, S. F. and Garfinkle, E. M. (1978). Male homophobia. *Journal of Social Issues, 34,* 29–47.

Morishima, M. (1982). *Why has Japan succeeded? Western technology and the Japanese ethos.* Cambridge: Cambridge University Press.

Morrison, A. M. (1992). *The new leaders: Guidelines on leadership diversity in America.* San Francisco, CA: Jossey-Bass.

Morrison, A. M. (1994). Building diversity. *Executive Excellence, 11* (10), 17–18.

Morrison, A. M. (1996). *Leadership diversity in America: New leaders.* San Francisco, CA: Jossey-Bass.

Morrison, A. M. and Von Glinow, M. A. (1990). Women and minorities in management. *American Psychologist, 45* (2), 200–8.

Morrison, A. M., White, R. P., Van Velsor, E., and the Center for Creative Leadership (1992). *Breaking the glass ceiling: Can women reach the top of America's largest corporations?* Reading, MA: Addison Wesley.

Morrison, E. W. and Herlihy, J. M. (1992). Becoming the best place to work: Managing diversity at American Express Travel related services. In S. E. Jackson and Associates (eds.), *Diversity in the workplace* (pp. 203–26). New York: Guilford Press.

Morrow, P. C., McElroy, J. C., Stamper, B. G., and Wilson, M. A. (1990). The effects of physical attractiveness and other demographic characteristics on promotion decisions. *Journal of Management, 16,* 723–36.

Murrell, A. J. (1996). Sexual harassment and women of color: Issues, challenges, and future directions. In M. S. Stockdale (ed.), *Sexual harassment in the workplace,* vol. 5 (pp. 51–66). Thousand Oaks, CA: Sage.

Murrell, A. J. and Tangri, S. S. (1999). Mentoring at the margin. In A. J. Murrell, F. J. Crosby, and R. J. Ely (eds.), *Mentoring dilemmas: Developmental relationships within multicultural organizations* (pp. 211–24). Mahwah, NJ: Lawrence Erlbaum Associates.

Murrell, A. J., Crosby, F. J., and Ely, R. (eds.) (1999). *Mentoring dilemmas: Developmental relationships within multicultural organizations.* Mahwah, NJ: Lawrence Erlbaum Associates.

Myers, S. L. (2000). Survey of troops finds antigay bias common in service. *New York Times*, March 25. Retrieved September 9, 2000, from http://www.nytimes.com

Naff, K. (1998). Progress toward achieving a representative federal bureaucracy: The impact of supervisors and their beliefs. *Public Personnel Management, 27*, 135–50.

Narayanan, L., Menon, S., and Spector, P. E. (1999). Stress in the workplace: A comparison of gender and occupations. *Journal of Organizational Behavior, 20*, 63–73.

Nash, D. (2000). Understanding dominance and subordination: One White man's experience. *Diversity Factor*, spring, 8–12.

National Center for Education Statistics (NCES) (2000). *Low-income students: Who are they and how do they pay for their education?* NCES 2000–169. Washington, DC: Author.

National Center for Education Statistics (2001). *Dropout rates in the United States: 2000.* NCES 2002–114. Washington, DC: Author.

National Institute for Occupational Safety and Health (NIOSH) (1996). *Violence in the workplace.* DHHS (NIOSH) 96–100. Cincinnati, OH: National Institute for Occupational Safety and Health.

National Institute for Occupational Safety and Health (NIOSH) (2001). *Fact sheet: Women's safety and health issues at work.* DHHS (NIOSH) 2001–123. Cincinnati, OH: National Institute for Occupational Safety and Health.

National University (1995). 1995 Global Cultural Diversity Conference Proceedings, Sydney. http://www.immi.gov.au/multicultura/confer/speech7a.htm

Neckerman, K. M. and Kirschenman, J. (1991). Hiring strategies, racial bias, and inner-city workers. *Social Problems, 38*, 433–47.

Nelson, D. L. and Hitt, M. A. (1992). Employed women and stress: Implications for enhancing women's mental health in the workplace. In J. C. Quick, L. R. Murphy, and J. J. Hurrell (eds.), *Stress and well-being at work: Assessments and interventions for occupational mental health.* Washington, DC: American Psychological Association.

Nelson, D. L., Quick, J. C., and Simmons, B. L. (2001). Preventive management of work stress: Current themes and future challenges. In A. Baum, T. A. Revenson, and J. E. Singer (eds.), *Handbook of health psychology* (pp. 349–63). Mahwah, NJ: Lawrence Erlbaum Associates.

Nelson, E. S. and Kreiger, S. L. (1997). Changes in attitudes toward homosexuality in college students: Implementation of a gay men and lesbian peer panel. *Journal of Homosexuality, 33*, 63–81.

Nelson, T. D. (2001). *The psychology of prejudice.* Boston, MA: Allyn and Bacon.

Nesiah, D. (1997). *Discrimination with reason? The policy of reservations in the United States, India and Malaysia.* Delhi: Oxford University Press.

Neville, H. A., Roderick, L. L., Duran, G., Lee, R. M., and Browne, L. (2000). Construction and initial validation of the Color-Blind Racial Attitudes Scale (CoBRAS). *Journal of Counseling Psychology, 47*, 59–70.

New Zealand, Statistics (2001). http://www.stats.govt.nz

Newman, B. S. (1989). The relative importance of gender role attitudes to male and female attitudes toward lesbians. *Sex Roles, 21*, 451–65.

Newport, F. (2001). American attitudes toward homosexuality continue to become more tolerant: New Gallop poll shows continuation of slow, but steady, liberalization of attitudes. Retrieved November 29, 2001, from the Gallop Organization website: http://www.gallop.com/poll/releases/pr010604.asp

Ng, E. S. and Tung, R. L. (1998). Ethno-cultural diversity and organizational effectiveness: A field study. *International Journal of Human Resource Management, 9*, 980–95.

NOD/Harris (2000). Survey of Americans with disabilities. Washington, DC: National Organization on Disability.

Northwestern National Life (1991). *Employee burnout: America's newest epidemic.* Minneapolis, MN: Northwestern National Life.

O'Connor, A. (2000). Poverty research and policy for the post-reform era. *Annual Review of Sociology, 26,* 547–62.

O'Flynn, J., Fisher, N., Sammartino, A., Lau, K., Ricciotti, A., and Nicholas, S. (2001). The Diversity Dividend. *HR Monthly,* June, 34–7.

O'Hanlan, K. A., Robertson, P., Cabaj, R. P., Schatz, B., and Nemrow, P. (1996). Homophobia is a health hazard. *USA Today Magazine, 235,* 26–30.

O'Neill, R., Horton, S., and Crosby, F. J. (1999). Gender and developmental relationships. In A. Murrell, F. Crosby, and R. Ely (eds.), *Mentoring dilemmas* (pp. 63–80). Mawah, NJ: Lawrence Erlbaum Associates.

O'Reilly, C. A., III, Caldwell, D. F., and Barnett, W. P. (1989). Work group demography, social integration, and turnover. *Administrative Science Quarterly, 34,* 21–37.

Offermann, L. R. and Phan, L. U. (2002). Culturally intelligent leadership for a diverse world. In R. E. Riggio, S. E. Murphy, and F. J. Pirozzolo (eds.), *Multiple intelligences and leadership* (pp. 187–214). Mahwah, NJ: Lawrence Erlbaum Associates.

Office of the Under Secretary of Defense (Personnel and Readiness) (1998). Report to the Secretary of Defense: Review of the effectiveness of the application and enforcement of the Department's policy on homosexual conduct in the military. Retrieved November 19, 2001, from www.defenselink.mil/pubs/rpt040798.html

Ogasawara, Y. (1991). *Office ladies and salaried men: Power, gender and work in Japanese companies.* Los Angeles: University of California Press.

Ohlott, P. J., Ruderman, M. N., and McCauley, C. D. (1994). Gender differences in managers' developmental job experiences. *Academy of Management Journal, 37* (1), 46–67.

Okun, B. F., Fried, J., and Okun, M. L. (1999). *Understanding diversity: A learning-as-practice primer.* Pacific Grove, CA: Brooks/Cole.

Olivolo, S. A. (2000). Air Force doc casts doubt on "Don't Ask, Don't Tell." *Boston Herald,* July 22. Retrieved September 9, 2001, from http://www.bostonherald.com

Olson, K. and Pavetti, L. (1997). *Personal and family challenges to the successful transition from welfare to work.* Washington, DC: Urban Institute.

Oncale v. Sundowner Offshore Servs., 523 US 75 (1998).

Oppenheimer, D. B. (1995). Exacerbating the exasperated: Title VII liability of employers for sexual harassment committed by their supervisors. *Cornell Law Review, 81.* Retrieved August 28, 2002, from Lexis–Nexis database.

Ouchi, W. C. (1981). *Theory Z.* Reading, MA: Addison-Wesley.

Owen, G., Shelton, E., Stevens, A. B., Nelson-Christinedaughter, J., Roy, C., and Heineman, J. (2000). *Whose job is it? Employers' views on welfare reform.* Paper presented at the Rural Dimensions of Welfare Reform Conference, Washington, DC.

Ozer, E. M. (1995). The impact of childcare responsibility and self-efficacy on the psychological health of professional working mothers. *Psychology of Women Quarterly, 19* (3), 315–35.

Ozer, E. M., Barnett, R. C., Brennan, R. T., and Sperling, J. (1998). Does child care involvement increase or decrease distress among dual-earner couples. *Women's Health: Research on Gender, Behavior, and Policy, 4* (4), 285–311.

Pagan, J. A. and Davila, A. (1997). Obesity, occupational attainment, and earnings. *Social Science Quarterly, 78,* 756–70.

Palmer, J. (1994). Diversity: Three paradigms. In E. Y. Cross, J. H. Katz, F. A. Miller, and E. W. Seashore (eds.), *The promise of diversity: Over 40 voices discuss strategies for eliminating discrimination in organizations* (pp. 252–8). Burr Ridge, IL: Irwin.

Parham, T. A. and Helms, J. E. (1981). The influence of black students' racial attitudes on preferences for counselor's race. *Journal of Counseling Psychology, 28*, 250–7.

Parker, C. P., Baltes, B. B., and Christiansen, N. D. (1997). Support for affirmative action, justice perceptions, and work attitudes: A study of gender and racial–ethnic group differences. *Journal of Applied Psychology, 82*, 376–89.

Paskoff, S. M. (1996). Ending the workplace diversity wars. *Training, 33*, 43–7.

Pasupathi, M., Carstensen, L. L., and Tsai, J. L. (1995). Ageism in interpersonal settings. In B. Lott and D. Maluso (eds.), *The social psychology of interpersonal discrimination* (pp. 160–82). New York: Guilford Press.

Pelled, L. H. (1996). Demographic diversity, conflict, and work group outcomes: An intervening process theory. *Organizational Science, 7*, 615–31.

Pelled, L. H., Eisenhardt, K. M., and Xin, K. R. (1999). Exploring the black box: An analysis of work group diversity, conflict, and performance. *Administrative Science Quarterly, 44*, 1–28.

Perkins, L. A., Thomas, K. M., and Taylor, G. A. (2000). Advertising and recruitment: Marketing to minorities. *Psychology and Marketing, 17* (3), 235–55.

Perry, E. L. and Bourhis, A. C. (1998). A closer look at the role of applicant age in selection decisions. *Journal of Applied Social Psychology, 28*, 1670–97.

Perry-Jenkins, M., Repetti, R. L., and Crouter, A. C. (2000). Work and family in the 1990s. *Journal of Marriage and the Family, 62*, 981–98.

Personal Responsibility and Work Opportunity Reconciliation Act of 1996 (1997). Pub. L. No. 104–193, 110 Stat. 2105.

Pervin, L. A. (1968). Performance and satisfaction as a function of individual–environment fit. *Psychological Bulletin, 69*, 56–68.

Peters, L. and Terborg, J. R. (1975). The effects of temporal placement of unfavorable information and of attitude similarity on personnel selection decisions. *Organizational Behavior and Human Performance, 13*, 279–93.

Pettigrew, T. and Martin, J. (1987). Shaping the organizational context for black American inclusion. *Journal of Social Issues, 43* (1), 41–78.

Pfeffer, J. (1983). Organizational demography. In B. Staw and L. L. Cummings (eds.), *Research in organizational behavior*, vol. 5 (pp. 299–357). Greenwich, CT: JAI Press.

Phillips, S. D. and Imhoff, A. R. (1997). Women and career development: A decade of research. *Annual Review of Psychology, 48*, 31–51.

Pilkington, N. W. and Lydon, J. E. (1997). The relative effect of attitude similarity and attitude dissimilarity on interpersonal attraction: Investigating the moderating roles of prejudice and group membership. *Personality and Social Psychology Bulletin, 23*, 107–22.

Piltch, C. A., Walsh, D. C., Mangione, T. W., and Jennings, S. E. (1994). Gender, work, and mental distress in an industrial labor force: An expansion of Karasek's job strain model. In G. P. Keita and J. J. Hurrell (eds.), *Job stress in a changing workforce*. Washington, DC: APA.

Pingitore, R., Dugoni, B. L., Tindale, R. S., and Spring, B. (1994). Bias against overweight job applicants in a simulated employment interview. *Journal of Applied Psychology, 79*, 909–17.

Piotrkowski, C. S. (1998). Gender harassment, job satisfaction, and distress among employed white and minority women. *Journal of Occupational Health Psychology, 3* (1), 33–43.

Piven, F. F. (2002).Welfare policy and American politics. In *From poverty to punishment: How welfare reform punishes the poor* (pp. 11–24). Oakland, CA: Applied Research Center.

Polasky, L. J. and Holahan, C. K. (1998). Maternal self-discrepancies, interrole conflict, and negative affect among married professional women with children. *Journal of Family Psychology, 12*, 388–401.

Ponterotto, J. G. and Wise, S. L. (1987). Construct validity study of the Racial Identity Attitude Scale. *Journal of Counseling Psychology, 34*, 218–23.

Population Projections Program (2000). Population Division, US Census Bureau, Washington, DC. Retrieved February 25, 2002, from http://www.census/gov/population/projections/nation/summary/np–t4–d.pdf

Population Reference Bureau (2002). Emerging trends in disability. Retrieved March 11, 2002, from PRB On–Line: www.prb.org

Porter, L. W., Lawler, E. E., and Hackman, J. R. (1975). *Behavior in organizations*. New York: McGraw-Hill.

Potts, J. (1996). Diversity assessment: Telling the story. *Diversity Factor*, summer, 33–9.

Potts, J. (2000). Measuring results. In E. Y. Cross (ed.), *Managing diversity: The courage to lead* (pp. 179–203). Westport, CT: Quorum.

Powell, G. N. (1980). Career development and the woman managers: A social power perspective. *Personnel, 57*, 22–32.

Powell, G. N. (1993). Promoting equal opportunity and valuing cultural diversity. In G. N. Powell (ed.), *Women and men in management* (pp. 225–52). Thousand Oaks, CA: Sage.

Powell, G. N. (1998). Reinforcing and extending today's organizations: The simultaneous pursuit of person–organization fit and diversity. *Organizational Dynamics, 26*, 50–61.

Powell, G. N. and Butterfield, D. A. (1989). The "good manager": Did androgyny fare better in the 1980s? *Group and Organization Studies, 14* (2), 216–33.

Powers, B. (1996). The impact of gay, lesbian, and bisexual workplace issues on productivity. *Journal of Gay and Lesbian Social Services, 4*, 79–90.

Prasad, P., Mills, A., Elmes, M., and Prasad, A. (1997). *Managing the organizational melting pot: Dilemmas of workplace diversity*. Thousand Oaks, CA: Sage.

Pratt, J. (1998). The rise and fall of homophobia and sexual psychopath legislation in postwar society. *Psychology, Public Policy, and Law, 4*, 25–49.

Presser, H. B. (2000). Nonstandard work schedules and marital instability. *Journal of Marriage and the Family, 62* (1), 93–110.

Priem, R., Harrison, D., and Muir, N. (1995). Structured conflict and consensus outcomes in group decision making. *Journal of Management, 21*, 691–710.

Progress of diversity initiatives (2002). Advantica/Denny's. Retrieved March 9, 2002, from http://www.advantica–dine.com

Pulakos, E. and Wexley, K. N. (1983). The relationship among perceptual similarity, sex, and performance ratings in management subordinate dyads. *Academy of Management Journal, 26*, 129–39.

Pyant, C. T. and Yanico, B. J. (1991). Relationship of racial identity and gender-role attitudes to Black women's psychological well-being. *Journal of Counseling Psychology, 38*, 315–22.

Quick, J. C. (1999). Occupational health psychology: The convergence of health and clinical psychology with public health and preventive medicine in an organizational context. *Professional Psychology: Research and Practice, 30* (2), 123–8.

Raber, M. J. (1994). Women in the workplace: Implications for childcare. *Employee Assistance Quarterly, 9* (3–4), 21–36.

Rabidue v. Osceola Ref. Co., Div. Of Texas–American Petrochemicals (CA6 1986), 805 F.2d 611.

Ragins, B. R. (1995). Diversity, power, and mentorship in organizations: A cultural, structural, and behavioral perspective. In M. M. Chemers, S. Oskamp, and M. A. Costanzo (eds.), *Diversity in organizations: New perspectives for a changing workplace* (pp. 91–132). Thousand Oaks, CA: Sage.

Ragins, B. R. (1999). Gender and mentoring relationships: A review and research agenda for the next decade. In G. N. Powell (ed.), *Handbook of gender and work* (pp. 347–70). Thousand Oaks, CA: Sage.

Ragins, B. R. and Cornwell, J. M. (2001). Pink triangles: Antecedents and consequences of perceived workplace discrimination against gay and lesbian employees. *Journal of Applied Psychology, 86,* 1244–61.

Ragins, B. R. and Cotton, J. L. (1991). Easier said than done: Gender differences in perceived barriers to gaining a mentor. *Academy of Management Journal, 34,* 939–51.

Ragins, B. R. and Cotton, J. L. (1999). Mentor functions and outcomes: A comparison of men and women in formal and informal mentoring relationships. *Journal of Applied Psychology, 84* (4), 529–50.

Ragins, B. R., Townsend, B., and Mattis, M. (1998). Gender gap in the executive suite: CEOs and female executives report on breaking the glass ceiling. *Academy of Management Executive, 12* (1), 28–42.

Rao, A., Stuart, R., and Kelleher, D. (1999). *Gender at work: Organizational change for equality.* West Hartford, CT: Kumarian Press.

Rapoport, R. N. (1970). Three dilemmas in action research. *Human Relations, 23,* 488–513.

Rapoport, R. N., Bailyn, L., Fletcher, J. K., and Pruitt, B. (2002). *Beyond work–family balance: Advancing gender equity and workplace performance.* San Francisco, CA: Jossey-Bass.

Register, C. A. and Williams, D. R. (1990). Wage effects of obesity among young workers. *Social Science Quarterly, 71* (1), 130–41.

Repetti, R. L. (1989). Effects of daily workload on subsequent behavior during marital interaction: The roles of social withdrawal and spouse support. *Journal of Personality and Social Psychology, 57,* 651–9.

Repetti, R. L. (1993). Short-term effects of occupational stressors on daily mood and health complaints. *Health Psychology, 12,* 126–31.

Repetti, R. L. (1994). Short-term and long-term processes linking job stressors to father–child interaction. *Social Development, 3* (1), 1–15.

Repetti, R. L. (1998). The promise of a multiple roles paradigm for women's health research. *Women's Health: Research on Gender, Behavior, and Policy, 4,* 273–80.

Repetti, R. L., Matthews, K. A., and Waldron, I. (1989). Employment and women's health: Effects of paid employment on women's mental and physical health. *American Psychologist, 44,* 1394–1401.

Repetti, R. L. and Wood, J. (1997). Effects of daily stress at work on mothers' interactions with preschoolers. *Journal of Family Psychology, 11* (1), 90–108.

Reskin, B. (1998). *The realities of affirmative action in employment.* Washington, DC: American Sociological Association.

Reyes, P. de los (2000). Diversity at work: Paradoxes, possibilities, and problems in the Swedish discourse on diversity. *Economic and Industrial Democracy, 21,* 253–66.

Reynolds, P. C. (1987). Imposing a corporate culture. *Psychology Today, 21* (3), 32–8.

Rhoads, G. K., Singh, J., and Goodell, P. W. (1994). The multiple dimensions of role ambiguity and their impact upon psychological and behavioral outcomes of industrial salespeople. *Journal of Personal Selling and Sales Management, 14* (3), 1–24.

Rice, F. (1996) Denny's changes its spots. *Fortune, 133*, May 13, 133–4.

Rice, J. K. (2001). Poverty, welfare and patriarchy: How macro-level changes in social policy can help low-income women. *Journal of Social Issues, 57*, 355–74.

Richard, O. C. (2000). Racial diversity, business strategy, and firm performance: A resource-based view. *Academy of Management Journal, 43*, 164–77.

Richard, O. C. and Kirby, S. (1997). Attitudes of white American male students toward workforce diversity programs. *Journal of Social Psychology, 137*, 784–6.

Richard, O. C. and Kirby, S. (1999). Organizational justice and the justification of workforce diversity programs. *Journal of Business and Psychology, 14*, 109–18.

Riemer, F. J. (1997). Quick attachments to the workforce: An ethnographic analysis of a transition from welfare to low-wage jobs. *Social Work Research, 21*, 225–32.

Riger, S. and Galligan, P. (1980). Women in management: An exploration of competing paradigms. *American Psychologist, 35*, 902–10.

Riordan, C. M. (2000). Relational demography within groups: Past developments, contradictions, and new directions. In G. R. Ferris (ed.), *Research in personnel and human resource management, 19* (pp. 131–73). New York: Elsevier Science Publishing.

Risser, R. (1993). *Stay out of court: The manager's guide to preventing employees' lawsuits.* Englewood Cliffs, NJ: Prentice-Hall.

Roberson, L. and Gutierrez, N. C. (1992). Beyond good faith: Commitment to recruiting management diversity at Pacific Bell. In S. E. Jackson and Associates (eds.), *Diversity in the workplace* (pp. 65–97). New York: Guilford Press.

Roberson, L., Kulik, C. T., and Pepper, M. B. (2001). Designing effective diversity training: Influence of group composition and trainee experience. *Journal of Organizational Behavior, 22*, 871–85.

Robinson, G. and Dechant, K. (1997). Building a business case for diversity. *Academy of Management Executive, 11* (3), 21–31.

Robinson, K. S. (2000). Temp workers gain union access, *HR News*, October, 1, 12.

Rockquemore, K. A. and Brunsma, D. L. (2002). *Beyond black: Biracial identity in America.* Thousand Oaks, CA: Sage.

Rodin, J., Silberstein, L., and Striegel-Moore, R. (1984). Women and weight: A normative discontent. *Nebraska Symposium on Motivation, 32*, 267–307.

Roehling, M. V. (1999). Weight-based discrimination in employment: Psychological and legal aspects. *Personnel Psychology, 52*, 969–1016.

Romano, M. (1993). Gay rights: Speak up or shut up? *Restaurant Business, 92* (12), 78–89.

Rosen, B. and Jerdee, T. H. (1974). The nature of job-related age stereotypes. *Journal of Applied Psychology, 61* (2), 180–3.

Rosen, B. and Jerdee, T. H. (1979). Coping with affirmative action backlash. *Business Horizons, 22*, 15–22.

Rosenbaum, J. E. (1984). *Career mobility in a corporate hierarchy.* San Diego, CA: Academic Press.

Rosin, H. M. and Korabik, K. (1991). Workplace variables, affective responses, and intentions to leave among women managers. *Journal of Occupational Psychology, 64*, 317–30.

Ross, C. E. and Huber, J. (1985). Hardship and depression. *Journal of Health and Social Behavior, 26*, 312–27.

Ross, C. E. and Mirowsky, J. (1989). Explaining the social patterns of depression: Control and problem solving or support and talking. *Journal of Health and Social Behavior, 30*, 206–19.

Ross, K. (1999). Can diversity and community coexist in higher education? *American Behavioral Scientist, 42*, 1024–40.

Rossilli, G. (1999). EU policy on equality of women. *Feminist Studies, 25* (1), 171–81.

Rothblum, E. D., Brand, R. A., Miller, C. T., and Oetjen, H. A. (1990). The relationship between obesity, employment discrimination, and employment-related victimization. *Journal of Vocational Behavior, 37,* 251–66.

Rothman, R. A. (2002). *Inequality and stratification: Race, class, and gender,* 4th edn. Englewood Cliffs, NJ: Prentice-Hall.

Ruderman, M. N. and Hughes-James, M. W. (1998). Leadership development across race and gender. In C. D. McCauley, R. S. Moxley, and E. Van Velsor (eds.), *The Center for Creative Leadership handbook of leadership development* (pp. 291–335). San Francisco, CA: Jossey-Bass.

Ruderman, M. N., Ohlott, P. J., Panzer, K., and King, S. N. (2002). Benefits of roles for managerial women. *Academy of Management Journal, 45* (2), 369–86.

Rush, L. L. (1998). Affective reactions to multiple social stigmas. *Journal of Social Psychology, 138,* 421–30.

Russo, N. F. and Zierk, K. L. (1992). Abortion, childbearing, and women's well-being. *Professional Psychology: Research and Practice, 23,* 269–80.

Rynes, S. and Rosen, B. (1995). A field survey of factors affecting the adoption and perceived success of diversity training. *Personnel Psychology, 48,* 247–62.

Saad, S. and Sackett, P. R. (2002). Investigating differential prediction by gender in employment-oriented personality measures. *Journal of Applied Psychology, 87,* 667–74.

Sackett, P. R. and Wilk, S. L. (1994). Within-group norming and other forms of score adjustment in preemployment testing. *American Psychologist, 49,* 929–54.

Sacks, P. (1999). *Standardized minds: The high price of America's testing culture and what we can do to change it.* Cambridge, MA: Perseus Publishing.

Sacks, P. (2001). How admissions tests hinder access to graduate and professional schools. *Chronicle of Higher Education,* June 8, B11.

Saenz, D. S. (1994). Token status and problem-solving capability deficits: Detrimental effects of distinctiveness and performance monitoring. *Social Cognition, 12,* 61–74.

Sagrestano, L. M., Heavey, C. L., and Christensen, A. (1998). Theoretical approaches to understanding sex differences and similarities in conflict behavior. In D. Canary and K. Dindia (eds.), *Sex, gender, and communication: Similarities and differences* (pp. 287–302). Mahwah, NJ: Lawrence Erlbaum Associates.

Sako, M. (1997). Introduction: Forces for homogeneity and diversity in the Japanese industrial relations systems. In M. Sako and H. Sato (eds.), *Japanese labor and management in transition* (pp.1–24). New York: Routledge.

Salgado, J. F., Viswesvaran, C., and Ones, D. S. (2001). Predictors used for personnel selection: An overview of constructs, methods and techniques. In N. Anderson, D. S. Ones, H. K. Sinangil, and C. Viswesvaran (eds.), *Handbook of industrial, work and organizational psychology, Vol. 1: Personnel psychology* (pp. 165–99). London: Sage.

Sanchez, J. I. and Brock, P. (1996). Outcomes of perceived discrimination among Hispanic employees: Is diversity management a luxury or a necessity? *Academy of Management Journal, 39* (3), 704–19.

Sanchez, M. (2000). Officials meet with slain soldier's parents. *Kansas City Star,* July 28. Retrieved September 9, 2001, from http://www.kcstar.com/newslibrary/

Santos, S. J., Bohon, L. M., and Sanchez-Sosa, J. J. (1998). Childhood family relationships, marital and work conflict, and mental health distress in Mexican immigrants. *Journal of Community Psychology, 26* (5), 491–508.

Saris, R. N. and Johnston-Robledo, I. (2000). Poor women are still shut out of mainstream psychology. *Psychology of Women Quarterly, 24,* 233–5.

Saso, M. (1990). *Women in the Japanese workplace.* London: H. Shipman.

Sauter, S. L., Hurrell, J. J., Jr., and Cooper, C. L. (eds.) (1989). *Job control and worker health.* New York: Wiley.

Sauter, S. L., Murphy, L. R., and Hurrell, J. J. (1990). Prevention of work-related psychological disorders: A national strategy proposed by the National Institute for Occupational Safety and Health (NIOSH). *American Psychologist, 45* (10), 1146–58.

Scandura, T. A. and Graen, G. B. (1984). Moderating effects of initial leader–member exchange status on the effects of a leadership intervention. *Journal of Applied Psychology, 71,* 579–84.

Scandura, T. A. and Lankau, M. J. (1996). Developing diverse leaders: A leader–member exchange approach. *Leadership Quarterly, 7* (2), 243–63.

Schaubroeck, J. and Jones, J. R. (2000). Antecedents of workplace emotional labor dimensions and moderators of their effects on physical symptoms. *Journal of Organizational Behavior, 21,* 163–83.

Schein, E. H. (1992). *Organizational culture and leadership.* San Francisco, CA: Jossey-Bass.

Schein, V. E. (1973). The relationship between sex role stereotypes and requisite management characteristics. *Journal of Applied Psychology, 57,* 95–100.

Schein, V. E. (1975). Relationships between sex role stereotypes and requisite management characteristics among female managers. *Journal of Applied Psychology, 60,* 340–4.

Schein, V. E., Mueller, R., and Jacobson, C. (1989). The relationship between sex role stereotypes and requisite management characteristics among college students. *Sex Roles, 20* (1/2), 103–10.

Schmerund, A., Sellers, R., Mueller, B., and Crosby, F. (2001). Attitudes toward affirmative action as a function of racial identity among African-American college students. *Political Psychology, 22,* 759–74.

Schneer, J. and Reitman, F. (1995). The impact of gender as managerial careers unfold. *Journal of Vocational Behavior, 47,* 290–315.

Schneider, B. (1987). The people make the place. *Personnel Psychology, 40,* 437–53.

Schneider, C. R. and Anderson, W. (1980). Attitudes toward the stigmatized: Some insights from recent research. *Rehabilitation Counseling Bulletin, 24,* 299–313.

Schneider, K. T., Fitzgerald, L. F., and Swan, S. (1997). Job-related and psychological effects of sexual harassment in the workplace: Empirical evidence from two organizations. *Journal of Applied Psychology, 82* (3), 401–15.

Schneider, K. T., Swan, S., and Fitzgerald, L. F. (1997). Job-related and psychological effects of sexual harassment in the workplace: Empirical evidence from two organizations. *Journal of Applied Psychology, 82* (3), 401–15.

Schneider, S. K. and Northcraft, G. B. (1999). Three social dilemmas of workforce diversity in organizations: A social identity perspective. *Human Relations, 52,* 1445–67.

Schreiber, C. T. (1983). Organizational effectiveness: Implications for the practice of management. In K. Cameron and D. Whetten (eds.), *Organizational effectiveness: A comparison of multiple models.* San Diego, CA: Academic Press.

Schultz, D. and Schultz, S. E. (2002). *Psychology and work today.* Upper Saddle River, NJ: Prentice-Hall.

Schuman, H., Steeh, C., Bobo, L., and Krysan, M. (1997). *Racial attitudes in America: Trends and interpretations.* Cambridge, MA: Harvard University Press.

Schweiger, D. M., Ridley, R. R., and Marini, D. M. (1992). Creating one from two: The merger between Harris Semiconductor and General Electric Solid State. In S. E. Jackson and Associates (eds.), *Diversity in the workplace* (pp. 167–202). New York: Guilford Press.

Scott, J. (1996). *Stratification and power: Structures of class, status, and command*. Cambridge, UK: Polity Press.

Seal, K. (1995). Gay business strengthens hotels in West Hollywood. *Hotel and Motel Management, 210* (7), 6, 15.

Sears, D. O., van Laar, C., Carillo, M., and Kosterman, R. (1997). Is it really racism? The origin of white Americans' opposition to race-targeted policies. *Public Opinion Quarterly, 61*, 16–53.

Seccombe, K. and Ishii-Kuntz, M. (1991). Perceptions of problems associated with aging: Comparisons among four older age cohorts. *Gerontologist, 31*, 527–34.

Seibert, S. E., Kraimer, M. L., and Liden, R. C. (2001). A social capital theory of career success. *Academy of Management Journal, 44*, 219–37.

Seike, A. (1997). Women at work. In M. Sako and H. Sato (eds.), *Japanese labor and management in transition* (pp. 131–50). New York: Routledge.

Sellers, R. M., Rowley, S. A., Chavous, T. M., Shelton, J. N., and Smith, M. A. (1997). Multidimensional Inventory of Black Identity: A preliminary investigation of reliability and construct validity. *Journal of Personality and Social Psychology, 73*, 805–15.

Seltzer, R. (1992). The social location of those holding antihomosexual attitudes. *Sex Roles, 26*, 391–8.

Senge, P. (1990). *The fifth discipline: The art and practice of the learning organization*. New York: Doubleday.

Senge, P., Kleiner, A., Roberts, C., Ross, R., and Smith, B. (1994). *The fifth discipline fieldbook: Strategies and tools for building a learning organization*. New York: Bantam Doubleday.

Servicemembers Legal Defense Network. (2000). Conduct unbecoming: The sixth annual report on "Don't Ask, Don't Tell, Don't Pursue, Don't Harass." Retrieved September 9, 2001, from http://www.sldn.org/templates/law/record.html?record=21

Servicemembers Legal Defense Network (2001). Army publishes first training guide on "Don't Ask, Don't Tell, Don't Pursue, Don't Harass" seven years after policy's implementation. Retrieved September 9, 2001, from http://www.sldn.org/templates/press/record.html?record=382

Sessa, V. I. (1992). Managing diversity at the Xerox Corporation: Balanced workforce goals and caucus groups. In S. E. Jackson and Associates (eds.), *Diversity in the workplace* (pp. 37–64). New York: Guilford Press.

"Sexual harassment in the Fortune 500" (1988). *Working Woman, 13* (12), 69.

Shaffer, M. A., Joplin, J. R. W., Bell, M. P., Lau, T., and Oguz, C. (2000). Gender discrimination and job-related outcomes: A cross-cultural comparison of working women in the United States and China. *Journal of Vocational Behavior, 57*, 395–427.

Shank, R. and Abelson, R. (1977). *Scripts, plans, goals, and understanding: An inquiry into human knowledge structures*. Hillsdale, NJ: Lawrence Erlbaum Associates.

Shaw, J. and Barrett-Power, E. (1998). The effects of diversity on small work group processes and performance. *Human Relations, 51*, 1307–25.

Shaw, L. B., Champlain, D. P., Hartmann, H. I., and Spalter-Roth, R. M. (1993). *The impact of restructuring and the glass ceiling on minorities and women*. Report to the Glass Ceiling Commission. Washington, DC: US Department of Labor.

Sheridan, A. (1995). Affirmative action in Australia – employment statistics. *Women in Management Review, 10* (2), 26–35.

Shofeld, J. W. (1986). Causes and consequences of the colorblind perspective. In J. F. Dovidio and S. L. Gaertner (eds.), *Prejudice, discrimination, and racism* (pp. 231–53). New York: Academic Press.

"SHRM releases new survey of diversity programs" (1998). *Mosaics, 4* (4), 1.

SHRM (2000). *Environmental scan 2000.* Retrieved January, 2002, from http://www/shrm.org/trends/

SHRM (2002). How is a diversity initiative different from my organization's affirmative action plan? Retrieved February 24, 2002, from http://www.shrm.org/diversity/diversityvsaffirmaction.htm

Sikora, M. (2000). Gearing M and A to meet 21st century demands. *Mergers and Acquisitions, 35* (8), 7, 8, 10, 12.

Silverstein, C. (1991). Psychological and medical treatments of homosexuality. In J. C. Gonsiorek and J. D. Weinrich (eds.), *Homosexuality: Research implications for public policy* (pp. 101–14). Newbury Park, CA: Sage.

Simpson, P. A. and Stroh, L. K. (under review). *Emotional labor in the workplace: Differences between men and women.*

Simpson, P. A. and Stroh, L. K. (2002). Revisiting gender variation in training. *Feminist Economist, 9,* 3.

Sinclair, A. (2000). Teaching managers about masculinities: Are you kidding? *Management Learning, 31* (1), 83–101.

Singh, J., Goolsby, J. R., and Rhoads, G. K. (1994). Behavioral and psychological consequences of boundary spanning burnout for customer service representatives. *Journal of Marketing Research, 31,* 558–69.

Sivaramayya, B. (1984). Affirmative action: The schedule castes and scheduled tribes. *International Perspectives on Affirmative Action.* New York: Rockefeller Foundation.

Skedsvold, P. R. and Mann, T. L. (1996). The affirmative action debate: What's fair in policy and programs? Special issue, *Journal of Social Issues, 52* (4).

Slocum, J. W., McGill, M. E., and Lei, D. T. (1994). The new learning strategy: Anytime, anything, anywhere. *Organizational Dynamics, 23,* 33–47.

Smircich L. and Stubbart, C. (1985). Strategic management in an enacted world. *Academy of Management Review, 10* (4), 724–36.

Smith, D. I. (1993). *We the Americans: Women* (WE–8). Washington, DC: US Department of Commerce.

Smith, K. K., Simmons, V., and Thames, T. B. (1989). "Fix the women": An intervention into an organizational conflict based on parallel process thinking. *Journal of Applied Behavioral Science, 25,* 11–29.

Sniderman, P. M. and Tetlock, P. E. (1986). Symbolic racism: Problems of motive attribution in political analysis. *Journal of Social Issues, 42* (2), 129–50.

Snowdon, R. (1996). Virgin's spirit of acceptance. *Marketing, 13.* Retrieved November 29, 2001, from ABI/Inform database (available through the California Digital Library, www.cdlib.org): http://128.48.120.7/mw/mwcgi?sesid=4025412102andZS2.1| CMandCScs=2andCdisplay(1,1cit.txt,abbrev)

Solomon, S., Greenberg, J., and Pyszczynski, T. (1991). A terror management theory of social behavior: The psychological functions of self-esteem and cultural worldviews. In M. P. Zanna (ed.), *Advances in experimental social psychology, 24,* 93–159. San Francisco, CA: Academic Press.

Soni, V. (2000). A twenty-first-century reception for diversity in the public sector: A case study. *Public Administration Review, 60,* 395–408.

South Africa Statistics (1996). Retrieved October 29, 2001, from http://www.statssa.gov.za/census96/html

Spence, J. T. (1985). Achievement American style: The rewards and costs of individualism. *American Psychologist, 40,* 1285–95.

Spielberger, C. D. and Reheiser, E. C. (1994). The job stress survey: Measuring gender differences in occupational stress. *Journal of Social Behavior and Personality, 9* (2), 199–218.

Staffieri, J. R. (1967). A study of social stereotype of body image in children. *Journal of Personality and Social Psychology, 7* (1), 101–4.

Stangor, C., Carr, C., and Kiang, L. (1998). Activating stereotypes undermines task performance expectations. *Journal of Personality and Social Psychology, 75,* 1191–7.

Statistics Canada. (1998). 1996 Census: Ethnic origin, visible minorities. http://www.statcan.ca/Daily/English/980217/d980217.htm

"Statistics on sexual harassment" (1994). Louis Harris and Associates. Retrieved August 18, 2002, from http://www.capstn.com/stats.html

Staw, B. M., Sandelands, L. E., and Dutton, J. E. (1981). Threat-rigidity effects in organizational behavior: A multi-level analysis. *Administrative Science Quarterly, 26,* 501–24.

Steeh, C. and Krysan, M. (1996). Affirmative action and the public, 1970–1995. *Public Opinion Quarterly, 60,* 128–58.

Steele, C. M. and Aronson, J. (1995). Stereotype threat and the intellectual test performance of African Americans. *Journal of Personality and Social Psychology, 69,* 797–811.

Steil, J. M. and Turetsky, B. A. (1987). Is equal better: The relationship between marital equality and psychological symptomatology. In S. Oskamp (ed.), *Applied social psychology annual 7* (pp. 73–97). Newbury Park, CA: Sage.

Stephenson, K. and Krebs, V. (1993). A more accurate way to measure diversity. In B. Abramms and G. Simons (eds.), *The cultural diversity sourcebook* (pp. 247–55). Amherst, MA: ODT.

Stewart, L. D. and Perlow, R. (2001). Applicant race, job status, and racial attitude as predictors of employment discrimination. *Journal of Business and Psychology, 16,* 259–75.

Stockdale, M. S. (1998). The direct and moderating influences of sexual harassment pervasiveness, coping strategies, and gender on work-related outcomes. *Psychology of Women Quarterly, 22* (4), 521–35.

Stockdale, M. S., O'Connor, M., Gutek, B. A., and Geer, T. M. (2002). The relationship between prior sexual abuse and reactions to sexual harassment: Literature review and empirical study. *Psychology, Public Policy and the Law, 8,* 64–95.

Stokols, D., Pelletier, K. R., and Fielding, J. E. (1996). The ecology of work and health: Research and policy directions for the promotion of employee health. *Health Education Quarterly, 23* (2), 137–58.

Stone, D. L. and Colella, A. (1996). A model of factors affecting the treatment of disabled individuals in organizations. *Academy of Management Review, 21,* 352–401.

Stone, D. L. and Stone-Romero, E. F. (2002). The religious underpinnings of social justice conceptions. In S. W. Gilliland, D. D. Steiner, and D. P. Skarlicki (eds.), *Emerging perspectives on managing organizational justice* (pp. 35–75). Greenwich, CT: Information Age Publishing.

Stone, E. F., Stone, D. L., and Dipboye, R. L. (1992). Stigmas in organizations: Race, handicaps, and physical unattractiveness. In K. Kelley (ed.), *Issues, theory, and research in industrial/organizational psychology* (pp. 385–457). Amsterdam, the Netherlands: Elsevier Science Publishers.

Stone-Romero, E. F. and Stone, D. L. (1998). Religious and moral influences on work-related values and work quality. In D. Fedor and S. Ganoush (eds.), *Advances in the management of organizational quality*, vol. 3 (pp. 185–285). Greenwich, CT: JAI Press.

Stone-Romero, E. F. and Stone, D. L. (in press). Cross-cultural differences in responses to feedback: Implications for individual, group, and organizational effectiveness. In G. R. Ferris (ed.), *Research in personnel and human resource management*, vol. 21. New York: Elsevier Science Publishing.

Stone-Romero, E. F., Stone, D. L., and Hartman, M. (2002). *Stereotypes of ethnic groups: Own versus assumed views of others*. Paper presented at the April meeting of the Society for Industrial and Organization Psychology, Toronto, Canada.

Stone-Romero, E. F., Stone, D. L., and Salas, E. (in press). The influence of culture on role conceptions and role behavior in organizations. *Applied Psychology: An International Review*.

Storey, J. (1999). Equal opportunities in retrospect and prospect. *Human Resource Management Journal, 9*, 5–10.

Stroh, L. K., Brett, J. M., and Reilly, A. H. (1992). All the right stuff: A comparison of female and male career patterns. *Journal of Applied Psychology, 77*, 251–60.

Stroh, L. K., Brett, J. M., and Reilly, A. H. (1996). Family structure, glass ceiling, and traditional explanations for the differential rate of turnover of female and male managers. *Journal of Vocational Behavior, 49*, 99–118.

Stroh, L. K., Northcraft, G., and Neale, M. A. (2001). *Organizational behavior: A management challenge*. Mahwah, NJ: Lawrence Erlbaum Associates.

Stroh, L. K., Varma, A., and Valy-Durbin, S. J. (2000). Why are women left at home: Are they unwilling to go on international assignments? *Journal of World Business, 35* (3), 241–55.

Stuhlmacher, A. F. and Walters, A. E. (1999). Gender differences in negotiation outcome: A meta-analysis. *Personnel Psychology*, October, 653.

Suro, R. (2000). New tack on gays at Air Force base. *Washington Post*, July 19. Retrieved September 9, 2001, from http://washingtonpost.com/

Suro, R. (2001). Military's discharges of gays increase. *Washington Post*, June 2. Retrieved September 9, 2001, from http://washingtonpost.com/

Sutherland, V. J. and Cooper, C. L. (1988). Sources of work stress. In J. J. Hurrell, L. R. Murphy, S. L. Sauter, and C. L. Cooper (eds.), *Occupational stress: Issues and developments in research* (pp. 3–39). London: Taylor and Francis.

Sutton v. United Airlines, Inc., 527 US 471 (1999).

Swanson, N. G., Piotrkowski, C. S., Keita, G. P., and Becker, A. B. (1997). Occupational stress and women's health. In S. J. Gallant, G. P. Keita, and R. Royak-Schaler (eds.), *Health care for women: Psychological, social, and behavioral influences* (pp. 147–59). Washington, DC: American Psychological Association.

Swedish Institute (1999). Immigrants in Sweden. *Fact Sheets on Sweden*. Retrieved July 20, 2002, from www.si.se/docs/infosweden/engelsca/fs63n.pdf

Swedish Institute (2000). Equality between women and men. *Fact Sheets on Sweden*. Retrieved July 2002, from www.si.se/docs/infosweden/engelsca/fs82n.pdf

Sweeney, J. J. (2001). The growing alliance between gay and union activists. In K. Krupat and P. McCreery (eds.), *Out at work: Building a gay–labor alliance* (pp. 24–30). Minneapolis: University of Minnesota Press.

Tajfel, H. (1969). Cognitive aspects of prejudice. *Journal of Social Issues, 25* (4), 79–97.

Tajfel, H. (1970). Experiments in intergroup discrimination. *Scientific American, 223* (5), 96–102.

Tajfel, H. (1981). *Human groups and social categories: Studies in social psychology.* Cambridge: Cambridge University Press.

Tajfel, H. and Turner, J. C. (1986). The social identity theory of intergroup behavior. In S. Worchel and W. Austin (eds.), *The psychology of intergroup relations,* 2nd edn. (pp. 7–24). Chicago, IL: Nelson-Hall Publishers.

Tasker, P. (1987). *The Japanese: A major exploration of modern Japan.* New York: Truman Talley Books.

Tatum, B. D. (1999). *Why are all the black kids sitting together in the cafeteria?* New York: Basic Books.

Taussig, M. and Fenwick, R. (2001). Unbinding time: Alternate work schedules and work–life balance. *Journal of Family and Economic Issues, 22* (2), 101–19.

Taylor, A. (1997). My life as a gay executive. *Fortune, 136* (5), 106–10.

Taylor, F. W. (1911). *The principles of scientific management.* New York: W. W. Norton.

Taylor, H. (2001). By more than 2-to-1 most Americans favor legislation to prohibit job discrimination against gays and lesbians. Retrieved November 29, 2001, from Harris Interactive/Harris Poll website: http://www.harrisinteractive.com/harris_poll/index.asp?PID=236

Taylor, S. E. (1999). *Health psychology,* 4th edn. New York: McGraw-Hill.

Taylor, S. E. and Brown, J. D. (1988). Illusions and well-being: A social psychological perspective on mental health. *Psychological Bulletin, 103,* 193–210.

Tharenou, P., Latimer, S., and Conroy, D. (1994). How do you make it to the top? An examination of influences on women's and men's managerial advancement. *Academy of Management Journal, 37* (4), 899–932.

"The Corporate Elite" (1991). *Business Week,* November 25. Issue no. 3241, pp. 185–214.

"The Diversity Industry" (1993). *The New Republic,* July 5, p. 23.

The Times of India Online (2001a). *Caste is not race: But let's go to the UN forum anyway.* Retrieved October 15, 2001, from http://www.timesofindia.com

The Times of India Online (2001b). *Straight answers: John C. B. Webster.* Retrieved October 15, 2001, from http://www.timesofindia.com

Theorell, T. and Karasek, R. A. (1996). Current issues relating to psychosocial job strain and cardiovascular disease research. *Journal of Occupational Health Psychology, 1* (1), 9–26.

Thermaenius, A. (2001). Who's washing the dishes now? *Focus on Member States.* Sigma 2/2001, pp. 37–8. Retrieved August 5, 2002, from http://www.scb.se

Thernstrom, S. and Thernstrom, A. (1997). *America in Black and White: One nation, indivisible.* New York: Simon and Schuster.

"35-year profile of M&A" (2000). *Mergers & Acquisitions 35* (8), 31.

Thoits, P. A. (1986). Multiple identities: Examining gender and marital status differences in distress. *American Sociological Review, 51,* 259–72.

Thomas, D. A. (1989). Mentoring and irrationality: The role of racial taboos. *Human Resource Management, 28* (2), 279–90.

Thomas, D. A. (1990). The impact of race on managers' experiences of developmental relationships (mentoring and sponsorship): An intra-organizational study. *Journal of Organizational Behavior, 2,* 479–92.

Thomas, D. A. (1993). Racial dynamics in cross-race developmental relationships. *Administrative Science Quarterly, 38,* 169–94.

Thomas, D. A. (1997). A question of color: A debate on race in the US workplace. *Harvard Business Review*, 119–32.

Thomas, D. A. (1999). Beyond the simple demography–power hypothesis: How blacks in power influence white-mentor–black-protégé developmental relationships. In A. J. Murrell, F. J. Crosby, and R. J. Ely (eds.), *Mentoring dilemmas: Developmental relationships within multicultural organizations* (pp. 157–70). Mahwah, NJ: Lawrence Erlbaum Associates.

Thomas, D. A. (2001). The truth about mentoring minorities: Race matters. *Harvard Business Review*, 99–107.

Thomas, D. A. and Ely, R. (1996). Making differences matter: A new paradigm for managing diversity. *Harvard Business Review*, 74 (5), 79–90.

Thomas, K. M. (1996). Psychological privilege and ethnocentrism as barriers to cross-cultural adjustment and effective intercultural interactions. *Leadership Quarterly Journal*, 7, 217–30.

Thomas, K. M. (1998). Psychological readiness for multicultural leadership. *Management Development Forum*, 1, 99–112.

Thomas, K. M. and Wise, P. G. (1999). Organizational attractiveness and individual differences: Are diverse applicants attracted by different factors? *Journal of Business and Psychology*, 13 (3), 375–89.

Thomas, L. T. and Ganster, D. C. (1995). Impact of family-supportive work variables on work–family conflict and strain: A control perspective. *Journal of Applied Psychology*, 80 (1), 6–15.

Thomas, R. R. (1990). From affirmative action to affirming diversity. *Harvard Business Review*, 2, 107–17.

Thomas, R. R., Jr. (1991). *Beyond race and gender: Unleashing the power of your total work force by managing diversity*. New York: AMACOM.

Thomas, R. R., Jr. (1992). Managing diversity: A conceptual framework. In S. Jackson and M. Ruderman (eds.), *Diversity in work teams: Research paradigms for a changing workplace* (pp. 306–18). Washington, DC: American Psychological Association.

Thomas, R. R., Jr. (1996). *Redefining diversity*. New York: AMACOM.

Thomas, R. R., Jr., and Woodruff, M. (1999). *Building a house for diversity: A fable about a giraffe and an elephant offers new strategies for today's workforce*. New York: AMACOM.

Thompson, A. D. and Kleiner, B. H. (1995). What managers should know about age discrimination. *Equal Opportunities International*, 14 (6, 7), 61–8.

Thompson, C. A., Beauvais, L. L., and Lyness, K. S. (1999). When work–family benefits are not enough: The influences of work–family culture on benefit utilization, organizational attachment, and work–family conflict. *Journal of Vocational Behavior*, 54, 392–415.

Thurow, L. (1992). *Head to head: The coming economic battle among Japan, Europe and North America*. New York: Morrow.

Tolman, R. M. and Raphael, J. (2000). A review of research on domestic violence. *Journal of Social Issues*, 4, 655–82.

Tomoskovic-Devey, D. (1993). *Gender and racial inequality at work: The sources and consequences of job segregation*. Ithaca, NY: ILR Press.

Tomkiewicz, J., Brenner, O. C., and Adeyemi-Bello, T. (1998). The impact of perceptions and stereotypes of the managerial mobility of African Americans. *Journal of Social Psychology*, 138, 92–9.

Tracy, C. S. (1996). Extending the advantage of an older workforce. *Business Quarterly*, 61 (2), 11–13.

Triandis, H. C. (1980). Vales, attitudes, and interpersonal behavior. In H. Howe and M. Page (eds.), *Nebraska symposium on motivation, 1979* (pp. 195–260). Lincoln: University of Nebraska Press.

Triandis, H. C. (1994). *Culture and social behavior*. New York: McGraw-Hill.

Triandis, H. C., Kurowski, L. L., and Gelfand, M. J. (1994). Workplace diversity. In H. C. Triandis, M. I. Dunnette, and L. M. Hough (eds.), *Handbook of industrial and organizational psychology* (pp. 767–827). Palo Alto, CA: Consulting Psychologists Press.

Trice, H. and Beyer, J. (1993). *The cultures of work organizations*. Englewood Cliffs, NJ: Prentice-Hall.

Trimberger, L. (1998). Deloitte and Touche: Retaining women means success. *HR Focus, 75* (11), 7–8.

Trompenaars, F. and Hampden-Turner, C. (1998). *Riding the waves of culture: Understanding cultural diversity in global business*, 2nd edn. New York: McGraw-Hill.

Tsui, A. S., Egan, T. D., and O'Reilly, C. A., III (1992). Being different: Relational demography and organizational attachment. *Administrative Science Quarterly, 37*, 549–79.

Tsui, A. S., Egan, T. D., and Xin, K. R. (1995). Diversity in organizations: Lessons from demography research (pp. 191–219). In M. M. Chemers, M. A. Costanzo, and S. Oskamp (eds.), *Diversity in organizations: New perspectives for a changing workplace*. Thousand Oaks, CA: Sage.

Tsui, A. S. and Gutek, B. (1999). *Demographic differences in organizations: Current research and future directions*. Lanham, MD: Lexington Books.

Tsui, A. S. and O'Reilly, C. A., III (1989). Beyond simple demographic effects: The importance of relational demography in superior–subordinate dyads. *Academy of Management Journal, 32*, 402–23.

Tsui, A. S., Xin, K. R., and Egan, T. D. (1995). Relational demography: The missing link in vertical dyad linkage. In S. E. Jackson and M. N. Ruderman (eds.), *Diversity in work teams: Research paradigms for a changing workplace* (pp. 97–127). Washington, DC: American Psychological Association.

Turner-Bowker, D. M. (2001). How can you pull yourself by your bootstraps, if you don't have boots? Work appropriate clothing for poor women. *Journal of Social Issues, 57*, 311–22.

"2000 M&A profile" (2001). *Mergers & Acquisitions, 36* (2), 23.

Uchitelle. L. (2002). The rich are different: They know when to leave. *New York Times*, January 20. Retrieved on February 20, 2002, from http://www.nytimes.com/2002/01/20/weekinreview/20UCHI.html

UK Office for National Statistics (2000). *UK resident population by ethnic group, 1999–2000*. Retrieved October 30, 2001, from http://www.statistics.gov.uk/compendia_reference/downloads/rifne.pdf

United Nations (1999). *The United Nations world population statistics*. Population Division: Department of Economics and Social Affairs. Retrieved October 30, 2001, from http://www.popin.org/6billion/b1.htm

United Nations (2001). *World population prospects: The 2000 revision*. Retrieved October 29, 2001, from http://www.un.org/popin/data.html#Globaldata

United Steelworkers v. Weber, 443 US 193 (1979).

University of California, Santa Barbara, Center for the Study of Sexual Minorities in the Military (2001). Suspension of gay ban has historical precedent. Retrieved September 20, 2001, from http://www.gaymilitary.ucsb.edu/PressCenter/PressReleasesHome.htm

Urban Institute (2001). *Welfare reform turns 5*. Retrieved April 26, 2002, from http://www.urban.org

Ursaki, T. J. (2001). Gender and promotion in Japan's largest employers. Administrative Sciences Association of Canada/Association des Sciences Administrative du Canada (ASAC). *2001 Conference Proceedings/Actes Volume 22, No. 11. Women in Management/Femmes et Gestion*.

US Bureau of Labor Statistics (1999). Contingent and alternative employment arrangements. *Labor force statistics from the current population survey*. US Bureau of Labor Statistics. Retrieved on October 10, 2000, from http://stats.bls.gov/news.release/conemp.nws/htm

US Bureau of Labor Statistics (2000). Number of jobs held, labor market activity, and earnings growth over two decades: Results from a longitudinal survey summary. *National longitudinal surveys*, April 25. Retrieved on October 10, 2000, from http://stats.bls.gov/news.release/nlsoy.nr0.htm

US Bureau of Labor Statistics (2001a). *Contingent and alternative employment arrangements, February 2001* (USDL 01–153). Washington, DC: US Department of Labor.

US Bureau of Labor Statistics (2001b). *Occupational injuries and illnesses: Counts, rates, and characteristics, 1998* (2538). Washington, DC: US Department of Labor.

US Bureau of National Affairs (1995). Good for business: Making full use of the nation's human capital fact-finding report of the Federal Glass Ceiling Commission released by the Labor Department, March 16, 1995.

US Census Bureau (1997). Census brief. Disabilities affect one-fifth of all Americans: Proportion could increase in coming decades. US Department of Commerce: Economics and Statistics Administration.

US Census Bureau (2001a). Black population in the US, March 2000 (Table 13). Earnings of full-time, year-round workers 15 years and over in 1999 by sex, and race, and Hispanic origin. Retrieved July 2, 2002, from http://www.censurs.gov/population/socdemo/race/black/ppl–142/tab13.txt

US Census Bureau (2001b). *Poverty in the United States: 2000*. Washington, DC: US Government Printing Office.

US Census Bureau (2001c). *Money income in the United States: 2000*. Retrieved on April 25, 2002, from http://www.census.gov/hhes/income/income00/inctab8.html

US Census Bureau (2002). Income 2000 (Table 7). Median income of people by selected characteristics: 2000, 1999, and 1998, published 22 August, 2002. Retrieved October 10, 2002, from http://www.census.gov/hhes/income/income00/inctab7.html

US Department of Commerce (1999). *Survey of Current Business, 79*, D28.

US Department of Health and Human Services (1999). Access to child care for low-income working families. Retrieved on April 26, 2002, from http://www.acf.dhhs.gov/programs/ccb/research/ccreport/ccreport.htm#3

US Department of Labor (1996). *Employed persons by occupation, race, and sex. Employment and earnings, 171*. Washington, DC: Department of Labor.

US Department of Labor (2001a). *Occupational employment and wages, 2000* (USDL 01-415). Retrieved March 7, 2002, from http://www.bls.gov/oes/

US Department of Labor (2001b). *National census of fatal occupational injuries in 2000* (USDL 01-261). Retrieved March 7, 2002, from http://stats.bls.gov/oshhome.htm

US Department of Labor (2001c). *Workplace injury and illness 2000* (USDL 01-472). Retrieved March 7, 2002, from http://www.bls.gov/iif/home.htm

US Department of Labor, Office of Public Affairs (1995). *The Glass Ceiling Commission unanimously agrees on 12 ways to shatter barriers.* Retrieved on September 9, 2002, from http://www.ilr.cornell.edu/library/

US EEOC v. Massey Yardley Chrysler Plymouth (CA11 1997) 117 F.3d 1244.

US General Accounting Office (1999). *Welfare reform: Information on former recipients' status* (GAO/HEHS 99-48). Washington, DC: Author.

US General Accounting Office (2000). *Pensions plans: Characteristics of persons in the labor force without pension coverage* (GAO/HEHS 00-131). Washington, DC: Author.

US General Accounting Office (2002). *Private pensions: Key issues to consider following the Enron collapse* (GA0-02-480T). Washington, DC: Author.

Van Velsor, E. and Hughes, M. W. (1990). *Gender differences in the development of managers: How women managers learn from experience.* Technical report no. 145. Greensboro, NC: Center for Creative Leadership.

Van Velsor, E., McCauley, C. D., and Moxley, R. S. (1998). Introduction: Our view of leadership development. In C. D. McCauley, R. S. Moxley, and E. Van Velsor (eds.), *The Center for Creative Leadership handbook of leadership development* (pp. 1–25). San Francisco, CA: Jossey-Bass.

Varma, A. and Stroh, L. K. (2001). Impact of the gender composition of supervisor–subordinate dyads on performance evaluations. *Human Resource Management, 40* (4), 309–20.

Vaux, A. (1993). Paradigmatic assumptions in sexual harassment research: Being guided without being misled. *Journal of Vocational Behavior, 42,* 116–35.

Venne, R. (2002). Population aging in Canada and Japan: Implications for labour force and career patterns. *Canadian Journal of Administrative Sciences/Revue Canadienne des Science de l'Administration, 18* (1), 40–9.

Voydanoff, P. and Donnelly, B. W. (1999). Multiple roles and psychological distress: The intersection of the paid worker, spouse, and parent roles with the role of the adult. *Journal of Marriage and the Family, 61,* 725–38.

Waclawski, J. and Church, A. H. (eds.) (2002). *Organization development: A data-driven approach to organizational change.* San Francisco, CA: Jossey-Bass.

Walker, B. A. and Hanson, W. C. (1992). Valuing differences at digital equipment corporation. In S. E. Jackson and Associates (eds.), *Diversity in the workplace* (pp. 119–37). New York: Guilford Press.

Wallerstein, N. (1992). Powerlessness, empowerment, and health: Implications for health promotion programs. *American Journal of Health Promotion, 6* (3), 197–205.

Wards Cove Packing Co. v. Atonio, 490 US 642 (1989).

Watson, W. E., Johnson, L., and Merritt, D. (1998). Team orientation, self-orientation, and diversity in task groups. *Group and Organization Management, 23,* 161–88.

Watson, W. E., Johnson, L., Kumar, K., and Critelli, J. W. (1998). Process gain and process loss: Comparing interpersonal processes and performance of culturally diverse and non-diverse teams across time. *International Journal of Intercultural Relations, 22,* 409–30.

Watson, W. E., Kumar, K., and Michaelsen, L. K. (1993). Cultural diversity's impact on interaction process and performance: Comparing homogeneous and diverse task groups. *Academy of Management Journal, 36,* 590–602.

Weakliem, D., McQuillan, J., and Schauer, T. (1995). Toward meritocracy? Changing social-class differences in intellectual ability. *Sociology of Education, 68,* 271–86.

Webber, S. and Donahue, L. (2001). Impact of highly and less job-related diversity on work group cohesion and performance: A meta-analysis. *Journal of Management, 27,* 141–62.

Weber, M. (1947). *The theory of social and economic organization*, trans. A. M. Henderson and T. Parsons. New York: Free Press.

Weber, M. (1958) [1904–5]. *The Protestant ethic and the spirit of capitalism*, trans. T. Parsons. New York: Charles Scribner's Sons.

Weeks, J. R. (1994). *Population: An introduction to concepts and issues*, 5th edn. Belmont, CA: Wadsworth.

Wegman, D. H. (1992). The potential impact of epidemiology on the prevention of occupational disease. *American Journal of Public Health, 82* (7), 944–54.

Weick, K. (1984). Small wins: Redefining the scale of social problems. *American Psychologist, 39*, 40–8.

Weinberg, G. (1972). *Society and the healthy homosexual*. New York: St. Martin's Press.

Weinberger, L. E. and Millham, J. (1979). Attitudinal homophobia and support of traditional sex roles. *Journal of Homosexuality, 4*, 237–45.

Weinger, S. (1998). Children living in poverty: Their perception of career opportunities. *Families in Society, 79*, 320–30.

Weisbord, M. R. (ed.) (1992). *Discovering common ground: How future search conferences bring people together to achieve breakthrough innovation, empowerment, shared vision, and collaborative action*. San Francisco, CA: Berrett-Koehler.

Weisbord, M. R. and Janoff, S. (2000). *Future search: An action guide to finding common ground in organizations and communities*, 2nd edn. San Francisco, CA: Berrett-Koehler.

Welch, J. (1996). The invisible minority. *People Management, 2* (19), 24–31.

Wentling, R. M. and Palma-Rivas, N. (1998). Current status and future trends of diversity initiatives in the workplace: Diversity experts' perspective. *Human Resource Development Quarterly, 9* (3), 235–53.

Wentling, R. M. and Palma-Rivas, N. (2000). Current status of diversity initiatives in selected multinational corporations. *Human Resource Development Quarterly, 11*, 35–60.

Wertlieb, E. C. (1985). Minority group status of the disabled. *Human Relations, 38*, 1047–63.

West, M. A. (2001). The human team: Basic motivations and innovations. In N. Anderson, D. S. Ones, H. K. Sinangil, and C. Viswesvaran (eds.), *Handbook of industrial, work and organizational psychology, Vol. 2: Organizational psychology* (pp. 270–88). London: Sage.

"What is this going to cost me?" (2002). *Delaware Employment Law Letter, 7* (6). Retrieved August 18, 2002, from Lexis–Nexis database.

Wheeler, M. L. (1995). *Diversity: Business rationale and strategies: A research report*. Report 1130–95–RR, The Conference Board, 845 Third Avenue, New York, NY, 10022.

Wheeler, M. L. (1999). Global diversity: A culture-change perspective. *Diversity Factor*, winter, 31–4.

Whitaker, M. (2000). General under fire over gays. *The Tennessean*. Retrieved September 9, 2001, from http://www.tennessean.com/sii/00/06/10/fort10.shtml

White, M. B. (1996). Strategies for success: The San Diego story. *Diversity Factor*, summer, 2–10.

Whitley, B. E., Jr. (1987). The relationship of sex-role orientation to heterosexuals' attitudes toward homosexuals. *Sex Roles, 17*, 103–13.

Whitley, B. E., Jr. (1999). Right-wing authoritarianism, social dominance orientation, and prejudice. *Journal of Personality and Social Psychology, 77*, 126–34.

Whyte, W. F., Greenwood, D. J., and Lazes, P. (1991). Participatory action research: Through practice to science in social research. In W. F. Whyte (ed.), *Participatory action research* (pp. 19–55). Newbury Park, CA: Sage.

Wildman, S. M. (1996). The dream of diversity and the cycle of exclusion. In S. M. Wildman (ed.), *Privilege revealed: How invisible preference undermines America* (pp. 103–37). New York: New York University Press.

Wildman, S. M. and Davis, A. D. (1996). Making systems of privilege visible. In S. M. Wildman (ed.), *Privilege revealed: How invisible preference undermines America*(pp. 25–42). New York: New York University Press.

Wilhelm, S. (2001). The impact of EEOC enforcement on the wages of Black and White women: Does class matter? *Review of Radical Political Economics, 33,* 295–304.

Williams, K. Y. and O'Reilly, C. A., III (1998). Demography and diversity in organizations: A review of 40 years of research. In B. Staw and L. L. Cummings (eds.), *Research in organizational behavior,* vol. 20 (pp. 77–140). Greenwich, CT: JAI Press.

Wilson, R. (2002). Stacking the deck for minority candidates? *Chronicle of Higher Education,* July 12, A10–A12.

Winett, R. A., Neale, M. S., and Williams, K. R. (1982). The effects of flexible work schedules on urban families with young children: Quasi-experimental, ecological studies. *American Journal of Community Psychology, 10* (1), 49–64.

Winkler, A. E. (1998). Earnings of husbands and wives in dual-earner families. *Monthly Labor Review,* 42–8.

Wirth, L. A. (1998). Women in management: Closer to breaking through the glass ceiling? *International Labour Review, 137* (1), 93–102.

Wise, L. R. and Tschirhart, M. (2000). Examining empirical evidence on diversity effects: How useful is diversity research for public-sector managers? *Public Administration Review, 60,* 386–94.

Witherspoon, G. (1977). *Language and art in the Navajo universe.* Ann Arbor: University of Michigan Press.

Witherspoon, P. D. and Wohlert, K. L. (1996). An approach to developing communication strategies for enhancing organizational diversity. *Journal of Business Communication, 33,* 375–99.

Wolff, E. N. (1998). Recent trends in the size and distribution of household wealth. *Journal of Economic Perspectives, 12,* 131–50.

Woodhams, C. and Danieli, A. (2000). Disability and diversity – a difference too far? *Personnel Review, 29,* 402–17.

Word, C., Zanna, M. P., and Cooper, J. (1974). The verbal mediation of self-fulfilling prophecies in interracial interaction. *Journal of Experimental Social Psychology, 10* (2), 109–20.

Wortman, C., Biernat, M., and Lang, E. (1991). Coping with role overload. In M. Frankenhaeuser, U. Lundberg, and M. Chesney (eds.), *Women, work, and health: Stress and opportunities* (pp. 85–110). New York: Plenum.

Wright, P., Ferris, S. P., Hiller, J. S., and Kroll, M. (1995). Competitiveness through management of diversity: Effects on stock price valuation. *Academy of Management Journal, 38,* 272–87.

Xie, J. L. and Johns, G. (1996). Job scope and stress: Can job scope be too high? *Academy of Management Journal, 38* (5), 1288–1309.

Yakura, E. K. (1996). EEO law and managing diversity. In E. E. Kossek and S. A. Lobel (eds.), *Managing diversity: Human resource strategies for transforming the workplace* (pp. 25–50). Cambridge, MA: Blackwell.

Yang, A. S. (2001). *The 2000 National Elections Study and gay and lesbian rights: Support for equality grows.* Retrieved November 29, 2001, from the National Gay and Lesbian Task Force Foundation website: http://www.ngltf.org/downloads/NES2000.pdf

Young, J. R. (2001). Scholars question the image of the internet as a race-free utopia. *Chronicle of Higher Education, 48,* A48.

Zane, N. C. (1994). Theoretical considerations in organizational diversity. In E. Y. Cross, J. H. Katz, F. A. Miller, and E. W. Seashore (eds.), *The promise of diversity: Over 40 voices discuss strategies for eliminating discrimination in organizations* (pp. 339–50). Burr Ridge, IL: Irwin.

Zedeck, S. and Mosier, K. L. (1990). Work in the family and employing organization. *American Psychologist, 45,* 240–51.

Zenger, T. R. and Lawrence, B. S. (1989). Organizational demography: The differential effects of age and tenure distributions on technical communication. *Academy of Management Journal, 32,* 353–76.

Zintz, A. (1997). Championing and managing diversity at Ortho Biotech Inc. *National Productivity Review,* 21–8.

Zucker, G. S. and Weiner, B. (1993). Conservatism and perceptions of poverty: An attributional analysis. *Journal of Applied Social Psychology, 23,* 925–43.

Zuckerman, A. J. and Simons, G. F. (1996). *Sexual orientation in the workplace: Gay men, lesbians, bisexuals and heterosexuals working together.* Thousand Oaks, CA: Sage.

Index